W9-ARJ-749

LOWNIK LIBRARY

IN OMNIBUS
GLORIFICETUR DEUS

A Gift From

The Class
of 1998

Senior Challenge
May 1998

Informing Today-Transforming Tomorrow

CAMBRIDGE COMPANIONS TO RELIGION
A series of companions to major topics and key figures in
theology and religious studies. Each volume will contain specially
commissioned essays by international scholars which provide
an accessible and stimulating introduction to the subject for new
readers and non-specialists.

Forthcoming titles in the series

THE CAMBRIDGE COMPANION TO BIBLICAL INTERPRETATION
edited by John Barton

THE CAMBRIDGE COMPANION TO LIBERATION THEOLOGY
edited by Christopher Rowland

THE CAMBRIDGE COMPANION TO DIETRICH BONHOEFFER
edited by John De Gruchy

THE CAMBRIDGE COMPANION TO KARL BARTH
edited by John Webster

CHRISTIAN DOCTRINE

Constructive Christian doctrine was for a long time in the doldrums, its contents progressively brought into question by representatives of intellectual modernism. But recent years have seen something of a revival in its fortunes. This is due to a number of factors, among them the critique of modernism and a stress on the particular and relative independence of the distinctive intellectual disciplines.

Theology has always taken a shape related to the culture in which it is set, and *The Cambridge Companion to Christian Doctrine* is no exception. The fourteen chapters, written by established theologians from Britain and America, attempt to develop the promise inherent in the changed intellectual situation, while at the same time introducing some of the central topics of theology. The book is divided into two parts, with the first six chapters examining Christian theology in its current setting, and the second eight treating major topics among those traditional in Christian doctrine. While it has not been possible to include an account of everything, there has nevertheless been built a framework within which detailed treatment of other doctrines could be developed. The advantage of the compression is that topics are brought into relation which might be worse treated in relative isolation.

New readers and non-specialists will find this an accessible and stimulating introduction to the content of the main themes of Christian doctrine, while advanced students and specialists will find a useful summary of recent developments which demonstrates the variety, coherence and intellectual vitality of contemporary Christian thought.

THE CAMBRIDGE COMPANION TO
CHRISTIAN DOCTRINE

Edited by Colin E. Gunton
King's College London

THEODORE LOWNIK LIBRARY
BENEDICTINE UNIVERSITY
5700 COLLEGE ROAD
LISLE, IL 60532-0900

CAMBRIDGE
UNIVERSITY PRESS

2 23508
C 178

Published by the Press Syndicate of the University of Cambridge
The Pitt Building, Trumpington Street, Cambridge CB2 1RP United Kingdom

Cambridge University Press
The Edinburgh Building, Cambridge CB2 1RP, United Kingdom
40 West 20th Street, New York, NY 10011–4211, USA
10 Stamford Road, Oakleigh, Melbourne 3166, Australia

© Cambridge University Press 1997

This book is in copyright. Subject to statutory exception
and to the provisions of relevant collective licensing agreements,
no reproduction of any part may take place without
the written permission of Cambridge University Press.

First published 1997

Printed in Great Britain at the University Press, Cambridge

Typeset in FF Celeste

A catalogue record for this book is available from
the British Library

ISBN 0 521 47118 4 hardback
ISBN 0 521 47695 x paperback

CP

Contents

Notes on contributors

Jeremy Begbie is Vice Principal of Ridley Hall, Cambridge. He lectures in systematic theology there and in the Faculty of Divinity at the University of Cambridge. He was originally trained as a musician and has worked on the interface between theology and the arts. He is author of *Music in God's Purposes* (Edinburgh: Handsel Press, 1989) and *Voicing Creation's Praise* (Edinburgh: T. & T. Clark, 1991).

Ralph Del Colle is Assistant Professor of Theology at Marquette University in Milwaukee, Wisconsin, USA. He is the author of *Christ and the Spirit: Spirit-Christology in Trinitarian Perspective* (New York: Oxford University Press, 1994).

David A. S. Fergusson is Professor of Systematic Theology in the University of Aberdeen, and is the author of *Bultmann* (London: Chapman, 1992) and the editor of *Christ, Church and Society: Essays on John Baillie and Donald Baillie* (Edinburgh: T. & T. Clark, 1993).

Colin Gunton has been Professor of Christian Doctrine at King's College London since 1984, and since 1975 Associate Minister of Brentwood United Reformed Church, Essex. Among his recent books are *The Promise of Trinitarian Theology* (Edinburgh: T. & T. Clark, 1991); *The One, the Three and the Many. God, Creation and the Culture of Modernity. The 1992 Bampton Lectures* (Cambridge: Cambridge University Press, 1993); *A Brief Theology of Revelation. The 1993 Warfield Lectures* (Edinburgh: T. & T. Clark, 1995); *Theology Through the Theologians: Selected Essays, 1972–1995* (Edinburgh: T. & T. Clark, 1996).

Trevor Hart is Professor of Divinity in the University of St Andrews. Recent publications include *Justice the True and Only Mercy. Essays on the Life and Theology of Peter Taylor Forsyth* (Edinburgh: T. & T. Clark, 1995); *Faith Thinking: The Dynamics of Christian Theology* (London: SPCK, 1995); 'Sinlessness and Moral Responsibility: A Problem in Christology' (*Scottish Journal of Theology*, vol. 48.1, 1995, pp. 37–54); 'Barth and Küng on Justification' (*The Irish Theological Quarterly*, vol. 59.2, 1993); 'The Word, the Words and the Witness: Proclamation as Divine and Human Reality in the Theology of Karl Barth' (*Tyndale Bulletin*, vol. 46.1, 1995).

Stanley Hauerwas is the Gilbert T. Rowe Professor of Theological Ethics at the Divinity School of Duke University. He has published such books as *The Peaceable Kingdom: A Primer in Christian Ethics* (Notre Dame, Indiana: University of Notre Dame Press, 1984); *Dispatches from the Front: Theological Engagements with the Secular* (Durham, N. Carolina: Duke University Press, 1994); *In Good Company: The Church as Polis* (Notre Dame, Indiana: University of Notre Dame Press, 1995) and the forthcoming *Christians Among the Virtues: Theological Conversations with Ancient and Modern Ethics.*

Robert W. Jenson is Professor of Religion at St Olaf College, Northfield, Minnesota; Associate Director of the Center for Catholic and Evangelical Theology; and co-founder and co-editor of the journal *Pro Ecclesia*. He was born in the United States and educated there and at the universities of Heidelberg and Basel. He has written on topics ranging across the spectrum of theology, perhaps especially on the doctrine of God. His most recent books are *Unbaptized God: The Basic Flaw in Ecumenical Theology* (Minneapolis: Fortress, 1992) and *Essays in Theology of Culture* (Grand Rapids, Michigan: Eerdmans, 1995).

Gerard Loughlin is Senior Lecturer and Head of the Department of Religious Studies at the University of Newcastle upon Tyne. He has contributed to a number of leading journals, including *Modern Theology* and *New Blackfriars*, and has published *Telling God's Story: Bible, Church and Narrative Theology* (Cambridge: Cambridge University Press, 1996).

Bruce D. Marshall is Associate Professor of Religion at St Olaf College, Northfield, Minnesota. He is the author of *Christology in Conflict* (Oxford and New York: Blackwell, 1987) and of the forthcoming *The Trinity and Truth* (Cambridge University Press), and editor of *Theology and Dialogue: Essays in Conversation with George Lindbeck* (Notre Dame, Indiana: University of Notre Dame Press, 1990).

Kathryn Tanner teaches Christian theology at the University of Chicago Divinity School. The author of *God and Creation in Christian Theology* (Oxford: Blackwell, 1988), and *The Politics of God* (Minneapolis: Fortress, 1992), she is currently writing a book on theological method and cultural theory.

Kevin J. Vanhoozer is Lecturer in Theology and Religious Studies at New College, University of Edinburgh. He is the author of *Biblical Narrative in the Philosophy of Paul Ricoeur: A Study in Hermeneutics and Theology* (Cambridge: Cambridge University Press, 1990) and *Is There a Meaning in this Text? the Bible, the Reader, and the Morality of Literary Knowledge* (Grand Rapids, Michigan: Zondervan/ HarperCollins, 1997) and the editor of *'Edinburgh Studies in Constructive Theology'*, a series of textbooks on Christian doctrine. He is a member of the American Academy of Religion, where he co-chairs the group of Systematic Theology, and of the Church of Scotland, in which he serves on the Panel of Doctrine.

Geoffrey Wainwright, a Minister of the British Methodist Church, is the Robert E. Cushman Professor of Christian Theology at Duke University. He holds the DrThéol. degree of the University of Geneva and the Cambridge DD. His books include *Christian Initiation* (London: Lutterworth Press, and Richmond, Virginia:

John Knox Press, 1969); *Eucharist and Eschatology* (London: Epworth Press, 1971; revised edn New York: Oxford University Press, 1981); *Doxology* (London: Epworth Press, and New York: Oxford University Press, 1980); *The Ecumenical Movement* (Grand Rapids: Eerdmans, 1983); *Methodists in Dialogue* (Nashville: Abingdon Press/Kingswood Books, 1995); *Worship With One Accord* (New York: Oxford University Press, forthcoming); *For Our Salvation: Two Approaches to the Work of Christ* (Grand Rapids: Eerdmans, forthcoming). He is an editor of *The Study of Liturgy* (London: SPCK, and New York: Oxford University Press, 1978; revised edn 1992); *The Study of Spirituality* (London: SPCK, and New York: Oxford University Press, 1986); *Keeping the Faith: Essays to Mark the Centenary of 'Lux Mundi'* (Philadelphia: Fortress Press, 1988, and London: SPCK, 1989); *A Dictionary of the Ecumenical Movement* (Geneva: World Council of Churches, and Grand Rapids: Eerdmans, 1991). For long a member of the Faith and Order Commission of the World Council of Churches, Dr Wainwright has since 1986 served as co-chair of the Joint Commission between the Roman Catholic Church and the World Methodist Council.

Francis Watson is Reader in Biblical Theology at King's College London. Publications include *Text, Church and World: Biblical Interpretation in Theological Perspective* (Edinburgh: T. & T. Clark/Grand Rapids, Michigan: Eerdmans, 1994) and *Text and Truth: Redefining Biblical Theology* (Edinburgh: T. & T. Clark/Grand Rapids, Michigan: Eerdmans, 1997).

Preface

Recent years have seen something of a revival in the fortunes of constructive Christian doctrine. Long in the doldrums by virtue of the apparent victory of 'criticism' – the ideology that everything before the modern era was almost by definition to be treated with heavy suspicion – its contents were progressively brought into question by representatives of intellectual modernism. The assumptions underlying modernism are that those things that cannot be justified at the bar of a particular kind of reason and a particular conception of what it is to be 'scientific' are thus far not justifiable as respectable intellectual exercises. Christian theology is particularly susceptible to a critique at the hands of this ideology, because its pretensions were among the first objects of Enlightenment criticism. As the Christian church has progressively lost its hold on Western social order, so its intellectual arm has appeared less essential a part of the universe of letters.

That things are changing is due to a number of factors, among them the critique of criticism and a stress on the particularity and relative independence of the distinctive intellectual disciplines. But the continuing vitality of Christian thought has made a contribution, from the engagement by theologians like Karl Barth with the cultural crises associated with both world wars to the part played by Christian faithfulness and sometimes intransigence both before and in the changes to the former Communist regimes in Eastern Europe. That does not mean that the tasks of constructive Christian theology can be taken up as if nothing had changed. Theology has always taken a shape related to the culture in which it is set, and this volume is no exception. It is a collection of papers by British and American writers dedicated to an attempt both to develop the promise inherent in the changed intellectual situation – what is sometimes called the postmodern world – and at the same time to provide an introduction for students and others to some of the central topics of theology. It is divided into two parts, with the first six chapters examining Christian theology in its current setting, the second eight treating major topics among those traditional in Christian doctrine.

Part one is dedicated to the nature of Christian theology, both historically and in the present, and with its relations to other forms of culture and religion. The first four chapters engage, chiefly but by no means only, with problems internal to theology, and of them two remarks can be made: that their authors belong to four different ecclesiastical traditions, as will be sometimes evident; and that, so far as content is concerned, the second and the fourth are particularly indicative of the contemporary situation. That ethics is here given a prominent place is to signal the fact that in Christian doctrine we are not engaged in 'mere' theory – with 'theology' in the pejorative sense once famously used by the former British Prime Minister Harold Wilson – but with truth claims that interact with life in its full breadth. Similarly, that the discussion of the interpretation of the Bible takes the form that it does indicates both that it is criticism of the Bible that is at the heart of the Christian encounter with the modern world which has so dominated recent years and that it is time for attitudes to change.

The latter two chapters in Part one consider the relation of Christianity first to Judaism and then to the arts. Judaism is chosen as a way of engaging with the question of the relation of Christianity to 'other religions'. In so wide-ranging a volume it is not possible to discuss all the problems in this area, but it is hoped that by taking one closely related faith the essay will throw some light on the broader questions that arise. Another of the matters it is no longer possible to avoid is the relation of Christianity to the often secular or atheistic culture that forms its context in the modern world, and the paper on the arts enables some focusing of this question.

Part two begins with an account of how the characteristic form of Christian belief in God as Trinity took shape, and it is succeeded by two chapters giving some account of this God's creative work, first with reference to the world as a whole, then of the human creature in particular. After that come two chapters showing how the triune God comes into relation with the created world with specific reference first to the fulfilment of the human destiny in Christ, understood as it must be against the background of sin and fallenness, and second as that destiny takes historical shape in the community of belief and practice known as the church. Finally there are three chapters which treat doctrinal questions consequent on the creative and redemptive activity of God. Eschatology is concerned with an understanding of the final outcome of the divine action; christology with the way its historical centre, Jesus Christ, is to be understood, especially in the modern world when traditional doctrines have come in for so much criticism; and the book comes to an end with an account of the doctrine of the third person of the Trinity, the Spirit, to whom is attributed the perfecting or completion of the work of God in relation to the world.

While it has not been possible to include an account of everything that would be included in a full treatment of the content of Christian doctrine, there has nevertheless been built a framework within which detailed treatment of other doctrines – for example, those of justification and sanctification – could be developed. Similarly, even in topics that have been treated, the constraints of space make some truncation inevitable, with fall and salvation in the same paper, when it might be argued that they need a full treatment of their own, and likewise with the church and the sacraments. The advantage of the compression is that topics are brought into relation which might be worse treated in relative isolation. In any case, it is hoped that any isolation that occurs will be no more than relative, for all the papers bear in some way upon all others. Sometimes it is the case that papers complement each other, as with the papers on the Trinity and christology, with one concentrating on the historical development of doctrine, the other on problems characteristic of the modern era. All in all, the claim is that here there is a beginning of exploration for those who would engage with this rich and diverse, yet common stream of tradition and thought.

It remains for the editor to thank, first, the contributors to the volume both for their papers and for their courtesy and co-operation; and second, Alex Wright, formerly of the Cambridge University Press, whose brainchild the volume is.

The theological world is immensely indebted to him for his enterprise and initiative over recent years.

Colin Gunton
King's College London.
Epiphany, 1996

Glossary

A word in italics refers to another glossary entry.

agnosticism 'unknowing-ism': the view that one cannot decide for or against the
truth of some, especially theological, claim

analogy distinguishing between different and related meanings of the same word

anthropocentric centred on the human; contrast *theocentric*

Apocalypse a way of speaking of the last book of the Bible, the Revelation of St John
the Divine

Apologists early Christian theologians, notably Justin Martyr, concerned with the
defence of Christianity

apophaticism a method of characterising divine qualities by 'speaking away' their
finite associations

apostolic proclamation the Christian faith as expressed in the preaching of the first
apostles

Arianism generally for any teaching that Jesus Christ is less than fully divine

Armageddon a symbol of the final battle between God and the powers of evil

atonement literally, 'at-one-ment', a way of characterising the work of Jesus Christ
in reconciling God and the world

canon, canonical literally, 'measuring rod'. The officially recognised texts – the Bible
– which act as the measure of Christian truth.

charism a human talent or capacity, understood as a gift of the grace of God

chiliastic associated with the *millennium*

christology the doctrine of the person of Jesus Christ

Constantinian to do with the Roman emperor, Constantine, who gave recognised
status to the Christian church in the fourth century. Generally, of any tendency
to make Christianity conform to contemporary conditions.

covenant God's commitment of himself to Israel and all humankind, particularly
involving the calling of people into relationship with himself; sometimes
distinguished into the old and new covenants (the contents of the Old and New
Testaments)

Decalogue the Ten Commandments

deism the doctrine that God, having created the world, has no continuing
interaction with it

diachronic happening over a period of time; contrast *synchronic*

dogma the formal teachings of an institution, particularly the church

doxology an ascription of glory to God

ecclesiology doctrine of the church

Emmaus road an allusion to the story related in Luke 24

Enlightenment a movement of thought, chiefly centred on the eighteenth century,
stressing human reason at the expense of authority and tradition

epistemology the theory of knowledge

eschaton the end of the world

filioque Latin for, 'and from the Son'. A chief cause of division between Eastern Orthodox and Western churches is the Western addition of 'and from the Son' to the credal confession that God the Spirit proceeds 'from the Father'. See chapter 14 for a discussion.

Gnosticism a religious teaching or system in which the stress is on the communication of knowledge, often knowledge available only to the initiated. It is contrasted in Christian theology with the public gospel centred on God's act in Christ.

Golgotha the place where Jesus was crucified

grace a way of characterising the action of God towards and in the world, and particularly the human agent

immanent within the world; contrast *transcendent*. For its technical use in connection with the Trinity, see chapter 7.

Immanuel 'God with us', usually a way of describing the presence of God in Jesus Christ; see *incarnation*

incarnation the teaching that in Jesus of Nazareth the eternal Son of God takes to himself 'flesh' – complete human being

Johannine logos the teaching of the gospel and letters of John that Jesus is the divine word

kerygma proclamation, particularly of the Christian gospel; see also *apostolic proclamation*

kyrios 'Lord'. A translation of the Hebrew word for God, but also attributed to Jesus Christ and the Holy Spirit in the New Testament.

levitical sacrifices rites performed by the official Jewish priests

liberal theology a school of late nineteenth- and twentieth-century theology; more generally, theology oriented to the *Enlightenment*

logion saying, especially one attributed to Jesus

logos word; often a way of describing Jesus Christ; see also *Johannine logos*

Manichaeism the teaching that evil, often attributed to the material world, is of near or equal power, to good

Messiah literally, 'the anointed one', a title for Jesus Christ and others expected or believed to inaugurate a new historical era in Israel

metaphysics 'after physics'; a philosophical theory of the nature of reality

metaphilosophy a theory of the nature of philosophy

millennium a thousand-year reign of Christ on earth

modalism see *Sabellianism*. Forms of modalism are defined in chapter 14.

monotheism belief in one God

natural theology theology developed by means of intrinsic human capacities, apart from divine revelation

nominalism the teaching, developed in opposition to Platonist and Aristotelian theories about the reality of universals or forms, and associated particularly with the late-medieval William of Ockham that only particular things exist

ontology, ontological thought or theory about the nature of being or reality

Palamite to do with Gregory Palamas, fourteenth-century Orthodox theologian

pantheism the doctrine that the universe as a whole is God

Paraclete advocate; one of the words for the Holy Spirit in the gospel of John

parousia 'coming'; usually of the second coming of Christ in glory at the end of time

perichoresis the teaching that each of the three persons of the Trinity is completely
involved in the being and acts of the others

phenomenological to do with descriptions of how things appear

pietism an approach to Christian faith seeing it as centred in the responsive side of
the person – the heart, emotions and moral seriousness

pneumatological to do with the doctrine of the Holy Spirit

polytheism belief in many gods

postmodern 'after the modern', often used to refer to a recent tendency of thought,
which stresses the plurality and variety of cultures and philosophies

predestination the doctrine that God has ordained in advance the destiny of human
beings

pro me, pro nobis Latin for, respectively, 'for me', 'for us'

Qur'an (sometimes written Koran) the sacred text of Islam

redactor a writer or editor who is held to have arranged the biblical texts into their
final form

Sabellianism the teaching that the three persons of the Trinity are manifestations
or modes of a single underlying reality

salvific to do with salvation

Second Temple the temple built after the return of the Jews from exile in 538 BC

Septuagint the Greek translation of the Old Testament, probably done in the third
century BC

Shema the central confession of the Old Testament faith, expressed in
Deuteronomy 6.4

Socinian associated with Faustus Socinus (1539–1604), and generally of the denial
of the divinity of Christ, of his atoning death and of the doctrine of the Trinity

soteriological to do with the doctrine of salvation

synchronic happening at the same time; contrast *diachronic*

synoptic gospels the first three gospels, because they, in contrast to John's gospel,
supposedly give a summary of the story of Jesus

telos Greek for 'end' or 'purpose'

theocentric centred on God; contrast *anthropocentric*

theophanies appearances of God or the divine

Thomist, thomistic of the school of Thomas Aquinas (*c.* 1225–1274)

Torah the Jewish law

transcendent outside or other than the world; contrast *immanent*

Trent the council held by the Roman Catholic Church, 1545–1563, to consolidate its
response to the Reformation

Tridentine to do with the council of *Trent*

typology, typological interpreting a thing or event in the light of a foreshadowing 'type', as when baptism is illustrated by reference to Noah's flood

univocal, univocity treating different meanings of a word as the same; contrast *analogy*

via moderna 'the modern way'; a term used for a school of late medieval theology; see also *nominalism*

Westminster Confession A confession of faith written by the Westminster Assembly of 1643 and one of the authoritative statements of the Christian faith for Presbyterian churches

Wisdom traditions a way of speaking of the writings such as Proverbs, Job and Ecclesiastes which are known as the Wisdom writings in the Old Testament

wisdom christology interpreting Jesus as the embodiment of divine wisdom

Chronology

1564–1642   Galileo Galilei, scientist
1596–1650   René Descartes, 'Father of modern philosophy'– and of the
             Enlightenment
1632–1677   Baruch Spinoza, pantheist philosopher
1632–1704   John Locke, philosopher
1642–1727   Isaac Newton, scientist and theologian
1703–1791   John Wesley. Methodism
1711–1776   David Hume, philosopher
1724–1804   Immanuel Kant, philosopher of the Enlightenment
1768–1834   Friedrich Schleiermacher, theologian. *The Christian Faith*
1770–1831   G. W. F. Hegel, philosopher
1801–1890   J. H. Newman, Anglican, later Roman Catholic, theologian
1809–1892   Charles Darwin, biologist
1813–1855   Søren Kierkegaard, writer and theologian
1848–1921   Peter Taylor Forsyth, theologian
1851–1930   Adolf Harnack, historian of doctrine
1884–1976   Rudolf Bultmann, New Testament scholar and theologian
1886–1968   Karl Barth, theologian. *Church Dogmatics* (1932–1967)
1886–1965   Paul Tillich, theologian
1889–1951   Ludwig Wittenstein, philosopher
1904–1984   Karl Rahner, theologian
1905–1988   Hans Urs von Balthasar, theologian

Part one

Christian doctrine in the late twentieth century:
the historical and intellectual context

1 Historical and systematic theology

COLIN GUNTON

Historical and systematic theology are disciplines concerned with the content of Christian teaching. Historical theology is that discipline whose task is to expound the course of Christian theology through time, within its different historical and cultural contexts. Systematic theology's distinctive character derives from its responsibility for articulating the meaning and implications of the church's claims for the truth of the Christian gospel. In some conceptions of its task, systematic theology is simply a fashionable way of speaking of what used to be called dogmatic theology; in others, a more conscious orientation to the characteristic conditions of the modern world is in view. We shall return to that question at the end of the chapter.

Despite their differences, however, the two studies do not follow entirely different courses, for their tracks cross in many places. One example will introduce what is meant. To study the *history* of the development of Christian theology in its formative years, the student needs to be aware not only of the *systematic* interconnections of – above all – the doctrines of God and of the person of Christ but also the relation of the Christian world of thought to other aspects of ancient culture, perhaps especially Greek philosophy and religion. To understand the history requires a measure of systematic awareness. The relation with classical civilisation is of particular importance, because there exist very different views of the interaction of the two worlds, a feature of the literature which helps to make historical theology the interesting and complicated study that it is. Conversely, what we make of questions of history will often have a bearing on how we see the faith today. We might ask, for example, whether the formation of Christian theology in the early days with the assistance of concepts borrowed from Greek philosophy is helpful or harmful as we attempt to articulate Christian theology systematically today. In sum, historical theology cannot be understood without some awareness of the nature of systematic theology; while systematic theology, particularly in view of the historical character of Christianity, cannot take shape without considerable historical awareness.

One other preliminary question concerns the distinction between theology and doctrine. It is sometimes suggested that doctrine is what is taught by the church, as the officially agreed teaching of the institution, while theology is a more open-ended activity, whose efforts may or may not be accepted as doctrine in the course of time. That is a useful distinction because it enables us to understand the nature of both ancient and modern discussions. Parts of the teaching of Origen came to be accepted as the doctrine of the church; other parts were condemned as heretical; but all he wrote was theological. Similarly, many modern systematic theologians have questioned some of the doctrines of the creed, for example that concerning the divinity of Jesus Christ, although no representative church body has yet accepted the validity of their contentions. But, like the distinction between historical and systematic theology, that between doctrine and theology cannot be treated as absolute, because Christian doctrines are theological, while theology is often centrally concerned with the church's official doctrine.

HISTORICAL THEOLOGY

A *theological* discipline

Historical theology is a characteristically modern form of theological thought. Jaroslav Pelikan notes that the history of doctrine emerged as a discipline only in the eighteenth century.[1] While it would be false and patronising to suggest that earlier eras had no historical sense at all, it is with the Renaissance that there first develops a definite sense that the form which Christian teaching takes varies with the era in which it is formulated. This understanding was deepened with the Reformation, whose claims to restore something truer to the original form of Christianity involved making historical judgements about the development or distortion of theology over the previous centuries.

Later, with the Enlightenment, the critical stance to the past became more pronounced and it was often assessed in the light of what were then claimed to be absolute standards of reason, objectively and impartially applied. While such claims are now no longer plausible, the belief that it is a primary duty of the present interpreter to be above all *critical* of the past leaves its traces in many accounts of the history of theology. Against this, the fact that there is available a wide range of approaches to the history of doctrine shows that interpretation is often coloured by theological and other beliefs. Here again systematic and historical questions are inseparable, so that the way in which the past should be approached is an open question, at least in the sense that there is room for discussion about which inter-pretation most faithfully accounts for the direction in which the Christian tradition developed.

The way in which interpretation of the past is ideologically or theo-logically loaded can be illustrated by the judgements made by different commentators about the history of theology. The work of the great nineteenth-century historian of dogma, Adolf Harnack,[2] which is still in many respects an excellent guide to much of the thought he describes, provides one clear example of the effect which his framework of interpreta-tion has on his exposition of the sources. According to him, theological thought in the early centuries achieved the transformation of the straight-forward gospel into a philosophy of religion in which a dogmatic Christ obscures the historical Jesus. Doctrinal developments are thus broadly characterised as accretions which distorted the faith. An altogether different picture had been produced earlier in the nineteenth century by J. H. Newman, who argued that later developments should be understood as being like the growth of an organism from a seed, so that additions to the creed are not necessarily foreign accretions but may be the unfolding of what was already implicit in the original faith.[3] Most more recent inter-preters, for example Pelikan, would understand the development of Christian doctrine in a way which falls somewhere between those two. In all cases, the interpretation of history is closely bound up with a view of what theology ought to be and do.

The account which follows is similarly based on a number of assump-tions. The first is that there is no such thing as pure objectivity, but that all interpretation involves some kind of provisional judgement that arises from the personal involvement of the scholar in the subject matter. This is not the same as a subjectivism which holds that all that we know is driven by mere prejudice, but a view that some form of personal commitment to that which is being studied is necessary if it is to be understood at all.[4] Study of the material in conversation with others who have also reviewed it will enable the initial judgements to be confirmed or refuted – most likely confirmed in some respects, refuted in others – but at any rate in such a way that under-standing is broadened and deepened, and the judgements modified. The (objective) truth about our theological past emerges when the past is taken seriously and our theories about it laid out for public debate.

A second assumption is that historical theology is a theological disci-pline. That is to say, our doctrinal past is best understood if its representa-tives are taken seriously as living voices with whom we enter into theological conversation. We shall sometimes agree and sometimes disagree with what they say, and that is what it means to take them seriously. In his *Church Dogmatics* Karl Barth is able to treat even opponents of the Christian faith as theological partners in conversation.[5] Accordingly it can be argued that historical theology should be a *theological* discipline not because we have decided in advance what to find, but because we approach our predecessors as theologians who have something to teach us.

The beginnings of theology: from the Bible to the Fathers

What we call theology emerged out of the biblical writings which, as the record of revelation, provide the source and criterion of Christian theology. But as soon as that is said, qualifications have to be made. Are not the biblical writings themselves theology? The answer is that in so far as there is speech about, from or involving God, there is theology, so that we can speak of the theology of the book of Genesis or of the writer of Revelation. There are other continuities, too, with later theology. The Bible contains and presupposes much doctrine or teaching, often as summaries or confessions of belief.

Yet there is a relative although not absolute difference of both style and content between the Bible and the theology found in later writings. For the most part, the New Testament writings, to concentrate on them, are occasional rather than systematic in their teaching. Although, in common with later theology, they hold that Jesus is the source of salvation, there is relatively little extended exposition or defence of Christian doctrinal teaching. Doctrine tends to be assumed or cited in the service of particular concrete concerns of the writers, often encouragement or exhortation, and so has to be teased out of scripture. For example, although the Bible contains the basis of the doctrine of creation its systematic expression as creation 'out of nothing' emerges only out of sustained engagement with *both* the biblical teaching *and* the challenges to articulate it in the world in which the early church was set.[6]

It is chiefly the change of situation which brought about the development of Christian theology proper. The transition appears to have been made through the development of the 'rule of faith'. This was a confession of faith which summarised, although not always in quite the same form of words, the heart of the Christian faith: belief in God the creator, Jesus Christ the saviour and coming judge, the Holy Spirit, and the church and the Christian life. The rule of faith is essentially a rehearsal of those central affirmations which make Christianity what it distinctively is, and is thus a precursor of the later, more formal creeds. By the end of the second century claims are made that this rule is universal in the church. Like the Bible, however, while it contains theology and doctrine, it is not yet theology in the sense we are approaching.

Theology as a rational or systematic discipline develops when elements of the rule are perceived to be denied or challenged from within or without the church. Internal challenges are those offered by heresy, which means a distortion of the gospel by church teachers of such a kind that it endangers the faith's integrity. External challenges come chiefly from opponents of the claims made by the church. But what from the point of view of the church of the time were dangers, to the historical theologian are seen to be opportunity, for it is through responding to the challenges – by being compelled to think hard about the content of the gospel – that the achievements of theology become possible. The unique significance of the first few centuries of Christian theology – the 'Patristic' period, the era of the early Church Fathers – is that there are then developed the main responses to two challenges in particular: the distinctively Christian doctrine of God and the understanding of the nature of Jesus Christ.

For the content of these two developments, the reader is directed to the articles devoted to them. In summary it can be said that both developments are consequent on the church's understanding of Jesus as the unique agent of divine salvation. It was this that led the Fathers to redefine what was meant by God, and so necessarily to come into conflict with the way in which God was understood in both Judaism and contemporary philosophy. The doctrine of the Trinity was thus developed in order to identify the God who made himself known in the way that Christians believed, so that a direct, if sometimes unsteady, line can be drawn from the baptism of early believers into the name of the Father, the Son and the Holy Spirit and the work of the Cappadocian Fathers and Augustine of Hippo several centuries later.

Similarly, the struggle in the early years was so to articulate the doctrine of the person of Christ that, without any denial of his unity, he could be understood as at once divine – for otherwise he could not save – and human – for otherwise he could not save *us*. The development of christology came to a kind of closure in 451 AD, when the Council of Chalcedon produced the Definition that has remained unquestioned in most parts of the church as a general expression of Christian belief until the modern era. Its central concern was to defend the unity of the person of Christ against those teachings which were suspected of endangering it, but at the same time to affirm that Jesus Christ was both God and man, and fully so.

'The Age of Faith': the age of the schools

The Middle Ages was, in both Eastern and Western parts of the church –
that is, on those communions centred on the rival authorities of Byzantium
and Rome, a period when beliefs were relatively settled. That is not to say
that there were no theological developments; on the contrary, the era was
one of great intellectual achievement. But it was an age in which the character
of theology, shaped as it was in a particular society, was marked by a number
of distinctive features. First, it was a Christian society in the sense that the
Christian religion had been adopted as its official basis, so that we are not now
so much concerned with the forging of a theology in a hostile intellectual environment as with its further articulation in the particular conditions of the time.

Second, just as the age saw a close combination of church and state,
so intellectually it was a synthesis of creed and philosophy – the era of
'Christian philosophy'.[7] Theologians performed their tasks with the help
of an almost universally adopted method, 'of discovering and illustrating
philosophical truth by means of a dialectic based on Aristotelian logic . . . '[8]
Although some scholastic thinkers were more indebted to Plato and some to
Aristotle, they were all concerned to perform in different ways the task set
for the era by Boethius in the sixth century, to combine faith – the creeds of
the church – with reason, the discoveries of philosophy.[9] The difference of
approach is to be seen in the fact that while platonisers tended to begin their
thought with a God whom they conceived to be intuited directly through a
process of divine illumination, the heirs of Aristotle – who was held in deep
suspicion until rather late in the Middle Ages – reached the deity by arguing
'from below', from features of the experienced world.

Third, the character of the theology of the time can be understood in the
light of the fact that it was by and large a credally static era. It was an age
when it was for the most part taken for granted that certain questions had
been settled beyond dispute, so that much thought was exercised on the
method of theology and on the elaboration of generally acknowledged
truths. It is not wholly the case that theologians were more concerned to
elaborate and defend doctrines taken on the church's authority than to strike
out in original ways, as is shown by the contributions made to the theology
of the atonement by Anselm, Abelard and Aquinas. But in general it can
be said that the Patristic period is that in which the doctrines of the great
creeds are being hammered out, the Middle Ages that in which they are
taken for granted, while the modern world that in which they come again
into question.

The theology of the era is no better illustrated than by the character and fate of the *Sentences* of Peter Lombard, a textbook on which hundreds of later theologians wrote commentaries. There were four books of *Sentences*, written around 1150 A D, and they took the form of a compilation rather than what we would call an original theological treatise. Their author applied the scholastic method of question and debate to a series of doctrinal proposi- tions, which were discussed not so much by argument as by citing for or against them various authorities, ranging from scripture, through the Councils and Canons (the official rulings of the Church), to the Fathers, especially Augustine. While this writer did in the course of the discussion develop his own interpretation of the tradition, his approach shows why 'scholasticism' later came to serve as a pejorative term. Theology in this form can easily appear as an unimaginative rearrangement of ideas, at the expense of the deeper penetration into the subject matter that always distinguishes the work of the greatest theologians, many medievals among them.

Just as the work of Lombard dominated developments in the West, so in the East did the achievements of John of Damascus and Gregory Palamas. The former's work in the eighth century achieved a kind of formalisation of the work of those Fathers who preceded him, while the latter in the four- teenth century gave the doctrine of the Trinity the form that it now takes in most theologies of Eastern Orthodoxy. While it would be an exaggeration to say that the Enlightenment and other modern movements have had no effect on Orthodox theology, it is the case that there has been no serious attempt to move beyond John and Palamas, who are themselves understood as authori- tative interpreters of the Fathers, particularly the Cappadocians and Maximus the Confessor. Their work in the fourth and seventh centuries defined, and still provides a final measure of, Eastern teaching on the Trinity, the heart- beat of the Eastern understanding of the faith.

Reconstruction and upheaval: the Reformation and beyond

Martin Luther's breach with the Roman Church in the early sixteenth century was the catalyst for the division of the Western Church into two main blocs. The Reformation is significant for the historical theologian for two reasons: it both represents the recovery of dimensions of theology that had tended to be neglected and begins the fragmentation of the Christian church and theology whose results remain with us today. It is here especially that our presuppositions will affect our interpretation of history. Those with Catholic sympathies will stress the latter, destructive, effects, while more Protestant thinkers will emphasise the reappropriation of what they believe had been neglected elements of the faith.[10]

What is notable about the Reformation is the change in form and atmosphere of its theological writings. First, they reveal a widespread belief that many of the writings of their predecessors had strayed into realms of abstract speculation which had little bearing on the life of the Christian believer. They set out to reverse the trend. Second, and consequently, there is a more directly biblical orientation to their writings. For example, while Aquinas had treated the doctrine of creation rather as a philosophical basis for the rest of theology, barely making use of the Bible except in rare and general references to Genesis and other texts, Luther and Calvin gave their teaching a more directly biblical form. Third, the churches become again theologically innovative – too innovative in the view of Rome – in a number of senses. The writing of credal confessions to teach and defend the faith begins again, as does a move towards a more direct engagement with earlier traditions of doctrine and with scripture. The Fathers are searched for their theology rather than for citations, while in its seeking to be primarily an introduction to scripture Calvin's *Institutes* could not present much more of a contrast to the *Sentences*. In place of the textbook of theology is a determined attempt to relate theology to the life of the ordinary believer and the church.

The real scandal of the way that the Reformation turned out was that it appeared to lead to ruinous quarrels and wars, and they in turn led many observers to the view that Christian dogma, authority and ecclesiastical tradition were the root of most evil. The modern age, therefore, begins with a sustained assault on pillars of traditional Christian doctrine that the Reformers had not questioned, particularly the doctrines of the Trinity, the divinity of Christ and his atoning death. Human individuality and freedom were elevated over the authority of the institution (the church), while reason came in the writings of many critics of Christianity to be opposed to revelation and church authority as the source of human wisdom.

The assault came on many fronts. The authority of the Bible came under attack from philosophical critiques of miracle and theories of interpretation which treated it as essentially the same as other ancient religious literature. Leading philosophers attacked the proofs of the existence of God which had been inherited from the Middle Ages, while in the writings of rationalist opponents of the faith science was exalted over religion as a way of knowing about the truth of the universe. In particular, although Isaac Newton, possibly the greatest of modern scientists, was a religious believer, the mechanist philosophy his discoveries suggested was developed by some of his disciples in a way that tended to exclude God's interaction with the world as the doctrines of the creeds, the atonement and the sacraments required. All this appeared to make theology of a traditional kind, if not impossible, then at least possible only on very different terms.

The question of what such terms should be was explored in the nineteenth and twentieth centuries by a series of theologians of genius. Just as the early period was one of construction and the middle one of consolidation, so now the challenge is of reconstruction or reformulation. Many modern theological discussions concern the relationship of Christianity with modern culture in all its forms. The challenge of rationalist philosophy and science threw into the centre the problem of knowledge, so that much modern theology is exercised with systematic questions about the relation between Christian truth claims with those of other disciplines and forms of life. One can place the different approaches on a spectrum, at one end of which would be attempts to make Christian theology conform to the patterns of enterprises which appear to be successful – history or science, for example – at the other a determination to preserve above all the distinctive content of Christian faith.[11] But it has to be said that the overall picture is more one of confusion than of a rich diversity, because the different responses to the challenges of modernity are often incompatible with one another. A number of guides to modern systematic theology, in which the developments are treated in detail, are available.

SYSTEMATIC THEOLOGY

Some complexities

To be systematic in some enterprise, whether the activity be laying a table, planting a garden or organising a body of thought, is to engage in it according to some rational order. When it comes to theological thought, however, the matter becomes complicated, because there are a number of different ways in which one might claim to be systematic. Someone, and, as we shall see, Irenaeus is a good example, may be considered a systematic thinker in the sense that he is aware of the implications of one aspect of belief on another, but never succeeds in ordering those thoughts in what could be called a system. In Brunner's words, he was able 'to perceive the connections between truths, and to know which belongs to which... No other thinker was able to weld ideas together which others allowed to slip as he was able to do.'[12] Or one may be systematic, as the philosopher Spinoza was systematic, in ordering all his thoughts on a topic in a tightly arranged and geometrically argued circle, which could be entered in any place and followed round back to the starting point.

Being systematic in theology involves, first, responsibility for the overall consistency of what one says. The systematic theologian must be aware of the relation to each other of different parts of the content of a theology. A simple example is the relation of the doctrine of God and Christ. If we say things about one that contradict what we say about the other, we shall be unsystematic. Once that is said, however, all kinds of questions arise. How systematic may we be in theology, given the fact that we, finite human beings, are seeking to speak about God? In book after book, Kierkegaard accused Hegel of so systematising the content of the faith that he turned it into a philosophy. The coming together of eternity and time in Christ, he believed, made theology essentially resistant to any kind of systematisation. Kierkegaard is in that respect undoubtedly in tune with the main traditions of Christian theology. Moreover, for eschatological reasons, we may wish to hold that because all our knowledge is provisional there are necessary limits to its completeness. It follows that our view of what it is to be systematic is closely bound up with our view of what the Christian faith is. And yet a fundamental point remains: if Christianity is to claim to be a true and rational faith, there must be consistency *of some kind* among its various doctrines.

This is a more than merely theoretical concern. Christian theology is concerned with practice as well as theory, especially in view of the fact that the gospel is centred on divine action in Jesus of Nazareth. That practice has a number of focuses, not only narrowly on what is called Christian ethics, but more broadly in the way the faith takes shape in communities and institutions, and in their forms of worship. No systematic theology is complete unless ethics and ecclesiology are in some way integral to its articulation.

A second feature of being systematic involves an awareness of the relation between the content of a theology and the contents of two other realms. The first of these is the sources specific to the faith, especially the Bible and the tradition of those writings, both official and unofficial, which are historical theology's main concern. Whatever stance one takes to the question of how these sources relate to each other, systematic theology manifestly stands in an intrinsic relation to them, for it could not be what it is without them. It is in somewhat more extrinsic relation to the second realm, which is constituted by claims for truth in human culture in general, especially perhaps philosophy and science. Here two extremes are possible. One may reject any interaction, and go one's own way in the firm belief that everything outside 'pure' theology is the work of the father of lies; or one may believe that God makes himself and the truth of his world known in all kinds of ways, so that we may draw broadly on 'secular' culture for theological insight. While no serious theologian belongs entirely in either camp, the focus of the discussion is the ways in which God is (1) understood to be the source of truth and (2) makes that truth known to the human mind. In what sense are our minds to be understood as fallen, so that they can know only if they are redeemed? And does this fallenness affect only theological knowledge, or all forms of knowledge? One example is the relation between the theology of creation and the world of scientific discovery. How far should the theologian ignore and how far be influenced by the claims – themselves not always consistent with one another – of natural scientists?

Much here depends upon the conception of reason with which a theologian operates. Contrary to some assumptions, what we mean by reason is by no means straightforward or agreed. All would agree that reason involves the use of general terms, argument, logic and the rest. That is the meaning of 'reason' in a neutral or merely technical sense. But one of the things inherited from the Greeks is a view of reason as ontological, in Paul Tillich's expression.[13] This is reason as it is conceived to be a capacity or endowment – a spark of the divine, perhaps – which in some way or other enables us to come to engage with the very nature of reality. The fact that, unless we are out and out subjectivists, we claim to be able to know the world, each other or God shows that there is something in that. But differences in conceptions of what reason is able to do *on its own* affect conceptions of the nature of systematic theology in various ways, especially in determining the place and relation of 'natural' and 'revealed' theology.

A number of different questions, therefore, will jostle for attention in the following examples. First is the question of the relation of a theology to its sources, and particularly to scripture and tradition. Second comes the internal relation of the various items held to belong to the Christian creed, while third is that of how far the content of theology should be affected by changing conceptions of truth in the world beyond the church. Fourth, and closely related to the first three, is the question of method, the relation between the way we go about constructing a body of theological thought and the content we believe it should have. In the following sections I shall try to bring out some of the aspects of this wide-ranging and complex matter with the help of three pairs of contrasting theologians: from the ancient world, from the medieval and from more recent times.

Theology and culture: Irenaeus and Origen

We begin with two early theologians who represent different styles of theology, and indeed continue today to provide models for the way in which the subject is approached. Both Irenaeus and Origen were church theologians, in that the articulation and defence of the Christian faith was their primary concern. Both adhered to very much the same doctrinal standards, and appealed in their work to scripture both in itself and as its teaching was summarised in the credal confessions which were shared by all parts of the early church. Where they differ is the way in which they responded to aspects of the Greek culture within which the church was set. A simple way of describing the difference between them is that they were, respectively, theologians of crisis and of culture.

For Irenaeus, the culture which dominated his concerns – 'Gnosticism' – was an enemy to be overcome by the use of every intellectual weapon at his disposal. His relation to the world outside the church was not negative, but he would not compromise on what he argued to be essential teaching about God who created and redeemed the world in Jesus Christ. His opponents represented – among other things – Greek philosophical influence in its more threatening form. Greek thought, like much modern thought, always had a tendency to dualism in the sense of a division of the world into two spheres of reality, the intelligible or rational and the material or sensible. The former, because it was apprehensible by mind, was understood as a higher reality, knowable and reliable; the latter, known through the bodily senses, was unreliable and therefore inferior.

In the thought of some of Irenaeus' Gnostic opponents this took the form of a disparagement of the material world and a denial that the God of Jesus Christ was the same God as the one who had created the world. This faced Irenaeus with a crisis for the faith, and his vigorous orientation to the fact that the Son of God had become flesh, and thus material, led him to be far more critical of his philosophical inheritance than his predecessors had been. He was anti-dualistic in that he affirmed the common createdness of all being, whether spiritual or material, and is therefore one of the earliest proponents of the view that God created everything out of nothing. The importance of the ethical dimension is also made very clear, and Irenaeus accused his opponents of adopting contradictory attitudes to life in the body, because they tended variously towards asceticism and licence, yet both for the same reason, that they despised the body. For him, because we shall be judged for what we do in the body, our life in it is of positive import.

From his place in the cultured city of Alexandria, Origen took a far more positive attitude to the philosophy of the age, and a correspondingly more negative one to life in the body, which he tended to treat as a preparation for a return to life with God outside it. Affirming the rule of faith, though rather more selectively than Irenaeus, he too taught the doctrine of creation out of nothing, and indeed showed in the first great system of theology, his *On First Principles*, how it fitted with all the other articles of the faith. But his qualifications of the doctrine of creation indicate a greater preparedness to compromise with culture. He was unable to be as positive as Irenaeus about the goodness of this material world, postulating a two-stage creation, in the first of which purely intellectual beings were created and only then the material world. This dualism led him to a relative disparagement of the world: it is indeed good, but only instrumentally so, for its main purpose is to provide a place of education whereby the fallen spirits should be able to find their way back to God. His is not a pure dualism, because the spirits, like matter, were all created by God, but dualism is by no means banished.

Our two early theologians, then, are systematic in different senses. As the originator of the first great system of Christian theology, Origen's achievement is to show how all the doctrines of the faith belong together as a coherent whole. In this way, he defended the consistency and philosophical respectability of the faith. Irenaeus is less concerned with systematic consistency, more with the integrity of the faith in the face of attack. As we have seen, he thought systematically in a broad sense, so that our contrast shows that different conceptions of consistency are at stake. It is my view that Irenaeus is a model for all systematic theologians.

Faith and reason: Anselm and Aquinas

In the Middle Ages Origen's vision of a synthesis of the heritage of the Bible and Greek reason became reality. The Father of the Western version of the synthesis was Augustine of Hippo, and all later theology in this tradition descends in some line or other from him. By virtue of the medieval preoccupation with the relation between theology and philosophy, Anselm and Aquinas are therefore systematic in ways that their two predecessors were not. Although they were concerned in many of their works to defend the truth and rationality of the faith, they wrote for a world which shared more of their assumptions than do the ancient and modern intellectual worlds. It was a culture where it was generally assumed that there was a divine order of some kind, and that therefore life and thought took place within a broadly just and rational world, whose features all interlocked.

That synthesis, however, did not rule out a variety of method and approach to theology. In Anselm, the Platonist, we see two characteristic features. First, following Augustine, he bases his theology on faith: all is faith in search of understanding, which means for him that theology derives from an essential directedness of Christian faith to rational understanding. All is of a piece: both his most famous proof of the existence of God and his study of the work of Christ are theological and philosophical *at the same time*. Philosophy is used in the service of the Christian vision and so integrated into it. Anselm's understanding of faith has both subjective and objective poles, referring as it does to his own personal commitment to God and to his confidence in the authoritative teaching tradition of the church. Thus no independent, or semi-independent, basis for his thought is to be sought from philosophy. This seems unusual to us, tending as we do to distinguish the philosophical from the theological content of theology, and seeing, for example, the proofs of the existence of God as belonging to the former, christology to the latter.

Second, Anselm had a strong, almost rationalist, confidence in what theological reason could achieve. He prefaces his christology with the intention to prove 'by necessary reasons' – irrefutable logic, we might say – that even laying aside our belief that Christ had indeed come to save us from our sins, we can demonstrate the rationality of the incarnation. Similarly, he held that once he had completed his proof of the existence of God, he could not now doubt God's existence even if he wanted to. Accordingly Anselm is a systematic theologian in the measure that he sets out to defend the inherent rationality of the faith with high confidence in its intellectual defensibility and reason's capacity to understand it, to a degree.

Like Anselm's, Aquinas' enterprise is one of faith in that it is based upon a prior belief in the unity of all truth, guaranteed by God. But his confidence in and employment of reason is rather different, above all in the respect that he held to a version of what is known as the two-source theory of truth. Although truth is one, there are two channels by which it comes, reason – the innate power of the mind to know God, a power left essentially unimpaired by the Fall – and revelation, by which Aquinas meant the authoritative deposit of faith, the truths of the Christian religion entrusted to the church. He believed that Anselm was wrong to treat belief in God's existence as part of the creed. For him, it was something that had to be established prior to the specific faith of the church, as part of a common structure of human belief in God.

Accordingly, he seeks to establish the existence and nature of God in the opening sections of his *Summa Theologiae* by means of concepts drawn from Aristotle, and appropriately adapted for his use. These opening gambits provide his basis for being a systematic theologian, and systematic he is, for once the existence of God is established, there follows discussion of all the articles of Christian belief, as well as detailed treatments of ethics. The difference from Anselm is that reason and faith are integrated by being set side by side, although it has also to be said that when Aquinas comes to treat the doctrines specific to the Christian faith, his method and content become similar to that of his great predecessor. Aquinas is the father of all those who hold that theology requires some basis in independent rational argument.

Content and method: Schleiermacher and Barth

Friedrich Schleiermacher and Karl Barth, from the nineteenth and twentieth centuries respectively, provide illustrations of different modern ways of going about systematic theology. They represent polar opposites in understanding the relation between method and content: between how we go about doing systematic theology and what we put into it.[14]

With Schleiermacher self-consciousness about theological method comes to the centre of the stage in a new way. Convinced above all by Kantian philosophy that one could no longer do theology in the old ways, by either proofs of the existence of God or appeal to God's action in history, he turned to experience as the matrix for a new approach to theology. Our experience, analysed in depth, demonstrates an awareness, given within that experience but not identical with it, of God understood as one on whom we are absolutely dependent. Theology's task is to explicate that experience as it takes shape at any given time. In the Christian church, theology is therefore the articulation of the experience of God mediated by Jesus of Nazareth. According to Schleiermacher's famous characterisation, 'Christian doctrines are accounts of the Christian religious affections set forth in speech.'[15] They therefore express the doctrine of God as essentially a function of human experience of the divine.

By contrast, Barth's attempt to overcome the Kantian restriction is to return to a theology of historical revelation, derived from scripture and conceived as God's demonstration that he is able to be present to the world in freedom and sovereignty. Kant had claimed that God cannot be known from the structures of worldly being. Rejecting this as mere a priori theory, Barth replied that because God did become present to the world in Christ, it followed that he was able to. The whole of Barth's theology is an outworking of the simple insight that in Jesus Christ God makes himself known as the triune God, whose activities towards and in the world take the form of creation, reconciliation and redemption.

The differences between the two lead to a strong disagreement about what it is to be systematic. Because Schleiermacher sees theology as the systematic articulation of an experience that is essentially above reason, the very fuzziness of the concept of God requires a correspondingly strong stress on the tight coherence of what is written, and a relative indifference to the language that is used. For Barth, on the other hand, the firmer outlines of the concept of God require at once a closer relation of revelation and language – which must be 'commandeered' by revelation if it is to be adequate to its task – and a more open structure to the theology. Barth disavows any desire for system, but understands Jesus Christ, as the Word of God, to operate as the centre or hub of a wheel from which various lines can be drawn in relative independence of one another.

CONCLUSION

The six examples are chosen to indicate a number of choices about the way the task should be approached. Irenaeus' approach is to be preferred to Origen's not only because we are faced, as he was, with a crisis for belief, but because his firm rooting in the Bible and the rule of faith enabled him to articulate a conception of the relation of creation and redemption which has never been surpassed. His awareness of the limits of the possibility of rationalisation was not perhaps shared by Anselm, but we can share the latter's view that faith is both prior to reason and of its own nature requires understanding. That twofold belief is an important reminder that theology is dependent upon grace for its very possibility. Barth's strongly trinitarian version of Anselm's method and approach has set the scene for what is arguably the most hopeful of the theological approaches jostling for attention today, the renewal of a trinitarian centre for Christian thought.

In what sense is Barth to be called a systematic theologian? If Schleiermacher, with his modern drive for system is a paradigm for a conception of the subject, he is not rightly so called. His concern is to articulate Christian theology in its own right, not in borrowed philosophical clothes, and Christianity of its very nature resists systematisation. But Barth himself said that after Kant theology could no longer proceed without some awareness of the method of reason which it employs. In the modern world, theology must be systematic in that sense. But if it is true to its character as mediator of a definite content, taking the form of gift, it must concentrate on the dogmatic task, which is to articulate its specific object, the being and action of the triune God. Systematic theology as a task of Christian thought is therefore best understood as dogmatics which is epistemologically self-aware.

Notes

1 Jaroslav Pelikan, *The Christian Tradition, A History of the Development of Doctrine*, 5 vols. (Chicago and London: Chicago University Press, 1971–89), vol. I, p. 3.

2 Adolf Harnack, *History of Dogma*, trans. in 5 vols. (London: Williams and Norgate, 1897–9).

3 John Henry Newman, *An Essay on the Development of Christian Doctrine*, 1945 edn (Harmondsworth: Penguin Books, 1974).

4 This position was argued by Michael Polanyi with respect to the philosophy of science. His *Personal Knowledge. Towards a Post-Critical Philosophy*, 2nd edn (London: Routledge, 1962) provides interesting insights into the relation of faith and reason in all spheres of human intellectual endeavour.

5 See especially his discussion of existentialists and others in *Church Dogmatics*, ed. G. W. Bromiley and T. F. Torrance (Edinburgh: T. & T. Clark, 1957–69), vol. III, part 3, pp. 334–49.

6 Gerhard May, *Creatio ex Nihilo. The Doctrine of 'Creation out of Nothing' in Early Christian Thought*, trans. A. S. Worrall (Edinburgh: T. & T. Clark, 1994).

7 Etienne Gilson, *History of Christian Philosophy in the Middle Ages* (London: Sheed and Ward, 1955).

8 David Knowles, *The Evolution of Medieval Thought* (London: Longman, 1962), pp. 87–8.

9 Josef Pieper, *Scholasticism* (London: Faber, 1960), p. 37. 'As far as you are able, join faith with reason.'

10 That this writer tends to the latter view does not mean that he would not prefer that reform had happened as many of its earlier advocates had hoped, with universal and peaceful renewal rather than polarisation, war and mutual condemnation.

11 See Hans Frei, *Types of Christian Theology*, ed. George Hunsinger and William C. Placher (New Haven and London: Yale University Press, 1992), for one, slightly restrictive, account of the range of possibilities.

12 Emil Brunner, *The Mediator. A Study of the Central Doctrine of the Christian Faith*, trans. Olive Wyon (Philadelphia: Westminster Press, 1947), p. 262.

13 Paul Tillich, *Systematic Theology* (London: Nisbet, 1968), vol. I, p. 80.

14 For an argument that Coleridge provides a third model for modern systematic theology, see my article, 'An English Systematic Theology?', *Scottish Journal of Theology* 46 (1993): 479–96.

15 The heading of section 15 of Friedrich Schleiermacher, *The Christian Faith*, ed. H. R. Mackintosh and J. S. Stewart (Edinburgh: T. & T. Clark, 1928), p. 76.

Further reading

Barth, Karl, *Church Dogmatics*, translation edited by G. W. Bromiley and T. F. Torrance, Edinburgh: T. & T. Clark, 1956–75, volume I, parts 1 and 2.

Protestant Theology in the Nineteenth Century: Its Background and History, translated by B. Cozens and J. Bowden, London: S C M Press, 1972.

Cunliffe Jones, Hubert, editor, *A History of Christian Doctrine*, Edinburgh: T. & T. Clark, 1978.

Dalferth, Ingolf, *Theology and Philosophy*, Oxford: Blackwell, 1988.

Frei, Hans, *Types of Christian Theology*, edited by George Hunsinger and William C. Placher, New Haven and London: Yale University Press, 1992.

Hart, Trevor, *Faith Thinking. The Dynamics of Christian Theology*, London: S P C K, 1995.

Heron, Alasdair, *A Century of Protestant Theology*, London: Lutterworth Press, 1980.

Nicholls, William, *Historical and Systematic Theology. The Pelican Guide to Modern Theology, volume I*, Harmondsworth: Penguin Books, 1969.

Pelikan, Jaroslav, *The Christian Tradition, A History of the Development of Doctrine*, 5 volumes, Chicago and London: Chicago University Press, 1971–89.

Tillich, Paul, *Systematic Theology*, 3 volumes, London: Nisbet, 1968.

2 On doctrine and ethics

STANLEY HAUERWAS

PROBLEMATISING THE RELATION BETWEEN DOCTRINE AND ETHICS

Strange as it may seem, [the] general conception of ethics coincides exactly with the conception of sin. So we have every reason to treat it with circumspection. We do take up the question of the good and we try to answer it. But there can be no more trying to escape the grace of God. On the contrary, we have to try to prevent this escape. When we speak of ethics, the term cannot include anything more than this confirmation of the truth of the grace of God as it is addressed to man. If dogmatics, if the doctrine of God, is ethics, this means necessarily and decisively that it is the attestation of that *divine* ethics, the attestation of the good of the command issued to Jesus Christ and fulfilled by Him. There can be no question of any other good in addition to this.[1]

Any account of the relation between Christian doctrine and ethics must take account of this passage from Karl Barth. By 'take account' I mean at the very least we need to understand Barth's claim that the general conception of ethics coincides with the conception of sin. What is entailed by the 'general conception of ethics' and why would such a conception seem so theologically problematic? What developments in theology and ethics would have led Barth to make such an exaggerated assertion? After all, is not one of the defining marks of being Christian, particularly in modernity, that Christians still believe they ought to be morally good? In fact most people, including most Christian people, assume that if Christianity is not about morality it is not about anything.

As a result many Christians remain relatively indifferent to 'doctrinal matters', but assume that one cannot make any compromises when it comes to moral questions. For liberal Christians one can be a Christian without being too concerned with questions, for example, about the Trinity, but one cannot remain indifferent to 'justice issues'. Conservative Christians often claim to care a great deal about doctrine, particularly doctrines about the Bible, but they assume that doctrines about the Bible are necessary to reinforce their prior established views about personal and sexual misconduct. For both, 'ethics' has become the justification for being Christian. Yet from Barth's standpoint both liberal and conservative Christians, Catholic and Protestant, mistakenly have assumed that a distinction can be drawn between doctrine and ethics. However, from Barth's perspective something has already gone wrong if Christians have to ask what the relation or relations might be between doctrine and ethics. To assume that a 'relation' between doctrine and ethics needs to be explicated unjustifiably presumes that something called 'ethics' exists prior to or independent from 'doctrine'. Yet it is exactly that assumption which has shaped Christian practice and reflection about ethics in modernity. For example, most Christians now assume that a word like 'justice' is about ethics, but a word like 'creation' is what you say if you are being theological. The burden of this chapter is to provide a narrative which explains how the disjunction between doctrine and ethics arose and why, as Barth claims, such a division cannot be justified theologically.

Yet surely, it may be asked, you are not saying that Christian ethics does not exist? After all, there is even a discipline called Christian ethics widely taught in colleges, universities and seminaries. That such a discipline does exist cannot be denied, but its existence may be an indication that something has gone wrong in basic Christian practices that makes such a discipline necessary.[2] Once there was no Christian ethics simply because Christians could not distinguish between their beliefs and their behaviour. They assumed that their lives exemplified (or at least should exemplify) their doctrines in a manner that made a division between life and doctrine impossible.

It is important that this point be not misunderstood. As I will indicate below, Christians of different times and in different ways have distinguished theology and ethics, life from doctrine, if only to emphasise various aspects of faith or underscore certain qualities of character. There is, moreover, always the danger that because such analytical distinctions can be made Christian reality itself can be so divided. As we shall see, the task of the theologian is not to deny that for certain limited purposes ethics can be distinguished from theology, but to refuse their supposed ontological and practical independence.

Unfortunately, the provisional nature of the distinction between theology and ethics is too often forgotten, leading some to presume that histories of Christian ethics in distinction from Christian theology can be written. Such histories cannot help but distort the character of Christian discourse.

At least it cannot help but distort the character of Christian discourse that we find in scripture and Christian theology through most of Christian history.

For example, too often it is assumed that 'biblical ethics' is to be found in materials in the Bible that look like 'ethics' to us. The Ten Commandments or the Sermon on the Mount are assumed to be prime candidates for ethics. This creates the problem of whether they must be taken literally, since at least some of the commandments, particularly in the Sermon on the Mount, seem impossible, or at least impractical, to follow. These assumed practical difficulties in following the 'ethics of the Bible' are often given quite sophisticated theological expression in terms shaped by the Protestant Reformation. For instance, the Bible is commonly read as an exemplification of the tension between law and gospel. From such a perspective the central question with which Christian ethics deals is how to understand the relation between creation and redemption or why justification precedes sanctification.

That we now think, for example, that there is a 'problem' in understanding the relation between Paul's discussion of justification in Romans 5:1–11 and the 'moral' instruction he gives in chapters 12–14 of Romans says more about us than it does about Paul. Our assumption that Romans 5 is theology and the later chapters of Romans constitute ethics is not a distinction Paul would recognise. There is no indication in Romans that Romans 5 is more significant than or foundational than Romans 12. The view that one of the tasks of Christian ethics is to provide some account of this 'problem' in Paul is but an indication that the Pauline text is being read through the polemics of the Reformation.

Of course it can be argued that we have learned much since Paul's day, or at least we face different challenges, and that we rightly ought to subject Paul's work to our own peculiarly modern questions concerning the relation of theology to ethics. The difficulty with such a response is that it fails to appreciate that the question of the relation between doctrine and ethics is not just a 'conceptual' matter but an institutional, or more accurately, an ecclesial issue. That Christians must begin to ask what relation might pertain between their theological convictions and their ethical practices indicates changes in the character of the church as well as the church's relation to the world.

For example, Paul saw no tension between his account of justification and the admonitions in Romans 12 because he assumed the church was the subject of God's imperatives. As Richard Hays points out, because Paul thought God was forming a covenant people, 'the primary sphere of moral concern is not the character of the individual, but the corporate obedience of the church. Paul's formulation in Romans 12:1–2 encapsulates the vision:

"Present your bodies (*somata*, plural) as a living sacrifice (*thysian*, singular), holy and well-pleasing to God. And do not be conformed to this age, but be transformed by the renewing of your mind . . . " The community, in its corporate life, is called to embody an alternative order that stands as a sign of God's redemptive purposes in the world.'[3] Our assumption that we must ask the question of the relation between doctrine and ethics indicates that we inhabit a quite different set of ecclesial practices from those assumed by Paul.

Which is a reminder that questions about the relations between doctrine and ethics are not simply a matter of the relation between 'ideas', but rather a reflection of the ever changing practices of the church.[4] Hence, the development of 'doctrine', which was at least in part determined by the church's response to heresy, can look quite different if and when the boundaries between church and the world have become blurred. If, for example, Christians are no longer distinguishable from the world by how they use their possessions, questions concerning the two natures of Christ may assume quite a different character, as questions of 'belief' now become the defining mark of the Christian rather than our willingness to share our possessions as part of our discipleship.[5]

I am not suggesting that questions about the two natures of Christ are unimportant. Rather, I am noting that only when such issues become 'doctrine' is one then led to ask what such doctrines have to do with how Christians are to live. What seem at first glance to be theological questions involving conceptual relations between ideas can in fact hide what are actually issues concerning the nature of the church. Barth's suggestion that any general conception of ethics is equivalent to sin is, therefore, a claim with implications about the church's relation to the world that is not immediately apparent. In order to understand better what is at stake in Barth's claim I must first provide the story that constitutes the background behind Barth's insistence that doctrine is ethics.

HOW CHRISTIANS HAVE THOUGHT ABOUT BEING CHRISTIAN: SOME HISTORICAL CONSIDERATIONS

I observed above that the notion of Christian ethics is a modern invention. At one time Christian ethics did not exist. That does not mean that Christians did not think about how best to live their lives as Christians. There are obvious examples of such reflection in the New Testament as well as among the Church Fathers. That may well put the matter too lamely just to the extent that the New Testament and the early Christian theologians thought about little else than how Christians were to live their lives. For the ancients, pagan and Christian, to be schooled in philosophy or theology meant to submit one's life to a master in order to gain the virtues necessary to be a philosopher or a Christian.[6] Ethics, in such a context, was not some 'aspect' of life, but rather inclusive of all that constituted a person's life.[7]

That we do not find explicit treatises on Christian ethics in scripture or in the work of the patristic writers does not mean they were unconcerned with giving direction to the church. They simply did not distinguish between theology and pastoral direction as we now do. Tertullian's *On Patience* may well have been the first treatise by a Christian on what we think of as a specifically moral topic, but there is no indication that he would have understood this treatise to be anything substantially different from his other theological and pastoral work.[8] Augustine, probably more than any of the early Church Fathers, did more to shape what would later be thought of as Christian ethics. On his *On the Morals of the Catholic Church*, he suggested that the fourfold division of the virtues familiar to pagan philosophers could rightly be understood only as forms of love whose object is God. Thus 'temperance is love keeping itself entire and incorrupt for God; fortitude is love bearing everything readily for the sake of God; justice is love serving God only, and therefore ruling well all else, as subject to man; prudence is love making a right distinction between what helps it towards God and what might hinder it'.[9]

Augustine's conflict with the Pelagians resulted in a particularly rich set of treatises dealing with topics such as grace and free will, but also marriage and concupiscence.[10] Equally important is Augustine's *The City of God*, in which he narrates all of human history as a conflict between the earthly and heavenly cities.[11] The earthly city knows not God and is thus characterised by an order secured only through violence. In contrast, the heavenly city worships the one true God, making possible the collection of 'a society of aliens, speaking all languages. She takes no account of any difference in customs, laws, and institutions, by which earthly peace is achieved and preserved – not that she annuls or abolishes any of those, rather, she maintains them and follows them, provided that no hindrance is presented thereby to the religion which teaches that the one supreme and true God is to be worshipped.'[12] How properly to understand the relation between the two cities becomes the central issue for the development of what comes to be called Christian social ethics. Of course, Augustine would have found the modern distinction between personal and social ethics at the very least questionable and more likely theologically a mistake.

The Church Fathers and Augustine did much to shape the way Christians think about Christian living, but equally, if not more important, is the development of the penitential tradition. In 1 Corinthians 5 Paul had insisted that the Corinthians were to 'root out the evil-doer from the community', but the question remained whether such an evil-doer should be received back into the community after due repentance. This was an issue that was not resolved until the Council of Nicaea in 325. That Council, which is primarily known for maintaining the full divinity of Christ against the Arians, also set a policy for the readmission of excommunicants after appropriate periods of penance. This was particularly significant since often the sin they had committed had been apostasy during times of persecution. Other major sins involved idolatry, adultery and homicide – all of which required public penance which was not only quite onerous but available only once in a person's life.[13]

A major development occurred in this tradition largely by accident. Drawing on the monastic habit of spiritual direction of one monk by another, there developed in Ireland the practice of private confession to a priest with forgiveness of sins offered after appropriate penance. This practice resulted in the development of books called Penitentials that were meant as aids to confessors so that the appropriate penance would be given for the corresponding sin. These books differed markedly one from the other, indicating different Christian practices at different times and places. Their organisation was quite varied with little or no attempt at theological rationale. For example, *The Penitential of Theodore* stipulated the following with regard to theft and avarice:

1 If any layman carries off a monk from the monastery by stealth, he shall either enter a monastery to serve God or subject himself to human servitude.
2 Money stolen or robbed from churches is to be restored fourfold; from secular persons, twofold.[14]

These books were carried by Irish missionaries across Europe and soon became the rule throughout Christendom. Though they were not explicitly theological, they depended on the continuing presumption that the church through baptism was to be a holy community. They were no doubt open to great misuse, but they also became the way the church grappled with the complexity of Christian behaviour through the development of casuistry, that is, close attention to particular cases. From these beginnings there developed as part of the church's theological mission a special task called moral theology. Under the guidance of Pope Gregory VII the church's practices concerning moral questions were made more uniform through canon law and the development of *Summae Confessorum*. The latter were pastoral handbooks that gave theological order to the penitentials so that priests might be given guidance in the administration of what had become the sacrament of penance.

Thus a clear tradition was established in the Penitentials, in canon law and in the *Summae Confessorum*, in which ethics was distinguished from theology and doctrine. There was, moreover, specialist training for each of these tasks, as canon lawyers, moral theologians and theologians were given distinctive training for their different roles. However, these diverse tasks were, in fact, one in so far as their intelligibility depended on the practices of the church. Ethics was not something done in distinction from theology, since both theology and moral theology presumed baptism, penance, preaching and eucharist as essential for the corporate life of the church.

Perhaps nowhere is this inseparable unity between the ethical and the theological dimensions of Christian living better exemplified than in the great *Summa Theologiae* of Thomas Aquinas. Though often characterised as a defender of 'natural theology', Aquinas' *Summa* is first and foremost a work in Christian theology. The structure of Aquinas' *Summa Contra Gentiles*, as well as the *Summa Theologiae*, draws upon the image of God as artist, such that all created realities are depicted as issuing from and returning to God.[15] In other words, Aquinas' great works evince a three-part structure. The story of creation begins in divine freedom; then Aquinas explains how all creation, and in particular that part of creation called human, returns to God. Finally, in the third part he provides an account of the means of creation's return to God through Christ and the sacraments. The *Summa*, rather than being an argument for the independence of ethics, as it is sometimes characterised, is concerned to place the Christian's journey to God squarely within the doctrine of God.

Indeed, it has been argued that one of Aquinas' main purposes in writing the *Summa* was expressed in the second part, which treats moral matters more specifically and directly. Aquinas thought the manuals far too haphazard in their presentation of the Christian moral life.[16] He therefore sought to place the discussion of morality in the context of a consideration of human nature and the virtues appropriate to our nature as creatures whose destiny was nothing less than to be friends with God. Drawing deeply on Aristotle's account of the virtues, Aquinas nonetheless argued that even the so-called natural virtues must be formed by charity if they are to be capable of directing us to God.

Aquinas' intentions, however, were subverted, as it was not long before the *secunda pars*, the second part, was abstracted from its context in the *Summa* and used as if it stood on its own.[17] This kind of anthologising in part accounts for the presumption by later commentators that law, and in particular natural law, stands at the centre of Aquinas' account. Yet Aquinas' understanding of the moral life is one that assumes the primacy of the virtues for the shape of the Christian life. Aquinas' work was either misunderstood or ignored through subsequent centuries, even to the point that he was used to support positions almost diametrically opposed to his own views.

The developments of the late Middle Ages are not unimportant, but in many ways they are now lost due to the profound effect the Reformation had for shaping how Protestant and Catholic alike began to think about the Christian life. It is not as if Martin Luther and John Calvin in their own work mark an entirely new way of thinking about the Christian life, but certainly the forces they unleashed changed everything. Neither Luther nor Calvin distinguished between theology and ethics. Certainly Luther stressed the 'external' character of our justification, yet in *The Freedom of a Christian* he equally maintained that 'a Christian, like Christ his head, is filled and made rich by faith and should be content with this form of God which he has obtained by faith; only he should increase this faith until it is made perfect. For this faith is his life, his righteousness, and his salvation: it saves him and makes him acceptable, and bestows upon him all things that are Christ's.'[18]

Yet the polemical terms of the Reformation could not help but reshape how ethics was conceived in relation to theology. From this time on, faith, not works, determined the Christian's relationship to God. Moreover works became associated with 'ethics', particularly as ethics was alleged to be the way sinners attempt to secure their standing before God as a means to avoid complete dependence on God's grace. So for Protestants the Christian life is now characterised in such a way that there always exists a tension between law and grace. The law is needed, but we can never attain salvation through the law and the works of the law. A similar tension constitutes the Lutheran understanding of the Christian's relation to what is now known as the 'orders of creation', that is, marriage, the legal order, the state. Christians are called to love their neighbours through submission to such orders, recognising that such service is not and cannot be that promised in the order of redemption.[19]

Calvin, and in particular later developments in Calvinism, was not as determined by the polemical context of the Lutheran Reformation. However, justification by faith is no less central for Calvin, who equally insists that 'actual holiness of life is not separated from free imputation of righteousness'.[20] Accordingly, Calvinists stressed the importance of the sanctification of the Christian and the Christian community. Christians were expected to examine their lives daily so they might grow into holiness. This theme was retained in the Anglican tradition and was given particularly strong emphasis in the Wesleyan revival in England as well as other forms of pietism.

Certainly the Protestant Reformation changed the way Christians understood 'ethics', but far more important were changes in the ways Christians related to their world. In earlier centuries, the Christian understanding of life could be articulated in the language of natural law, but it was assumed that natural law was only intelligible as part of divine law as mediated by the church. What was lost after the Reformation was exactly this understanding of the church as the indispensable context in which order might be given to the Christian life. For example, with the loss of the rite of penance in Protestantism, casuistry as an activity of moral theologians was lost. Such a loss did not seem to be a problem as long as it was assumed that everyone 'knew' what it meant to be Christian. However, as it became less and less clear among Protestants what it 'means' to be Christian there have increasingly been attempts to 'do' ethics. The difficulty is that no consensus about what ethics is or how it should be done exists. As a result, theologians have often turned to philosophy for resources in their search for an ethic – resources that ironically helped create the problem of how to relate theology and ethics, because now it is assumed that 'ethics' is an autonomous discipline that is no longer dependent on religious conviction.

HOW ETHICS BECAME A PROBLEM IN MODERNITY

The birth of modernity is coincident with the beginnings of 'ethics' understood as a distinguishable sphere or realm of human life. Faced with the knowledge of the diversity of moral convictions modern people think of themselves as haunted by the problem of relativism. If our 'ethics' are relative to time and place, what, if anything, prevents our moral opinions from being 'conventional'? If they are conventional some assume they must also be 'arbitrary'. But if our morality is conventional how can we ever expect to secure agreements between people who disagree? Is it our fate to be perpetually at war with one another? 'Ethics' becomes that quest to secure a rational basis for morality so we can be confident that our moral convictions are not arbitrary.

The great name associated with this quest is Immanuel Kant. Kant sought to secure knowledge and morality from the scepticism that the Enlightenment, by its attempt to free all thought from its indebtedness to the past, had produced. Kant also wanted thought to be free from the past; thus his famous declaration – 'Enlightenment is man's release from his self-incurred tutelage. Tutelage is man's inability to make use of his understanding without direction from another. Self-incurred is this tutelage when its cause lies not in lack of reason but in lack of resolution and courage to use it without direction from another.'[21]

Kant's commitment to this Enlightenment ideal was his response to the breakdown of the Christian world. If ethics depended on or was derived from religious belief, then there seemed to be no way to avoid the continuing conflict, as heirs of the Reformation,[22] between Catholics and Protestants. Accordingly, Kant sought to ground ethics in reason itself, since, in his words, 'it is there I discover that what I do can only be unconditionally good to the extent I can will what I have done as a universal law'.[23] Kant called this principle the 'categorical imperative' because it has the form: 'Act only according to that maxim by which you can at the same time will that it should become a universal law.'[24]

Only an ethics based on such an imperative can be autonomous, that is, free of all religious and anthropological presuppositions. Only by acting on the basis of such an imperative can an agent be free. Such an ethic is based on reason alone and can therefore be distinguished from religion, politics and etiquette. Yet Kant did not understand his attempt to make ethics independent of religion to be an anti-religious project but rather one that made faith possible. Indeed in many ways Kant becomes the greatest representative of Protestant liberalism; that is, Protestant liberal theology after Kant is but a series of footnotes to his work.[25]

For example, Protestant theologians no longer sure of the metaphysical status of Christian claims, have sought to secure the ongoing meaningfulness of Christian convictions by anchoring them in anthropological generalisations and/or turning them into ethics. No longer convinced that Jesus is the resurrected Messiah, his significance is now said to be found in his proclamation of the kingdom of God. The kingdom is the outworking in human history of the Fatherhood of God and the Brotherhood of Man.[26] Theology, at least Protestant liberal theology, became ethics, but the ethics it became were distinctively Kant's ethics dressed in religious language.

Such a generalisation must be qualified in the light of Friedrich Schleiermacher's theology and philosophy. Schleiermacher was part of the

Romantic revolt against the rationalism of Kant, but it was a revolt that sought to stay within the presuppositions of the Enlightenment. Schleiermacher's great work, *The Christian Faith*, has no section devoted to ethics.[27] Yet Barth rightly argues that Schleiermacher's work was motivated by the ethical project of drawing people into the movement of education, the exaltation of life, which he understood at bottom to be religious and, thus, Christian. Barth goes so far as to suggest that 'Schleiermacher's entire philosophy of religion, and therefore his entire teaching of the nature of religion and christianity was something secondary, auxiliary to the consolidation of this true concern of his, the ethical one. The fact that, in academic theory, he ranked theology below ethics, is but an expression of this state of affairs.'[28]

Schleiermacher sought to support Christian theology through the development of a philosophical theology which could demonstrate that the existence of the church was necessary for the development of humanity. This project was ethical just to the extent that ethics is understood to express those principles of history by which reason permeates nature and gives it form. In short, ethics is the study of how nature comes to consciousness. The most determinative form of such consciousness Schleiermacher identifies with the 'feeling of absolute dependence'. Thus he begins *The Christian Faith* with a long prolegomenon to establish the proposition: 'the totality of finite being exists only in dependence upon the Infinite is the complete description of that basis of every religious feeling which is here to be set forth'.[29]

Christian theology and ethics for Schleiermacher are descriptive disciplines inasmuch as their task is to set forth the ideas and behaviour of Christian communities in different times and places. Though Schleiermacher often lectured on philosophical and Christian ethics, unfortunately he never published his ethics. From his lectures and posthumous writings we know that he was critical of what he considered the formalism and legalism of Kant's ethics. As a great Plato scholar, he reintroduced the language of virtue and the highest good, though he identified the latter with the rational content of life as a whole. His account of the Christian life was that of 'a continuum between the beginnings of one's desire for communion with God and the culmination of that desire in absolute blessedness'.[30]

More important, however, than Schleiermacher's explicit views about ethics was his conception of the dogmatic task as a civilisational and thus ethical task. The crucial institution for such a civilisational task for Schleiermacher was the university, and in particular, the University of Berlin.[31] Theology could be part of the university, according to Schleiermacher, in so far as it meets, like medicine and the law, human needs indispensable for the state.[32] Since the state needs religion, theology is justified for the training of clergy who are thus seen as servants of the state. The theology that is so justified is now the name of a cluster of disciplines (scripture, church history, dogmatics and practical theology), that are understood to be descriptive in character. Accordingly, theology is no longer understood to be practical knowledge necessary for the acquisition of wisdom, but as a 'science' for the training of semi-public officials.

This reconstrual of the tasks of theology shaped and continues to shape the curricula not only in Germany but in universities and seminaries around the world and, in particular, in the United States. Of course the division of the curriculum into scripture, church history, dogmatics and practical disciplines in these different contexts does not mean that theology was or is necessarily understood in Schleiermacher's terms. But the curriculum so structured created and continues to create the 'problem' of what relation there might be between theology and ethics. In other words, it is unclear exactly where 'ethics' should be located. Is its proper place in 'dogmatics' or in the 'practical disciplines'? The rise and importance of Christian ethics as a discipline in the United States (associated with such people as Reinhold and H. Richard Niebuhr, Paul Ramsey and James Gustafson) has not resolved this fundamental issue. If anything, it has only deepened and further obscured the issue. Indeed, the institutional shape of the theological curriculum, particularly in Protestant seminaries – and increasingly Catholic institutions at least in America have imitated the Protestants – has resulted in intellectual developments that distort the character of theological discourse. The assumption, for example, that students should take 'systematic theology' before they take ethics invites the presumption that theology is in some sense more basic than ethics. In such a context theology begins to look like a 'metaphysics' which one might get straight before one can turn to questions of ethics. Yet as I have indicated above, through most of Christian history Christians have *not* thought it possible to distinguish so easily between what they believe and what they do. At stake is the question of whether theology is first and foremost a discipline of the church or the university.

Thus the significance of Karl Barth's challenge quoted at the beginning of this chapter. For Barth, undisputedly the greatest Protestant theologian of this century, there can be no ethics that is not from beginning to end theological. Indeed, ethics is theological through and through because for Barth theology is more than simply one discipline among others. Theology rather is the exposition of how God's word as found in Jesus Christ provides not only its own ground but the ground for all that we know and do. Barth, therefore, rejects Schleiermacher's attempt to make theology part of a 'larger essential context, of a larger scientific problem-context', by returning theology to its proper role as servant to the church's proclamation of Jesus Christ.[33] For Barth dogmatics cannot have access to a higher or better source of knowledge than that which is found in the church's proclamation that the God Christians worship is triune.

Barth, thus, begins his *Dogmatics* with the doctrine of the Trinity, since it is from that doctrine that 'we actually gather who the God is who reveals Himself and therefore we let it find expression as the interpretation of revelation'.[34] For Barth 'ethics' is but an integral part of the dogmatic task and, therefore, cannot be treated as an independent subject. Barth's explicit reflections on ethics occur in several places in his multi-volume *Church Dogmatics*,[35] but it would be a mistake to assume that his ethics is to be found only in those sections explicitly devoted to ethics. As John Webster argues, Barth's *Dogmatics* is

> a moral ontology – an extensive account of the situation in which human agents act. Barth's ethics has, therefore, a very particular character, both materially and formally. It is primarily devoted to the task of describing the 'space' which agents occupy, and gives only low priority to the description of their character and to the analysis of quandary situations in which they find themselves. Barth's ethics tends to assume that moral problems are resolvable by correct theological description of moral space. And such description involves much more than describing the moral consciousnesses of agents. A Christianly successful moral ontology must be a depiction of the world of human action as it is enclosed and governed by the creative, redemptive, and sanctifying work of God in Christ, present in the power of the Holy Spirit.[36]

The 'ethics' that animates Barth's project is thus quite different from that of Schleiermacher. Barth does not seek to make the church a servant of a civilisational project and thus a supplement for what is a prior conception of ethics. Rather, just as Israel 'annexed' the land of Palestine so Christians must appropriate 'ethics' as a secular, Enlightenment subject matter.[37] For example, notions such as 'the good' or the 'categorical imperative' are far too abstract to give the guidance that can come only from the concreteness of God's command as found in Jesus Christ.[38]

Barth provides extensive discussions of such matters as suicide, euthanasia, marriage and singleness, the ethics of war, the Christian calling to serve the neighbour, but denies that casuistry can ever predetermine

'God's concrete specific command here and now in this particular way, of making a corresponding decision in this particular way, and of summoning others to such a concrete and specific decision'.[39] Accordingly Barth's ethics are often criticised for being too 'occasionalistic', since he denies that we can ever predetermine what we should do prior to God's command. While he may be vulnerable to such criticism what should not be lost is that Barth in his *Dogmatics* has sought to do nothing less than displace human self-consciousness as the legitimating notion for the creation of ethics independent of God's revelation in Christ. By doing so he has returned theology to the presumption that there can be no 'ethics' separate from theology, particularly when theology is understood as an activity of the church.

THEOLOGY AND ETHICS AFTER BARTH

By ending the last section with Barth I do not suggest that Barth's position has won the day. In fact, he remains a minority voice among those Christians presently doing theology and ethics. Barth is particularly unwelcome among those who seek to develop practical or applied ethics in such areas as medicine, business and the professions in general. Those working in such areas assume that the particularity of Christian convictions must be suppressed in the interest of developing an ethic for 'anyone'. Many working in these fields originally had theological training, but they now have come to assume that at most consideration of Christian doctrine is a methodological afterthought to the real business of ethics.

Those trained to do theology 'proper', however, seldom stray into 'ethics' as part of their job description. Too often theologians spend their time writing prolegomena, that is, essays on theological method meant to show how theology should be done in case anyone ever got around to doing any. Those who do try to do theology too often assume that their primary task is to construct a systematic presentation of theological *loci* and their interrelations. Ethics is what is done *after* one has accomplished these more primary tasks, or ethics becomes the responsibility of those who teach courses in ethics.

Happily there are some exceptions to this state of affairs that are signs of hope. For example, James McClendon begins his projected three-volume *Systematic Theology* with *Ethics*, to be followed by *Doctrine*, and then by a last volume dealing with philosophical questions raised within our cultural context.[40] McClendon does not think that by beginning with ethics he is delaying the theological task, but rather he begins with ethics in order to remind us that theology gains its intelligibility through the practices of the church. Therefore, he commences his project with ethics not because he assumes that Christian theology can be reduced to ethics, but to reclaim theology's task in the shaping of the Christian life. Accordingly, his *Ethics*, like Barth's, requires discussion of baptism and forgiveness, cross and resurrection, but also is built around the display of lives like those of Jonathan and Sarah Edwards, Dietrich Bonhoeffer and Dorothy Day, whose directions were shaped by and in turn shape our understanding of Christian doctrine.[41]

What McClendon helps us see is that what we do not need, if we are better to understand the nature of our existence as Christians, are further nuanced accounts of the relation of doctrine *and* ethics. For such accounts too often simply reproduce the presuppositions that created the 'and' which divides theology and ethics into separate realms, the conjunction against which we must now struggle. Rather what is needed are Christian speakers for whom doctrine is speech that does work. Rowan Williams, a theologian and bishop, offers us another fine indication of what a truly ethical–theological discourse might look like in an address before the Wales and Chester Judges' Circuit on 'Administering Justice'.[42] At first glance, this would not appear to be a particularly promising context for the display of doctrine, yet Williams begins with justice and ends with the Trinity.

Williams observes that justice means giving to each their due, but that requires that we must reflect back to others what they truly are. 'Doing justice' begins in our effort to respond to the reality of one another, which demands that we see one another as God sees us. We only see one another, therefore, when we look towards God, so justice is impossible without the vision of God. This leads Williams to observe that the administration of justice, as is increasingly evident in our times,

> becomes harder and harder, the more we cease to take it for granted that God is to be honoured. Ultimately, all that can be said by the Christian about justice rests on the doctrine of God, not simply as the God whose truthful love is directed towards us, but as the God whose very life is 'justice', in the sense that Father, Son and Holy Spirit reflect back to each other perfectly and fully the reality that each one is, 'give glory' to each other ... So the Uxbridge Magistrates' Court and its local equivalents point us towards the contemplation of the Holy Trinity, and that contemplation, with all that it says about truth and reciprocity, grounds, for the Christian, the vision of a just society. Administering justice is a ministry of the truth of God's life to our imaginations, whether we know it or not.[43]

Both Williams and McClendon exemplify the rediscovery that Christians have little reason to disjoin doctrine from ethics. To speak truthfully and intelligibly of one will always require speaking of the other. And if, with Williams, Christians learn to speak to the magistrate as if Jesus and Trinity matter, then the church may indeed have some interesting times ahead. Indeed, one might argue that it is precisely because Christians in modernity have presumed that ethics can safely be treated apart from theology (if only to provide a non-particularistic, tradition-independent ethic suitable for 'anyone') that their attempts to speak truthfully and convincingly to magistrates and other civil officials have proved so ineffectual. That is, the persuasive power of Christian discourse rests upon the indissociable unity of the theological and the ethical aspects of Christian faith, not their separation.[44]

Notes

1 Karl Barth, Church Dogmatics, trans. ed. G. W. Bromiley and T. F. Torrance (Edinburgh: T. & T. Clark, 1957), vol. II, part 2, p. 518.
2 See, for example, my 'Why Christian Ethics Is A Bad Idea', in Hilary Regan, Rod Horsfield and Gabrielle McMullen (eds.), Beyond Mere Health: Theology and Health Care in a Secular Society (Kew, Victoria: Australian Theological Forum, 1996), pp. 64–79.
3 Richard Hays, 'Ecclesiology and Ethics in I Corinthians', Ex Auditu 10 (1994): 33.
4 One of Ernst Troeltsch's insights was how 'doctrine' often reflected prior assumptions about the church. Even though I find his typology (i.e., church, sect and mysticism) problematic, at least it rightly emphasises how our theologies reflect prior assumptions about the church's relation to the world. Ernst Troeltsch, The Social Teachings of the Christian Churches, trans. Olive Wyon and introduced by James Luther Adams (Louisville, Kentucky: Westminster/John Knox Press, 1992).
5 James McClendon observes, 'Is it not worth considering, finally, how different might have been the history of Christianity if after the accession of the Emperor Constantine the church's leaders had met at Nicaea, not to anathemize each other's inadequate Christological metaphysics, but to devise a strategy by which the church might remain the church in light of the fateful political shift – to secure Christian social ethics before refining Christian dogma?' Ethics, vol. I of Systematic Theology (Nashville: Abingdon Press, 1986), p. 42.
6 Robert Wilken provides a very helpful account of how such schools worked in his, 'Alexandria: A School for Training in Virtue', in Patrick Henry (ed.), Schools of Thought in the Christian Tradition (Philadelphia: Fortress, 1984), pp. 15–30.

7 For example, Aristotle thought how a person laughed not unimportant for morality. See his *Nicomachean Ethics*, trans. Martin Ostwald (Indianapolis: Bobbs Merrill, 1962), 1128a33–5.

8 Tertullian, 'On Patience', in A. Cleveland Loxe (ed.), *The Ante-Nicene Fathers* (Grand Rapids, Michigan: Eerdmans, 1989), pp. 707–17. For a further discussion of Tertullian's account of patience as well as that of Cyprian, Augustine and Aquinas see my 'Practicing Patience: How Christians Should Be Sick', in Regan et al. (eds.), *Beyond Mere Health*, pp. 80–102. Dr Robert Milken rightly directs attention to the importance of the lives of the saints for Christian reflection as the moral life in his *Remembering The Christian Past* (Grand Rapids, Michigan: Eerdmans, 1995), pp. 121–44.

9 Augustine, *On the Morals of the Catholic Church*, in Waldo Beach and H. Richard Niebuhr (eds.), *Christian Ethics: Sources of the Living Tradition*, with Introductions by the editors (New York: The Ronald Press, 1955), p. 115. It would be hard to underestimate the significance of the Beach and Niebuhr anthology for the creation of Christian ethics as a discipline. Their anthology, which in many ways remains unsurpassed, made it seem apparent that for all of its diversity something called Christian ethics is a distinctive subject running through Christian history. Their selections range from *The Didache*, to Clement of Alexandria, the ethics of monasticism, Luther, Calvin, Wesley, Edwards, Kierkegaard and Rauschenbusch. It would be carping to criticise whom they chose to include as it is impossible to include everyone that might have a claim to have done 'ethics'. More important is the impression the volume gives, which may even be contrary to some aspects of Beach's and Niebuhr's own views; namely, that ethics is a subject that can be 'abstracted' from ecclesial and theological practices.

10 These treatises can be found in the *Nicene and Post-Nicene Fathers of the Christian Church: Saint Augustine's Anti-Pelagian Works*, trans. Benjamin Warfield (Grand Rapids, Michigan: Eerdmans, 1956), vol. v.

11 Augustine, *The City of God*, trans. Henry Bettenson and introduced by David Knowles (New York: Penguin Books, 1972).

12 *Ibid.*, pp. 877–8.

13 I am indebted to John Mahoney's *The Making of Moral Theology: A Study of the Roman Catholic Tradition* (Oxford: Clarendon Press, 1987), and John A. Gallagher's *Time Past, Time Future: An Historical Study of Catholic Moral Theology* (New York: Paulist Press, 1990) for their accounts of the penitential tradition.

14 Gallagher, *Time Past, Time Future*, p. 7.

15 As Aquinas says in the *Summa Contra Gentiles*, 'All creatures are compared to God as artifact to artist. Whence the whole of nature is like a certain artifact of the divine art. It is not, however, opposed to the nature of an artifact that the artist should work in a different way on his product even after he has given it its first form. Nor therefore is it against nature that God should work otherwise in natural things than the customary course of nature operates.' (3, 10). Quoted

38 Stanley Hauerwas

in Thomas Hibbs, *Dialectic and Narrative in Aquinas: an Interpretation of the Summa Contra Gentiles* (Notre Dame: University of Notre Dame Press, 1995).

16 Leonard Boyle, OP, *The Setting of the Summa Theologiae of St. Thomas* (Toronto: Pontifical Institute of Medieval Studies, 1981).

17 For an extraordinary account of why Aquinas' *Summa* must be read as a whole as well as evaluated as a whole see Alasdair MacIntyre, *Three Rival Versions of Moral Enquiry: Encyclopedia, Genealogy, and Tradition* (Notre Dame: University of Notre Dame Press, 1990), pp. 133–7. MacIntyre argues, rightly I think, that integral to Aquinas' understanding of becoming a person of virtue, particularly the virtues of faith, hope and love, is a recognition of our disobedience (p. 140).

18 Martin Luther, *The Freedom of a Christian*, in John Dillenberger (ed.), *Martin Luther: Selections from His Writings*, with an introduction by the editor (Garden City, New York: Anchor Books, 1961), p. 75.

19 Luther maintains that Christians must bear the 'secular' sword even though they have no need of it for their own lives, since the sword is 'quite useful and profitable for the whole world and for your neighbour. Therefore, should you see that there is a lack of hangmen, beadles, judges, lords, or princes, and find that you are qualified, you should offer your services and seek the place, that necessary government may by no means be despised and become inefficient or perish. For the world cannot and dare not dispense with it.' *Secular Authority: To What Extent It Should Be Obeyed*, in Dillenberger (ed.), *Martin Luther*, pp. 374–5. The contrast between Lutheran and Calvinist positions about such matters are frequently overdrawn. See, for example, Quentin Skinner, *The Foundation of Modern Political Thought* (Cambridge: Cambridge University Press, 1978), vol. ii, pp. 189–238.

20 John Calvin, *Institutes of the Christian Religion*, ed. John MacNeill and trans. Ford Lewis Battles (Philadelphia: Westminster Press, 1960), Book i, ch. 3.

21 Immanuel Kant, *Foundations of The Metaphysics of Morals and What is Enlightenment?*, trans. with an Introduction by Lewis White Beck (New York: Liberal Arts Press, 1959), p. 85. The quotation comes from the first paragraph of *What is Enlightenment?*

22 It should never be forgotten that one of Kant's last projects was his *On Perpetual Peace*, in which he sought to provide an account for how nations determined by republican principles based in his ethics had a better chance of maintaining a world free of war.

23 Kant, *Foundations*, p. 23.

24 *Ibid.*, p. 39.

25 The liberal presuppositions that shape Kant's religious views are nicely exemplified in his observation that 'in the appearance of the God-Man [on earth], it is not that in him which strikes the sense and can be known through experience, but rather the archetype, lying in our reason, that we attribute to him (since, so far as his example can be known, he is found to conform thereto), which is really the object of saving faith, and such a faith does not

differ from the principle of a course of life well-pleasing to God'. Immanuel Kant, *Religion Within the Limits of Reason Alone*, trans. with an Introduction by Theodore Greene (New York: Harper Torchbooks, 1960), pp. 109–10.

26 Though this position is associated with Albrecht Ritschl and Adolf Harnack, it perhaps found its most powerful expression in the American social gospel movement.

27 Friedrich Schleiermacher, *The Christian Faith*, ed. H. R. Mackintosh and J. S. Stewart (Edinburgh: T. & T. Clark, 1960).

28 Karl Barth, *Protestant Thought from Rousseau to Ritschl*, trans. Brian Cozens (New York: Harper and Row, 1959), p. 317.

29 Schleiermacher, *The Christian Faith*, p. 142.

30 Friedrich Schleiermacher, *Introduction to Christian Ethics*, trans. with an Introduction by John Shelley (Nashville: Abingdon Press, 1989), p. 27 of Shelley's Introduction.

31 For a wonderful account of the significance of the University of Berlin, as well as Schleiermacher's decisive role in its shaping, see Hans Frei's *Types of Christian Theology*, ed. George Hunsinger and William C. Placher (New Haven and London: Yale University Press, 1992), pp. 95–132.

32 Edward Farley provides an extremely helpful account of the importance of Schleiermacher's views on these matters in *Theologia: The Fragmentation and Unity of Theological Education* (Philadelphia: Fortress, 1983), pp. 73–98. Schleiermacher's position concerning the university was quite similar to Kant's. Schleiermacher, in spite of his criticism of Kant, continued to presuppose the basic structure of Kant's position.

33 Karl Barth, *Church Dogmatics*, ed. G.. Bromiley and T. F. Torrance (Edinburgh: T. & T. Clark, 1960), vol. I, part 1, p. 39.

34 *Ibid.*, p. 358.

35 Barth's first treatment of ethics is to be found in *Church Dogmatics*, vol. II, part 2, as part of his exposition of the doctrine of election. His special ethics is in *Church Dogmatics*, vol. III, part 4, that is, the last volume in his doctrine of creation. The ethics volume that was meant to be the culmination of his account of the doctrine of reconciliation was not completed, but in it Barth was to explicate the Christian life in terms of baptism with the Holy Spirit and water. *Church Dogmatics*, vol. IV, part 4, trans. G. W. Bromiley (Edinburgh: T. & T. Clark, 1969). Further lecture fragments of Barth's last reflections on the Christian life can be found in his *The Christian Life*, trans. G. W. Bromiley (Grand Rapids, Michigan: Eerdmans, 1981). In this last volume Barth builds his reflections around the Lord's prayer.

36 John Webster, *Barth's Ethics of Reconciliation* (Cambridge: Cambridge University Press, 1995), pp. 1–2. For another excellent secondary source on Barth's ethics see Nigel Biggar, *The Hastening that Waits: Karl Barth's Ethics* (Oxford: Clarendon Press, 1993).

37 Barth, *Church Dogmatics*, vol. II, part 2, p. 518.

38 *Ibid.*, pp. 665–9.
39 Barth, *Church Dogmatics*, vol. IV, part 4, p. 9.
40 McClendon, *Ethics*. McClendon's second volume, *Doctrine*, was published in 1994 by Abingdon.
41 Also to be noted is the work of Gregory L. Jones, who argues in his *Transformed Judgment: Toward a Trinitarian Account of the Moral Life* (Notre Dame: University of Notre Dame Press, 1990) that 'the moral life, when understood in terms of Christian life, receives its shape and pattern from God's Trinity. The vocation of the moral life is to learn to see and act rightly by participating in the mystery of the Triune God' (p. 120). Jones has developed this position further in his *Embodied Forgiveness* (Grand Rapids, Michigan: Eerdmans, 1995).
42 This address is in Rowan Williams, *Open to Judgement* (London: Darton, Longman and Todd, 1994).
43 *Ibid.*, pp. 245–6.
44 I am indebted to Mr Scott Saye and Professors Jim Fodor and Greg Jones for their suggestions and criticisms of this chapter.

Further reading

Gill, Robin, *A Textbook of Christian Ethics,* Edinburgh: T. & T. Clark, 1995.
Gustafson, James, *Christian Ethics and the Community*, Philadelphia: Pilgrim Press, 1971.
Häring, Bernard, CSSR, *The Law of Christ: Moral Theology for Priests and Laity*, translated by Edwin Kaiser, CPPS, Westminster: Newman Press, 1961.
Hauerwas, Stanley, *The Peaceable Kingdom: A Primer in Christian Ethics*, Notre Dame: University of Notre Dame Press, 1983.
Jones, L. Gregory, *Embodying Forgiveness: A Theological Analysis*, Grand Rapids, Michigan: Eerdmans, 1995.
MacIntyre, Alasdair, *Whose Justice? Which Rationality?*, Notre Dame: University of Notre Dame Press, 1988.
Ramsey, Paul, *Basic Christian Ethics*, Louisville, Kentucky: Westminster/John Knox Press, 1993.
Wogaman, J. Philip, *Christian Ethics: A Historical Introduction*, Louisville, Kentucky: Westminster/John Knox Press, 1993.

3 The basis and authority of doctrine

GERARD LOUGHLIN

POSTMODERN PREAMBLE

At the end of the second Christian millennium it has once again become possible for the church to remember itself as a people called to bear witness to the *future now*. It has no settlement in past or present, but looks forward to that which it awaits even as it arrives. Through trust in the promises of Christ the church has hope of tomorrow: looking for that which it recollects in the present, in its ever renewed meeting with its Lord, in the table-fellowship he gives of himself. This is the old news that is forever new: the announcement of an ancient postmodernity.[1]

The church's postmodernity is different from that which Fredric Jameson identifies as the cultural logic of late capitalism,[2] yet it is the arrival of the latter which allows the church to once more recall its freedom from the law of the present. For the passing of modernity – in so far as it is passing – is the weakening of modernity's claim to arbitrate the legitimacy of all human enterprises and institutions, including the church; judging them by a universal law in the court of reason – which was the project of Enlightenment. Modernity replaced the divine Logos with human Reason – God with Man – making the latter the present measure of all claims to knowledge and truth. Without God, reason alone had to secure the foundations of new practices and polity: the new physical and social sciences and the modern nation-state. Reason was deliberately unable to found other undertakings, such as religion and art, and they became mere leisure pursuits: diverting, even lucrative, but inessential. All was well for as long as reason and its rule appeared to be what its proponents claimed, an impartial universal that preserved human autonomy, furthered freedom and exposed those partial *mythoi* – religions and primitive cultures – that were but socially constructed and rhetorically defended, and subjugated men and women to the rule of the priests. However, this story – as in the classic fiction of modernity, Mary Shelley's *Frankenstein; or, the Modern Prometheus* (1818) – ended badly.[3]

The twentieth century has witnessed the failure of the Enlightenment project in all its diversity. Sometimes quietly and obscurely, sometimes in spectacular fashion, the attempt to make the world anew in the image of rational Man has had to admit that its law is but one more socially constructed and rhetorically defended – often violently defended – *mythos*; one more example of priestcraft. Yet what comes after – postmodernity – is the celebration of this defeat: a jubilant relief because there are no more universal laws, only local customs. Now everything is permitted. As Jean-François Lyotard has taught, postmodernity announces the demise of the meta-narratives, the stories – whether religious, political or scientific – that would put us in our place.[4] But this is not the whole story.

It is a paradox of postmodern culture that its pluralism obscures a deep homogeneity: a universal reason no less socially constructed and rhetorically maintained than those supposedly overcome, yet more insidious and ferocious because the condition of the very pleasures of postmodern pluralistic society. This 'reason' is the material law of the market-place, predicated upon the metaphysical concept of the Void.

The question of the basis and authority of doctrine in modern theology has to be set against the story of modernity-cum-postmodernity because so many theologians in the Western church, rather than refusing to acknowledge the jurisdiction of Enlightenment, accepted the challenge to defend the church's doctrine at the bar of an impartial and universal reason. It was a trial they could not win. This was not just because reason is never impartial – because always the reason of particular people with particular interests – but also because Enlightenment reason was conceived in opposition to Christian faith, claiming to exist in its own right as pure reason. The Enlightenment imagined reason sovereign in its own domain, *sola ratione*, taking no account of its relation to the font of all true reason, the divine Logos (Reason). Theologians not only accepted philosophy's right to rule its own domain, but its right to rule everything else, including God. Philosophy sought to judge doctrine by a wholly human *ratio*. As a consequence, the legitimate foundations of doctrine – scripture and tradition – were transformed in subtle and not so subtle ways into history and experience, which individually and together were to prove unstable and too weak for anything other than a liberal theology that is finally no theology at all.[5]

These transformations – of scripture into history and tradition into experience – were made possible by a fundamental development within theology itself, constituting both its own demise and the birth of modernity. This development consisted in the acceptance of a universal reason as a common measure between theology and philosophy; and in the abandon-ment, by Christian apologists, of what was distinctively Christian in the church's theology – Jesus Christ. It is perplexing that the theologians lost interest in theology, as Nicholas Lash puts it,[6] but it follows from the inven-tion of a homogeneous universe ruled by a univocal reason. The modern is the invention of one metaphysical world, in which God proves to be a null entity.

This chapter seeks to show how theology's invention of modernity – first in the fourteenth century, and then more fully in the sixteenth and seven-teenth centuries – undermined the ancient establishment of doctrine within, rather than upon, the church's tradition of performing the scrip-tures. The modern attempt to underwrite doctrine by appeal to history and experience was bound to fail because the latter were conceived according to a univocal reason that was and is the antithesis of Christian faith. This does not mark an impasse between reason and faith, but between an absolute human reason and a divine *ratio*; between different rationalities, indeed, between a singular and a plural economy of reason. The later part of this essay will suggest how the church in postmodernity – which, in principle if not in fact, declares against all univocity – may again understand its doctrine as the grammar and rule, the stage-direction, of a traditioned performance of the story that alone calls it into being: the life, death and resurrection of Jesus Christ.

ONE WORLD

Different writers locate the decisive point differently – the point at which the modern began to arrive – though all are agreed that it had fully arrived with the eighteenth-century Enlightenment. Hans Frei (1922–88), whose interest is primarily the collapse of scripture into history, points to the work of the English deist, Anthony Collins (1676–1729), as paradigmatic of reason's triumph.[7] However, as Frei also shows, the establishment of reason against scripture had already been accomplished in the seventeenth century by Baruch Spinoza. For Spinoza, in his *Tractatus Theologico-Politicus* of 1670, the scripture is merely an imaginative rendering for the unlearned of the religious truths that reason alone establishes. Reason teaches 'that there exists a God, that is, a supreme Being, Who loves justice and charity, and Who must be obeyed by whomsoever would be saved; that the worship of this Being consists in the practice of justice and love towards one's neighbour'.[8]

The new rationalism, differently represented in Spinoza and Collins, saw orthodox Christianity as superstitious and intolerant, leading to atheism. But in espousing a natural religion founded upon reason alone, it was continuing a development already promoted by theologians in the earlier part of the seventeenth century. Michael Buckley, in his magisterial study of the origins of modern atheism, points to Marin Mersenne (1588–1648), and before him Leonard Lessius (1554–1623), as two influential Catholic theologians who constructed Christian apologetics in purely philosophical terms, as a discourse that could appeal to any educated person, irrespective of nationality or creed.[9]

Lessius, in his *De providentia numinis* (1613), undertook to show the necessity of believing in God for both moral and political life. Without fear of divine judgement, morality and polity lose all final sanction and collapse into arbitrariness. But while this explains the necessity of religious belief it does not establish its truth, for which Lessius turned, not to the gospel of the church, but to the 'design' of the world. Though arguing against the atheists of his day, Lessius did not feel that he could name them – 'since the feare of the lawes doth impose silence to these kind of men, and only secretly among their familiars do they vomit out their Atheisme'[10] – and so he took as his opponents the 'atheists' of antiquity. In this way his argument with contemporary atheism had to be conducted as a philosophical one, the Christian centuries having been overstepped.[11] Lessius became a latter-day Balbus, the stoic protagonist in Cicero's *De natura deorum* (*On the Nature of the Gods*, *c.* 45 BC).

> In question, interest, evidence, and argument, Balbus and Lessius are virtually one. The question is about the provident god; the interest lies with social or moral importance; the evidence is the *notae* [marks] and *vestigia* [traces/footprints] which indicate the presence of a designing intelligence; and the arguments include the consent of the universal world, the nature of physical things, and the portentous events and life-stories which have occurred in human historical experience.[12]

In so far as Jesus Christ figures in the debate, he does so as one more portentous event and life-story, even if the most important. He is, finally, just another providential effect of the world's designing deity. There is no suggestion that one might begin an account of Christian doctrine with the story of Jesus Christ as the Word of God. In part this is because Lessius, and after him Mersenne, wished to dissociate themselves from those Christian 'sceptics' who presented the claims of revelation at the expense of reason, such as Michael de Montaigne (1533–92) and Pierre Charron (1541–1603). For such sixteenth-century Pyrrhonists, reason could never provide certitude and would eventually lead to atheism: only faith was certain.[13]

A second reason, suggested by Buckley, why Lessius and Mersenne conceived a purely philosophic apologetic, was the influence of St Thomas Aquinas. The replacing of Peter Lombard's *Sententiae* (*Book of Sentences*) with Aquinas' *Summa theologiae*, as the prime theological text for the teaching of doctrinal theology in the sixteenth century, marked not only a new factionalism in the teaching of theology, but helped produce a philosophical 'habit of mind', since the *Summa* appeared to teach that the truth of Christian doctrine could be demonstrated from common evidence by reason alone.[14] Buckley's argument really only concerns the reception and use of the *Summa* in the sixteenth century, though there is a suggestion that already in the thirteenth century Aquinas had opted to found Christian doctrine by way of nature rather than Christ, a choice that was to bear fruit in Enlightenment understanding of Jesus as little more than a moral teacher.[15] But this is to misread Aquinas.

While it is true that Thomas allows a place to philosophy without as well as within theology,[16] and does not consider the doctrines of Christ until the third part of the *Summa*, after first considering those of God and man, including the virtues, it is important to understand these moves within what Buckley acknowledges as the organic theology of the whole work. The *Summa* is really no more than 'grammatical' notes upon the church's reading of scripture, being entirely determined by the scriptural story of the world redeemed in Christ.[17] It has a narrative flow (even if intercalated with a synchronic pattern unfolded in the telling), being first and last a narrative of the Word. Thus Christ is present in every part of the *Summa* as the condition of its possibility. At the end of the prologue to the first part (*prima pars*) of the *Summa*, where the plan of the whole work is set forth, Thomas tells us that he will treat 'first, of God, secondly, of the journey to God of reasoning creatures, thirdly, of Christ, who, as man, is our road to God'.[18] Thus the third part (*tertia pars*) of the *Summa* embraces the other two parts, since it is Christ who makes the journey to God possible. Some readers of the *Summa* seem to be misled by the fact that though Thomas sought to discuss everything pertaining to holy teaching, or nearly everything, he could not do so all at once, but had to begin at one place and end at another.[19]

Though it would be an inattentive reader who supposed Aquinas to have already relativised revelation and scripture with regard to reason, it is possible to trace a theological origin for univocal reason in the work of another thirteenth-century theologian, Duns Scotus. In wishing to demarcate the domains of theology and philosophy, Scotus made God and Being their respective objects.[20] It is given to philosophy to think Being in itself, as a universal concept that applies to all things, great or small, infinite or finite. Being is conceived univocally, as a neutral 'essentiality' which applies to both God and world (*esse univocum*).[21] In doing this, Scotus developed a philosophical concern that came to him from Aristotle via Averroës,[22] and helped to constitute what Amos Funkenstein has called the 'nominalistic revolution' of the fourteenth century.[23]

Scotus and the fourteenth-century nominalists, chief among whom was William of Ockham, sought – beyond a univocal concept of Being – a univocal language and reason; a transparency of thought. For everything there is a name, but not every name denotes a thing. Universals exist in name only; they do not denote universal things, but only connote the attributes of sets of things. This must be related to Ockham's development of Scotus' formal principle of individuation – the 'thisness' (*haecceitas*) of things, so that in reality there are only individual things. When these ideas are combined with Ockham's 'voluntarism', his privileging of the divine 'will' over the divine 'intellect' in the act of creation – so that God creates as he wills, and he could as well will one thing as its opposite – the modern concept of the 'singular' is born. A thing is what it is only in virtue of itself as freely willed by God, and not in virtue of its matter or through relation or participation in any universal or transcendental. There is thus a need for a language that will mirror this world of arbitrarily posited singulars, a language that clearly denotes what there is, without suggesting any real relations between them.[24] With these ideas in place theology is already walking the *via moderna*. If all things, including God, are purely singular and denotable in a univocal discourse, then God, albeit the one who wills all the rest, is but another object of philosophic scrutiny.

For Hans Urs von Balthasar, these ideas came to the seventeenth century by way of Francisco Suárez (1548–1617),[25] but once arrived they helped make possible what we have already seen: the handing over of Christian apologetic to a purely philosophic discourse; a defence of doctrine on the basis of reason alone. But it was of little avail. Once the univocity of concept and language had been established, analogy and metaphor belittled and God conceived as but another, if unique, 'extended' thing (*res extensa*)[26] it was only a matter of time before Ockham's 'razor' was used to remove an unnecessary hypothesis. It can have been only the interests of morality and polity – the want of sovereignty for social order – that made the seventeenth and eighteenth centuries so fearful of atheism while contemptuous of ecclesial Christianity. In the twentieth century that fear has been overcome, and modernity-cum-postmodernity is the imagining of a godless voluntaristic nominalism: a world of self-willed singularities, without participation or relation. If, as Balthasar suggests,[27] the voluntarist God of pure freedom – who might as easily demand one thing as another – was a fearful image, how much more so is a multitude of such gods, since now there can be no reason – other than coercion – why anyone should do anything other than they like.

SCRIPTURE BECOMES HISTORY

Traditionally, doctrine was founded upon scripture and piety; but that changes with the coming of nominalism. Now the scripture – the canonical texts of 'old' and 'new' testaments – is but one more singular text, the meaning of which is transparent and singular also. The allegorical reading of former centuries, which had produced a multivalent text, gives way to a rational univocity. Now the text has only one literal meaning, which is understood as its historical reference, in a wholly positivistic manner. Anthony Collins, who has already been cited as exemplary of the new rationalism, not only identified literal and historical meaning – which had occurred earlier – but placed them in complete opposition to figurative or typological meaning. This meant that the literal/historical significance of one passage of scripture could no longer be the 'figure', the type or emblem – the re-presentation – of another literal/historical passage of scripture. Scriptural meaning is either literal/historical *or* it is figurative; it cannot be both. As Frei argues, this represents the modern invention of the literal sense as *purely* referring to a historical domain, which, as such, is accessible only by an extra-biblical historical science.[28] The distinction between the history-like and the historical is abolished, so that a text without historical reference is without significance.[29] From the eighteenth century onwards, scripture will increasingly be considered a querulous site wherein to find the remains of what really happened; but what *really happened* is known to science, not scripture.

Scripture is no longer understood as mutually constituted by the story it narrates and the community to whom it is narrated – a community already contained within the story, as the story within it. Rather, the scripture is seen as unreliable, and that which it distorts only really available through the labours of historical science, which looks behind the scriptural narratives to the historical events they partially and quaintly disclose. These events are available to anyone with an interest; there is no longer required a discipline of pious reading and liturgical enactment. When historical science, rather than scripture, becomes the basis of doctrine, the latter becomes as hypothetical and prone to fashion as its new foundation.

At the same time as history replaced scripture, reason was championed as the true basis of doctrine. Collins was a disciple of John Locke, who, like Spinoza, argued that 'reason leads us to the knowledge of this certain and evident truth, that there is an eternal, most powerful, and most knowing Being', whose attributes are finally but an enlarged idea of our own perfections.[30] But reason was to prove a false friend, becoming the enemy rather than support of doctrine. While Immanuel Kant insisted that he denied religious knowledge 'in order to make room for faith',[31] his advocacy of God as a postulate of practical reason was to set the tone for all later modernity: God as wishful thinking. Throughout the nineteenth and twentieth centuries scholars sought to establish doctrine through biblical criticism, but to little avail, since any success was the result of a sentimentally motivated and logically arbitrary refusal to go so far and no further along the path of historical scepticism.

TRADITION BECOMES EXPERIENCE

The changing status of scripture must also be related to the growing misunderstanding and suspicion of tradition, since scripture as such only functions when embedded within a tradition of pious use it both informs and is informed by. But tradition, as the accumulated wisdom of the past, the record, as we may think, of previous conversations initiating new discussion in the present, was uncongenial to a radically homogeneous world, which looks to the present rather than the past for its truth. In such a world – as conceived, for example, by René Descartes – knowledge rests upon the consciousness of the present moment: the 'I am' built upon the 'I think'.[32] Reason must build on *terra nullius* (empty ground), free from the constraints of the past, the ordinances of dead men. Each person must found his or her own world, beholden to no one else. For, as Locke wrote, 'we may as rationally hope to see with other men's eyes as to know by other men's understandings. So much as we ourselves consider and comprehend of truth and reason, so much we possess of real and true knowledge. The floating of other men's opinions in our brains makes us not one jot the more knowing, though they happen to be true.'[33]

It seemed to many in the nineteenth century, that with reason, scripture

and tradition no longer able to support the house of doctrine, it might be possible to close, even demolish various parts, and support what remained with
an appeal to 'experience'. Present experience has the inestimable value of
being of the moment. It has no need of the past (scripture and tradition), and
is indubitable in the face of rational argument. You cannot doubt what you
know immediately, and in a world where immediacy matters, who can gain-
say your right, nay your duty to believe? Here the work of William James
(1842–1910) is paradigmatic. In *The Varieties of Religious Experience* (1902)
James not only displays an array of religious experiences, but concerns himself with the question of religion's veracity, its basis and authority. For James
'feeling' is the source of religion, and 'philosophic and theological formulas
are secondary products, like translations of a text into another tongue'.[34] As
an argument for the veracity of religion, 'feeling' offers poor support, since
any philosophic or theological translation must beg the question; though, as
we shall see, James deliberately begs the question. While James sets himself
against an 'intellectualism in religion' which 'assumes to construct religious
objects out of the resources of logical reason alone',[35] his position, popular
throughout the twentieth century, repeats the modern presumption of a
homogeneous world constituted from radical singularities. For James, religious feelings are always private feelings, the experiences of fundamentally
isolated individuals. Thus prayer, which is the 'very soul and essence of religion', is understood, not as the mere 'vain exercise of words' or repetition of
'sacred formulae', but as an 'interior' happening, the 'very movement itself
of the soul, putting itself in a personal relation of contact with the mysterious
power of which it feels the presence'.[36] At the same time, these 'interior' feelings are understood to follow a universal pattern, being 'practically indistin-
guishable' for 'Stoic, Christian, and Buddhist'.[37] Beneath the secondary
'individualistic excrescences' there is a 'nucleus' of 'common elements'.[38]
Each singularity is finally the same as all the others.[39] It need hardly be
said that James' conception of this common concern – a feeling of 'union'
with something 'more' that defeats ennui[40] – fails, in its banality, to underwrite Christian doctrine, which has anyway been dismissed as secondary
excrescence.

What is most remarkable about James' discussion of religious experience is his total disregard for what actually constitutes the religious experience
of most people: the communal traditions of story, belief and practice, of
liturgy and ritual, that form the experience of the people who make and are
made by these traditions of communal behaviour.[41] James has a reason for
doing this, since he believes that real life is finally psychic life,[42] and the

burden of his study is to present a psychological account of religion. People who experience a religious feeling of 'union' with something 'more', are in fact united with more of themselves: the 'subconscious continuation' of their 'conscious life'.[43] To think it any more than this is to indulge in 'over-beliefs' which, while they cannot be rationally established, may be treated with 'tenderness and tolerance so long as they are not intolerant themselves'.[44] Despite describing himself as a supernaturalist,[45] it would seem that James' own 'over-belief' was in fact what he described as an 'under-belief',[46] that the God who has real effect is the incursion of the subconscious into conscious life.[47] At the very end of his book James suggests a form of polytheism, whereby people carry their own god within them.[48] We may think this the inevitable outcome of the 'nominalistic revolution'.

Before William James, the German theologian Friedrich Schleiermacher had sought, in his monumental study of *The Christian Faith* (1821; revised 1831), to establish not only 'religion' abstractly conceived, but concrete Christian faith and doctrine on the basis of 'feeling' – 'Christian doctrines are accounts of the Christian religious affections set forth in speech'.[49] Unlike James, he did so with some understanding that religious feeling does not simply well up from within, but is shaped and formed through belief and practice. For Schleiermacher the consciousness of God, which is the basis of doctrine, depends upon Jesus Christ's 'God-consciousness', mediated through the preaching and piety of the church. It is the church which kindles Christ's 'God-consciousness' in its members, and it is this which constitutes 'redemption'.[50] Nevertheless, for Schleiermacher a Christ-formed God-consciousness is finally a modality of a more basic 'feeling' given in the condition of humanity itself: 'the consciousness of being absolutely dependent, or, which is the same thing, of being in relation with God'.[51] This consciousness of absolute dependence gives rise to a universal piety, or at least a universal potential that awaits kindling.[52] Schleiermacher thus has the problem of showing how Christian 'God-consciousness' differs from other modes of the feeling of absolute dependence, in such a way that Christ might be thought to precede and exceed those other ways.

Despite the undoubted magnificence of Schleiermacher's undertaking and achievement – to conceive the entirety of Christian doctrine upon the basis of feeling alone – it marks a fatal move. Though it seeks to honour and not disparage doctrine (as in James), and though it seeks to locate the fundamental piety of 'absolute dependence' within ecclesial tradition, it nevertheless founds doctrine upon a present psychological moment, rather than within histories of narrative performance, communal practices of prayer and charity, which it both informs and is informed by. Just as James begs the question of the 'more' with which believers feel themselves united – is it something beyond or within themselves? – so also Schleiermacher begs the question of the 'whence' upon which believers feel themselves dependent. For many, it will be Sigmund Freud who decisively answers the question.

It would thus seem that modernity has done with religion, having undermined any and all foundations upon which it may be thought to rest. The ironic theological invention of a homogeneous 'being' presented in singularities, together with a univocal reason, has not only denied any route from the world to a transcendent God, but divested scripture of its difference and redefined tradition as death, so that only an appeal to the singularity of present experience, dependent on nothing but itself, has seemed to offer the same security as it already offered to the physical sciences. But now everything has changed.

In so far as postmodernity is the weakening of univocal reason, the church is freed to recover its own self. No longer need the church – nor anyone else – accept the claim of an absolute science to render a single domain; rather many domains are described by a multiplicity of sciences. Nor need the church – nor anyone else – submit to the requirements of a dominant discourse, for there are to be no more dominant discourses, only a friendly babble of different tongues: a benign babel. Even the physical sciences are now freed from the need to find an absolute, unified theory of everything. With the passing of Einsteinian physics, they too can develop multiple theories for manipulating the cosmos, the heterogeneity of which can now be freely explored.[53] In this way postmodern science almost returns us to an Aristotelian universe.[54]

However, postmodernity does not quite return the church to how it was before the nominalist inauguration of modernity. For in the new freedom there is still an order; a law of equitable trading. Everything is permitted except one thing: denial of the Void which our fictions – religious and political, commercial and aesthetic – are used to keep at bay. As long as everyone keeps exchanging their stories, no one should notice, let alone care, that the basic story of postmodernism constitutes the world a zone of singularities, each one of which must assert itself against the rest in order to delay its final oblivion. In this world each person is obliged only to him or herself. It is a world of plans without purpose, structures without order, information without knowledge, speed without movement and connections without relations. It is a world with a past but no memory or faithfulness; with a future but no patience or hope; and with a present but no dispossession or charity. This world will tolerate anything except that which will not tolerate it; that which tells of a world differently founded.

The question of the basis and authority of doctrine in postmodernity must tell of such a different world, since the story I have sketched above, of modernity's assault upon Christian doctrine, finally reminds us that doctrine is not based on history or experience, not even, finally, upon scripture or tradition, but only on that of which it is, at the last, the doctrine. In the concluding two sections of this essay I seek to sketch an account of doctrine that will return us to the ancient postmodernity of Aquinas' *Summa*, written as it was on the eve of modernity.

THE FOUNDATION OF DOCTRINE IN POSTMODERNITY

All Christian doctrines hang together. They support and inform one another. Starting from any one doctrine you can find your way to all the rest. This is even true of those doctrines some consider secondary, such as the marian doctrines which concern Christ's first disciple, his mother Mary. From the doctrines of her immaculate conception and assumption one comes to the church's doctrines concerning her son and our salvation. All doctrines are intimately related. This is not surprising, since all Christian doctrines are finally about one thing: the charity of the triune God. Everything comes from the Father through the Son in the Spirit, and is called to return likewise; doctrines are merely signposts to the route that the divine dispersion has taken in history, reminders of the story of God's love for us.

Remembering and showing the inter-linked nature of doctrine has always been a task of systematic or doctrinal theology; displaying, as it were, its perichoretic relations. In modern theology a marvellous example of this is provided in Karl Rahner's *Schriften zur theologie (Theological Investigations)*: a multi-volume collection of essays, each one of which is discrete and yet linked to others, so that starting from any one essay a reader will eventually find his or her way to all the rest.[55] The essay form displays both the multiplicity and unity of doctrine, as well as its endless diversity, since the work only ends because Rahner wrote a last essay, and not because he concluded his exposition of doctrine. It is always possible to say something more or in a new way, to supplement what has already been said, so that doctrine is both complete and never complete: it resists closure. This understanding of doctrine's unified but multiple form, and of its ceaseless supplementarity, its ever burgeoning exposition, is not a modern insight, but one already understood by medieval theology.

The *Summa theologiae* of St Thomas Aquinas remains one of the most vibrant expositions of Christian doctrine as an ever growing interrelated whole, where any one part is ultimately related to all other parts. To read the *Summa* is to find oneself in a space without perceptible boundaries; a manifold for theological exploration. One can start to read at the beginning, where Aquinas began because he had to begin somewhere, but the work has no proper beginning because in Christian doctrine all points are beginning and end. In so far as the *Summa* has a structure it is, as Thomas Gilby suggests, that of the sea, following the flow of the divine charity.

> Its arguments are less like a progressive series of theorems than like waves in the ebb and flow of the tide, the grand Platonic sweep of the whole work which follows the *exitus* [egress] and *reditus* [return] of Creation – the going forth of things from God and their coming back to him, the setting out and returning home, the first birth in which we are possessed by God and the second birth from which he is possessed by us.[56]

Doctrine has no proper starting point; there is no one doctrine which is the basis upon which the others rest. It may seem obvious that the doctrines of the immaculate conception and assumption of the Virgin Mary could not be the basis of other doctrines, but neither could the doctrines of creation or incarnation, fall or redemption, resurrection or salvation. Rather, each doctrine supports and is supported by all the other doctrines. Thus while the doctrines of the immaculate conception and assumption are not primary, neither are they secondary.

Nevertheless, doctrine is pericentric as well as perichoretic, it has a centre to which it always finally returns us: the story or person of Jesus Christ. Here I do not distinguish between story and person because I take it that a person is his or her story: the narrative of what he or she does and undergoes, and of the relationships, however fleeting or tentative, that constitute his or her narrative persona.[57] Only the telling of the whole story delivers the truth of the person; and of no person is this more true than Jesus Christ. For he is known only as he is received in the community to which the Spirit is given, so that only in telling the stories of all its members can his story be fully told. (The full disclosure of the mystery of Christ waits upon the *parousia*.) His story is the non-doctrinal basis upon which doctrine rests. Yet this is too static a conception, like that of a building upon its foundations, for while we must distinguish story from doctrine, and accord primacy to the former, the two are mutually constituted.

The story comes first. It is told in the four canonical gospels; in the entire canon of scripture when it is read figuratively; and in the continuing life of the church, in so far as it repeats Christ faithfully: the imitation of Christ (*imitatio Christi*) being the rule of the saints. The story is different from the narratives in which it is recounted, for they are always partial, often diverse, sometimes contradictory narrations. Matthew, Mark, Luke and John each tell the story somewhat differently, yet each tell the same story, and it is given not by attending to any one narration, or by constructing a composite out of them, but by attending to the differences between them. The evangelists' fourfold narration is the form of the story, and it is by reading for the form that one learns the story.[58]

The story is not identical with any one of the narratives, but is nevertheless known in the prayerful reading and performing of the narratives in the church's liturgies and common life. The story is known to piety, in and through the faithful practice of ecclesial life; learned through its telling in the sacramental and virtuous life of the community. It is above all a practical knowledge, *phronesis* rather than *theoria*, and doctrine is simply the rule and discipline of the practice.

Doctrinal teaching grew out of the formulation of baptismal creeds and so-called 'rules of faith' in the early church: pertinent summaries of the gospel story for teaching the catechumenate and reminding the baptised.[59] All later developments, from the creeds of the ecumenical councils to the great *summae* of the medieval period, and on to the conciliar and other doctrinal statements of the twentieth century, are finally no different in intent: to rule the proper and faithful telling of Christ's story in the life of the church. We can thus think of doctrine as the grammar of Christian discourse; the stage directions for the church's performance of the gospel.

The idea of doctrine as direction, rule or grammar has achieved recent prominence in the work of George Lindbeck,[60] who can be read as articulating a remark made by the philosopher Ludwig Wittgenstein: 'Grammar tells us what kind of object anything is. (Theology as Grammar)'.[61] This idea is not original to Wittgenstein, having been suggested in 1901 by Harold Fielding-Hall (1859–1917): 'the creeds are the grammar of religion, they are to religion what grammar is to speech'.[62] Lindbeck, however, finds a more ancient provenance for creed as grammar in St Athanasius. Following Bernard Lonergan (1904–85), Lindbeck argues that Athanasius has learned from Greek philosophy how to formulate propositions about propositions, and understood the credal doctrine of the 'consubstantiality' of Father and Son as expressing the rule that 'whatever is said of the Father is said of the Son, except that the Son is not the Father (*eadem de Filio quae de Patre dicunter excepto Patris Nomine)'.*[63] For Athanasius the doctrine of Nicaea was a second-order rule for Christian speech, and to accept the doctrine meant agreeing to speak in a certain way.[64]

An understanding of Nicene doctrine similar to that of Lonergan and Lindbeck had been advocated by Ian T. Ramsey (1915–72) in his 1957 study of *Religious Language.* For Ramsey, the notion of substance is used to 'maintain a logically necessary connection between "God" and "Jesus" despite the use of a father–son model by plain men'.[65] It is not used as a first-order proposition or description, but as a logical qualifier of a more basic 'model' (story/symbol/metaphor),[66] just as for Lindbeck it is a second-order or grammatical proposition that informs the way the story of Jesus is 'told and used'.[67] As Ramsey teaches, doctrines are 'rules for our talking'.[68]

The rule theory of doctrine – variously expressed in Ramsey, Lonergan and Lindbeck – is not uncontested, and certain related ambiguities and tensions need to be clarified. Firstly, it should be noted that while doctrines are understood as second-order propositions referring to other propositions, symbols and stories, they can *also* be taken as first-order propositions concerning worldly entities and divine mysteries. Lindbeck insists that a 'doctrinal statement may also function symbolically or as a first-order proposition'. But when it does so, the statement is no longer functioning as a 'church doctrine'.[69] The doctrinal character of the statement is constituted by its grammatical use.

Secondly – and this is the burden of my exposition – doctrine construed as ecclesial grammar is intimately dependent upon that which it rules: the telling of the story. Doctrine is always secondary to that which it informs – the church's performance of the gospel – which is alone its basis or foundation. Doctrine rests upon nothing other than the church's telling of Christ's story, upon the enacted reading, the non-identical repetition, of Christ's charitable practices, heeding the command to 'follow', to do as he does; in short, upon the ecclesial tradition of discipleship. As Rowan Williams teaches, it is only in so far as doctrine brings the church to the point of 'judgement and conversion worked out through encounter with the telling of Jesus' story', that it finds its proper basis and function.[70] There is thus no legitimation of doctrine, in history or experience, outside of Christian practice itself.

While doctrine is secondary, it is at the same time *creatively* dependent upon churchly discourse and practice, a constitutive factor in the speech and performance of the church. This is the third point of clarification, and it can be addressed by considering a certain ambiguity in the idea of doctrine as grammar. Wittgenstein's therapeutic philosophy is said to leave everything as it is, for it is finally no more than a reminder of what we already know. It is descriptive rather than prescriptive; a recalling of how we speak, the 'language games' we play and the 'forms of life' they inform. This follows from thinking philosophical investigation a reflection upon grammar. 'Grammar does not tell us how language must be constructed in order to fulfil its purpose, in order to have such-and-such an effect on human beings. It only describes and in no way explains the use of signs.'[71] Is doctrine likewise wholly descriptive, a recalling of how Christians speak and act? This was certainly Fielding-Hall's understanding of the creeds, which are to religion as grammar is to speech. 'Words are the expression of our wants; grammar is the theory formed afterwards. Speech never proceeded from grammar, but the reverse. As speech progresses and changes from unknown causes, grammar must follow.'[72] Yet grammar can also be understood prescriptively, as setting forth the rules of well-formed speech; and this is how the doctrinal grammar of theology must be understood, as not just describing but prescribing the proper ordering of story and symbol, praise and prayer.

Many doctrinal arguments proceed by recollecting the church's faithful practice, reminding us of its ecclesial grammar; yet at the same time there is also the argument that seeks to convince the church of well-formed as opposed to deformed speech and practice. Doctrine is not just description but prescription, not just recollection but invention. There is undeniably a creative aspect to doctrinal development, a further imagining of the story through its conceptual articulation.[73] Here we need to realise that the distinction between speech and grammar, story and doctrine, is finally a formal distinction, since the latter terms are always already at play in the former. (In the same way there is always an element of prescription – or interpretation – in description, since every object is patient of more than one, contestable, description.) From the first, the gospel narratives are informed by doctrinal considerations, and the church's telling of the story ruled by grammatical clarifications. The story and how it is told are not finally separable items. It is, however, the prescriptive and inventive aspect of doctrine that raises the question of its authority. How does the church decide between well- and ill-formed rules of practice? How does it decide on what should and should not be said and done?

THE AUTHOR(ITY) OF DOCTRINE

For Aquinas, sacred doctrine is 'science' (knowledge), the principles of which are neither self-evident (as in arithmetic or geometry) nor established by a higher science (as when geometry establishes the principles of optics or arithmetic the principles of harmony), but received in faith from a superior knowledge, 'namely God's very own which he shares with the blessed'.[74] It is this *scientia Dei et beatorum* – given to us in the scriptural revelation through the tradition of the church – which is at one and the same time the basis and authority of doctrine, its authoring source and final context. The principles of doctrine are not otherwise known; yet to know them – and the world in their light[75] – is to begin to share in that life which God wills for all as their final end, and which is given through incorporation in Christ. The unfolding of doctrine in the practices of the church – for it is both a doing and a saying[76] – serves to enfold the church into the very life of God. Thus all theology is finally mystical, a *habitus* (habit/habitat) or 'wisdom' given by the Spirit.[77]

It should be clear that doctrine is not vouchsafed by anything external to the life of the church, by an extra-ecclesial discipline or rationality. To think so is to suppose the demise of the church; and it is only liberalism which implicitly supposes such a catastrophe, when it advances the individual's experience as sole determinant of doctrinal propriety.[78] Liberalism teaches autonomy, the self-making and ruling of the individual, whose greatest fear is to fall into heteronomy, and whose greatest boast is to be self-made, the person who did it his or her way (no matter how disastrously).[79] While this is a pure form of (secular) modernity, its invocation of a radical singularity is, as we have seen, of theological origin and finds a purportedly Christian expression today.[80] However, other possible doctrinal authorities are no less the fruit of modernity for being internal to the church.

The requirement of doctrinal exactitude for the faithful rendition of the story (which can become a paranoiac quest for personal certainty), has led people to suppose the church blessed with an unequivocal authority, whether this is taken to be a text or a person, the Bible or a bishop (more properly the bishops of the church in council), or some other cognate. While an appeal to one or other of these authorities is not in itself mistaken, it becomes so when they are held to yield an unequivocal guarantee of faithful practice. The phantom of univocity that haunts modernity is present whenever it is supposed that Bible or bishop delivers a guidance that can be received without, at the same time, being in part constituted by that reception.[81] Meaning is always a relationship between that which gives and that which receives, and where both parties are alike giver and receiver, so that it is never simply a movement from one to the other, but of both to each other. One might say that real meaning is always constituted in dialogue, not monologue; but a dialogue that is more nearly the form than the means of ecclesial understanding. Thus the Bible has no real meaning for the church – has no authority over its doctrine – outside of that conversation which is finally the tradition of the church in all its diversity, in all its conversations, both intra- and extra-ecclesial; and the same is true for any person or group of people designated as teachers within the church. They are only teachers in so far as they are also taught, since, at the last, the only true teacher of the church – the only measure of its doctrine – is Jesus Christ, who through the Spirit gives himself, from within and 'without', not to one person or group within the church, but to the whole community, which alone, in all its parts, is the Body of Christ.

It is not that Bible or episcopate are unauthoritative for the church and its doctrine, but that they are only constituted as authoritative within the complex life of the church, where they must always be received in the circumstances of the day through those processes of discerning interpretation which are at the same time a prayerful reciprocation.[82] Outside of Christ, there is no text or person that guides the rule of the church's speech and practice; and Christ – through his resurrection and gift of the Spirit – has become the charity of the church in history, so that only within its tradition of charitable practices can we find true doctrine. As Maurice Blondel (1861–1949) teaches, we find the basis and authority of doctrine not in any one place or person, but in the 'mediation of collective life, and the slow progressive labour of the Christian tradition'.[83]

Near the beginning of his study on the origins of modern atheism, Michael Buckley notes that Peter Lombard's *Sententiae* provided the medieval church with a 'focus or a unity precisely within dispersion, a common series of theological statements, a vocabulary and a common intellectual tradition which allowed substantial disagreements, and an irreducible pluralism within a shared culture'.[84] It may be a forlorn hope, but perhaps at the beginning of the third Christian millennium, after the demise of modernity, the church can renew its confidence in that *sacra doctrina* (holy teaching) which, preserved in scripture and creeds, classic commentaries and treatises, including those of the modern period, together with the prayers and charitable deeds of humble people, constitutes its common tradition and culture and allows for that perichoretic unity in diversity which mirrors its one true foundation: the abiding charity of the triune *ratio*.[85]

> Let us speak the truth in love; so shall we fully grow up in Christ. He is the head, and on him the whole body depends. Bonded and knit together by every constituent joint, the whole frame grows through the due activity of each part, and builds itself up in love.
> *(Ephesians 4: 15–16)*

Notes

1 See further Gerard Loughlin, *Telling God's Story: Bible, Church and Narrative Theology* (Cambridge: Cambridge University Press, 1996), ch. 1.

2 See Fredric Jameson, *Postmodernism, or, the Cultural Logic of Late Capitalism* (London and New York: Verso, 1991).

3 Mary Wollstonecraft Shelley, *Frankenstein or the Modern Prometheus: The 1818 Text*, ed. Marilyn Butler (London: William Pickering, 1993).

4 Jean-François Lyotard, *The Postmodern Condition: a Report on Knowledge*, trans. Geoff Bennington and Brian Massumi (Manchester: Manchester University Press, 1984).

5 For an example of liberal theology on the same subject as the present essay, see David A. Pailin, 'Reason in Relation to Scripture and Tradition', in Richard Bauckham and Benjamin Drewery (eds.), *Scripture, Tradition and Reason: A Study in the Criteria of Christian Doctrine* (Edinburgh: T. & T. Clark, 1988), pp. 207–38. 'Theologians . . . are to use scripture and tradition as resources which they *ransack* for insights' (p. 237; emphasis added).

6 Nicholas Lash, 'When Did the Theologians Lose Interest in Theology?', in Bruce D. Marshall (ed.), *Theology and Dialogue: Essays in Conversation with George Lindbeck* (Notre Dame: University of Notre Dame Press, 1990), pp. 131–47.

7 Hans Frei, *The Eclipse of Biblical Narrative: a Study in Eighteenth and Nineteenth Century Hermeneutics* (New Haven and London: Yale University Press, 1974), p. 76.

8 *The Chief Works of Benedict de Spinoza*, 2 vols., trans. R. H. M. Elwes (New York: Dover Publications, 1951), vol. I, p. 186.

9 Michael J. Buckley, SJ, *At the Origins of Modern Atheism* (New Haven and London: Yale University Press, 1987), ch. 1.

10 Quoted in *ibid.*, p. 46.

11 *Ibid.*, p. 47.

12 *Ibid.*, p. 50.

13 See Richard H. Popkin, *The History of Scepticism from Erasmus to Spinoza* (Assen, The Netherlands: Koninklijke Van Gorcum, 1960), pp. 42–65.

14 Buckley, *Origins*, p. 66. On the relationships between the *Sententiae* and the *Summa* see W. J. Hankey, *God in Himself: Aquinas' Doctrine of God as Expounded in the Summa Theologiae* (Oxford: Oxford University Press, 1987), ch. 1.

15 Buckley, *Origins*, p. 55. Colin Gunton reads Buckley in this way, supposing him to have shown that the form of St Thomas' analogy underlies 'the development of modern atheism, the erection of theological structures independently of christology and pneumatology'. *The One, the Three and the Many: God, Creation and the Culture of Modernity: The Bampton Lectures 1992* (Cambridge: Cambridge University Press, 1993), pp. 138–9.

16 St Thomas Aquinas, *Summa Theologiae*, I (1a.1): *Christian Theology*, trans. Thomas Gilby, OP (London: Eyre and Spottiswoode, 1964), 1a.1, 1 (pp. 5–9).

17 See Lash, 'When Did the Theologians Lose Interest in Theology?', pp. 140–3.

18 St Thomas Aquinas, *Summa Theologiae*, II (1a.2–11): *Existence and Nature of God*, trans. Timothy McDermott, OP (London: Eyre and Spottiswoode, 1964), 1a (p. 3).

19 For example, it is sometimes held against Thomas that he discussed the one God before he discussed the Trinity, as if the latter were not one God and the one God not the Blessed Trinity.

20 It might even be suggested that it was the Scotist demarcation of philosophy and theology that inaugurated modernity, since it imagines a domain whose truth is not given first and last by theology. In this regard see John Milbank, 'Only Theology Overcomes Metaphysics', *New Blackfriars* 76 (1995): 325–43. Milbank can be read as seeking to again locate philosophy (metaphysics) within theology.

21 See Hans Urs von Balthasar, *The Glory of the Lord: a Theological Aesthetics*, 7 vols., ed. Joseph Fessio, SJ and John Riches (Edinburgh: T. & T. Clark, 1991), vol. v, pp. 16–19.

22 See Balthasar (*ibid.*, pp. 10–11), who locates thirteenth-century 'Averroism' as the point at which medieval thought begins to turn modern.

23 Amos Funkenstein, *Theology and the Scientific Imagination: From the Middle Ages to the Seventeenth Century* (Princeton, New Jersey: Princeton University Press, 1986), pp. 26–7.

24 *Ibid.*, p. 57.

25 Balthasar, *Glory to the Lord*, vol. v, pp. 21–9.

26 On the 'extension' or 'body' of God see Funkenstein, *Scientific Imagination*, pp. 23–31.

27 Balthasar, *Glory of the Lord*, vol. v, p. 20.

28 Frei, *Eclipse*, pp. 76–7.

29 For Frei, Collins located scriptural meaning outside the text, in the intention of the author and the events of history; so that meaning is empirically verifiable or it is nothing (*ibid.*, pp. 78–85).

30 John Locke, *An Essay Concerning Human Understanding* (1690), abridged and ed. A. S. Pringle-Pattison (Sussex: Harvester Press, [1924] 1978), book 4, ch. 10, section 6 (p. 313); see also book 2, ch. 23, section 33 (p. 172).

31 Immanuel Kant, *Critique of Pure Reason* (1781), trans. Norman Kemp Smith (London: Macmillan, 1933), p. 29.

32 See further John Carroll, *Humanism: The Wreck of Western Culture* (London: Fontana Press, 1993), ch. 7.

33 Locke, *Essay*, p. 40.

34 William James, *The Varieties of Religious Experience: A Study in Human Nature*, ed. Martin E. Marty (Harmondsworth: Penguin Books, 1985), p. 431.

35 *Ibid.*, p. 433.

36 *Ibid.*, p. 464.

37 *Ibid.*, p. 504.

38 *Ibid.*, pp. 503–4.

39 James – his work a mixture of scepticism and pragmatism, tinged with sentiment – is a prime exemplar of modernity; indeed a champion of positivistic reason who endorses a utilitarian conception of religion – belief in God is useful in so far as it increases vivacity (*ibid.*, pp. 506–7).

40 *Ibid.*, pp. 508–9.

41 This is the burden of Nicholas Lash's critique in *Easter in Ordinary: Reflections on Human Experience and the Knowledge of God* (London: SCM Press, 1988), pp. 18–104.

42 James, *Varieties*, pp. 501–2.

43 *Ibid.*, p. 512.

44 *Ibid.*, pp. 514–15.

45 *Ibid.*, p. 521.

46 *Ibid.*, p. 515.

47 *Ibid.*, p. 523.

48 *Ibid.*, pp. 525–6. Unlike Lash, I find the idea of psychic polytheism, rather than theism, makes better sense of *Varieties*. Either way, James fails to conceive the 'more' as the transcendent creator God of Christian theology. See Lash, *Easter*, pp. 78–83.

49 Friedrich Schleiermacher, *The Christian Faith*, ed. H. R. Mackintosh and J. S. Stewart (Edinburgh: T. & T. Clark, 1928), section 15 (p. 76).

50 *Ibid.*, section 100 (pp. 425–31).

51 *Ibid.*, section 4 (p. 12).

52 *Ibid.*, section 11 (p. 55).

53 See Martin H. Krieger, *Doing Physics: How Physicists Take Hold of the World* (Bloomington and Indianapolis: Indiana University Press, 1992).

54 See Funkenstein (*Scientific Imagination*, pp. 35–7), who argues that Aristotle sought univocity without homogeneity: 'Aristotle's *nature* is a ladder of *natures*' (p. 36).

55 Karl Rahner, *Theological Investigations* (London: Darton, Longman and Todd, 1961–81).

56 Thomas Gilby, OP, 'Appendix 1: structure of the *Summa*', in Aquinas, *Summa*, 1, 43–6 (p. 43).

57 See further Hans Frei, *Theology and Narrative: Selected Essays*, ed. G. Hunsinger and W. C. Placher (New York and Oxford: Oxford University Press, 1993).

58 See Balthasar, *Glory of the Lord*, vol. 1: *Seeing the Form*.

59 See Frances Young, *The Art of Performance: Towards a Theology of Holy Scripture* (London: Darton, Longman and Todd, 1990), pp. 45–65.

60 George A. Lindbeck, *The Nature of Doctrine: Religion and Theology in a Postliberal Age* (London: SPCK, 1984), pp. 73–111. For a fuller discussion of Lindbeck's rule theory of doctrine see Loughlin, *Telling God's Story*, pp. 46–51.

61 Ludwig Wittgenstein, *Philosophical Investigations*, 2nd edn, trans. G. E. M. Anscombe (Oxford: Basil Blackwell, [1952] 1958), section 371.

62 H[arold] Fielding[-Hall], *The Hearts of Men* (London: Hurst and Blackett, 1901), p. 313; quoted in James, *Varieties*, p. 436 n. 1.

63 Lindbeck, *Nature of Doctrine*, p. 94. See Bernard Lonergan, *De Deo Trino* (Rome: Gregorian University Press, 1964), partly trans. Conn O'Donovan as *The Way to Nicea* (London: Darton, Longman and Todd, 1976). See also his *Method in Theology* (London: Darton, Longman and Todd, 1972), p. 307.

64 Lindbeck, *Nature of Doctrine*, p. 94.

65 Ian T. Ramsey, *Religious Language* (London: SCM Press, 1957), p. 160.

66 *Ibid.*, p. 164.

67 Lindbeck, *Nature of Doctrine*, p. 80.

68 Ramsey, *Religious Language*, p. 173.

69 Lindbeck, *Nature of Doctrine*, p. 80.

70 Rowan Williams, 'The Incarnation as the Basis of Dogma', in Robert Morgan (ed.), *The Religion of the Incarnation: Anglican Essays in Commemoration of Lux Mundi* (Bristol: Bristol Classical Press, 1989), pp. 85–98 (p. 87).

71 Wittgenstein, *Philosophical Investigations*, section 496.

72 Fielding, *Hearts*, p. 313; quoted in James, *Varieties*, p. 436 n. 1.

73 See further John Milbank, *Theology and Social Theory: Beyond Secular Reason* (Oxford: Basil Blackwell, 1990), pp. 382–8; and Gerard Loughlin, 'Christianity at the End of the Story or the Return of the Master-narrative', *Modern Theology* 8 (1992): 365–84 (pp. 375–81).

74 Aquinas, *Summa* 1, 1a.1, 2 responsio (p. 11).

75 *Ibid.*, 1, 1a.1, 3 (pp. 13–15).

76 *Ibid.*, 1, 1a.1, 4 (pp. 15–17); James 1:22.

77 Aquinas, *Summa*, 1, 1a.1, 6 (pp. 21–5). On doctrinal science as a means for our return to God see Thomas Gilby, OP, 'Appendix 6: Theology as Science', in *ibid.*, 1 (pp. 67–87).

78 The liberal authority of individual experience should be distinguished from the Catholic idea of personal conscience, which is the idea of a communally formed moral reason.

79 On the emergence of the heroic autonomous agent in Renaissance humanism see Carroll, *Humanism*, ch. 2.

80 See Don Cupitt, *Taking Leave of God* (London: SCM Press, 1980).

81 When the episcopate (or Bible) is conceived as simply giving (*ecclesia docens*) and not also receiving (*ecclesia discens*), it is conceived as somehow, impossibly, *outside* the church; and this is, as Nicholas Lash says, 'ecclesiologically intolerable'. *Change in Focus: a Study of Doctrinal Change and Continuity* (London: Sheed and Ward, 1973), p. 98. The theme of constitutive reception derives, of course, from John Henry Newman. See *ibid.*, pp. 100–3.

82 On the reciprocal nature of teaching within the church see the essays in the special issue of *New Blackfriars* on Catholic teaching, 70 (1989): 55–104; in particular Edmund Hill, OP, 'Who Does the Teaching in the Church?', pp. 67–73.

83 Maurice Blondel, *History and Dogma* (1904), in *The Letter on Apologetics and History and Dogma*, trans. Alexander Dru and Illtyd Trethowan (Edinburgh: T. & T. Clark, [1964] 1995), pp. 221–87 (p. 269). The last section of Blondel's essay – on 'The Vital Role and the Philosophical Basis of Tradition' (pp. 264–87) – is entirely pertinent to the present essay.

84 Buckley, *Origins*, p. 43.

85 I would like to thank Gavin D'Costa, Colin Gunton, Nicholas Lash and Graham Ward for comments on some earlier drafts of this chapter; remaining infelicities are my own.

Further reading

Bauckham, Richard, and Benjamin Drewery, editors, *Scripture, Tradition and Reason: A Study in the Criteria of Christian Doctrine*, Edinburgh: T. & T. Clark, 1988.

Blondel, Maurice, *The Letter on Apologetics and History and Dogma*, translated by Alexander Dru and Illtyd Trethowan, Edinburgh: T. & T. Clark, (1964) 1995.

Buckley, Michael SJ, *At the Origins of Modern Atheism*, New Haven and London: Yale University Press, 1987.

Congar, Yves, *Tradition and Traditions*, translated by Michael Naseby and Thomas Rainsborough, London: Burns and Oates, 1966.

Funkenstein, Amos, *Theology and the Scientific Imagination: From the Middle Ages to the Seventeenth Century*, Princeton, New Jersey: Princeton University Press, 1986.

Lash, Nicholas, *Newman on Development: the Search for an Explanation in History*, London: Sheed and Ward, 1975.

Lindbeck, George, *The Nature of Doctrine: Religion and Theology in a Postliberal Age*, London: SPCK, 1984.

Newman, J. H., *An Essay on the Development of Christian Doctrine*, London, 1845.

4 The scope of hermeneutics

FRANCIS WATSON

Whatever its other responsibilities may be, Christian theology cannot evade the task of biblical interpretation. It is in the biblical texts that the irreplaceable primary testimony to the God acknowledged in Christian faith is to be found. According to Christian faith, this God cannot be directly deduced from general features of the world and our human experience of it, and the effect of this is to emphasise our dependence on a highly particular stream of religious and cultural tradition: the history of Israel, which for Christians reaches its climax in the events that brought the Christian church into being, and which at its deepest level is not merely a component of the general history of the world but the privileged 'place' in which God is uniquely disclosed and acknowledged. There is no access to this 'place' except by way of the biblical texts, and biblical interpretation is therefore theology's primary task – the object of interpretation being the biblical texts in their integral relation to that to which they bear witness.

Because biblical interpretation is so fundamentally important for Christian theology, it is necessary to reflect on how this task is to be carried out. For example, one might enquire whether interpretation should confine itself to the so-called 'literal' sense of the text or whether there is also a less obvious, secondary meaning, sometimes described as the 'spiritual' or 'allegorical' sense; and this is an issue that Christian theology has reflected on from the earliest period. This question is a genuinely theological one, but it belongs more particularly to the sphere of theological *hermeneutics*. In general terms, hermeneutics may be defined as *theoretical reflection on the practice of textual interpretation*. In a theological hermeneutics, the theoretical reflection would be informed by theological criteria and would take as its subject matter the practice of interpreting the biblical texts. On this definition, theological hermeneutics has always been an integral part of Christian theology. Yet the term 'hermeneutics' has had a complex history within modern theology, and if it is to be usefully employed some preliminary clarifications are necessary.

Under the influence of a mid-twentieth-century theological programme known as the 'new hermeneutic', it is still widely assumed that the role of hermeneutics is to investigate how an ancient text, determined by quite specific historical factors, can transcend the limitations of its historical origin and be 'meaningful' today.[1] The 'new hermeneutic' sought to answer this question by appealing to an ontology of human existence according to which to be human is to be confronted with the question of existence and of God; the biblical texts (or privileged parts of them) are to be read as testimony to God's answer to this universal question in and through Jesus Christ. The 'Christ-event' to which they testify is not simply a historical occurrence of long ago: on the basis of that past occurrence, it occurs above all in the present, in the moment in which one encounters through the biblical text God's own word or address, challenging the illusion of human self-sufficiency and disclosing the reality of human dependence upon God. One feature of this theological programme was its willingness to employ a radical historical criticism which sought to strip away 'inessentials' such as the bodily resurrection of Jesus in order to attain a supposedly more fundamental understanding of the divine–human relationship. This remained a *hermeneutical* programme, in the sense that reflection on textual interpretation was central to it; and yet this reflection was concerned only with the highly specific question of present meaningfulness in the face of the problem posed by historical distance. Hermeneutics was identified with theology, and there was also a tendency to blur the dividing-line between hermeneutics and biblical interpretation itself, between theory and practice. The 'new hermeneutic' makes it impossible to enquire about the *distinctive* contribution of hermeneutics to the theological enterprise, for 'hermeneutics' now defines and encompasses that enterprise as a whole.

In this chapter, I shall advocate a more modest understanding of hermeneutics as theoretical reflection on interpretative practice. This theoretical reflection will normally occur within communities of interpreters concerned with particular types of text, and will respond in the first instance to the 'local' concerns of an interpretative community. Where the interpretative community consists of theologians striving to interpret the biblical texts, the appropriate theoretical reflection on interpretative practice will take the form of a specifically theological hermeneutics. I shall first develop this understanding of hermeneutics in greater detail, and then outline a possible role for hermeneutics within contemporary theology and biblical interpretation.[2]

LOCAL HERMENEUTICS

Texts are written in order to be read. They may be addressed to a single reader, as in the case of a personal letter, or they may attain 'classic' or 'canonical' status and be read by an unlimited number of readers in very different historical and cultural contexts. Readers make sense of texts on the basis of a previously acquired knowledge of the language in which the text is written, the genre to which it belongs and the subject matter to which it directly or indirectly refers. On this basis, it is normally assumed that the act of reading will be accompanied by an understanding of what is read; for to read without understanding is futile and frustrating. Understanding, however, often appears to be provisional and partial. It is a common experience that one 'gets more out of' a text on reading it a second time, suggesting that an initial understanding is always subject to correction and extension. An obvious reason for this is that the second reading can utilise a knowledge of the text as a whole which was not yet available in the course of the first reading. An increased knowledge of the language, genre or subject matter of the text will also assist the correction and extension of an initial understanding. It seems that there is always more to be understood.

In some cases, understanding may be so valued that readers make use of secondary texts which *interpret* the primary text, assisting and enhancing the process of understanding through the specialised skills and knowledge of the interpreter. Texts that attract to themselves the activity of interpreters are likely to be 'canonical', separated from the vast mass of non-canonical writing by the fact that they continue to be read and reread by significant numbers of people long after they were written, and by a public, quasi-official recognition of their value that will find institutional expression in, for example, educational practice. Most texts have only a short life; canonical or classic texts are those texts that enjoy an indefinitely extended afterlife. Such texts are read in the knowledge that they have already been much read, perhaps over a period of centuries, and the consensus of so many different readers that they are worth reading perpetuates a belief in their enduring value and an expectation that they will repay prolonged, careful attention. This belief and this expectation underlie the practice of interpretation, in which 'professional' readers deploy various analytical techniques in order to further the process of understanding and to expose something of that 'value' which the text is held to contain.

'Interpretation' may also imply that communication has been impeded. Where the language of the speaker is unfamiliar to the hearer, an 'interpreter' is needed if successful communication is to occur, and a textual interpreter must similarly devote particular attention to those aspects of texts that are likely to impede readers' understanding. Indeed, interpretation may in some contexts amount to little more than a series of explanations relating, for example, to unfamiliar names or practices referred to in the text. Yet it is widely assumed that the interpreter is responsible for the *whole* text and that solving local difficulties is only one element in his or her role. If, however, the text in its entirety stands in need of interpretation, then it is presupposed that the entire text is 'difficult'. The phenomenon of the local difficulty – the obscure expression, the unfamiliar term – is, as it were, universalised: a canonical or classic text is held to be a 'difficult' text which does not yield up its real value to a merely casual and uninformed reading. The classic text is the text that needs interpretation, and it is both the perceived value and the difficulty of the classic text to which interpreters appeal in order to legitimate their activities.

So long as a text retains its classic status, interpretation continues; its duration is as unlimited and indefinite as the text's. There is, it seems, no such thing as the definitive interpretation, the interpretation that causes interpretative activity to cease because the text has now been rightly and exhaustively understood. Where an interpretative text establishes itself as canonical, it will itself become subject to various processes of interpretation. The infinite value and the infinite difficulty of the classic text are held to preclude the definitive solution one might hope for in, for example, trying to decipher a coded message. The difficulty of the text is also presupposed in the phenomenon of interpretative conflict. Interpretations are in part constructed out of the perceived inadequacies of their predecessors, the failure of all interpretation hitherto to identify or surmount the difficulties that are now to be addressed. Each act of interpretation implies some kind of claim to definitive status, however modest; it does so by denying definitive status to earlier interpretations, and it cannot avoid the tacit acknowledgement that its own claim will in turn be challenged by interpretations that are yet to come.

Disagreement with other interpreters is fundamental to a great deal of interpretative activity. Disagreements may be minor and insignificant, but they may relate to precisely those aspects of a text in which its value is held to reside. Interpretative disagreement becomes serious when a particular construal of that which makes the text valuable is denied and a radically different reading is proposed. Whether minor or major, however, disagreements between interpreters are commonplace: those whose role it is to guide and shape the way in which classic texts are to be read cannot agree among themselves. Hermeneutics – theoretical reflection on the practice of textual interpretation – arises in part out of this 'scandal' of interpretative disagreement. Hermeneutical thinking recognises that interpretative disagreement often originates in the differing assumptions, criteria and priorities that interpreters bring to the text. It tries to establish which assumptions, criteria and priorities are appropriate, or, if this proves impossible, how different approaches to interpretative practice can learn to co-exist with one another. It shifts the focus of attention away from the texts to the act of interpretation itself, seeking to make explicit the tacit understanding presupposed in its various practices. Hermeneutics does not recommend interpreters to abandon the study of texts and to practise self-examination instead; but it does suggest that texts will be studied with greater insight where the act of interpretation has itself been subjected to critical scrutiny.

Different types of canonical or classical text are studied by different communities of interpreters, and interpretative disagreement normally occurs within – rather than between – these interpretative communities. Hermeneutical thinking is therefore, in the first instance, local in nature. It arises out of disagreements about the meaning and significance of a particular body of texts. It will no doubt have much to learn from hermeneutical reflection in other fields, but the interpretative problems to which it must respond may well be specific to a particular field. A general (that is, philosophical) hermeneutics would seek to establish the conditions presupposed in any interpretative act, but its abstraction from local issues would restrict its usefulness in practice. In the case of Christian theology, for example, the manner of the church's past investment in the biblical texts and their interpretation raises hermeneutical questions that are unique to this particular context, even if there may be analogies elsewhere. This suggests the need for a Christian theological hermeneutics distinct from the project of a general hermeneutics intended to apply to all forms of interpretation. It also suggests that it is a mistake to address issues in biblical interpretation with conceptuality drawn from a general hermeneutics, unless at the same time one attends carefully to those issues which are specific to the local context.

Examples of local and of general hermeneutical thinking will help to clarify this point. A local, specifically theological example will be taken from the work of the third-century Alexandrian theologian, Origen; a general, philosophical example, from the work of the twentieth-century German philosopher Hans-Georg Gadamer.

In book 4 of his work *de Principiis* (*On First Principles*), Origen presents the first Christian hermeneutical treatise. His starting point is in the disagreements and problems that arise out of an excessively literalistic interpretation of the scriptures of the Old and the New Testaments. In the Old Testament utterances such as the following are ascribed to God: 'I am a jealous God, visiting the iniquities of the father upon the children unto the third and fourth generation' (Exodus 20:5); 'I repent of having anointed Saul to be king' (1 Samuel 15:11); 'I am a God that maketh peace and createth evil' (Isaiah 45:7). Heretics appeal to such statements to prove that the God of the Jews, the creator of heaven and earth, cannot be the same as the God revealed in Jesus Christ. Simple-minded orthodox believers are almost as much in error when they assume that the true God really is as he is depicted in such texts: thus 'they imagine concerning him such things as would not be believed of the most savage and unjust of humankind'.[3] The problem is both theological and hermeneutical. A literalistic hermeneutic assumes an exact correspondence between what is said and what is meant, and this results in erroneous beliefs about God and conflict within the Christian community. It fails to distinguish between the letter of the text and its deeper, spiritual meaning; it does not recognise that, in the gospels as well as in the Old Testament, literal falsehood may nevertheless point towards theological truth. One unfortunate effect of this narrow-mindedness is to damage the credibility of the church's proclamation among educated non-Christians. For Origen, the dual meaning of scripture is related to its unique status as inspired by the Holy Spirit; he is not proposing a general hermeneutic that could be applied to all texts indiscriminately.

For Gadamer, on the other hand, the task of hermeneutics is to enquire into the basis for the possibility of understanding presupposed in all of the *Geisteswissenschaften*, that is, in all study of cultural artefacts as opposed to natural objects. (This broad conception of hermeneutics is inherited from the nineteenth century, and especially from F. D. E. Schleiermacher and W. Dilthey.)[4] Gadamer is particularly concerned to resist the encroachment into the humanities of a view of 'objectivity' derived from the natural sciences, according to which the scientist must study his object of investigation from a standpoint of detachment and neutrality. Whether or not this is an appropriate account of scientific practice, it becomes untenable when transformed into the 'purely historical' approach to cultural artefacts in humanities disciplines. Gadamer's point is that all human beings are historically and culturally located, and that within a particular stream of historical becoming one encounters certain cultural artefacts that have been elevated to the status of 'classics', wherein 'truth' is to be sought and found. To study these artefacts as purely historical objects, restoring them to their circumstances of origin, is simply to ignore the classic or canonical status that cultural tradition has assigned to them – a self-contradictory position, since these works are only selected for historical treatment in the first place because of their continuing canonical status. The 'purely historical' approach mis-understands both the phenomenon of the canonical text and the situation of the interpreter, who is never without a specific place but is always situated within particular horizons, from within which he or she engages in dialogue with the text. This dialogue is or should be oriented towards the question of the truth mediated by the text; truth will occur when, through the dialogue, the horizons of interpreter and text expand so as to merge into one another.

Gadamer's philosophical hermeneutics has proved immensely influen-tial across a range of disciplines; in theological contexts, it is often employed in criticism of the dominance of historical approaches to the Bible. Such criti-cism is largely justified: in its exclusive concern with circumstances of origin, historical-critical practice overlooks or negates the phenomenon of the canonical text in just the way that Gadamer identifies. Yet this general hermeneutics, for all its merits, is no substitute for a theological hermeneu-tics attentive to the specificities of Christian usage of holy scripture. For example, Origen's question about the relationship between literal and theo-logical senses is still with us in various forms; but it must be answered by way of criteria internal to theological discourse, and not by appealing to a general hermeneutics which, if it is interested in this issue at all, will see it only as an instance of a more universal problem. Theological hermeneutics will have much to learn from general hermeneutics, but it will have much more to learn from theology itself.

A ROLE FOR THEOLOGICAL HERMENEUTICS

What role, then, might a theological hermeneutics play within contem-porary theological discussion? At this point we must begin practising theo-logical hermeneutics, and not just talking about it. Theological hermeneutics should be primarily concerned with the use of the Bible in theological construction, and it must identify and criticise interpretative assumptions that hinder that task. Insights drawn from non-theological hermeneutical reflection may prove valuable to it, but it must go its own way if it is to be theologically relevant. I shall give two examples of the kind of contribution that theological hermeneutics might offer.

(1) Hermeneutical awareness may help us to identify certain problems arising from the post-Enlightenment rewriting of the theological curriculum. Under this regime, the total theological task is divided up between various groups of specialists. The Bible itself is the preserve of two groups, Old Testament and New Testament scholars, whose disciplinary structures – as indicated by journals, monograph series, conferences and so on – allow the two interpretative communities to operate in almost complete isolation from each other. This division of labour already ensures that one can only reflect on the relation between the Testaments by, as it were, encroaching upon another professional domain – trespassing on someone else's intellectual property. In practice, biblical scholars keep safely within their own customary territory, and the result is that the theologically indispensable question of the relationship between the Testaments is systematically marginalised at all levels, from teaching to research. As the writings of the Christian 'Old Testament' are also the scriptures of the Jewish community, there is good reason for caution and sensitivity at this point – but not to the extent of a *de facto* concession that these writings cannot really be understood as Christian scripture at all.

The territory assigned to the systematic theologian is much more extensive: he or she must have acquired an expertise in the entire history of Christian theology, from the apologists to the present, together with an acquaintance with the history of philosophy and a range of contemporary intellectual trends. In practice, of course, specialisation will occur within this vast field; no individual can be equally at home in all of it. But the same is true within biblical studies, where a scholar may devote the best part of an academic career to the study of the Deuteronomic history or the Gospel of Mark. Despite these sub-specialisations, the respective fields of Old and New Testament studies and systematic theology retain a high degree of internal coherence. There is no difficulty in shifting the focus of one's research from one part of the field to another. Teaching conventions require scholars to take some responsibility for the field as a whole: the specialist in the Gospel of Mark will probably deliver a course of lectures on Pauline theology without undue strain, and the specialist in modern Protestant theology will probably not feel seriously ill at ease in the company of Athanasius, Augustine or Aquinas. Yet freedom of movement within disciplinary boundaries is not matched by a freedom to cross these boundaries. The Old Testament scholar will only venture into Pauline theology in exceptional circumstances, despite the fact that this theology has been the single most important factor in shaping the Christian Old Testament. The New Testament scholar probably knows little of Athanasius, Augustine or Aquinas, who are assigned a negative role in the alleged history of biblical misinterpretation that preceded the dawn of critical enlightenment. The systematic theologian cannot avoid the Bible as thoroughly as the biblical scholar can avoid systematic theology; and yet the use of the Bible in theological construction is severely inhibited by the anxiety engendered by the disciplinary boundary. To cross the boundary into someone else's territory is to be liable to anxiety, however much one may believe that one has every right to be here.

Like political boundaries, disciplinary boundaries may be arbitrary conventions that have come into existence through a variety of highly contingent factors. They are not 'natural' entities. On the other hand, institutional pressures may make them very hard to change once they have been established. In order to establish credentials in a particular scholarly discipline, one must subject oneself to a process of socialisation into that discipline's traditions, procedures and assumptions; and in the process – perhaps contrary to one's intentions – one will internalise that discipline's view of its own proper boundaries with respect to neighbouring disciplines. The postgraduate training that equips a person to become a New Testament scholar will foster a view of the Old Testament as a mere repository of background information, of no interest in its own right. If systematic theology is the chosen discipline, serious exegetical engagement with the biblical tests will in practice be regarded as superfluous, the province of another discipline which can always be consulted should the need arise; and this despite the foundational significance of the biblical texts and biblical interpretation for almost all forms of Christian theology. Disciplinary boundaries are *convenient:* faced with the difficulty of mastering an already extensive field, it is a relief to know that this field has its limits and that one has no responsibility for that which lies outside those limits. Disciplinary boundaries – again like political ones – may also be reinforced by a history of hostilities between the divided communities. A discipline that engages enthusiastically in a 'quest of the historical Jesus' does so on the assumption that the real (historical) Jesus is qualitatively different from the Jesus Christ of Christian faith and theology. A discipline uneasy about continuing to label its object of study as 'the Old Testament', on the grounds that this term is contaminated by Christian presuppositions, is similarly alienated from the concerns of Christian theology. It is regarded as reprehensible when a biblical scholar is caught in possession of a 'theological agenda', for it is assumed that theological engagement with the texts is bound to distort the autonomous processes of historical understanding. Even where it is acknowledged that everyone has an 'agenda' of some sort, whether theological or anti-theological, the structure of the discipline operates in such a way as to marginalise this insight and to prevent the appropriateness or otherwise of these varying commitments from being explicitly considered.

As Werner Jeanrond has written, 'It simply does not make sense that theologians today are not actively engaged in studying the primary texts of their traditions, while their biblical colleagues are on the whole not involved in discussing the intellectual, cultural, political, social and ecclesial context in which the textual objects of their study could play a transformative role.'[5] Indeed, the anomaly goes still deeper than this: the disciplinary boundaries are not only restrictive, they also grossly distort precisely the objects that they are intended to demarcate and protect. A systematic theology which has surrendered the biblical texts to other disciplines will tend to construe the history of Christian theology as a self-contained tradition and to overlook the dependence of classic theologies on sophisticated practices of biblical inter-pretation. The christologies of Athanasius and of Schleiermacher are not autonomous productions springing from abstract theological premises, but are shaped and permeated by their authors' reading of the biblical texts. A dialogue with such christologies that is not at the same time and explicitly a dialogue about biblical interpretation will be seriously flawed. It seems that theologians have tacitly accepted biblical scholarship's negative assessment of the biblical interpretation of classic Christian theologies, concluding that their exegetical shortcomings need not affect the way in which they are eval-uated: if bad exegesis produces good theology, then the exegesis can be regarded as mere scaffolding and discarded. But it would first be necessary to show by what criteria the exegesis is judged to be deficient, and to ask how far those criteria are appropriate to this material. The exegesis and hermeneu-tics underlying classic Christian theologies should be accorded the same nuanced and discriminating treatment that is often extended to their other constituent parts. If attentiveness to God's self-disclosure as attested in the biblical texts is required of Christian theology, then it is inconceivable that bad exegesis could produce anything other than bad theology. And a con-temporary theology that is content to abandon biblical interpretation to a non-theological discipline can hardly be regarded as Christian.

An inappropriate disciplinary boundary also distorts the object of bibli-cal studies, the biblical texts themselves. The overwhelming concentration of scholarly work on the texts' historical circumstances of origin has had the effect of marginalising all informed reflection about these texts' real significance. At the moment of origin, significance is uncertain. It is not initially clear whether the Christian community as a whole will accept the testimony of, say, the Gospel of John to God's self-disclosure in the incarnate Word, or whether and how far it will allow itself to be shaped by that testimony. The significance of a text takes time to unfold: and an exegesis that is interested only in the process of origination deprives it of the time that has actually been bestowed on it by virtue of its canonical status. It abstracts the text from its past, present and future roles in the ongoing dialogue of Christian theology, converting it into an inert object, viewed as if from a great distance. This object is subjected to a series of manipulations out of which a securely grounded knowledge of its circumstances of origin is expected to materialise; yet the repeated failure to achieve the desired knowledge, as one hypothesis after another is found to be inadequately grounded, does not seriously dent the discipline's confidence in the viability of its historical projects. Needless to say, Old and New Testament scholarship has also produced substantial, well-grounded work from which theology can only benefit. But here too, progress is hindered by the fact that biblical scholars fail to take responsibility for an informed theological development of their own insights. The insights themselves would be richer and more varied if theological concerns were incorporated into the interpretative framework within which they arise.

In the long run, as Jeanrond has argued, institutional change is needed: 'In view of the new hermeneutical connection between biblical studies and theological studies today, it seems not to be a premature proposal to suggest a reorganisation of the division of labour in our theological faculties and schools.'[6] In the meantime, however, a patient hermeneutical investigation is required that will trace, in detail, the distortions engendered by the assumption that the study of the Bible and the study of Christian theology are best kept apart. One such distortion, to which we now turn, concerns the status accorded to the 'final' or 'canonical' form of the biblical text.

(2) What is meant by a text's 'final form'? It might be argued that there is no such thing. As it is transmitted through copying and translation, a text is subjected to a continual process of addition, subtraction and adjustment. For the majority of readers of biblical texts, translation is necessary; and, since language is constantly changing, translation is an unending task which must produce ever new renderings of biblical texts as old ones lose their appeal and their intelligibility. Even if we ignore translation and identify the 'final form' with the text in its original language, ambiguities abound. Does the 'final form' of the Gospel of Mark include or exclude the account of resurrection appearances (16:9–20)? This has been added by someone other than the

evangelist; yet it is part of the Gospel of Mark as transmitted by the majority of Greek manuscripts, and can only be excised by way of complex techniques developed by modern textual criticism. A textual difficulty on this scale does, however, appear to be unusual: the vast majority of variant readings are relatively minor, and are compatible with the view that at a particular point a text attained a relative stability which is preserved in the process of transmission. The fact that the concept of the 'final form' of a text has slight residual ambiguities does not affect its usefulness. One might similarly speak of the 'final form' of an eighteenth-century novel, contrasting the published version with earlier drafts or notes, even though variations in spelling, layout, capitalisation and so on will continue to accumulate as the novel appears in successive editions.

For Christian theology, the significance of the final form of the biblical texts is that this is the form in which they were taken into the canon and thereby 'authorised' for various kinds of communal usage. In the case of a novel, it is conceivable that a modern scholar might edit and publish a significantly different earlier draft, arguing that this is in certain respects superior to the version originally published and that the newly issued text should henceforth be the basis for scholarship and literary criticism. In the case of the biblical texts, however, no such possibility exists either in practice or in principle. It is the texts now known as the book of Genesis and the Gospel of Matthew that were accepted as canonical, not 'J' or 'Q' – if these shadowy entities ever existed in any of the forms envisaged by modern scholarship. The canonical texts could not be displaced or supplemented by reconstructions of 'J' or 'Q', even if these reconstructions were more securely grounded than they actually are. It is true that the exact content of the Christian canon has never been definitively settled, as variations in the Old Testament canons of various Christian communities indicate; yet it is hard to imagine how an effective challenge to the basic structure of the Christian canon could ever be possible or defensible. One of the tasks of theological hermeneutics is therefore to establish the reality of the canonical form of the texts, and to defend its integrity against interpretative practices that undermine it. Two such practices may be described as *archaeology* and *supplementation.*

Modern biblical scholarship is often *archaeological* in character. The surface of the text is valued not for itself but for the information it may yield up about its historical circumstances of origin. If the information is to be extracted, excavation must occur. Various strata must be identified and differentiated, the downward movement through the strata corresponding to a backward movement through time. Near the surface will be the stratum of the 'redactor'; beneath this, earlier forms of the tradition as shaped and handed on in communal usage; and, further down still, there may perhaps be a few fragments dating back to the moment of origin. The ambiguity of these findings and the difficulty in achieving a clear differentiation of strata ensure that the circulating scholarly discussion achieves a kind of perpetual motion. In the process, however, the surface of the text has been destroyed. It is no longer fit for its customary uses. A text that had once seemed to testify to the reality of Jesus Christ, who is Immanuel, God-with-us, has now been compelled to speak about many other things: the problems of early Christian communities, the distinctive concerns of an individual evangelist, the enigma of a so-called 'historical Jesus' who is qualitatively different from the Jesus Christ of Christian faith. Analysis requires the differentiation of strata, and so the possibility that there may be continuities between the real Jesus and the Christ-image of the evangelist is systematically marginalised; the distortions that occur here originate not in the ambiguity of the evidence but in the interpretative model itself. In opposition to this, theological hermeneutics must develop more adequate ways of conceptualising the *truth-content* of the gospel texts in their single but many-sided testimony to the Word made flesh. Small-scale archaeological operations may still be desirable – for no possible source of insight can be ruled out in principle as theologically irrelevant; but there can be no question of accepting the archaeological model's right to dictate the structure of the entire field.

Modern biblical scholarship is also anxious to *supplement* the biblical texts with information about their broader linguistic, social and cultural environment. This information is in general more reliable than the hypotheses generated by the archaeological model, and there can be no question of dispensing with it. The biblical texts cannot be understood and translated without a broad knowledge of biblical languages stemming in part from extra-biblical sources. Individual obscurities are often clarified by an awareness of current practices or beliefs. To abstract the biblical texts entirely from their original environment would be to treat them docetically, as originating directly from above without the mediation of historically and culturally located human agency. Christians in the early centuries who already read Josephus alongside the gospels were undoubtedly right to do so.

There are, however, a number of ways in which 'supplementation' tends to undermine the integrity of the biblical texts in their canonical form:

(a) The integrity of the text may be threatened by the quantity of information with which it is supplemented. The 'background' to every text, and to every part of every text, is in principle unlimited. Every significant word has a rich and diverse history of usage; and parallels, analogies and sources can be postulated for every significant idea. Yet in locating the word or idea within this unlimited network, one may not be sufficiently attentive to the particularity of its role within its immediate biblical context. A broadly conceived background may take precedence over a sharply defined context. For example, an investigation of the 'background' of the term *logos* in the Johannine prologue (John 1:1–18) might be extended over many pages without any serious consideration of its particular role in inaugurating and grounding the entire Johannine narrative. This problem is exacerbated by a 'quantitative' view of scholarship according to which the amassing and processing of large quantities of information is valuable in itself, even when there is no obvious use for much of it.

(b) Supplementation may also threaten the integrity of a text when excessive claims are made for the relevance of single elements in the background. The claim that the Johannine Logos may be explained entirely on the basis of Jewish 'wisdom' traditions will tend to exaggerate the area of overlap and to underestimate the area of difference. But it is in the difference that permeates even the overlap that the term's theological significance is to be found. The Word through whom all things were made is also the Word who became flesh, and the enfleshment of the Word transforms utterly the well-known theme of the Word's role in creation. To explain the text out of its 'background' is to construe it as an intelligible effect of a known cause, despite the fact that this text traces its own origin back to an event in which normal historical processes of cause and effect are overturned.

(c) Supplementation may threaten the integrity of the text where it is used to disparage its representation of reality. To take a fairly minor example, it may be that biblical chronology is at some points incompatible with apparently accurate data from elsewhere in the ancient near east or in the Graeco-Roman world; yet the distinctive theological role of chronological data in biblical history-writing would still need to be clarified. Identifying biblical inaccuracies and misrepresentations on the basis of supplementary material is at best a necessary but trivial procedure, and at worst an expression of deep alienation from the substance of Christian faith as attested in these texts. Attentiveness to the text in its canonical form makes it possible to counter the arbitrariness and overstatement sometimes evident in this area.

In this chapter, I have outlined a view of hermeneutics as theoretical reflection on interpretative practice, and have suggested that this should be

understood in 'local' terms, in relation to the practice of a specific interpretative community. I have also argued that contemporary theological
hermeneutics must take as its main subject matter the distortions arising out
of inappropriately drawn disciplinary boundaries, thereby mediating
between the separated disciplines of biblical interpretation and Christian
theology. An example of this mediating activity was then given: the concept
of the final form of the text made it possible to identify and correct the
particular distortions that arise from the practices of 'archaeology' and of
'supplementation'. Needless to say, a great deal of further investigation is
required if the full reality of the present situation is to be brought to light,
and if remedies are to be found.

Notes

1 For an introduction to the 'new hermeneutic', see Werner Jeanrond,
  Theological Hermeneutics: Development and Significance (Basingstoke:
  Macmillan, 1991), pp. 148–58.
2 For a more extensive statement of the position outlined here, see my *Text,*
  Church and World: Biblical Interpretation in Theological Perspective
  (Edinburgh: T. & T. Clark; Grand Rapids, Michigan: Eerdmans, 1994).
3 Origen, *de Principiis* iv.1.8 (translation from *The Anti-Nicene Fathers* (Grand
  Rapids, Michigan: Eerdmans, 1976), vol. iv, p. 357).
4 Gadamer's major work is his *Truth and Method* [1960] (English translation,
  London: Sheed and Ward, 1975). For a useful anthology of the German
  hermeneutical tradition, including texts from Schleiermacher, Dilthey and
  Gadamer, see K. Mueller-Vollmer, *The Hermeneutics Reader* (Oxford: Basil
  Blackwell, 1986).
5 Werner Jeanrond, 'After Hermeneutics', in F. Watson (ed.), *The Open Text:*
  New Directions for Biblical Studies? (London: SCM Press, 1993), pp. 85–102;
  p. 99.
6 *Ibid.*, p. 99.

Further reading

Childs, Brevard, *Introduction to the Old Testament as Scripture*, London:
  SCM Press, 1979.

Frei, Hans, *The Eclipse of Biblical Narrative: A Study in Eighteenth and Nineteenth Century Hermeneutics*, New Haven and London: Yale University Press, 1974.
Theology and Narrative: Selected Essays, edited by G. Hunsinger and W. C. Placher, New York and Oxford: Oxford University Press, 1993.

Gadamer, Hans-Georg, *Truth and Method*, English translation, London: Sheed and Ward, 1975.

Jeanrond, Werner, *Theological Hermeneutics: Development and Significance*, Basingstoke: Macmillan, 1991.

Mueller-Vollmer, Kurt, *The Hermeneutics Reader*, Oxford: Basil Blackwell, 1986.

Ricoeur, Paul, *Essays on Biblical Interpretation*, edited by Lewis S. Mudge, Philadelphia: Fortress, 1980.

Thiselton, Anthony, *New Horizons in Hermeneutics: The Theory and Practice of Transforming Biblical Reading*, London: HarperCollins, 1992.

Watson, Francis, *Text, Church and World: Biblical Interpretation in Theological Perspective*, Edinburgh: T. & T. Clark; Grand Rapids, Michigan: Eerdmans, 1994.

Text and Truth: Redefining Biblical Theology, Edinburgh: T. & T. Clark; Grand Rapids, Michigan: Eerdmans, 1997.

Young, Frances, *The Art of Performance: Towards a Theology of Holy Scripture*, London: Darton, Longman and Todd, 1990.

5 Christ and the cultures: the Jewish people and Christian theology

BRUCE D. MARSHALL

The century now drawing to a close has seen a searching reconsideration by Christians of their relationship to the Jewish people. In part this new perception has stemmed from momentous historical events: the Holocaust, in which Christians have had to recognise their own complicity, and the return of the Jewish people, after two millennia, to the land God gave to Abraham. These events have forever altered the intellectual and social conditions under which Christian theology is practised. But Christian theologians have also found themselves prompted to re-evaluate traditional Christian assumptions about the Jews by reflection on some of their own community's most basic and central convictions. This too promises to have a far-reaching effect, the full extent of which is still not wholly clear, on what Christian theologians say about God and all God's works.

The theological point of departure for our century's critical reassessment of the church's relation to the Jewish people is the proposal, now commonly made, that Christians ought to share a wider range of beliefs with Jews than they have in the past, and one belief in particular: that the biological descendants of Abraham, Isaac and Jacob are permanently and irrevocably the elect people of God. Correlatively, Christians ought to do away with a belief which their community has held for a long time, namely the conviction that the church has displaced Israel (that is, the Jewish people) as God's elect. Christians should reject, that is, their long-held supersessionist interpretation of their relationship to the Jewish people.

The extent to which the rejection of supersessionism has had an impact on the belief and practice of Christians is of course hard to gauge with any precision, but many Christian communities, and not just individual theologians, have made the repudiation of supersessionism part of their public teaching.[1] In coming to share with Jews a belief in God's permanent election of Abraham's children, Christians have accepted a conviction which is not peripheral for Jews, but central to historic Jewish communal identity and to Jewish views of the world. As the Jewish theologian Michael Wyschogrod observes, 'The foundation of Judaism is the family identity of the Jewish people as the descendants of Abraham, Isaac, and Jacob. Whatever else is added to this must be seen as growing out of and related to the basic identity of the Jewish people as the seed of Abraham elected by God through descent from Abraham.'[2] We should expect, therefore, that in accepting this central Jewish belief Christians will find themselves engaged with further Jewish beliefs about God and God's works; rejecting supersessionism will be likely to involve reassessment in other areas of Christian theology as well.

The notion of 'supersessionism', however, has a wide and sometimes confusing variety of associations. Christian theologians sometimes use the term to cover any elements in traditional Christian conceptions of the church's relation to Israel which they believe can no longer be maintained. So for some theologians the belief that Jesus is Israel's promised Messiah is itself inherently supersessionistic, and must be discarded if the church is to have a morally tolerable relation to the Jewish people; others insist on the importance of rejecting supersessionism, but do not include this traditional christological claim in the very definition of what must be rejected.[3]

In this chapter the term will be used in a much more specific way: to denote the belief that the church has taken the place of the Jews as the elect people of God. The point of defining supersessionism in a relatively precise and limited fashion is not to decide any substantive issues in advance, but to be clear and to avoid begging questions. Virtually all Christians who reject 'supersessionism' agree at least that in so doing they affirm the permanent election of the Jewish people, and so rule out the possibility that the Jews could be replaced as God's elect; they disagree about what this affirmation does, and what it does not, entail for the rest of Christian belief. In order to explore some possible entailments, we need first to consider Israel's election, traditional Christian supersessionist teaching about it and the mutant form that teaching took in modern Protestant theology.

SUPERSESSIONISM

That the Jewish people are elected or chosen by God turns out to be a complex thought. 'You are,' as Moses says to the children of Abraham gathered on the outskirts of the promised land, 'a people holy to the Lord your God; the Lord your God has chosen you out of all the peoples on earth to be his people, his treasured possession' (Deuteronomy 7:6). This suggests that Israel's election involves at least the following elements. The elect are (1) the biological descendants of Abraham, Isaac and Jacob. This descent 'according to the flesh' (as Romans 9:3 has it) constitutes membership in the elect people and identifies for themselves and others who the elect are; that Abraham's descendants are the elect thus (2) presupposes a distinction between this biological family and all the other peoples of the earth. The elect people (3) receive God's favour; they are his 'treasured possession', those upon whom the God who owns heaven and earth has 'set his heart in love' (Deuteronomy 10:14–15), not because of any achievements for which they could claim credit, but simply because of God's spontaneous affection (see Deuteronomy 7:7–9; 9:4–7). As the larger narrative context of these Deuteronomic passages makes clear, to God's beloved (4) belongs God's promise of blessing, both the promise that they will be blessed by God, and the promise that through them God's blessing will ultimately come to all the peoples of the earth (see Genesis 12:1–3). With God's favour and promise towards the elect people go (5) special responsibilities of the elect people towards God, namely that they are expected to keep God's law, enjoined only upon them among all the nations (for example, Deuteronomy 5:32–3); perhaps the most obvious legal mark of election is circumcision ('So shall my covenant be in your flesh', Genesis 17:13). If (1) and (2) specify who the elect people are, (3)–(5) specify the content and consequences of God's election of this people. Characterised in this way, the notion of divine election seems to presuppose (6) that God wills a world with a perceptible diversity of peoples, among whom he can then choose to bestow his favour.

On a supersessionist account of divine election, the church has displaced Israel as the chosen people of God. From Abraham to John the Baptist, belonging to God's elect people – those upon whom God has 'set his heart in love' – was a family affair: being a descendant of Abraham made one a member of the chosen people. From Jesus' resurrection and the outpouring of the Holy Spirit at Pentecost to the end of time, election is no longer a matter of biological descent, but of baptism and faith – no longer a matter of being a Jew, but of being a Christian. God has, as it were, changed the rules of divine election, the rules by which he 'sets his heart in love' on his creatures. Or more precisely, the old rules have been superseded by new ones: God's favour (points 3–5, above) is now bestowed according to different criteria than it was before (see points 1–2). Now that the new has come, the old, having served its preparatory purpose, must be left behind.

So according to the church's historic supersessionist teaching, Abraham's descendants according to the flesh no longer enjoy any special favour with God. Indeed, this teaching has tended to suggest the view that the Jews now have a special claim on God's *dis*favour, since Jesus Christ was one of their own, and they not only handed him over to death, but continue to reject his messianic mission. This punitive element, however, while a common feature of traditional Christian teaching, is not a logically inevitable consequence of supersessionism; one could hold that in the advent of Jesus Christ and the church the election of the Jews has fully accomplished its divinely appointed purpose without supposing that God has abandoned the Jews, or that the Jews are subject to any special divine punishment (as, for example, Karl Barth basically seems to do).[4]

Supersessionism, it should be observed, played a crucial role in keeping the Hebrew Bible (or more precisely its Greek translation, the Septuagint) in the Christian canon of scripture. As early as the second century, Gentile Christians were able to make sense of Jewish scripture, alien though it was to them, by reading the election of Israel and the details of Israel's life as a necessary prelude to the salvation accomplished for all humanity in Christ, and so as a witness to their own irrevocable inclusion as Gentiles in the saving plan of God. In particular, traditional supersessionism maintained, against the Gnostics and Marcion, that the Old Testament's depiction of God's engagement with the Jewish people provides the permanently necessary narrative context for grasping Jesus' redemptive significance. The Old Testament alone adequately acquaints us with the God who creates the world and sends his Son for the sake of all humanity: the one who does these things is, quite specifically, Israel's God. Thus Irenaeus, one of the architects of traditional supersessionism, insists that the being whom Jesus calls 'Father' is not only 'the maker of heaven and earth', but none other than the one 'whom the prophets proclaimed . . . whom also the law announces, saying "Hear, O Israel, the Lord your God is one God" '.[5] While the role of the Jewish people in the economy of redemption is for traditional supersessionism purely preparatory, the church until the end of time remains linked to and dependent upon the Jews, in that a knowledge of their narrated history from Abraham to Jesus is indispensable for Christians: without a grasp of Israel's history, and so without Jewish scripture, Christians cannot locate the Father of the Lord Jesus Christ, and so cannot know the God whom they are to worship.

But supersessionism also had a considerable cost: on this reading God's dealings with Israel do indeed have permanent significance for Christians, but only in so far as they prepare for and anticipate what happens in Jesus Christ and in the church. The abiding significance of the Jewish people consists in, and is limited to, Israel's preparatory role; the election of the Jewish people – God's favour towards them and the special responsibilities by which they respond in love to God's gracious election – ends with the coming of Christ. In a formulation of Justin Martyr often repeated in later Christian theology, the church is 'the true spiritual Israel'. The true 'descendants of Judah, Jacob, Isaac, and Abraham ... are we who have been led to God through this crucified Christ'. 'You deceive yourselves,' Justin therefore warns the Jews, 'while you fancy that, because you are the seed of Abraham after the flesh ... you shall fully inherit the good things announced to be bestowed by God through Christ ... It becomes you to eradicate this hope from your souls.'[6]

We cannot here trace the complex history of supersessionism.[7] The picture is, however, far from uniform. Augustine in particular introduced ideas which had a tremendous influence on the way subsequent Western theology understood the Jews. With characteristic clarity, he articulates a sense of the continuity between the church and biblical Israel markedly deeper than that of his theological predecessors. The believing Israelites depicted in the Old Testament had the same faith as believing members of the Christian church now enjoy, a faith which joined them to Jesus Christ the mediator and so brought them salvation. To be sure, they believed that Christ was to come in the flesh while the church believes he has come; their faith depended on 'sacraments' (circumcision and the levitical sacrifices) which pointed ahead to the mediator still to come, the church's faith depends on sacraments (baptism and the eucharist) which look back upon the media-tor already come, who makes himself present in the sacraments he instituted with a personal directness previously unavailable.[8] But they relied for salva-tion upon the very same person the church does, and so had the church's faith. Indeed, the church begins with Abel, the first righteous person, and extends to the end of time, embracing all – Jews, pagans and Christians – who in one way or another have faith in the one mediator and so belong to his one body.[9]

To propose this sort of underlying unity between Israel and the church naturally tends to downplay the notion that the church supersedes Israel, precisely because it downplays the election of physical Israel as such. On this view, the rules of election have not so much changed as become more explicit. Divine election was never chiefly a matter of descent according to the flesh, but always of faith and obedience; the one elect people of God is that collection of individuals who, whether in the midst of physical Israel or the mixed body (*corpus mixtum*) of the Constantinian church, truly believe God's word and hearken to his commands. But from Augustine to the dawn of modernity, theologians in the Latin West remained haunted by an awareness, rooted in their close reading of scripture, that the God whom they worshipped had in fact elected one line of Abraham's biological children. This compelled them to account for the place of the Jewish people even after Christ in God's plan of salvation, despite the poor fit this made with their inclination to think of the elect as coextensive with the members of the church from Abel to the end of time.

So, for example, the conviction that God's faithfulness will see to the eschatological salvation of the Jews, despite their previous rejection of Christ, was a medieval theological commonplace. Augustine's picturesque scenario for this, suggested by Malachi 4:5–6, was that Elijah would return 'in the last days before the judgement' and convert the Jews (those alive at the time, it seems) to Christ.[10] Intensifying this line of thought, Thomas Aquinas takes Romans 11:26 to teach a future healing and restoration of the Jews, when 'not only particular [Jews], as now, but all universally' will attain salvation.[11] As Aquinas reads Paul this *reparatio* is only fitting: 'if God permitted the trespass and failure of the Jews [see Romans 11:12, upon which Aquinas here comments] for the benefit (*utilitas*) of the whole world, all the more will he make good their ruin, again for the benefit of the whole world'.[12] To be sure, such ideas proved compatible with approval of appallingly harsh social measures against the Jews, rooted in the conviction that they were subject to divine punishment for their unbelief. Here too, however, there were noteworthy differences of outlook.[13]

Interestingly, the rise of self-consciously modern forms of Christian theology saw the emergence of a new theological conception of the Jewish people, but not one rooted in a concern that traditional theology had made too little of the role of the Jewish people in God's creative and redeeming work. On the contrary: supersessionism made too much of the Jews. For example Friedrich Schleiermacher, perhaps the greatest theologian of liberal Protestantism, argued that the connection of Christianity to Judaism, and in particular the fact that Jesus was a Jew, is simply a historical accident which has nothing to do with the essence of Christianity or with Jesus' redemptive significance. Schleiermacher deliberately removes Jesus from the narrative context of the Old Testament, and proposes instead to make sense of Jesus as redeemer against the background of a universal 'consciousness of the need for redemption' (13,2).[14] The Hebrew scriptures are in principle superfluous for the church; they contain nothing of value which is not more clearly stated in the New Testament, and much Jewish material which is of no value at all – indeed, the more characteristically Jewish the text is, the less useful it is (see 27,3; 12,3). It would be permissible to leave them, especially the Psalms and the prophets, as a kind of historical appendix to the New Testament, a suggestion intended to highlight the irrelevance, indeed deceptiveness, of the traditional canon's narrative sequence for Christian faith and theology (see 132,3).

Judaism is therefore no closer to Christianity than any other religion, and in particular is equidistant with ancient paganism (see 12,2). Quite consistently with this outlook, Schleiermacher regards the notion of God's special electing love for Israel as a remnant of fetishism – the lowest form of religious consciousness, because it ascribes to God a spatially particular location, in the midst of this one people (8,4). An adequately developed monotheistic religious consciousness recognises that God can have no such spatial location (8,1–3), and cannot be conceived as favouring one human clan over another; unsurprisingly, the Jewish people never come in for consideration in Schleiermacher's own extensive account of divine election (117–20).

Thus Schleiermacher denies that the God of Jesus Christ is or ever was in any distinctive sense the God of Israel. Though this is probably a mutation of traditional Christian ideas about God's abandonment of unbelieving Jewry, it is not supersessionism, because on Schleiermacher's account Christian faith has no stake in the claim that the church has in any sense *replaced* Israel; this would assume that the Jewish people were once God's elect, and that in some way Christian faith remains dependent on both the history and the scripture of this elect people, all of which Schleiermacher is consistently concerned to deny. So Schleiermacher, and liberal Protestantism more broadly, cut the tie between Jews and Christians which even traditional supersessionism had always maintained: their common claim that to worship the only God there is, we must know the story in which Moses said of this God to the children of Abraham, 'Hear O Israel, the Lord your God, the Lord is one' (Deuteronomy 6:4).

REJECTING SUPERSESSIONISM

There might be many different reasons not to be a supersessionist. One might, for instance, reject supersessionism for moral reasons, on the grounds that it encourages, or at least tolerates, hostility towards the Jews. But if Christians are convinced that their own most central beliefs require a supersessionist view of Israel, they will naturally be inclined to argue that a morally sustainable Christian posture towards the Jewish people is compatible with supersessionism. Surely, it might be argued, the Great Commandment applies to Christian treatment of Jews as much as of anyone else, regardless of the status of Jewish election; the church's historic abuse of the Jewish people stems, so the argument might go, from the sinful failure of Christians to keep the commandment of love towards Jewish neighbours, rather than from supersessionist belief. So if there are going to be effective reasons for the church as such to reject supersessionism, they will have to be theological as well as moral. They will, in other words, have to show that the Christian community's most central beliefs are incompatible with supersessionism, and require its rejection.

Once noticed, the theological reasons for rejecting supersessionism seem obvious and compelling. The apparent theological problem with supersessionism is that were it true, no one could take the God of Israel at his word. Now we Christians believe that this God has in Jesus Christ promised salvation to all humanity. This promise, Christians suppose, is permanent and irrevocable; God will never do anything to take it back – or supersede it. The same God also promised Abraham that his descendants would be God's own people forever (see Genesis 17:7: 'an everlasting covenant'). God made, in other words, the same sort of promise to Abraham as Christians believe he has made to all the world in Christ: a permanent and irrevocable one. If Christians suppose that this God has revoked his promise to Israel, then we suppose that when this God declares a promise permanent and irrevocable, he may be lying. So if Christians want to believe that God's promise of salvation to all the world in Jesus Christ is permanent, then we have to believe that the election of Israel is permanent. Or as it is sometimes put: if God's pledge of salvation to the world in Jesus Christ is unsurpassable, then the election of Israel is unsurpassable. Christians cannot therefore be supersessionists about Israel unless they are willing to be supersessionists about Jesus – which is to say, unless they are willing to stop being Christians.

In recent theological discussion this sort of argument has emerged largely from exegesis of the New Testament, above all of Romans 9–11. Paul there reflects on, indeed agonises over, a perplexing state of affairs. Israel has for the most part rejected the Messiah given to it by Israel's God, while the Gentiles have embraced him. The passage is extraordinarily complex, but one basic feature of Paul's outlook seems clear: this astonishing reversal of expectations is the intention of Israel's God. He has hardened the hearts of Israel so that the Gentiles may receive in Jesus Christ the blessing which God promised to all the nations in Abraham (Romans 11:25). This does not mean that God has rejected Abraham's children according to the flesh, as some Gentile Christians at Rome seem erroneously to have supposed. Rather

Israel's rejection of the gospel is God's own will, to give the Gentiles time and space to accept it. This is a great mystery of Israel's God, which we Gentiles must ponder in awe and fear: 'As regards the gospel,' Paul writes, 'they [the Jews] are enemies for your sake; but as regards election they are beloved on account of their forefathers; for the gifts and the calling of God are irrevocable' (Romans 11:28–9; see 11:1–2). Paul's reason here why God loves Israel – namely on account of Abraham, and in spite of Israel's own action – is not concessive; this is exactly the same reason Deuteronomy 10 gives why God has set his heart in love upon Israel. The election of Israel, Paul seems to say, is as much in force after Christ as it was when Israel was poised to enter the promised land.[15]

For the church's relation to the Jewish people and for Christian theology, what follows – and does not follow – from the end of supersessionism?

One obvious consequence of dropping supersessionism is that it enables Christians to see clearly a possibility which for so long they could at best only dimly perceive: that the salvation of the Jews is in the bag. Here again Paul is the chief teacher. In the end, after the temporary hardening of the Jews for the sake of the salvation of the Gentiles, 'all Israel will be saved' (Romans 11:26). In Jesus Christ eschatological salvation comes to light as the ultimate blessing which God promised to Abraham's children and, through them, to the nations (see point 4 in the description of election, above); if God's gifts are irrevocable, then this supreme blessing will not be withheld from those to whom it was first promised. This suggests that Christians may engage in a non-proselytising conversation with Jews; since we do not have to assume that we are talking to the damned, we do not have to feel responsible for converting and thus saving them. Such a conversation is likely to be mutually more instructive than the sort which has traditionally taken place between Jews and Christians. Whether Paul or the New Testament as a whole permits, or even requires, the church to drop the idea of a mission to the Jews in view of their promised salvation remains in dispute, though even the most profoundly christocentric theologians have entertained doubts on this score.[16]

Post-supersessionist reflection leads some Christian theologians not only to reject the notion of a mission to the Jews, but to take the further step of arguing that Jesus Christ has saving relevance only for Gentiles, and not for Jews. On this view, since the election of Israel is still in full force, the salvation of the Jews depends on their descent from Abraham, while the salvation of Gentiles depends on Jesus Christ. There are in effect two parallel but not overlapping covenants which the God of Israel has made with humanity, one with Jews and one with Gentiles.

It is not entirely clear, however, that this is a position which Christians can coherently maintain. It seems quite basic to the New Testament that in the slaying and raising of the Jew Jesus, the God of Israel has acted definitively – unsurpassably – on behalf of all humanity, Jews as well as Gentiles. Of course the ways Jews and Gentiles are each related to what happens on the cross and the Emmaus road may differ quite significantly, but the New Testament seems deeply committed to saying that what happens here is decisive for the destiny of both. As Acts 15 has Peter observe, speaking as a Jew to the Jewish Christians of the Jerusalem church, 'we believe that we' – that is, we Jews – 'will be saved by the grace of the Lord Jesus, just as they' – that is, the Gentiles – 'will' (Acts 15:11).

It seems implausible to take Paul's insistence on the permanence of Israel's election as a repudiation of this conviction that salvation comes through Jesus Christ alone, or as a suggestion that the salvation of the Jewish people will come about, in the end, without their own recognition of Jesus as Israel's promised Messiah. Paul's argument in Romans turns on the assumption that the gospel which proclaims Jesus as Israel's Messiah is for Jews as well as Gentiles, indeed primarily for Jews (Romans 1:16). He depicts the eschatological salvation of the Jews precisely as their 'full inclusion' (Romans 11:12) in the community, of which they remain the elected root (Romans 11:16–24), that is now open to Gentiles and gratefully receives the gospel of Christ as God's decisive saving power for Jews and Gentiles alike (Romans 1:17; see 11:23). Rather than suggesting separate saving arrangements (that is, 'covenants') for Jews and Gentiles, Romans 9–11 assumes that there is only one such arrangement, which depends as a whole on Jesus' death and resurrection (see Galatians 3:13–14); present Jewish rejection of the gospel is only a *problem* for Paul – the problem which leads him to write these chapters in the first place – because it threatens to exclude them from this arrangement. It thus seems that while Abraham's descendants will surely not be rejected, their acceptance depends finally not on their descent, but on what happens with the one Jew Jesus of Nazareth. This is not to suggest that the 'rules' of divine election have changed – Abraham and his descendants, once elected, will never lose anything which election involves or entails. But it does imply a distinction between what visibly guarantees Jewish election (descent from Abraham) and what ultimately and mysteriously causes it (Jesus' death and resurrection); for most Jews, Paul seems to say, there is at this point a divinely willed disharmony between the order of knowing and the order of being which will only be overcome at the end of time (see Romans 11:25–7).

SOME CONSEQUENCES OF REJECTING SUPERSESSIONISM

The discovery that Christians ought to share with Jews a belief in the permanent election of Abraham's children poses a challenge for Christian theology, one which in some respects has not been faced seriously since the second century: how can Christians coherently maintain a commitment both to the permanent election of Israel and to the unsurpassability of Jesus Christ? We can explore this question by looking at two theological topics where the difficulties of being coherent press particularly hard in a post-supersessionist environment: the law and the Trinity.

The law

The permanent election of Israel seems to require that the identifiable existence of the Jewish people also be permanent. Israel's election would be void if the biological descendants of Abraham indeed received God's promised blessing, but had ceased to be identifiable as Abraham's descendants, that is, as Jews. The permanence of Israel's election thus entails the permanence of the distinction between Jew and Gentile.[17] To be sure, Christians maintain, God has now extended his favour and salvation to the Gentiles in Jesus Christ; they too are now 'his treasured possession'. But it remains God's favour towards *Israel* which finds in Christ both its unsurpassable fullness and its extension to the nations. Jews remain the root on to which the Gentile branches are grafted; the branches neither replace the root, nor may they be confused or identified with it (Romans 11:16–24). So the coming of Christ reinforces the distinction between Jews and Gentiles, but it also eliminates some of the elements in which that distinction, and so Israel's election, had formerly consisted; the *content* of divine election is now largely shared with the Gentiles (specifically points 3 and 4 in the description above). How then is the distinct identity of the Jews, and so Israel's election, to be maintained?

The obvious answer is by Jewish observance of the full range of traditional Jewish law (*halachah*, which embraces both the written and oral Torah, that is, both biblical and rabbinic law – see point 5, above). This observance, in which the Gentiles will surely have no interest and to which God's electing will does not obligate them, will be the chief means by which Abraham's descendants can be identified, and indeed will keep the Gentiles at a certain distance, thus ensuring that Abraham's children do not, through intermarriage, vanish into the sea of nations. The ancient and distinctive responsibilities of the Jewish people towards God are, as it were, that mark of Israel's primordial and permanent election which remains *post Christum.*

But the New Testament also includes vigorous polemics against the Old Testament law. Jesus seems to reject various fasting, Sabbath, ritual purity and dietary laws (Mark 2:23–3:6). Paul proclaims that those in Christ have 'died to the law' and are now 'discharged from the law', so that they might 'belong to him who has been raised from the dead', and so 'bear fruit for God' (Romans 7:4–6; see Galatians 2:19); the law was given only for a time, as 'our tutor until Christ came' (Galatians 3:24–5; see 3:19), and was in fact a covenant of slavery (see Galatians 4:24–5). Now that Christ has come those who still want to keep the law (for example, by being circumcised) cut themselves off from Christ and lose his benefits (see Galatians 5:2–6). Passages like these make it seem at best unnecessary, and at worst positively harmful – a rejection of Christ – for anyone to keep the law after Christ has come.

Precisely because they read the New Testament in a supersessionist way, traditional accounts of the law in Christian theology saw no problem here. With the coming of Christ, they supposed, God's election of the Jews – and in particular his will that they be distinct from the Gentiles – is at an end. As a result there is no further need for practices which would distinguish Jews from Gentiles; on traditional views the only legitimate functions of the law after Christ are universalisable ones (such as accusing the conscience of sin or guiding the moral life of believers), confined on most accounts to the Decalogue, broadly interpreted. But a post-supersessionist theology does have a problem here. The Jewish people cannot be permanently elect unless they can be distinguished at all times from the nations, and the observance of traditional Jewish law seems to be the one mark by which this distinction can be sustained *post Christum.* How then can the New Testament, and Paul in particular, be for the permanent election of Israel but against keeping the law?

A theological account of the law which aimed to uphold both Israel's permanent election and the unsurpassability of Jesus Christ might take its point of departure from an exegetical commonplace: the heart of the New Testament polemic against the law is the rejection of the law as a way to salvation. Jesus Christ is the saving righteousness of God come to dwell in the world with complete historical finality, 'apart from the law' (Romans 3:21); that his death and resurrection, not the law, is God's eternally intended way of delivering the world from evil is the divine mystery long hidden, but now revealed at the last (Romans 16:25–7). If much of the New Testament polemic is not against the law itself, but against treating the law and its observance as the way to salvation, it would so far seem compatible with that polemic for Jews, as the people upon whom the law was once enjoined, to keep on observing it even after the coming of Christ. Observant Jews have, indeed, traditionally understood their obedience to the commandments as an act of gratitude and thanksgiving to God for his electing love towards the Jewish people, and not as a means to salvation or to some other end. Jews are to observe the Torah 'for its own sake', and so be 'like servants that minister to the master without the condition of receiving a reward'.[18]

Moreover, the New Testament itself contains significant (if not wholly unambiguous) suggestions that Jews are to keep the law even after the coming of Christ. As depicted in Acts 15:4–21 the decisions of the 'Jerusalem Council', even as they affirm salvation through Christ alone for both Jews and Gentiles, imply that Jews who come to believe the gospel should continue to observe the commandments; the vigorous debate over whether *Gentiles* who believe in Christ ought to be circumcised and keep the Jewish law (to which Acts 15:13–21 gives a negative answer) would make little sense unless both sides assumed that Jewish believers ought to keep the law (see also the depiction of Paul's 'zeal for the law' in Acts 21:17–26). To be sure, this passage deals only with Christian Jews, and not with Jews generally. But in a post-supersessionist context it seems to provide support for an argument *a fortiori*: if Christians are committed to the permanent election of the Jewish people, and so (we have argued) to the halachic mark by which this people may always be distinguished from the nations, must they not be yet more committed to the halachic distinctiveness of the baptised Jews in their own midst?[19]

In fact even classically supersessionist interpretations of the Old Testament law, and especially of the Levitical cult, made a distinction between the figural significance of the cult (to 'sketch out' for Israel, as John Calvin puts it, the Christ who was to come) and its literal significance – to worship the true God.[20] Supersessionist accounts bound the two aspects of the cult together, in such a way that when the prefigured Christ had come the cult forever lost its literal meaning, and with that the possibility of being legitimately observed (a judgement which does, to be sure, get some support in the New Testament, especially in Hebrews).[21] But it seems possible for post-supersessionist Christians, acknowledging as they do God's commitment to the enduring existence of the Jews as a distinct and identifiable people, to hold that God wills continued Jewish observance of the law, as the means by which Abraham's children may always be distinguished from the nations. The Old Testament cult, to put the point in traditional terms, might be understood as retaining its literal significance when practised by the people to whom God commanded it; this would not by itself rule out the view that the cult is in its totality a figuration of or witness to Jesus Christ, now come in the flesh.

This suggestion gives rise, however, to certain perplexities. In traditional Judaism it is of course not the biblical cult, but its rabbinic reinterpretation for a people without temple or land, which in practice gives the norms by which every Jew is to worship God in daily life. Traditional Jewish law is quite complex, and the extent to which its continued observance is compatible with the New Testament's re-evaluation of the law might depend on which of its commandments were under consideration. Repentant observance of the fasting ordinances for Yom Kippur (rooted in the biblical legislation for the day of atonement in Leviticus 16) is, for example, understood by rabbinic Judaism to bring forgiveness for sins, if not exactly eschatological salvation. This case surely tests the claim that Christians can regard halachic practices as compatible with the New Testament's insistence on salvation through Christ alone. In the case of Christian Jews the matter becomes yet more complicated, since it seems unlikely that they can regard rabbinic law (and thus a substantial part of traditional halachic observance) as binding; this would in effect give them a canon of scripture different from that of Gentile Christians. But the compatibility with Christian worship of continuing to observe some of the biblical legislation is also open to question; could, for example, a Christian Jew faithfully participate in both the Jewish Passover rituals and the Christian Easter Vigil, when the latter speaks precisely of Jesus Christ as the true Passover for all humanity?

Such are the practical perplexities which pose for contemporary Christian theology the challenge of showing how belief in both the unsurpassability of Jesus Christ and the permanent election of the Jews may coherently be maintained. If Christians can meet this challenge, the consequences for their theology and practice would be momentous. Christians would thereby grant that their own most central convictions not only permit but require them to regard the Jewish religion as willed by God to endure to the end of time, despite the rejection of the gospel by virtually everybody who practises this religion. This would amount to regarding observant Jews not as practitioners of a dead religion, but as worshippers of the true God – and that not simply in the remote and elusive depths of their hearts (where, to be sure, many modern theologians have wanted to say that all people do, or at least can, worship God), but in their public communal practice.

having *identified* them. After all one can, to use a rough analogy, refer to an approaching human being without actually being able to tell who it is that approaches (without, that is, being able to identify the one approaching as Peter, Paul, Priscilla or someone else). Indeed: given the way the persons of the Trinity actually come to be grasped in their personal uniqueness as the biblical drama unfolds, it seems not just a logical possibility, but a practical necessity, that at least one of the divine persons – namely the Father – could be referred to before he could be identified. The one who sends his Word and his Spirit into the world for the world's redemption is not a previously unheard-of deity, but rather, as Christian theologians maintained early on, the God of Israel, who in these actions fulfils his promises to Abraham. Just this God is the one whom both Jews and Gentiles will finally identify, in his personal uniqueness as 'the Father', through the 'mighty saviour' whom he will raise up from David's line (see Luke 1:68–9), and the Spirit whom he will pour out on all flesh (see Acts 2:17). Just because the missions of the Son and the Spirit, so Christians traditionally maintain, teach us to identify the God of Israel as the Father of Jesus Christ, it must be possible to refer to this God *without* referring to the events which lead from Bethlehem to Golgotha – without referring to the missions of Christ and the Spirit. Otherwise these very events would not enable us to identify just this God, the one who promised to bless all the nations through Abraham's children, as the one whom Jesus calls 'the Father'; nor, conversely, could we say that in the sending of Christ and the Spirit from the Father, the promises precisely of the God of Israel to Abraham had been fulfilled. Thus the church's identification of the one true God as the Trinity does not preclude, but rather requires, that Abraham and his children know how to refer to this God, and so are able to worship him.

Now if the rejection of supersessionism requires Christians to suppose that it is the will of the God whom they worship that Abraham's biological descendants observe, in some basic and publicly observable way, the law he gave to them alone, it also apparently permits them to regard this observance as worship of the one true God. If Abraham's children before Christ were able to refer to and so to worship this God, without identifying him as the Trinity, nothing appears to stand in the way of saying that they worship him also after Christ, except the assumption that after Christ God does not will the observance which constitutes this worship – except, that is, for supersessionism.

This is not to say, of course, that Christians and Jews agree about the identity of God. Christians think God is the Trinity, and Jews do not; both can perhaps concur that there will be no resolution of this disagreement before the eschaton. The foregoing reflections are meant rather to suggest an especially important consequence of a post-supersessionist outlook for Christian belief: that without making Jews secret believers in the Trinity, trinitarian Christians can coherently regard themselves as worshippers of the same God in whom the Jewish people, past and present, believe.

Notes

1 Perhaps most influentially the Roman Catholic Church at Vatican II; cf. *Nostra Aetate*, section 4 and *Lumen Gentium*, section 16 (in Norman Tanner, SJ, ed., *Decrees of the Ecumenical Councils*, 2 vols., [London: Sheed & Ward, 1990], vol. II, pp. 861, 970–1). Many Protestant denominations, along with the World Council of Churches, have made similar statements; cf. the documents collected in *The Theology of the Churches and the Jewish People* (Geneva: WCC Publications, 1988).

2 Michael Wyschogrod, *The Body of Faith: Judaism as Corporeal Election* (Minneapolis: Seabury Press, 1983), p. 57. Of course not all Jews continue to believe in Jewish election; this includes some who place a high value on maintaining a distinctive Jewish identity (Mordecai Kaplan is one prominent example). Rejecting supersessionism thus tends to ally Christian theology with traditionalist Jews more than with some revisionist ones. For a spirited historical analysis and theological defence of belief in Israel's election from a Jewish point of view, see Novak in the suggestions for further reading.

3 On this see the works by van Buren and Soulen in the recommendations for further reading.

4 See, for example, *Church Dogmatics*, ed. G. W. Bromiley and T. F. Torrance (Edinburgh: T. & T. Clark, 1956–75), vol. II, part 2, pp. 267–70 (on God's faithfulness to disobedient Israel after Christ); vol. III, part 2, pp. 582–7 (on the fulfilment and completion of Israel's history by the coming of Christ).

5 Irenaeus, *Against Heresies*, IV, 2, 2 (in *The Ante-Nicene Fathers*, ed. A. Cleveland Coxe [Grand Rapids, Michigan: Eerdmans, 1977], vol. I, p. 464a, translation slightly altered).

6 Justin Martyr, *Dialogue with Trypho*, chs. 11, 44 (in *The Ante-Nicene Fathers*, vol. I, pp. 200a, 216b–17a); cf. chs. 123, 135.

7 For a detailed survey of the history of Christian–Jewish relations, including the varieties of historic Christian supersessionism, cf. Karl Heinrich Rengstorf and Siegfried von Kortzfleisch (eds.), *Kirche und Synagoge. Handbuch zur Geschichte von Christen und Juden: Darstellung mit Quellen*, 2 vols. (Stuttgart: Ernst Klett Verlag, 1968–70).

8 Cf. *inter alia* Letter 102, in *St Augustine: Letters 83–130*, trans. Sister Wilfred Parsons, SND (*The Fathers of the Church*, vol. xvii) (New York: Fathers of the Church, Inc., 1953), especially pp. 155–6.

9 On this cf. Yves Congar, 'Ecclesia ab Abel', in Marcel Reding (ed.), *Abhandlungen über Theologie und Kirche* (FS Karl Adam) (Düsseldorf: Patmos-Verlag, 1952), pp. 79–108, with abundant references to Augustine and later Western theologians.

10 Cf. *The City of God* xx, 29; trans. Marcus Dods (New York: Random House, 1950), pp. 757–8.

11 *Super Epistolam ad Romanos Lectura* (=*In Rom.*), (caput) 11, (lectio) 4, no. 916 (in Raphael Cai, OP (ed.), *S. Thomae Aquinatis Super Epistolas S. Pauli Lectura*, 8th edn, 2 vols. [Turin: Marietti, 1952]). Thomas qualifies, it should be noted, the sense in which 'all' Jews will be saved; cf. *In Rom.* 11, 4, no. 932.

12 *In Rom.* 11, 2, no. 884.

13 For example, on whether Jewish children should be taken forcibly from their families, baptised and raised as Christians, a practice Aquinas (with most of the preceding tradition) opposed (*Summa Theologiae* ii–ii, 10, 8; 12), but Duns Scotus favoured (*Ordinatio* iv, 4, 9); cf. the discussion, with full citations, in Rengstorf and Kortzfleisch, *Kirche und Synagoge*, vol. i, pp. 217–20. See also John Y. B. Hood, *Aquinas and the Jews* (Philadelphia: University of Pennsylvania Press, 1995), especially pp. 88–92.

14 Parenthetical references are to paragraph and section of Friedrich Schleiermacher, *The Christian Faith*, ed. H. R. Mackintosh and J. S. Stewart (Edinburgh: T. & T. Clark, 1976).

15 For the current exegetical debate, see the works by Hays and Wright among the suggested readings.

16 For example Karl Barth, though he remained a supersessionist, was prompted by his reading of Paul to reject Christian missions to the Jews (cf. *Church Dogmatics*, vol. iv, part 3, pp. 876–8).

17 Passages like Galatians 3:28–9 ('There is no longer Jew or Greek ... male and female; for all of you are one in Christ Jesus'), cannot by themselves plausibly be taken to propose that the distinction between Jew and Gentile has been eliminated in Christ, any more than they can be taken to propose that the distinction between men and women has been eliminated.

18 Mishnah tractate *Pirkei Avot* 1:3; cf. the discussion in Robert M. Seltzer, *Jewish People, Jewish Thought* (New York: Macmillan, 1980), pp. 297–8.

19 For a lively discussion of this question, see the essays in *Modern Theology* 11/2 (1995): 165–241.

20 *Commentary on Galatians* (3:23), in D. W. Torrance and T. F. Torrance (eds.), *Calvin's New Testament Commentaries*, 12 vols., trans. T. H. L. Parker (Edinburgh: Oliver & Boyd, 1965), vol. xi, p. 66; cf. also *Institutes* ii.vi.2; vii.1; ix.1. See also the discussion in Thomas Aquinas, *Summa Theologiae*, i–ii, 101, 2; 102, 2.

21 See, for example, Calvin, *Commentary on Galatians*, pp. 67–8; Aquinas, *Summa Theologiae*, i–ii, 103, 4 (observance of the ceremonial law after Christ is a mortal sin), though cf. ii–ii, 10, 11 (even after Christ Jewish worship retains its figural significance; Christians should therefore not try to compel Jews to give it up).

22 For one traditional account of this claim, cf. Thomas Aquinas, *Summa Theologiae*, iii, 16, 1–2. For a contemporary version, with considerable attention to exegetical detail, cf. Hans Urs von Balthasar, *Mysterium Paschale*, trans. Aidan Nichols (Grand Rapids, Michigan: Eerdmans, 1990).

23 This is not, of course, to say that the later trinitarian doctrine of the church is explicitly in the New Testament (as the formulators of that doctrine were well aware). The church's developed trinitarian doctrine may be regarded, rather, as an effort to make explicit the logic of scripture's talk of God.

Further reading

Barth, Karl, *Church Dogmatics*, translation edited by G. W. Bromiley and T. F. Torrance, Edinburgh: T. & T. Clark, 1956–75, volume ii, part 2, especially section 34.

van Buren, Paul M., *A Theology of the Jewish–Christian Reality*, 3 volumes, San Francisco: Harper & Row, 1980–8.

Hays, Richard B., *Echoes of Scripture in the Letters of Paul*, New Haven: Yale University Press, 1989.

Novak, David, *The Election of Israel: The Idea of the Chosen People*, Cambridge: Cambridge University Press, 1995.

Soulen, R. Kendall, *The God of Israel and Christian Theology*, Minneapolis: Augsburg Fortress Press, 1996.

Wright, N. T., *The Climax of the Covenant: Christ and the Law in Pauline Theology*, Edinburgh: T. & T. Clark, 1991.

Wyschogrod, Michael, *The Body of Faith: Judaism as Corporeal Election*, Minneapolis: Seabury Press, 1983.

6 Christ and the cultures: Christianity and the arts

JEREMY BEGBIE

In the Kunsthistorisches Museum in Vienna hangs one of the most arresting of sixteenth-century paintings, Pieter Bruegel's *The Tower of Babel*. It is the kind of work which repays diligent attention, not least because many of the pivotal aspects of the complex interaction between Christianity and the arts will be brought to the surface.[1] To begin with the obvious, the painting reminds us that for large tracts of the church's history there has been a close intertwining of Christian faith and artistic practice. There have of course been times when the church's stance towards the arts has been marked by uncertainty and suspicion, but more often than not the arts have played a crucial role in her life and mission. More specifically, Christian doctrine has profoundly affected the form, content and development of the arts. (Despite the disdain in some quarters for treating the artist's circumstances as aesthetically significant, it would be hard to interpret Bruegel's output without any reference to the doctrinal traditions he espoused.) And this has worked in the opposite direction also: the arts have frequently had a decisive impact on the shape of Christian belief. In Bruegel's age, many received their doctrinal tutoring chiefly through one or more of the arts.

However, comparatively little attention has been paid by Western theologians to exploring systematically the connections between the arts and central doctrinal topics, with some notable exceptions (for example, Augustine, Aquinas). Certainly, in this century one searches in vain amongst prominent continental theologians. Paul Tillich and the Dutch Neo-Calvinist tradition are the chief exceptions in the Protestant world; Jacques Maritain and Hans Urs von Balthasar in the Roman Catholic. Some recent works may indicate that the tide is turning[2] but it would be safe to say that of the three ancient universals – truth, goodness and beauty – much more time has been given by theologians to the first two than to the third. At least four interrelated reasons may be suggested for this. In the first place, there is the fear of idolatry. In almost every period of church history there has arisen an anxiety that God's place as creator will be threatened by any sustained focus on human creativity: the artist or the artwork will all too easily be idolised. Second, bound up with this have been serious misgivings about the materiality of the arts and their emotional power. Third, as far as the modern era is concerned, a cluster of socio-cultural factors needs to be borne in mind. For Bruegel, the church was by far the most significant patron of the arts, but for a variety of reasons, those days are no longer. Further, we have witnessed a wane of explicitly religious symbolism in the arts over the last few centuries (although we should remember that broadly religious themes have been explored extensively and much so-called 'popular' art does employ religious icono-graphy (for example, that of Madonna and the artist formerly known as Prince), albeit primarily as a stylistic device).

Fourth, perhaps most significant in contributing to the relative neglect of the arts by theologians, is a broader feature of the way the arts have been treated in the West: an uncertainty about how to relate the arts effectively to other forms of human activity, which leaves the status of the arts profoundly ambivalent. In modernity this typically emerges in a cast of mind which tends to demote the arts in favour of other spheres of human endeavour and, more fundamentally, regard them as essentially discontinuous with the rest of our experience. In the first part of this chapter I want to examine some of the streams of thinking and practice which have led to this attitude in the Enlightenment and post-Enlightenment periods. This will serve to bring to the fore five key theological issues at the interface of Christianity and the arts which we shall explore in the second part.

ART'S MARGINALISATION

First, put crudely, there is the Enlightenment assumption that the nat-ural sciences grant us public, reliable and verifiable truth – 'dry truth and real knowledge' (John Locke) – while the arts are to do with private taste, ornament or self-expression, and have little or no bearing on the way things actually are. In reaction to this, the Romantic tradition sought various means of giving art an especially privileged position, some seeing it as the gateway to absolute truth. And others have tried to accord art some kind of quasi-scientific respectability. But by far the commonest attitude over the last two hundred years, generated in part by what is perceived to be the ever increas-ing success of the scientist, assigns science to the realm of certainty and art to the realm of private opinion.

With this go assumptions about scientific and artistic discourse – that of science is literal and common-sense, concerned with conveying information, while that of art primarily concerns inward thoughts and dispositions. Supporting this are often a set of epistemological suppositions. Immanuel Kant – in so many ways the father of modern aesthetics – propounded an emphatic distinction between the sphere of knowledge and the sphere of aesthetic objects and judgements. Aesthetic pleasure comes about when two mental faculties, the imagination and the understanding, engage in a 'free play'. It is this free play which we enjoy, arising from the contemplation of beautiful objects characterised by 'purposiveness without purpose'. Aesthetic judgements are based not primarily on features of the world to which we respond but on features of *our response* – specifically the interplay of the imagination and understanding. When someone makes an aesthetic judgement, 'nothing in the object is signified, but [only] a feeling in the subject as it is affected by the representation'.[3] It is simplistic to say that Kant represents the subjectivisation of aesthetics, for, as Andrew Bowie has argued, his aesthetics was designed to relate a world seen as governed by natural necessity and a world in which we are free agents.[4] But Kant's passionate belief that aesthetic experience has its own distinctive role and character – it must not be subsumed under cognition, nor (unlike the Romantics) must it be allowed to swallow up all else – led him perilously close to isolating (and enervating) the aesthetic realm altogether. One result is that evaluative judgements about art and beauty become virtually impossible to articulate and sustain – a situation with which we are all too familiar today.

It is not surprising, therefore, that we should find a prominent strand in both art theory and practice celebrating and encouraging the autonomy of art. In the eighteenth century, the concept of 'disinterestedness' began to be applied to the 'fine' (as opposed to the 'useful') arts, a notion reinforced by Kant. If we are to treat a work of art as art, it was urged, we should never regard it as a means to an end but attend to the work itself for its own sake. Only in the seventeenth and eighteenth centuries do we see the rise of the museum, art gallery and concert hall, but today even a brief survey of what our society commonly calls 'works of art' would probably show that the majority were intended for some form of disinterested contemplation. Kant's aesthetics quickly spawned the idea of 'art for art's sake' – the view that art is answerable only to itself, has no social responsibility, and must not be assessed according to any correspondence it might have to phenomena beyond itself, such as a moral order, the artist's intentions or the circumstances of its production. Bowie contends that the increasing separation of music from words in the nineteenth century had a crucial role to play here:

'the divorce of music from representation is the vital step in the genesis of a notion of aesthetic autonomy which removes the work of art from any obligation to represent anything but itself'.[5] In this century, theories sometimes called 'formalist' hold that what is crucial in the enjoyment of art is its 'significant form'; representation has no aesthetic value at all and is often an aesthetic disvalue.[6] In the 1950s and 60s, the sculptures of David Smith and Anthony Caro and the paintings of Ad Reinhardt are instances of work produced by those convinced that art should pursue its own self-referring ends. In literary criticism, the complex movement known as structuralism (Viktor Shlovsky, Roman Jakobson, Northrop Frye), in which language and literature are treated as essentially closed systems, is a further example of the same general phenomenon.

Needless to say, denied the dignity of any kind of referral, eventually art can only talk to itself. Anthony Giddens has argued that this self-critical 'reflexive' aspect of the Enlightenment project is intrinsic to modernity[7] and it is certainly not hard to discover in the arts. So, for example, the artist becomes the subject of art: 'Never has so much art been made on the subject of its maker' (Waldemar Januszczack).[8] Or the process of producing art takes central place: as with the so-called Action Painters of the 1950s, and many of the novels of Samuel Beckett. Or again, the focus becomes the identity of art: many of the musical pioneers of the twentieth century have been those who, in their music, have pressed the question: what is music? (John Cage, Karlheinz Stockhausen). It is in this light that so-called 'postmodern' art may perhaps be best approached. In so far as there are features which distinguish it from modern art, often they represent not so much the contradiction of modernism but its extension. Now, not only is the connection between art and extra-artistic reality questioned, but also the very meaningfulness of the distinction, for it assumes a privileged viewpoint from which we can check out an 'appearance' against some alleged 'reality'. No such Archimedean viewpoints are available. So it is that postmodern art can take on 'the appearance of appearance', 'a rush of filmic images without density' (Fredric Jameson). David Lynch's film *Blue Velvet* (1986) portrays a small-town 1950s world co-existing with an underworld of nightmarish perversion. One is a mask for the other but neither is presented as authentic. In much postmodern theatre (for example, the work of Richard Foreman) the line between theatre and non-theatre is deliberately erased. Postmodern fiction offers 'metafiction': fiction about fiction.[9] Perhaps most notorious of all is the cluster of post-structuralist writing which sometimes goes under the heading 'deconstruction' (Jacques Derrida, Paul de Man), in which language is regarded as a system of signifiers detached from any stable thing or things, and meaning inherently unstable and endlessly deferred. We have no way of attaining an a-cultural position to assess whether a text is being true to a purported 'outside' reality. The distinction between history and fiction is bound to evaporate, for texts do not direct attention to authors or things or events, they point to other texts, and within this intertextuality writing becomes a playful, ceaseless process in which writer is already reader and reader necessarily becomes writer.[10]

Bemused perplexity is not an uncommon reaction to such apparently self-defeating and counter-intuitive writing, but seen against the background of the eighteenth and nineteenth centuries (and assumptions stretching far back into antiquity) it represents an understandable (if not inevitable) outcome. To put it at its simplest, the artistic imagination, previously spurned by the world of factuality and made irrelevant to that world, now returns with a vengeance to swallow up the very world it was reluctant to describe and could not transform. As Andrew Bowie and Roger Lundin make clear, the story of modern aesthetics since Kant can in large part be recounted as a struggle by aestheticians to make grand what they have already made trivial.[11]

RESPONDING RESPONSIBLY

This very rough sketch of one major strand in modernism and post-modernism has been designed to highlight what would seem to be a major requirement of a constructive aesthetics of the future: that a proper stress on the distinctiveness and integrity of the arts – against functionalism, commercialism or anything which would force art into its own mould – needs to be combined with a refusal to divorce and alienate the arts from other forms of human action, thought and language. But this needs to be related to a much wider issue, perhaps the most important at the interface of the arts and Christian faith, namely the relatedness of artist (and art) to a world which is irreducibly other. What we shall argue below is that we require a rich notion of *responsibility* in artistic thinking and practice, a concept deeply rooted in the Judaeo-Christian tradition, based on a recognition that we live in a world of concrete otherness which calls forth from art and artists an attitude of perceptive trust, 'a courtesy or tact of heart' (George Steiner). For Steiner it is the encounter with the other which lies at the source of art: 'The meaning, the existential modes of art, music and literature are functional within the experience of our meeting with the other. All aesthetics, all critical and hermeneutic discourse, is an attempt to clarify the paradox and opaqueness of that meeting as well as its felicities.'[12] He continues: 'The issue is that of civility ... towards the inward savour of things.' Arguably, only when art rediscovers this 'civility' will it find its proper place in relation to other human activities. In the remaining part of this chapter, we shall explore something of what this civility might mean, drawing especially on a theology of responsibility grounded in the triune God.

The good integrity of the material world

To begin with, much hinges on whether we believe the material order is itself the bearer of meaning and can therefore elicit our trust. It is worth recalling that Bruegel's *The Tower of Babel* is more than a portrait of human pride: it is also a magnificent landscape, typically Flemish with its elevated viewpoint, high horizon and attention to detail, counterbalancing the ugliness of the tower in the foreground. Landscapes were Bruegel's first love: 'If in his figure compositions he must be regarded as fundamentally a pessimist ... [the] landscapes appeal first and foremost in their power to capture our own feeling for the physical beauty of the world.'[13] Yet it is here that Western aesthetics has been decidedly hesitant. Art has frequently come to be seen as fulfilling its highest function in so far as it leaves materiality behind, so to speak. The roots of this go back at least as far as Plato, and that the Christian church is not exempt is well illustrated in the case of Augustine, whose influential aesthetics exhibits so clearly the unease about physicality of which I am speaking. For him, beauty is not so much something the world embodies as something towards which it directs us. Physical beauty is the lowest grade of beauty, being mixed up with all sorts of imperfections. We are urged to seek the beauty of the soul, and that incorporeal beauty which gives form to the mind and through which we judge that all actions of the wise man are beautiful. But above all we are directed towards the supreme beauty, that of God himself.[14] Consequently, although a consummate artist, Augustine exhibits a deep wariness of art, for it can so quickly tug us away from the Creator towards merely physical realities.

This probably relates to a broader tendency in Augustine to lose sight of the biblical stress on the integrity of the physical world.[15] But whatever the truth of that, he gives expression to a tendency which, though not universal, has certainly been prominent in the West. In the modern era the shift away from the physical has been less towards eternal forms than the inner rational and emotional life of the individual subject. The German and English Romantics of the early nineteenth century are perhaps the most pointed example, for whom art characteristically becomes the expression of inner emotion, 'the spontaneous overflow of powerful feelings' (William Wordsworth). Ernst Kris sees the whole development of visual art from the sixteenth century as from the artist as manual worker to artist as individual creator. 'The work of art is for the first time in human history considered as a projection of an inner image. It is not its proximity to reality that proves its value but its nearness to the artist's psychic life.'[16] The seminal aesthetics of G. W. F. Hegel is especially instructive, with its intellectualist thrust: for him the key drawback of art was its dependence on the material world, the physical being only one stage in the unfolding of cosmic Spirit. Art reaches its highest form in poetry for poetry comes closest to pure thought. (It is this aesthetics which the Congregationalist theologian, P. T. Forsyth, attempts to baptise in his book *Christ on Parnassus* (1911).) The work of painter Wassily Kandinsky provides an intriguing illustration of the same trend. Sometimes hailed as one of the foremost 'religious' painters of our time, it is worth recalling that his major work hinged on the opposition of spiritual value to nature. His painting was to prepare people for the ultimate dissolution of all things physical. And on a wider front, the view of reality as wholly transient, fragmented and insubstantial, which has characterised so much art of this century, and which is so evident in the more vaporous instances of post-modern art, begins to make much more sense in the light of a long-term and pervasive Western suspicion about the inherent rationality of matter.

In response to this, it is not enough simply to affirm that art takes place through engaging with a physical world with its own inherent order. Theologically, at the very least, there needs to be an appropriation of the doctrine of God's creation of all things out of nothing, and thus a stress on the liberty of the creation in its contingent but ordered (and beautiful) otherness. Creation flows from the free love of God in which he posits another with its own distinctive integrity which is neither God (and therefore not to be worshipped), nor chaotic matter (and therefore to be respected in its own orderliness). Moreover, the Son through whom all things took shape has become incarnate: in Christ the integrity of the finite world is affirmed as well as judged and redeemed. This carries positive encouragement for the artist to treat the sensible world as a proper, meaningful environment to enjoy and explore, worthy of attention, cultivation and adornment. Ironically, the most full-blooded argument along these lines in recent years has come from the professed atheist, Peter Fuller, in *Theoria: Art, and the Absence of Grace*. Fuller bemoans what he calls the 'collapse of the idea of art as a channel of grace' and looks back to the tradition embodied in John

Ruskin's *theoria* – a moral response to beauty rooted in the awareness of natural order.[17] Whatever our questions about Fuller – and there are many – the call for an aesthetic grounded in natural structure is noteworthy, especially since it issues from someone who was both steeped in the visual art of the last thirty years and highly acute to its theological dimensions.

Courteous interaction

If the intrinsic goodness of the created world is held in question, what might broadly be called the Platonic tendency – to press beyond the material – is certainly not the only option open to the artist. Commoner in modernity has been the conception of the artist as the contributor or imposer of individually or socially constructed meaning. In its strongest form, the belief is that the only meaning the world can have is that which we give it.

Of course, there can be no such thing as pure discovery; all our commerce with reality involves a contribution on our part which affects the content and character of our experience. This is probably the most celebrated and widely accepted of Kant's insights. More questionable is the Kantian stress on the mind's imposition of a *fixed* conceptual order on essentially *unknown* reality. For Kant, the crucial factor in the experience of beauty is the 'form of purposiveness', and the 'form' is given by the subject's mind. Despite his belief that it is the aesthetic object which evokes aesthetic pleasure, this pleasure is derived primarily from those powers which enable us to arrange the plurality of sense data, not from a cognitive apprehension of order beyond ourselves: 'the understanding is itself the source of the law of nature, and so of its formal unity'.[18] The Romantics, though far from Kant in important respects, are not distant from him here. Although they could wax eloquent about the beauties of the natural world, many were intensely aware of its darker sides, its ambiguity and cruelty (see the paintings of Caspar David Friedrich). In this setting there arose the belief that nature needs the artist in order to realise itself and that the world of poetry and painting is in some sense more real than anything else (Ferdinand Delacroix, Percy Bysshe Shelley, Novalis). The underlying drive, of course, is towards according the artist Godlike status: the artist works the wonders of the imagination on the chaos of nature, wresting coherence out of that which is essentially incoherent. There is at least some evidence to support Ernst Kris' (exaggerated) claim that in artistic modernism, 'the artist does not "render" nature, nor does he "imitate" it, but creates it anew. He controls the world through his work ... The unconscious meaning is *control at the price of destruction*.'[19] Some of the music of the French composer Pierre Boulez provides a striking illustration, in which patterns of strict mathematical consistency are impressed upon sound out of a desire for absolute control over musical material.

But even bearing in mind the 'tragic' aspects of the physical world, the question posed by Oliver O'Donovan is soon bound to arise: 'How can creativity function with its eyes closed upon the universe? For man does not encounter reality as an undifferentiated raw material upon which he may impose any shape that pleases him.' Love, he continues, 'achieves its creativity by being perceptive'.[20] If the arts are a means of engaging with the material world whose peculiar integrity demands an attentive respect, a crucial part of human creativity is to be perceptive to this integrity, to discover it and to bring it to light. Accordingly we will need to question views of art which lay the main weight on *bringing* value and meaning *to* a reality whose value and meaning is constantly under suspicion. This need not render the artist's work purely passive, for we can speak of a dialectic of welcoming reception and shaping, in which physical reality is neither ignored nor overridden, but enabled to take on another, hopefully richer, meaningful form. In this connection, we might think of Vincent Van Gogh's landscapes and interiors, Albrecht Dürer's meticulously detailed drawings of the human body, or J. S. Bach's exploration of the harmonic series.

To set this in a more theological perspective, the arts can be seen as part of our calling to voice creation's praise, to extend and elaborate the praise which creation already sings to God. The doxology of creation has found its summation in Christ: the one through whom all things were created became part of a creation whose praise has been corrupted, and in the crucified and risen Lord, creation is offered back to the Father, redirected towards its originally intended goal. The Spirit now struggles in creation to bring about what has already been achieved in Christ. We are now invited into this movement in order to enable creation to be more fully what it was created to be. I have set out more fully what this could imply for the arts elsewhere;[21] here we mention only three features of the responsible interaction with creation which a 'doxological aesthetics' involves.

First, artistic responsibility will apply as much as anything to the medium the artist employs – paint, notes, wood or whatever. Professor Alexander Goehr of Cambridge has spoken of the composer needing 'to love sound'. Much depends here on whether we see creation's order as essentially constrictive or as gift, the gracious gift of God. If the latter, the properties of a medium can be regarded as a stimulant to artistry rather than a strait-jacket. In this regard, the musical improviser has much to teach all artists: the best jazz pianists are extremely alert to the attributes of sound, engaging in an intense process of monitoring and listening. It is not a matter of imposing a preconceived grid of pure thought on acoustic entities, but indwelling them, thinking *in* notes, melodies, harmonies, metres and so on.

Second, the physical embeddedness of the arts is mediated through our own physicality. The theological tradition affirms that we are not disembodied spirits or intellects but unities of spirit and matter inhabiting a physical world with which we are intimately bound up and have a large measure of continuity. A loss of some such vision has arguably distorted our understanding of what most art involves. It is far from obvious that we should construe art as necessarily shifting us beyond the material order, or see the heart of an artist's work as giving outward expression to inner, non-physical realities, as if the 'real' work was carried out in the sanctuary of the self and the piece of art merely served to externalise this interior experience. That the sensory matrix of an artwork is integral to its being, and that when we inscribe marks on paper, pile stone on stone or whatever, we are dealing with things which bear to us the most intimate of relations, are matters which several theologians are now asserting with renewed vigour.[22] The composer Igor Stravinsky once wrote:

> The very act of putting my work on paper, of, as we say, kneading the dough, is for me inseparable from the pleasure of creation ... The word *artist* which, as it is most generally understood today, bestows on its bearer the highest intellectual prestige, the privilege of being accepted as a pure mind – this pretentious term is in my view entirely incompatible with the role of the *homo faber*.[23]

Congruent with this, we will be seriously hampered by epistemologies which do not do full justice to our physical indwelling of the world, to the material dimensions of the relation of person to reality. (The notion of 'disinterested' contemplation in the arts – with its sharp split between subject and object – is in the last resort Descartes transported into the arts.)[24] Participatory models of knowledge, stressing our bodily engagement with reality, will help us see that the arts can be regarded as (potentially) a means of responsible, truthful engagement with the world we inhabit as physical creatures. A way is thus opened up for treating art as authentically cognitive while still holding (with Kant) that it is distinctive and irreducible. The proper autonomy of art will best be safeguarded not by wrenching it apart from knowledge nor by equating it with conceptual or moral knowledge, but by seeing it as a distinct but genuine vehicle of knowing the world.[25]

Third, we might cautiously speak of a 'redemptive' calling of the artist. Sentimentality about the created world is as damaging as unrestrained pessimism. (Bruegel's later landscapes, we might note, took on a particularly tragic turn.) The very fact that artists frequently describe their work in terms of a struggle with their chosen material speaks of an encounter with the destructive dimension of created existence, and a desire to recreate that which is subject to corruption. This applies not only to the medium but to a myriad of other realities encountered by artists – such as the suffering of the innocent, terminal disease, the inevitability of death. Sadly, as Tillich used to point out repeatedly, much so-called 'Christian' art has degenerated into a superficial *Kitsch*.[26] But if it is into the very heart of evil that God has penetrated in Christ, there can be no attempt to diminish the horror of the tragic by reducing it to appearance or subsuming it into a monistic whole.

Nevertheless, redemption also achieves a renewal of that which is distorted, in such a way that we are granted a promise of the ultimate transformation of all things. Theologies of art which begin with the incarnation and end with the cross are woefully inadequate. Whatever else 'Christian art' is, it will be art which takes for its final reference point the raising of the crucified Son of God from the dead. Such art will inevitably resound with an inner joy, though it may only be a joy won through despair. It will be 'realistic' in that it will be propelled by the irreversible reality of the raising of Jesus from the dead. And in so far as this happens, there will be an anticipation of the ultimate goal of creation. Do we not see something of this quality in Rembrandt's *Christ Healing the Sick* or El Greco's representation of Christ in Gethsemane (*The Agony in the Garden*), Duke Ellington's 'Come Sunday', and the extraordinary music of the Scottish Roman Catholic composer James Macmillan (for example, *The Confessions of Isobel Gowdie*)?

Of course, to speak of the redemptive possibilities of art is dangerous. We might infer that Christ's work is no more than an aesthetic reordering of creation (when it is clearly much more than that). But the redemption effected in Christ has an aesthetic dimension to it and there would seem no good reason to deny that we can give voice to this in and through the arts. More seriously, to claim that art can be redemptive might detract from the decisiveness of what has been established in Christ. So we need to insist that the incarnation, crucifixion and resurrection provide not simply a detached pattern for the artist to work from but actually constitute God's unique liberation *of* creation *within* creation. The task of the artist is not to complement (or add to) the work of Christ but to share, by the Spirit, in its outworking.

Beyond the first person

The patterns of responsibility we are attempting to uncover also extend to relations between people. Conceptions of the human person in which relationships are seen as incidental or epiphenomenal have exercised a considerable impact on the arts. In many respects the image of the artist which has dominated modernity is that which reaches its apex with the Romantics: the lone creative individual, estranged from the flow of mundane history, misunderstood, eccentric, making his or her distinctive 'mark', faithful only to an inner creative urge. Paul Vitz notes how frequently the word 'creative' has cloaked a narcissist self-indulgence: 'Today in the secular world creativity is simply a gift from the self *to* the self, it has degenerated into a synonym for any form of personal pleasure without reference to others.'[27] With this can go an intense distrust of past tradition and a tendency to exalt originality and novelty as artistic virtues. One only need think of the number of supposedly 'fresh starts' in modern visual art, Boulez's struggle to free himself from the 'burden of memory', and Piet Mondrian's declaration that 'The past has a *tyrannic* influence which is difficult to escape … The worst is that there is always something of the past *within* us.'[28] The examples could be multiplied many times over.

In the postmodern sensibility, the solitary Cartesian and Kantian ego of modernity is said to collapse and give way to the 'de-centred' subject, shaped essentially through language and culture. For some indeed, the human self is no more than an ideological construction or an effect of language (Jacques Lacan). Consequently, 'the artist' is at most a vehicle or field for a range of social forces. In some respects, this can be read as the outcome of modernist philosophies of the person: the non-related, self-constituting individual undergoes inevitable disintegration. What appears to be required is the avoidance both of the ultimately suffocating individualism of modernism and the erasure of personal distinctiveness of postmodernism. The most promising way forward – and it is really only the recovery of an ancient tradition – is to recognise that persons discover their particularity in mutually constitutive relations. The self is indeed always and already a social product, and yet is 'centred' when addressed and treated as a distinct 'you' by another person or other persons. From this angle, the church can be seen as God's given social matrix where distinctive persons are formed through relations of unconditional love. And the church takes its being and life from the life of the triune God, whose being is the eternal and undistorted communion of mutually constituted persons-in-relationship.

Set against this horizon, a piece of art may fruitfully be regarded not as a 'gift from the self to the self' (Vitz), nor an imposition of individual or group, but a medium of personal exchange, a 'trial of encounter' (Steiner). Originality can never be absolute because it arises within a network of communicative conventions which make up every social world. Moreover, past tradition, as T. S. Eliot urged in a famous essay, can become not only something to be understood and respected but a means of personal growth as our own deeply cherished beliefs are enriched, modified and perhaps surrendered; ironically, it is often in this way that an artist's particularity is brought more fully into relief.[29] It may well be that if the church is to play a significant part in the future renewal of art, this will come about through the emergence of fresh forms of corporate art, in which the distinctive relationships generated by the Holy Spirit are allowed to shape the very character of artistic creativity.

Towards an enriching particularity

Our fourth issue relates closely to the last: the ancient problem of the one and the many, a matter crucial to Christianity's engagement with the arts and raised acutely in modern and postmodern culture: 'Aesthetic theory from Kant onwards faces the problem of finding a whole into which the particular can fit in a meaningful way, once theological certainties have been abandoned.'[30] One account of modernism in the arts would see it as more than anything else a quest for unity in a world without God. In architecture, the project associated with the Bauhaus pursued a vision characterised by a reduction and renunciation of the unnecessary or frivolous: architecture with 'no noodles' (Mies van der Rohe). By the 1950s, the world was familiar with the self-contained geometrical intensity of the lean glass and steel boxes. A strong strand in modern painting has been concerned with the search for the fundamental core of this art form – Clement Greenberg charts the history of painting in the last two centuries as a progressive discovery of painting's essence (which he believed to be its two-dimensionality).[31]

However, modernist conceptions of unity, as the postmodernist is quick to point out, are often oppressive (not least in architecture). Totalising schemes and all-embracing theories (including, some say, the Christian faith) are ultimately tools of domination and enemies of freedom. Bruegel was not unfamiliar with these dangers when he painted *The Tower of Babel* (the terrors of the Inquisition were known to him well). The story of Babel is that of a people given the faculty of one language but misusing this to reach for a unity which comes not from God nor from the world, but from the attempt to escape finitude and particularity and displace God, to achieve a

God's-eye view and dominate the earth (to make 'a name for themselves'; Genesis 11:4). Bruegel does not paint the subsequent divine judgement, but the tininess of the human figures in contrast to the panoramic space they inhabit underlines powerfully the frailty and folly of purely human projects (a favourite Bruegel theme). Present here is the ancient concept of the *Theatrum Mundi*: the world as an amphitheatre with humanity as the absurd spectacle. The tower's likeness to Rome's Colosseum is not accidental. Bruegel knew that monument from his Italian tour and for his contemporaries the parallel between Rome and Babylon was well established. Rome was the eternal city, designed by the Caesars to last for ever. This painting is as much as anything else an invitation to view any form of human imperialism with a discerning pity.

In contrast to grasping after the divine perspective, the postmodernist is at ground level, celebrating the limitations of the finite particular, the local, the marginal. Elevated viewpoints and unifying theories have been left behind. In postmodern art, typically, a host of disconnected images and fragments of earlier styles are playfully juxtaposed (for example, many rock videos, the paintings of Pat Steir, the architecture of G. Aulenti, Michael Graves). Some even allude to the Babel story to speak of postmodernism's rehabilitation of the particular: to avert evil, we are reminded, God confused the languages. Gianni Vattimo applauds the 'emancipatory' confusion of dialects in postmodern culture, the absence of a crippling 'central' co-ordination and the elimination of total domination.[32] Yet it is debatable whether the liberation is as great as Vattimo would believe. Commentators on 'political correctness' are not the only ones to observe how stultifying inclusivity for inclusivity's sake can be. In the arts, in some quarters, even to raise the possibility of differences in quality is to risk ridicule. The diversity of postmodern culture can be at least as homogenising as the worst of modernism. 'The problem faced by postmodernist theory is how to speak of and bring plurality into being, in a way that does not itself limit and neutralise that plurality.'[33] Moreover, what we often experience today is not an enriching plurality but a fragmentation of competing communities, fuelled by greed, without dialogue or mutual responsibility. It is precisely this which is brought out in Genesis 11: there the linguistic plurality is presented as alienating, not enriching.

The cardinal issue here can be put in the form of a question: can we have concrete particularity and diversity in the world *and* the presence and activity of a God who is one? All too often in the West the answer has been in the negative. Yet a conception of God which embraces both distinct particularity and unity moves us in a rather different direction. The world's multiplicity of particulars could then be seen as flowing from and pointing to not a closure of diversity but an infinitely generative life, which, interwoven with our own, brings plurality to fruition in a multi-levelled relational unity. The unity of this God is the unity of mutually constitutive particularity – Father, Son and Spirit – and it is this form of oneness which God is committed to enabling within creation.[34]

It would take more space than we have here to spell out the implications of this in different art-forms. The medieval polyphonic motet comes to mind as a sonic parable of the kind of unity-in-diversity of which I am speaking. But at the very least we can ponder Bruegel's work again. One of the reasons for his almost universal esteem and popularity is the combination of a unified composition *and* diversity of incident and accuracy of detail. There is an endearing worldliness, a concern to let particular things be particular, which goes much further than a craving for cramming information into a small space. Further, as commentators never cease to point out, there is an extraordinary dynamism and sense of movement in the particularity, in contrast to the often static monumentality of the High Renaissance.[35] For Bruegel at least there was no necessary contradiction between glorying in particulars and seeking their unity in God.

Come, Creator Spirit

The trinitarian dynamic behind our discussion will be clear by now. But, more specifically, it may be that a richer doctrine of the Holy Spirit than has often been apparent in the West will be the most significant contribution of theologians to a vigorous interaction between Christianity and the arts in the future. The initial concept to grasp here is *responsiveness*. It is the Spirit who makes possible the responsible interaction of the artist with other people, the physical world and the Creator of which I have been speaking. The Spirit is the Spirit of interplay, of that mutual giving and receiving integral to an artist's work. To be 'inspired' by the Spirit, accordingly, is above all to be responsive. As John Taylor points out in *The Go-Between God*, the Spirit 'enables us not by making us supernaturally strong but by opening our eyes. The Holy Spirit is that power which opens eyes that are closed, hearts that are unaware and minds that shrink from too much reality.'[36] If we are to speak about inspiration, it may be best to regard the artist not simply as a tool in the hands of an irresistible force, nor as effortlessly receiving visions from above which flow out to the world, but of the Spirit generating a process of interaction between artist and subject, artistic medium, fellow artists, community or whatever. Authentic inspiration will then not be a violation of human freedom but the actualisation of freedom, for freedom is a matter of being rightly related to what is not of our own making. This is an immensely costly business: art is painful and hard work. In all responsible relating there is inevitably a loss of pride, a laying aside of cherished ideas and practices. But far from this being a sign of the Spirit's absence, it is here that the Spirit is probably most active, for the Spirit is 'that in virtue of which God is an everlasting movement of *giving away'.*[37]

But there is another dimension to be noted here. For the last time we turn to the tower of Babel. Pentecost is sometimes spoken of as the 'reversal' of Babel, a return to one language. In fact, the crowds heard the disciples *in their own tongues* (Acts 2:6). There is no suppression of cultural diversity; quite the opposite. The coming of the Spirit means particularity is preserved and indeed encouraged, as Paul's vision of the Spirit-directed Church makes clear (1 Corinthians 12). This is rooted in the person and work of Christ: in him, our humanity (and provisionally) the whole of creation, has been freed by the Spirit to be responsive to the Creator, but in such a way that humanity and the created order become more authentically themselves. The Spirit's work through us is to bring creation to praise its maker in such a way that both creation and our character as finite and contingent creatures are not disrupted but enabled to flourish. Applied to the arts, this would mean that both an artist and the realities with which he or she engages become more fully themselves in their distinctive particularity.

Finally, a more focused concentration on the Spirit would lend extra weight to our previous comment about the ability of art to prefigure the final consummation of creation. In the New Testament, the Spirit is the one who brings us a foretaste here and now of the new age, the age anticipated in the resurrection of Christ. Art which truly bears the imprint of the Spirit – 'inspired art' – will thus not so much hark back to an imagined lost paradise, as depict within space and time, imaginatively and provisionally but nonetheless substantially, the final transfiguration of the cosmos.

Notes

1 I shall adopt a broad use of the word 'art', to embrace the activities and products associated with music, poetry, drama, literary fiction, visual depiction and patterning, architecture, dance, film and sculpture.

2 In addition to the 'Further reading' list for this chapter, see Richard Harries, *Art and the Beauty of God: A Christian Understanding* (London: Mowbray, 1993).

3 *Critique of Judgement*, trans. J. H. Bernard, 2nd edn (New York and London: Hafner, 1968), p. 38.

4 Andrew Bowie, *Aesthetics and Subjectivity: from Kant to Nietzsche* (Manchester: Manchester University Press, 1990), ch. 1.

5 *Ibid.*, p. 30.

6 Clive Bell, *Art* (New York: Capricorn Books, 1958).

7 *The Consequences of Modernity* (Oxford: Blackwell, 1990); *Modernity and Self-Identity* (Cambridge: Polity Press, 1991).

8 *The Guardian*, 2 December 1986: 24.

9 For a clear survey of these phenomena, cf. Gene Edward Veith, *Postmodern Times* (Wheaton: Crossway, 1994).

10 Cf. Christopher Norris, *Deconstruction: Theory & Practice* (London and New York: Methuen, 1982); Hugh J. Silverman and Don Ihde, *Hermeneutics and Deconstruction* (Albany: State University of New York Press, 1985).

11 Bowie, *Aesthetics and Subjectivity*; Roger Lundin, 'Our Hermeneutical Inheritance', in Roger Lundin, Anthony C. Thiselton, Clarence Walhout (eds.), *The Responsibility of Hermeneutics* (Grand Rapids, Michigan: Eerdmans, 1985), pp. 14f.

12 George Steiner, *Real Presences* (London: Faber and Faber, 1989), p. 138.

13 Marguerite Kay, *Bruegel* (London: Hamlyn, 1969), p. 26.

14 Cf. e.g. *Confessions* (Oxford: Oxford University Press, 1991), iii:6; xi:4.

15 Cf. Robert J. O'Connell, *Art and the Christian Intelligence in St. Augustine* (Oxford: Blackwell, 1978).

16 As quoted in Brandon Taylor, *Modernism, Post-Modernism, Realism: A Critical Perspective for Art* (Winchester: Winchester School of Art Press, 1987), p. 36.

17 *Theoria: Art, and the Absence of Grace* (London: Chatto and Windus, 1988).

18 *Critique of Pure Reason*, trans. Norman Kemp Smith (London: Macmillian, 1929), p. 127.

19 As quoted in Taylor, *Modernism*, pp. 36f. My italics.

20 *Resurrection and Moral Order* (Grand Rapids, Michigan: Eerdmans, 1986), pp. 25f.

21 Cf. Jeremy S. Begbie, *Voicing Creation's Praise: Towards a Theology of the Arts* (Edinburgh: T. & T. Clark, 1991).

22 John Dixon, *Nature and Grace in Art* (Chapel Hill: University of North Carolina Press, 1964); Aidan Nichols, *The Art of God Incarnate: Theology and Image in the Christian Tradition* (London: Darton, Longman and Todd, 1980); George Pattison, *Art, Modernity and Faith* (Basingstoke: Macmillian, 1991); Nicholas Wolterstorff, *Art in Action* (Grand Rapids, Michigan: Eerdmans 1980).

23 *Poetics of Music in the Form of Six Lessons*, trans. Arthur Knodel and Ingolf Dahl (Cambridge, Massachusetts: Harvard University Press, 1947), p. 51.

24 Lundin, 'Our Hermeneutical Inheritance', pp. 9ff.
25 For fuller discussion of this, cf. Begbie, *Voicing Creation's Praise,* pp. 233–52.
26 'Existentialist Aspects of Modern Art', in Carl Michalson (ed.), *Christianity and the Existentialists* (New York: Charles Scribner's Sons, 1956), pp. 142f.
27 *Psychology as Religion: The Cult of Self-Worship* (Grand Rapids, Michigan: Eerdmans, 1977), p. 61.
28 As quoted in Robert Hughes, *The Shock of the New: Art and the Century of Change* (London: Thames and Hudson, 1993), p. 203.
29 'Tradition and the Individual Talent', in *Selected Essays* (London: Faber & Faber, 1932), pp. 13–22.
30 Bowie, *Aesthetics and Subjectivity,* p. 5.
31 'Modernist Painting', in Francis Frascina and Charles Harrison (eds.), *Modern Art and Modernism: A Critical Anthology* (London: Harper and Row and Open University Press, 1982), pp. 5f.
32 *The Transparent Society,* trans. David Webb (Cambridge: Polity Press, 1992), pp. 1–11.
33 Stephen Connor, *Postmodernist Culture* (Oxford: Blackwell, 1989), p. 80.
34 Cf. Colin E. Gunton, *The One, the Three and the Many: God, Creation and the Culture of Modernity* (Cambridge: Cambridge University Press, 1993).
35 Kay, *Bruegel,* p. 22.
36 London: SCM, 1972, p. 19
37 *We Believe in the Holy Spirit,* Report of Doctrine Commission of the Church of England (London: Church House, 1991), p. 67.

Further reading

Begbie, Jeremy S., *Voicing Creation's Praise: Towards a Theology of the Arts,* Edinburgh: T. & T. Clark, 1991.
Bowie, Andrew, *Aesthetics and Subjectivity: from Kant to Nietzsche,* Manchester: Manchester University Press, 1990.
Burch Brown, Frank, *Religious Aesthetics,* Basingstoke: Macmillan, 1990.
Dillenberger, John, *A Theology of Artistic Sensibilities: The Visual Arts and the Church,* London: SCM, 1987.
Fuller, Peter, *Theoria: Arts and the Absence of Grace,* London: Chatto and Windus, 1988.
Pattison, George, *Art, Modernity and Faith,* Basingstoke: Macmillian, 1991.
Steiner, George, *Real Presences,* London: Faber and Faber, 1989.
Wolterstorff, Nicholas, *Art in Action,* Grand Rapids, Michigan: Eerdmans, 1980.

Part two

The content of Christian doctrine

7 The triune God

RALPH DEL COLLE

INTRODUCTION

Friedrich Schleiermacher, the great 'Father of Modern Theology', at the end of his *magnum opus, The Christian Faith,* insightfully identified the 'being of God in Christ and in the Christian Church' as the main pivot for the ecclesiastical doctrine of the Trinity, only to go on to state that in his judgement they could stand independent of it.[1] No evaluation before or since better captures both the necessity and ambiguity of the doctrine. It is the perspective of this essay that the Christian doctrine of God requires a confession of the Holy Trinity.

Clearly, though, one cannot separate the Christian understanding of God as Trinity from the religious monotheism of its closest two relatives, both of whom along with Christianity lay claim to Abraham as their ancestor. The conviction that the one unsurpassable God is self-revelatory in word and deed is the common testimony of Judaism, Christianity and Islam. The unique One has spoken and the divine Word which is mediated by a prophetic figure constitutes the theological genesis of their traditions and communities. Torah, Gospel and Qur'an all bear witness to the speaking God as do the personalities of Moses, Jesus and Muhammad. Peculiar to the Christian tradition is the notion that although the mediation of God's speech to the world still requires the prophetic mouthpiece it goes much beyond the attestation of another prophet, even a final prophet. The nature of the communication is so intrinsic to the divine life that the understanding of God can no longer be rendered as simple, absolute, undifferentiated monotheism. The conjunction between divine revelation and the self-giving of the hidden and revealing God is so intimate that God's very self is unveiled and communicated in the event. The more proper inter-religious comparison, then, is not just that Jesus is the originative or final mediator of revelation analogous to Moses or Muhammad (although he is that) but that he like the Torah and Qur'an is in his person and work the revelation itself. Gospel and mediator converge in the self-communication of divine life that is at the heart of Christian faith known and received in the Spirit.

Whether one considers the doctrine of the Trinity as the capstone of Christian dogmatics as did Schleiermacher or the necessary prolegomenon for its execution as did his modern critic, Karl Barth, the common presupposition ought to be that its truth pervades the very nature of Christian faith, life and worship. Whether the preferred theological methodology is 'from below' with the Christian experience of grace (Schleiermacher) or 'from above' with the self-revealing God (Barth), one is distinctly reminded that testimony to the presence of the risen Christ in and with the Holy Spirit alters the confession of God's oneness. The passage from the Judaic Shema, 'Hear, O Israel: the LORD our God, the LORD is one' (Deuteronomy 6:4) to Paul's triadic benediction, 'The grace of the Lord Jesus Christ and the love of God and the fellowship of the Holy Spirit be with you all' (2 Corinthians 13:14) implicitly entails what Larry Hurtado calls 'the early Christian mutation' of ancient Jewish monotheism.[2] This observation does not immediately settle either the dogmatic definition or the underlying theology of the Trinity. It simply alerts the Christian believer to the fact that faith in the risen Christ and testimony to the outpoured and indwelling Spirit require a theological explication of the monotheistic confession that is consistent with the awareness of a more pluralist dimension to the saving action of God and the graced recognition of the same in worship and doctrine.

BIBLICAL FOUNDATIONS

As with most Christian doctrines the driving force for dogmatic construction of the Trinity and its theological understanding is soteriological, that is, God's saving action, a point that is more than insisted upon by the Church Fathers. The naming of God as triune – Father, Son and Holy Spirit – is not a fondness for numeration or dialectic. It is the faithful attempt to represent the One known in the person of Jesus and in the life of the ecclesial community grounded as they are in the covenant history of Israel. Therefore, the Christian confession begins with the one God of Israel whose redeeming hand in the call and election of the patriarchs and the deliverance from Egyptian slavery establishes the matrix out of which Jesus' own affirmation of the Shema (Mark 12:29) is heard. But the oneness of the God of Abraham, Isaac and Jacob is already subject to an apprehension of his being that lends itself to a diversified array of symbolic conceptualisations and actual naming, not the least of which includes representations of God by means of the divine Word, Wisdom and Spirit.

The New Testament foundations for the doctrine of the Trinity are construed at the level of the saving activity of the God of Israel as this was realised in the person and event of Jesus Christ and in the reception of the gift of the Holy Spirit. The resurrection/exaltation of Jesus is determinative for christological origins and while not negating the significance of his earthly/historical ministry it casts it in a new light. Here the relationship between Jesus and the God whom he addressed as Abba (Father) also informs the understanding of God. However, in neither case, the post-Easter witness to the risen Lord nor the evangelical narratives of the written Gospels, is a formal trinitarian theology suggested or worked out. What is conveyed is a 'primary trinitarianism', that is, testimony to God's identification with Christ in the Spirit in the rhetoric of Christian proclamation.[3]

Three aspects of this primary trinitarianism are decisive for subsequent trinitarian reflection since they establish the contours for trinitarian doctrine. First, the identification between God and Jesus Christ does not obliterate the distinction between them. This is to state the obvious in reference to the New Testament but it figures importantly for later theological debates between orthodox and modalist positions, the latter of which argued that the distinctions of Father, Son and Holy Spirit applied only to the activity of God in the world and did not bespeak any distinction inhering in the divine being itself. For the most part as well these modes of divine activity were transitional in nature. God became Father, then Son and then Spirit.

This New Testament differentiation, however, also holds not simply for a distinction between God and the humanity of Christ but also in more nuanced fashion between 'God our Father' and the 'Lord Jesus Christ' in such a manner that the pluralism now embodied in the naming of the divine, namely, *theos* (God) and *kyrios* (Lord) each with their respective referents, does not compromise biblical monotheism. Second, the God who is revealed in the Christian proclamation is in fact identified by the mutual conditioning of these two referents, the Father and Jesus. Neither one is known apart from the other. Third, lest we misrepresent the apostolic proclamation's witness to the divine in binitarian fashion, it is necessary to register the distinction between the exalted Christ and the Spirit with respect to their inseparable agency and their personalised representations.

On the first count the various christologies of the New Testament identify Jesus at the very least as God's eschatological agent of salvation, distinct from God but the mediator of God's salvific activity. More than that, the so-called 'high' christologies, specifically, Pauline Wisdom christology and Johannine Logos christology, utilise notions in their formulations which lend themselves to later affirmations of pre-existence. These affirm the pre-existence and divinity of Wisdom at the time of creation (Colossians 1:15–20) or that of the Logos-Son before (John 1:1–18). While these are not the only sources for the attribution of deity to Christ, they set such attribution within the framework of the divine life itself. Divine titles, for example, *kyrios* and *theos*, as well as divine functions or honours, for example, judgement (John 5:26–8) and Christ being the object of worship (Revelation 5:12), support it. The pre-existence christologies imply that the attribution of divinity to Christ might require the recognition of differentiation within the divine being.

The Word (*Logos*) in John 1:1 was *with* (towards) God and *was* God. Clearly the Fourth Gospel presents the highest christology in the New Testament. From the prologue (1:1–18) to the 'I am' statements (6:35; 8:12; 10:9,11; 11:25; 14:6; 15:1) to Thomas' christological confession, 'My Lord and My God' (20:28), both the identity and differentiation between Christ and the Father are maintained. The Johannine Jesus can assert his unity with God, 'I and the Father are one' (10:30), precisely because of the dialogical relationship he possesses with the Father, for example, his 'high priestly prayer' in chapter 17. Jesus will receive glory from the Father in his paschal death because of the mutual glory they possessed from before the world's foundation (17:5).

While the distinction between the Father and Son/Word will become normative for subsequent trinitarian reflection it is important to note that a trinitarian understanding of God is dependent not only on an intra-divine distinction but also on the mutual conditioning of the terms of this distinction. The early Christian innovation to refer to God as 'Father' clearly derives from the prayer practice and 'Abba experience' of Jesus. Any inferences drawn from this towards the meaning of either term can only proceed on the basis of their interdependence. As much is suggested by the so-called 'Johannine logion' in the Q tradition common to both Matthew (11:27) and Luke (10:22): 'No one knows the Son except the Father, and no one knows the Father except the Son and anyone to whom the Son chooses to reveal Him.'

A full-blown trinitarian theology cannot be derived from the saying. Nevertheless, it is proper to deduce that the meaning of Father must be determined by the life and praxis of Jesus of Nazareth and that likewise that Jesus of Nazareth is only known within the matrix of the God already revealed in the covenant with Israel. With a similar logic it is also proper to speak of Father and Son as they are revealed within the divine economy of salvation and within the divine life itself in the relational terms that the saying suggests. Interestingly enough this will be a pressing issue for the Fathers, especially Athanasius, from whom the principle is actually derived, and for contemporary theology in light of feminist concerns. It is not fatherhood relative to the world as his creation *per se* that is of moment but rather the relation between Jesus and God that the name Father signifies. From this perspective the notion of fatherhood is transformed (Ephesians 3:14–15).

Our third point is intended in formal dogmatic terms as a caution against modalism of the second and third persons of the Trinity. Exegetes dispute the issue of identity or non-identity between the exalted Christ and the Spirit in the New Testament, particularly in the Johannine and Pauline literature. Is it the case that the Johannine Paraclete is nothing other than Christ himself pneumatically present in the community of faith? Or, is the relationship between the risen Christ and the Holy Spirit in Paul's pneumatological exhortations one of total identity? Dogmatically, these are important questions. A trinitarian view of God would be undermined if on the basis of the New Testament we could only posit a biunity between God and Christ. Much depends on what the scripture conveys regarding the Holy Spirit.

Aside from the prevailing view in the Synoptic gospels and Acts that God anointed Jesus with the Spirit to inaugurate and empower his messianic mission, it is to Paul and John that we must turn for the more developed pneumatologies. In each case the Christian life is understood as life in the Spirit. At times the christological and the pneumatological referents are almost interchangeable (Romans 8: 9–10a) or they appear to be entirely conflated (1 Corinthians 15:45; 2 Corinthians 3:17–18). It is also suggested by some scholars that in the experience of the believer there is no difference between the risen Christ and the Spirit.[4] While contemporary exegetes and theologians debate this issue there are two factors which uphold the primary trinitarianism embedded in the biblical language.

First, the Spirit is instrumental in mediating the relationship between the Father and the exalted Christ. The Spirit's identification as the Spirit of God and the Spirit of Christ amounts to an attribution of agency to the risen Jesus as much as to the Father in the sending of the Spirit (John 15:26). In this mission the Spirit mediates or executes the activity of the exalted Christ. Rather than an identity between Christ and the Spirit in either an ontological or functional manner in which any distinction between the two would be obliterated there is the conjunction of their saving activity. This is supported by other Pauline passages in which Christ and the Spirit are clearly distinguished (Romans 15:30) or where a 'soteriological trinitarianism' is evidently at work, that is, triadic references to the salvific agencies of God, Christ and Spirit (1 Thessalonians 1:4–5; 2 Thessalonians 2:13; 1 Corinthians 1:4–7, 2: 4–5, 2:12, 6:11; 2 Corinthians 1:21–2; Galatians 3:1–5; Romans 8: 3–4, 15–17).[5]

Christ's relationship to the Spirit is not just construed in terms of his lordship vis-à-vis the Spirit, namely, as Lord he sends the Spirit. The Spirit is indeed the Spirit of God and the Spirit of Christ and the Paraclete sayings of the Fourth Gospel indicate the Spirit is sent by the Father in Christ's name to bear witness to him and continue his work. There the Spirit is the modality of the presence of Christ.[6] However, the Spirit also mediates the relationship of Jesus to the Father. Both the origin and unfolding of Jesus' sonship is pneumatologically grounded, extending from conception (Luke 1:34–5) to messianic inauguration into public ministry (Luke 3:21–2) and culminating in redemptive death (Hebrews 9:14), resurrection (Romans 1:4) and exaltation (John 15:26). The Holy Spirit as the Spirit of Sonship (Romans 8:15–16; Galatians 4:4) implies that the Spirit is constitutive of the Son's fellowship with the Father and therefore of its extension by grace in the hearts of believers.[7]

A second dimension of biblical pneumatology (that is, theology of the Holy Spirit) which underscores the trinitarian tendencies of the New Testament is the personalised agency of the Spirit's presence and activity. From the Spirit as a revelatory (Acts 20:23) and providential (Acts 16:6–7) actor in the Lucan narrative to the Spirit as the wellspring of prayer and pathos in the believer's life (Romans 8:26–7), pneumatological agency and identity are almost as prominent as that which is more properly christological and theological. This robust pneumatology integrated with christology and theology completes the foundation for a thoroughgoing trinitarian understanding of God.

PATRISTIC DEVELOPMENTS

As the church moved into its formative era doctrinal disputes became part and parcel of its efforts to understand and pass on the apostolic faith. The period of the Apostolic Fathers and the Apologists well into the second century witnessed the beginnings of what we may now describe as 'economic trinitarianism'. That is, the recognition of God's triunity was confined to the revelation of God's activity in the economy of creation and redemption. It did not investigate the being of God apart from this, as to whether for instance God was triune before the creation of the world. This would have been a question of God's immanent being. Trinitarian theologians have thus come to distinguish between the economic Trinity, namely, the divine persons revealed in salvation history, and the immanent Trinity, namely, the triune nature of God's being even apart from salvation history.

The path to a clear trinitarian doctrine was therefore some three centuries in coming. Fluidity in language and conceptuality was the rule rather than the exception. The terms of this early discussion were also informed by the inculturation of the gospel message within the world of Graeco-Roman philosophy. The Johannine Logos christology – 'the Word became flesh' – was especially suitable for this, particularly in regard to Platonic and Stoic conceptualities.

Irenaeus of Lyons was the first to develop a more explicit trinitarian theology based upon the divine economy of salvation. The Son and the Spirit are the 'two hands of God' who mediate the creation of human being (*Against Heresies* IV, Preface), are the agents of revelation and redemption and are respectively seen as God's Word and Wisdom, 'His offspring and His similitude' (IV, 7). There is no hint of an immanent intra-divine relationship among three eternal persons but the trinitarian structure of salvation history – from the Father through the Son in the Holy Spirit and in the Spirit through the Son to the Father – with its end in the recapitulation of all things in Christ is clear. Irenaeus moved beyond the Apologists in asserting the eternal Sonship of the Word which is generated from the Father, therefore, not delimiting the name of Son only to the incarnation (III, 30).

Although Irenaeus' theology is an instance of 'economic trinitarianism', his contributions to trinitarian theology are noteworthy. Endemic to trinitarian thinking is the problem of how to distinguish the work of the three persons without violating the divine unity, that is, to avoid tritheism. Irenaeus offered the following, again relative to the economy (in this instance to the creation of human being): 'the Father planning everything well and giving His commands, the Son carrying these into execution and performing the work of creating, and the Spirit nourishing and increasing [what is made]' (IV, 38, 3). This pattern, which attributes to each person a specific work within the one activity of God, that is, an appropriation to each person, was utilised by subsequent theologians and became typical. On the other hand, Irenaeus with the metaphor of the Son and the Spirit as the two hands of God also bequeathed a legacy of implicit subordinationism that would have to be resolved, especially among the Greek Fathers. It came to a head in the Arian controversy when the theological descendants of Origen contested the Son's relationship to the Father. Meanwhile the Latin West proceeded on somewhat different lines.

The North African theologian, Tertullian, provided the West with its trinitarian terminology. The formula, three persons (*personae*) of one substance (*unius substantiae*), is still the mainstay of Western trinitarianism. It also perennially raised the question of what is meant by 'person'. Nevertheless, it provided a framework for subsequent trinitarian discussion. Tertullian's explanation of *trinitas* (he was the first to use the Latin term) did not endure beyond the terminology except to say that his opposition to modalistic monarchianism was decisive. Except for a minority wing of the Pentecostal movement known as 'Oneness', no Christian church has affirmed a modalist or Sabellian position wherein the trinitarian names are referred to the same divine person/being under different modes or manifestations. This is not to say that theologians have not tended in that direction, especially those for whom the notion of three persons is just a step short of tritheism.

Another legacy of Tertullian was subordinationism, that somehow the Son is less than the Father. Even more so was this the case for the Greek Fathers, especially since Logos christology had taken such a hold. Origen of Alexandria, the first truly Christian systematic theologian, left a legacy that his intellectual disciples would contest in the church's path to doctrinal and credal orthodoxy. While affirming that the transcendent and ingenerate nature of God, that is, God (the Father) is without origin, he is also clear that the generation of the Son by the Father is an 'eternal and everlasting begetting' (*On First Principles* 1.2.4). Here Origen moves beyond Tertullian and Irenaeus and sets the stage for the resolution of the trinitarian question.

Contributing to the scenario and provoking the split among his followers was his subordinationism. As in Tertullian the Son is God by derivation and is referred to simply as 'God' (*theos*) or as the second God (*Contra Celsum* 5.39) rather than 'the God' (*ho theos*), the designation given to the Father (3.39). Arius, a priest in the Church of Alexandria, accentuated this subordinationist strand in Origen's thought and clearly placed the Son/Word on the side of the creature, thus ruling out his eternal generation from the Father. His great opponent Athanasius countered, and with the conciliar introduction of a new term, *homoousios* (that the Son was *of the same substance* as the Father), Arius' position was condemned.

Introduced at the Council of Nicaea by the Emperor Constantine at the behest of his chaplain Ossius, *homoousios*, while a non-biblical term, fits well with the intentions of the opponents of Arius. It became part of the creed professed by the Council and spoke to at least three formative dimensions of trinitarian doctrine. First, it emphasises the priority of the Father as does the phrase 'begotten, not made' in the creed itself. Second, it assures equality in being between Father and Son. Third, it maintains the distinction between the two, although this took some bit of convincing for a number of Greek theologians. One is not *homoousios* with oneself but with another, and thus modalism was precluded.

Athanasius in defence of Nicaea contributed to a major breakthrough in trinitarian theology. By resolving the generation of the Son on the side of God rather than the creature, he established an intra-divine basis for the divinity of the Son and the Spirit, without excluding the soteriological principle that the Word became flesh in order that 'He might minister the things of God to us, and ours to God' (*Contra Arianos* 4.6). The consequence is that the Father is designated such not on the basis of his relationship to creation as the source of all that is but primarily as the one who generates the Son.

It is more godly and accurate to signify God from the Son and call him Father, than to name him from his works and call him unoriginate. (*Contra Arianos* 1.34)

If God is without Offspring, then he is without work; for the Son is his Offspring through whom he works. (*Contra Arianos* 4.4)

The Cappadocian Fathers, Basil of Caesarea, Gregory of Nyssa and Gregory of Nazianzus, finalised the distinction between *ousia* (essence or substance) and *hypostasis* (an individual instance of a given essence), hitherto synonyms, and in so doing clarified an important trinitarian principle. It was the same issue implied in the Latin formula used by Tertullian, *tres personae, una substantia,* except for the fact that translation and mutual understanding between East and West on this matter was not a simple process. One *ousia* and three *hypostases* provided Greek theology with a language and conceptuality by which to undergird and complement the *homoousios* of the Nicene symbol.

Three other contributions by the Cappadocians are noteworthy. First, in order to underscore the numerical identity in the essence or substance (*ousia*) of the three hypostases they posited the *perichoresis* or coinherence of each person in the other. This accented both the Trinity in unity and unity in Trinity. Faithful to the economic pattern that the Father works through the Son in the Holy Spirit, the doctrine of *perichoresis* is able to affirm that the distinction of persons does not compromise the divine unity. *Perichoresis* prevents distinction from becoming separation or division.

Second, along with Athanasius, the Cappadocians contested with the so-called Pneumatomachians ('Spirit-fighters') for the divinity of the Holy Spirit. It is more than a truism to suggest that trinitarian theology stands or falls on the basis of whether or not it maintains a vibrant pneumatology. Athanasius had already made the soteriological argument that the Spirit must be divine in order to enable the creature to participate in the divine nature. The fact that the *homoousios* of the Holy Spirit was not dealt with until the fourth century is natural enough considering the impersonal connotations associated with spirit. However, once the equality of the Son with the Father was established then the co-equality of all three persons including the Spirit followed.

Third, by the time of Athanasius and the Cappadocians a restrictive economic trinitarianism had been overcome. The distinction between *theologia* and *oikonomia*, that is, between God in the trinitarian mystery of his being, and the mediatorship of the Son and the Spirit in creation and redemption, was essential for the maturation of the doctrine. Even as this is affirmed care should be taken to note that it was precisely because of the soteriological necessity of the *homoousios* of the Son and Spirit as they are revealed in the divine economy that one ought to posit an equality of being in the internal relations of each to the Father. No longer does a relationship of 'sending' and 'being sent' between the Father and his 'two hands' imply a subordinationist ontological status, a common problematic among pre-Nicene theologians.

The issue concerns more than just the status of the Son and the Spirit *vis-à-vis* the Father. Endemic to the older theology was the notion that the Son/Word is the visible representation of the invisible God. So, for example, it was not uncommon to attribute Old Testament theophanies to the manifestation of the pre-incarnate Son. Taken to its logical outcome this could reinforce a bipolarity in God between transcendence and immanence, between the hidden and revealed. While there is truth even biblically speaking for such an approach, it is not simply a matter of transcendent (and immutable) mystery versus visible historical revelation. Rather, the trinitarian naming of God points to the Christian understanding that the event of Jesus Christ and the sending of the Holy Spirit reveal the loving mystery of the saving God whose transcendence in the mystery is the basis for its communication and invitation to the creature. The saving economy points to the relations of the trinitarian persons to one another, a matrix of divine life in which all three persons are transcendent and immanent via their coinherence and the *homoousios*. But here we must note the different trinitarian models and the possibilities they present.

In fact it was the Cappadocians, Gregory of Nazianzus to be exact, who introduced the notion of mutual relations (*scheseis*), a fertile concept that informed both Greek and Latin thought. It has also become the subject of much contemporary theological reappropriation. The divine persons may be distinguished on the basis of one principle and two criteria. The principle is simply one of identity and non-identity. Athanasius said as much: 'But they are two, because the Father is Father and is not also the Son, and the Son is Son and not also the Father; but the nature is one' (*Contra Arianos* 3.3). The identity of each person with the divine nature is offset by the non-identity of each with the other.

The two criteria focus on the distinguishing characteristics of the persons based on relation and relationality. Regarding the latter the Fathers were not hesitant to identify the persons on the basis of distinctive marks of their work, for example, Paternity, Sonship and Sanctity, even when considered within the exclusive perspective of the divine economy. However, this principle is not sufficient to sustain the doctrine without inviting subordinationist tendencies. On the other hand, neither is it insignificant for the contemporary discussion. The recognition of the divine persons in their proper relations to the world is essential if trinitarian theology is to be prevented from losing its grounding in the salvific activity of God.

Yet it is also the case that the manifestation of the divine persons to the world reveals their relations to one another. When Gregory of Nazianzus spoke of the mutual relations which distinguish the three hypostases he built on the distinguishing characteristics of the persons that Gregory of Nyssa identified as Unbegotten, Begotten and Proceeding. The relations are those of origin *vis-à-vis* the Father. The Son and the Spirit who respectively are begotten and proceed from the Father can be distinguished by virtue of the ineffable difference between generation and procession. The Latins employed similar notions on slightly other grounds in part because the Cappadocians (and Greek theology in general) differ from Athanasius (to whom the Latin West is much closer) on one significant point.

The dividing line between Eastern and Western trinitarian theology (not simply dogma!) is not so much the *filioque* (that is, that the Holy Spirit proceeds from the Father and the Son), although that is often the flashpoint, as it is the weight given to the monarchy of the Father. The Cappadocians (although here Gregory of Nazianzus is something of an exception) as the orthodox culmination of Greek theology still held to the monarchy of the first person even as they overcame the last vestiges of subordinationism with their doctrine of *perichoresis*. The Father is the *arche* (origin) of the Son's begetting and the Spirit's proceeding. For Athanasius (and for the Latin West) the configuration of how the Son and the Spirit were related to the Father was conceived differently. It was not so much from the person as from the being of the Father that the Son was begotten and the Spirit breathed forth. The *homoousios* ensured the equality of Father, Son and Spirit while their non-identity distinguished them. For Athanasius it was clear that something could not be *homoousios* with itself. Add to this the concept of relation and there is even more solid basis for the distinction among the persons, as became especially clear in Augustine's *De Trinitate*.

In the West the Father is still the principle by which the Son is generated and the Spirit breathed forth. In the Latin model, since relation is qualified more by opposition than by origin, the *filioque* is required in order to maintain the trinitarian distinctions; specifically, because the Holy Spirit proceeds from the Father and the Son the Spirit must be distinct from the Father and Son. For the most part this has become the standard account of the difference between East and West regarding this key notion of relation. While the East proceeds largely on the basis that the unity of the three hypostases is theologically conveyed by the monarchy of the Father in conjunction with the *perichoresis* of the persons, in the West the emphasis has been on the unity of the divine nature as identical with the differentiation in the divine being constituted by the relations.

MEDIEVAL CONSOLIDATIONS

Subsequent developments in both East and West basically refine what was achieved during this period. Augustine implicitly introduced the notion of the divine persons as subsisting relations, a point that Thomas Aquinas would bring to theological maturity in a virtual trinitarian metaphysics. The relation to the other (*ad alium*), for example, the Father actively generates the Son and the Son is passively generated by the Father, is coincident with subsistence in oneself (*in se*).

Other debates and proposals surround the development of trinitarian theology. They range from the usefulness of psychological models to advance trinitarian understanding, for example, Augustine's analogical patterning of the three persons as memory, intellect and will; to appropriate definitions of person, for example, Aquinas works with both Boethius' definition (a person is an individual substance of a rational nature – *rationalis naturae individua substantia*) and that of Richard of St Victor (person as the incommunicable existence of the divine nature – *divinae naturae incommunicabilis existentia*) in order to posit the trinitarian persons as subsisting relations; to, in the Eastern Church, the Palamite distinctions between the divine essence (*ousia*) and energy (*energeia*) as well as recurrent debates about the *filioque*. For the most part, however, even though the theological routes of East and West are quite different a certain equivalency has settled in regarding their respective formulae regarding the one divine nature, substance, or being and the three persons or hypostases – *mia ousia, treis hypostaseis; tres personae, una substantia*.

Classical representations of trinitarian theology which have become the norm by which to measure the Christian doctrine of God or against which to reconstruct it would point to Thomas Aquinas in the West and Gregory Palamas in the East. The dynamics of the two traditions of East and West that come to maturity in Aquinas and Palamas are such that while each along with the Fathers evokes the possibility for *ressourcement*, that is, a constructive return to the sources of doctrine, the quite different tendency for revision and reconstruction of the doctrine of the Trinity has affected the former more than the latter. Nevertheless, a critical appreciation of the contrast between Thomistic and Palamite emphases helps illuminate the agenda of modern and contemporary trinitarian theology and the issues which have generated something of a renaissance in the genre.

The contrast is not so much between different approaches to the doctrine in which the Latins focused on the *unitas in Trinitate* and the Greeks on the *Trinitas in unitate*. While there is some truth to this characterisation and while much contemporary trinitarian theology stresses either the modal (that is, the unity in distinction of persons) or social (that is, the distinction of persons in the unity) dimensions of the doctrine, it is another issue of contention that is the more formidable. Here the matter is the relationship between the epistemological approach to the doctrine and ontological affirmations that can be made about the being and nature of God.

The Palamite distinction between the essence and energies of God, with the former inaccessible to creaturely knowledge, and the Thomistic insistence that it is only through the habit (*habitus*) of created grace that the human mind is enabled to grasp divine truth, provoked charges and counter-charges in the trinitarian stand-off between East and West. Ironically, the complaints are very similar, namely, that the redeemed human creature does not actually know or participate in the actual being of God. It never was the case for either side that one should affirm the human comprehensibility of the divine or that the divine mystery be reduced to the revelation of God in the economy of salvation. It was really whether or not each theological model was able to clearly state that indeed God was known in the trinitarian revelation. The Palamites of course responded that the uncreated energies are God and that in fact they are enhypostasised in the tripersonal revelation of the divine. The Thomists could argue that the consequence of the created *habitus* of grace was the actual human knowing of God in the beatific vision (*visio beatifica*). The supernatural light of glory (*lumen gloria*) equipped the creaturely mind to see God, the foretaste of which is now known via the reception of sanctifying grace. What is impressive about both accounts is the confidence with which both East and West kept in focus that the graced knowledge of God did in fact concern God's tripersonal identity. There were no bouts of theological agnosticism except for a very healthy apophaticism (that is, the contemplation of God without images) that shows up in the spiritual and mystical traditions of each ecclesial stream. Such was not easily the case for the post-Enlightenment modern.

MODERN ISSUES

Between the formative period in the development of trinitarian doctrine and any contemporary trinitarian theology lies the epistemological disruption in theological method that is a consequence of the Enlightenment. The issue may be simply put, namely, how can one know the reality of God or that God is triune in nature? Does one begin with God, or with the works of God known in creation and redemption? Through a combination of the classical Protestant soteriological emphasis – 'to know Christ is to know his benefits' – and the post-Kantian limits upon knowledge-claims (Immanuel Kant claimed that we cannot know things in themselves but only as they appear to us), it was merely a matter of logic before trinitarian doctrine found itself on the margins of Christian theology.

Clearly there were rescue attempts not the least of which was the ambitious effort of G. W. F. Hegel to reconstruct metaphysics on a trinitarian basis. However, his concerns had more to do with a meta-philosophy than a revitalised church dogmatics. Even so, his trinity of Absolute Spirit as the divine subject dialectically coming to itself through the historical process influenced a good number of theologians.

More directly relevant to the concerns of Christian doctrine were the efforts of Friedrich Schleiermacher. Recalling the tack with which this chapter began, it is with a great deal of circumspection that one considers the contribution of the Father of modern theology to trinitarian dogma. With doctrine proceeding from a critical examination of the religious affections, any affirmation of the trinitarian being of God comes by way of a phenomeno-logical contrast between the hidden and revealed God. As the former is not accessible to human knowledge the latter takes its cue from the two pivots of the christological confession and the divine indwelling of the community of faith. Each entails the union of the divine essence with human nature, either with the human nature of Jesus or the common spirit of the church as the community of faith. Such analysis, however, does not necessarily constitute the doctrine of the Trinity. It only asserts that Christian faith has to do with the reality of God, namely, the divine essence via its reception by humanity in Christ and the Spirit. Trinitarian statements are at best the consequence of secondary combinations of several utterances regarding the Christian reli-gious consciousness.

All things considered, Schleiermacher preferred a Sabellian accounting of the relationship between the hidden divine essence and the revelation of God in the economy of salvation. The Trinity is more a matter of circum-scriptions in the divine being enacted in revelation than intrinsic to the divine essence itself. Therefore while it is clear that nothing less than God is known in the divine economy, it is by no means certain that God is triune apart from his relation to the world in creation and redemption.

Here it may be useful to borrow from Claude Welch, who posited three distinct expressions of trinitarian assertions: the economic, the essential and the immanent Trinities. The revelation of God via Christ and the Spirit in the history of salvation constitutes the economic Trinity. The doctrines of the *homoousios* along with the coeternity and coequality of the hypostases or persons is indicative of the essential Trinity. Only with the assertion of the internal relations (that is, generation and procession) along with the coin-herence (*perichoresis*) of the persons may we speak of the immanent Trinity.[8] Even if we posit that Schleiermacher would subscribe to the essential Trinity there is no doubt that he excluded an immanent Trinity and raised serious questions concerning proper theological warrants for such a step.

The twentieth century, however, would witness a rebirth of trinitarian theology in some of its most notable theologians. Karl Barth certainly led the way with his assertion that the doctrine of the Word of God is the only ade-quate prolegomenon for dogmatics and itself requires a clear affirmation of the divine triunity. In revelation we come to know 'God himself in unim-paired unity yet also in unimpaired distinction [as] Revealer, Revelation, and

Revealedness'.[9] As a counter-point to Schleiermacher the contrast could not be clearer. What is mediated and indirect for Schleiermacher is still mediated but direct for Barth. The triadic revelation bespeaks the very being of God who immanently must be triune in nature for it to be a *divine* revelation. Trinitarian doctrine is not the consequence of combining several Christian affirmations so much as the prerequisite for any Christian affirmation. It is not that the three persons are the revelation of the hidden God who is an absolute undifferentiated unity, possibly implying a 'God beyond God' (Paul Tillich), but that the three are the revelation of the Christian God who is Trinity.

Among all the problematics for contemporary trinitarian theology this is the most telling. Other issues such as the question of God's impassibility (that is, not being subject to suffering) and the divine missions; temporality and eternality; history and the revelation of the triune God; the nature of the trinitarian symbols and names including the issue of inclusive language and discourse about God, are derivative of this one. Either the Christian knowledge of God identifies the very being of God in the revelation of the divine persons and in this manner preserves the divine transcendence, or trinitarian language amounts to a triadic representation of God in history according to the receptive capacity of the human subject and nothing more. In ultimate terms this latter position eventually yields to an apophatic agnosticism concerning the being of God.

Hence in the recent renaissance of trinitarian theology presaged by Karl Barth and Karl Rahner, respectively reinvigorating the Evangelical and Catholic traditions, one may take the latter's trinitarian axiom – *The 'Economic' Trinity is the 'Immanent' Trinity and the 'Immanent' Trinity is the 'Economic' Trinity*[10] – as indicative of this decisive issue. The axiom begs for either qualification or radicalisation. First of all, it should be recognised that the axiom represents a necessary turn in trinitarian theology to rescue it from possible theological irrelevance. The intent is to demonstrate that the separation of the doctrinal tract on the trinity (*De Deo Trino*) from that on the one God (*De Deo Uno*) as well as from the substance of christology, soteriology and the theology of grace isolates the doctrine from its proper formative influence for all of Christian doctrine. Second, this is only reinforced by focusing the tract on the intricacies of trinitarian terminology and definition relative to the nature of the intra-trinitarian distinctions. By beginning with the divine economy the foundational importance of the doctrine of the Trinity for the entire scope of Christian dogmatics is underscored.

Once the intent of the axiom is accomplished, namely to ground the basis for trinitarian reflection in the economy of salvation, what scholastic theology identified as the trinitarian missions of the Son and the Holy Spirit, the formative influence of the doctrine with respect to the other dogmatic *loci* is relatively secure. The only qualification for the axiom is that the immanent being of God may not be exclusively reduced to the revelation of the divine persons in the incarnation and the outpouring of the Holy Spirit. It is to suggest a *kenosis*, that is, a self-emptying, of the trinitarian persons, especially of the Son and the Spirit in their joint mission for the world's redemption, the source of which is none other than the divine freedom itself. Necessity as constitutive for the being and enactment of the divine Trinity in the world process (*à la* Hegel) is excluded.

The radicalisation of the axiom proceeds in a different direction and recalls the pre-Nicene 'economic trinitarianism' discussed above. It confines the object of the Christian trinitarian confession to the divine economy with the supposition that the immanent Trinity is a vacuous concept or simply the inner dimension of God revealed in the economy. Epistemologically it delimits the speculative moment in trinitarian thought, either ruling it out or confining it to the divine economy. It also confounds the epistemological intent of the Thomistic and Palamite trinitarian theologies which, each in their own way, attempted to ensure that knowledge of the divine persons was in fact the pinnacle of creaturely knowledge of God. Theologically, it is consistent with the notion that the divine essence recedes beyond the triune revelation. Are we then left with the conundrum that in the divine economy we have to do with God in some way but not according to the very nature of the divine being?

In consideration of the latter position a few concluding comments are in order. One should not divorce theological reflection about the triune God from God's salvific activity and isolate it in the realm of a metaphysics of immanent trinitarian life. While there is much truth to this position, and an integral trinitarian theology that informs the whole spectrum of Christian doctrine is necessary, three considerations from our survey of the long road towards the development of an adequate doctrine of the Trinity are noteworthy.

First, the soteriological principle essentially means that what God is in his saving activity is what God is in the divine being itself. Anything less would compromise the nature of divine revelation and the communion of grace that is constitutive of Christian life and community. Second, in the revelatory events of the sending of Jesus Christ and the outpouring of the Holy Spirit there clearly exist dialogical relations of Christ and the Spirit to the

Father and to each other. The presumption in favour of such relations in the immanent being of God is strong if we are not to violate our first principle. Third, the nature of relation and personhood so important for a Christian understanding of the human person and of ecclesial life would then be grounded in the very nature of the divine being, both revealed in the economy of salvation and implanted in human being by virtue of God's creative act culminating in the image of God.

Needless to say, the Christian doctrine of God is constructed on the foundation and capstone of Christian existence enacted in praise and worship. It is in this doxological event and context as the source and summit of Christian vision and understanding that the one God who is Father, Son and Holy Spirit is known, proclaimed and adored.

Notes

1 *The Christian Faith*, ed. H. R. Mackintosh and J. S. Stewart (Philadelphia: Fortress, 1976), p. 741.

2 *One God, One Lord: Early Christian Devotion and Ancient Jewish Monotheism* (Philadelphia: Fortress, 1988), pp. 93–114.

3 The phrase is introduced by Robert W. Jenson, *The Triune Identity: God According to the Gospel* (Philadelphia: Fortress, 1982), pp. 40–8. In a similar fashion Hurtado identifies six features of early Christian religious devotion which bear the same rhetorical function. They are: '(1) hymnic practices, (2) prayer and related practices, (3) use of the name of Christ, (4) the Lord's Supper, (5) confession of faith in Jesus, and (6) prophetic pronouncements of the risen Christ', *One God, One Lord*, pp. 100–14.

4 James D. G. Dunn, '1 Corinthians 15.45 – Last Adam, Life-giving Spirit', in B. Lindars and S. S. Smalley (eds.), *Christ and Spirit in the New Testament* (Cambridge: Cambridge University Press, 1973), p. 139.

5 The phrase is used by Gordon D. Fee, who argues contra Dunn for trinitarian distinctions in the Pauline corpus. See his 'Christology and Pneumatology in Romans 8:9–11', in Joel B. Green and Max Turner (eds.), *Jesus of Nazareth: Lord and Christ: Essays on the Historical Jesus and New Testament Christology* (Grand Rapids, Michigan: Eerdmans, 1994), pp. 312–21. In the same vein and in the same volume see Max Turner, 'The Spirit of Christ and "Divine" Christology', pp. 413–36.

6 See especially Gary M. Burge, *The Anointed Community: The Holy Spirit in the Johannine Tradition* (Grand Rapids, Michigan: Eerdmans, 1987), p. 41.

7 Wolfhart Pannenberg, *Systematic Theology*, trans. Geoffrey W. Bromiley

(Grand Rapids, Michigan: Eerdmans, and Edinburgh: T. & T. Clark, 1991), vol. i, p. 268.

8 Claude Welch, *In This Name: The Doctrine of the Trinity in Contemporary Theology* (New York: Scribners, 1952), pp. 293–4.

9 *Church Dogmatics*, ed. G. W. Bromiley and T. F. Torrance (Edinburgh: T. & T. Clark, 1975), vol. i, part 1, p. 295.

10 Karl Rahner, *The Trinity*, trans. Joseph Donceel (New York: Herder & Herder, 1970), p. 22.

Further reading

What follows is a brief selection of books which specifically highlights recent developments in trinitarian theology. I would draw the reader's attention to several areas. They include new accounts of trinitarian theological development (Studer, de Margerie) including the modern period (Gunton [1995]); earlier classic texts on the importance of the doctrine for modern theology (Hodgson, Welch); restatement of the doctrine with application to a variety of contemporary theological issues (Hill, Gunton [1991], Jenson, Jüngel, Kasper, Kelly, Moltmann, Peters, Torrance [to whom much of my own thought in this essay is owed]) including liberation (Boff) and feminist theology (Johnson).

Boff, Leonardo, *Trinity and Society*, Maryknoll, New York: Orbis, 1988.

Congar, Yves, *I Believe in the Holy Spirit: Volumes i–iii*, London: Geoffrey Chapman, 1983.

   The Word and the Spirit, London: Geoffrey Chapman, 1986.

De Margerie, SJ, Bertrand, *The Christian Trinity in History*, Still River, Massachusetts: St Bede's Publications, 1982.

Gunton, Colin E., *The Promise of Trinitarian Theology*, Edinburgh: T. & T. Clark, 1991.

   'The Trinity in Modern Theology', in P. A. Byrne and J. L. Houlden, editors, *Companion Encyclopedia of Theology*, London: Routledge, 1995.

Hill, William J., *The Three-Personed God: The Trinity as a Mystery of Salvation*, Washington, DC: The Catholic University Press of America, 1982.

Hodgson, Leonard, *The Doctrine of the Trinity*, New York: Scribners, 1944.

Jenson, Robert W., *The Triune Identity: God According to the Gospel*, Philadelphia: Fortress, 1982.

Johnson, Elizabeth A., *She Who Is: The Mystery Of God in Feminist Theological Discourse*, New York: Crossroad, 1992.

Jüngel, Eberhard, *The Doctrine of the Trinity: God's Being is in Becoming*, Grand Rapids, Michigan: Eerdmans, 1976.

Kasper, Walter, *The God of Jesus Christ*, New York: Crossroad, 1989.

Kimel, Alvin F., *Speaking the Christian God: The Holy Trinity and the Challenge of Feminism*, Grand Rapids, Michigan: Eerdmans, 1992.

LaCugna, Catherine Mowry, *God For Us: The Trinity and Christian Life*, San Francisco: Harper, 1991.

Moltmann, Jürgen, *The Trinity and the Kingdom: The Doctrine of God*, San Francisco: Harper & Row, 1981.

Studer, Basil, *Trinity and Incarnation: The Faith of the Early Church*, Collegeville, Minnesota: The Liturgical Press, 1993.

Torrance, Thomas F., *The Trinitarian Faith: The Evangelical Theology of the Ancient Catholic Church*, Edinburgh: T. & T. Clark, 1994.

Trinitarian Perspectives: Toward Doctrinal Agreement, Edinburgh: T. & T. Clark, 1988.

Welch, Claude, *In This Name: The Doctrine of the Trinity in Contemporary Theology*, New York: Scribners, 1952.

Zizioulas, John D., *Being as Communion: Studies in Personhood and the Church*, London: Darton, Longman and Todd, 1985.

8 The doctrine of creation

COLIN GUNTON

THE DOCTRINE OF CREATION

All cultures, ancient and modern alike, seek for a way of accounting for the universe that will give their lives coherence and meaning. Creation theology, in the broadest sense of an enquiry into the divinity or divinities that shape or make our world, is a universal human concern, however different the forms that it can take. But among all the theologies, myths and theories, Christian theology is distinctive in the form and content of its teaching. It is credal in form, and this shows that the doctrine of creation is not something self-evident or the discovery of disinterested reason, but part of the fabric of the Christian response to revelation. 'I believe in God the Father, maker of Heaven and Earth.' Here the word 'maker' is understood in a particular sense. As it stands, it is ambiguous. It may refer to one who is like a human maker, a potter for example, who makes an object out of a material that is already to hand. But Christian theology has rejected that sense as inadequate. The unique contribution to thought made by Christian theologians of creation lies in their development of a view that God creates 'out of nothing'. This became possible by virtue of the trinitarian form of the doctrine. When in the late second century Irenaeus taught that God the Father created by means of his 'two hands', the Son and the Spirit, he was able to complete one stage in a process of intellectual development during which the implications of the Christian form of creation belief were drawn out.

To understand the distinctiveness of the development, it is important to realise that these three themes – creation as an article of the creed; creation out of nothing; and creation as the work of the whole Trinity, Father, Son and Holy Spirit – are in some way bound up with each other, both historically and systematically. Doctrinally, they produce the following features. First, the teaching that creation was 'out of nothing' affirms that God, in creating the world, had no need to rely on anything outside himself, so that creation is an act of divine sovereignty and freedom, an act of personal willing. It further implies that the universe, unlike God who is alone eternal and infinite, had a beginning in time and is limited in space. Here Christian teaching is in contradiction of almost every cosmology that the world has known. The biblical stress on the sovereignty of God, allied with the demonstration of that sovereignty in the resurrection of Jesus from the dead, led in due time to the realisation that to attribute eternity to anything other than God was to make that in effect divine.

But, second, it does not follow that creation was an arbitrary act upon the part of God. It was, rather, purposive, and in two senses: that it derives from the love of God, not simply his will; and that it exists for a purpose – to go somewhere we might say. Rather like a work of art, creation is a project, something God wills for its own sake and not because he has need of it. It is here that we can begin to understand something of the place of the doctrine of the Trinity in the development. Because that doctrine teaches that God is already, 'in advance of' creation, a communion of persons existing in loving relations, it follows that he does not need the world, and so is able to will the existence of something else simply for itself. The universe is therefore the outcome of God's love, but not its necessary outcome. It did not have to be, but rather is *contingent*, meaning – among other things, as we shall see – that the world is given value as a realm of being in its own right. In the words of Genesis it is 'very good', not only partly good or as a means to an end, but good simply as and for what it is and shall be: the created order.

A third feature of the doctrine, also deriving from its trinitarian structure, is that God remains in close relations of interaction with the creation, but in such a way that he makes it free to be itself. God's transcendence as the maker of all things is not of such a kind that he is unable also to be immanent in it through his 'two hands'. According to the New Testament, creation is *through* and *to* Christ, and this means that it is, so to speak, structured by the very one who became incarnate and as such part of the created order of which we are speaking. It follows that it is good because God himself, through his Son, remains in intimate and loving relations with it. Similarly, we can understand something of what it means for creation to be a kind of project if we recall that Basil of Caesarea described the Holy Spirit as the *perfecting cause* of the creation.[1] It is the work of God the Spirit, by relating the world to God the Father through Jesus Christ, to enable the created order to be truly itself, and so to move to that completedness which God intends for it. Thus although the doctrine of creation is chiefly concerned with God's establishing an order of things, in our past, so to speak, it is not merely concerned with that. It is a matter also of the *kind* of world that there is.

There is then an eschatology of creation, an understanding of a destiny which is something more than a return to its beginnings. The created world is that which God enables to exist in time and through time to come to its completion.

Fourth, a focus on the way the transcendent Creator is involved in the world through his two hands makes possible an understanding of the place of other concepts which are in close relation with the doctrine, especially 'conservation', 'preservation', 'providence' and 'redemption'. They are all to do with the way God works in and towards the creation, and we know about them because they are revealed in the characteristic forms of action of the Son and the Spirit. Conservation and preservation express God's continuing upholding of and care for his creation. God does not, like the machine-maker deity of some conceptions, simply leave his world to go its own way, but actively maintains it in being. Providence and redemption have a more forward-looking orientation, and refer to the forms of action by which God provides for the needs of the creation and enables it to achieve the end that was purposed for it from the beginning. All of them take their centre in the incarnation, perhaps particularly as it is understood by Athanasius in *On the Incarnation*. In Jesus of Nazareth, the Word made flesh, the one through whom the world was created comes in person to his world to remake that which threatened to fall into dissolution through sin and evil.

Fifth, the term 'redemption' reminds us that we cannot escape some engagement in this context with the question of evil. On the account being developed here, evil is that which prevents the created order from fulfilling its proper purpose. While Greek thought tended to trace the origin of evil to matter, Christian theology came to the view that, because all that God creates is good, evil must be something extraneous to or parasitic upon creation as a whole. If the universe is created good, and with an end in view, evil becomes that which corrupts the good creation and so thwarts God's purpose for it. At the centre of the problem is the doctrine of the Fall or fallenness of the human race, according to which human sin in some way involves the whole created order in evil. The human fall is sometimes traced to the fall of angels, or to some other force or agency, so that evil in some way corrupts the creation even before the Fall. However the matter is understood, the point for our purpose is that evil is attributed not to a fault in God's creating activity or in the created order as such, but to something which subverts it and must be overcome. Its existence means that creation's purpose can be achieved only by its redirection from within by the creator himself. Here once again, we encounter the centrality of christology and pneumatology. Given the all-polluting power of evil and its centre in human sin, redemption can be achieved only by the action of the one through whom the world was created. His becoming incarnate, dying and being raised by the Creator Spirit is the way through which the creation is redeemed (bought back) from its bondage to destruction, from within, without loss to its created integrity. The final redemption of creation will be completed only at its end, but in the meantime, anticipations of creation's final perfection are achieved whenever and wherever Christ and the Spirit hold sway.

Sixth, it follows from a number of features of the above that no theology of creation is complete without attention being paid to the place of humankind in the project. According to Genesis 1:27, God 'created man in his own image ... male and female he created them', and there has been in the tradition much discussion of what this means both for man and for his relation to the remainder of the created order. The traditional tendency to locate the image of God in reason or some other human endowment or quality is now much disputed in favour of a conception of the whole of human being as existing in relation to God, other human beings and the rest of the created order. The latter relation is in terms of 'dominion' (Genesis 1:26), which means a calling to be and to act in such a way as to offer the whole created order as a response of praise to its maker. But the distinctive place of the human creation cannot be understood apart from christology. Genesis makes the human race both the crown of, and uniquely responsible for, the shape that creation takes. By speaking of Jesus Christ as the true image of God, the New Testament shows that this responsibility takes shape through him.

Seventh, and related to the previous section, there are the ethical dimensions. These have come into the centre in the light of recent concerns about the environment, but it must be remembered that sexual relations, abortion, genetic engineering and war are also among the human activities that involve the doctrine of creation because they concern relationships between created persons and between them and the material world. If God's purpose is for the redemption and perfection of the creation, all human action will in some way or other involve the human response to God that is ethics.

As we now move to trace some of the central episodes in the history of the doctrine of creation, we shall find that all of these themes will figure in different ways. How each of them is treated determines the shape that any particular articulation of the doctrine takes. It is because of the different forms that the doctrine has taken over nearly two millennia that a historical account is indispensable to understanding the doctrine.

THE RISE AND FALL OF THE DOCTRINE OF CREATION

The doctrine of creation, like other Christian teaching, emerged out of two backgrounds: the Bible and the leading philosophies of the cosmos in the Greek culture which provided the context. Because the two worlds are both distinctively different from each other and themselves internally diverse, their interaction is very complex. During the development of the earliest doctrine, the Greek world was represented by a very wide range of influences, from some of the richest philosophies ever developed to the weirdest of speculations, but they do exhibit some common features. We shall for the sake of clarity take the two worlds one at a time, though it should be remembered, particularly when speaking of the Bible, that the books which make it up are themselves the product of a complex cultural history and are not hermetically sealed off from the worlds in which they were written.

When the biblical doctrine of creation is discussed, particularly in the light of modern disputes about science and religion, the opening chapters of Genesis are nearly always in the thick of things. This is scarcely surprising in the light of their profundity and position in the Bible, although they have often been misunderstood or misused, and become an unnecessary stumbling block to belief. But Genesis is by no means the only text for a theological account of creation. The reasons are two. First is the fact that Genesis crystallises what is found in other parts of the Old Testament, although sometimes in rather different form. The Psalms, 104 and 139 for example, celebrate God's creation of everything without the framework of days or an allusion to a first human couple. The famous speech of God from the whirlwind in Job 38–9 celebrates what is surely the main point of Old Testament witness, the sheer freedom and sovereignty of God over all the things that he has made, a note to be found nowhere outside the Bible, for in all other accounts, certainly in those of the Greeks, there are always constraints on divine action.

Second, it must be remembered that the primary source for Christian doctrine, through which the Old Testament is interpreted, is the New Testament, where the theology of creation is more prominent than is sometimes suggested. There are two formal statements: in Hebrews 11:3 the author claims that belief in creation is the object of faith; and in Revelation 4:11 there is what perhaps amounts to a summary credal confession: 'thou didst create all things, and by thy will they existed and were created'. Perhaps even more important are the writings which link creation with Jesus Christ in general and his resurrection in particular. In 1 Corinthians, Colossians and Hebrews, as well as the famous opening verses of the Gospel of John, Jesus Christ is celebrated as the mediator of creation, the one through whom God the Father created and continues to uphold the universe, and to whom it moves. The doctrine of creation is linked with the resurrection in Romans 4:17, which speaks of Abraham's faith in the God 'who gives life to the dead and calls into existence the things that do not exist'. That is scarcely surprising, for in raising Jesus from the dead God shows his lordship over the created order, the very freedom and sovereignty celebrated in the Old Testament.[2]

The work of the Spirit in creation is less prominent in the New Testament, except in one crucial respect. In reliance on texts such as Romans 8:11, some early theologians argued that it is by his Spirit that God the Father raised Jesus from the dead. Similarly, later in that chapter the Spirit appears in connection with the transformation of creation. If we take this along with other passages, we can see that the theologians who later spoke of the 'Creator Spirit' were not simply conjuring ideas out of thin air. Luke's gospel speaks of the Spirit's work in forming the child Jesus in the womb of his mother Mary, suggesting that the birth of Jesus is an act of divine re-creation, while behind it lie those Old Testament passages which suggest the Spirit as the vehicle of God's sovereign power over the created order, particularly, perhaps, Ezekiel's (37:1–14) prophecy of the dry bones, which are transformed by the divine Spirit in an act of visionary resurrection.

When we come to the Greeks, a very different atmosphere prevails. At the centre of their contribution to the discussion was a concern with reason, with seeking the explanation for why things are as they are. The early Greek poets, especially Homer and Hesiod, referred the world to two sets of forces: a number of gods and goddesses, often vying with one another for influence; and impersonal forces like 'chance', 'necessity' and 'fate', powers to which even the gods were subject. Unlike the sovereign God of the Bible, these gods could do only what had to be. The characteristic form of Greek philosophy arose out of an attempt to do something better than this, but these thinkers never freed themselves from some kind of dependence upon 'necessity', as is shown by Plato, who is often thought to be nearest to the Christian view.

Plato is not a static thinker, so that it is difficult to state categorically what his 'doctrine' was. But two features of his writings have shaped Christian theology, and it is these which I shall summarise. The first is his doctrine of forms, particularly as it appears in the *Republic*. This teaches that there is a set of eternal realities, discerned by the mind, which are more or less successfully incorporated in the material things that we perceive with our senses. These forms comprise the world of 'being': that which is always and unchanging, and so can be known by the mind. Over against them is the world of 'becoming': those things which cannot truly be the objects of knowledge because they are here today, but may tomorrow change into something else or disintegrate. Plato's world is dualist not in the sense that it distinguishes God from the world, but in dividing the world into two orders of being, the material or sensible and the ideal or intelligible. The latter is more real than the former, and later philosophers, particularly the Neoplatonists, were to develop this into a doctrine of degrees of being, according to which reality takes the form of a hierarchy, with pure matter at the foot and pure form at the top.

The potential for clashes between this teaching and the teaching of Genesis that all things God created are very good is manifest. For the Neoplatonist Plotinus, matter is not good at all, but evil, and at the very best becomes good only when *informed* by the higher realities. To put it simply: there is, if not a contradiction then certainly a tension, between saying that all things are good and saying that some things are so low on the scale of being that they are scarcely good at all. But the tension was hidden, if not removed, by some of the things said by Plato in the other work that is influential for later developments, the *Timaeus*. This is an odd and speculative work, but two things in particular should be noted. The first is that, like Genesis, it is affirmative of the created order. 'The world is beautiful and its maker good.'[3] The second, however, is that it remains tied to the Greek tradition of subjecting the Creator to some form of outside necessity. God is not the sovereign lord of all but one of three coeternal realities, matter, form and himself. He is the maker – the Greek word is *demiourgos*, workman – in the weaker sense of the word, for he does not *create* but only *forms* that which is already to hand.

The Christian doctrine of creation was developed when Christian thinkers entered the world of Greek thought and articulated their understanding of the creed in its shadow. Crucial episodes are as follows. In the work of Justin Martyr, we see the beginnings of a process of disentangling theology from Platonism. Justin did not develop a doctrine of creation out of nothing, but did see clearly that the Bible conceives the relation of God and the world differently from the Platonists. In his *Dialogue with Trypho*, sections 3–7, he tells of his conversion to Christianity in conversation with an old man who taught him to question whether we can know God by virtue of some affinity with God or some continuity between our mind and the divine. Justin's achievement is to suggest that to know God as Creator we need to be taught by the Holy Spirit rather than to rely on community of being between God and ourselves, as the Greeks believed to be the case. Here we see emerging one of the essential articles of a doctrine of creation, that because God is universal Creator, everything, whether matter or spirit, is alike created, and nothing but God is eternal and divine.

By strengthening the trinitarian aspects of the doctrine of creation, Irenaeus was able, first, to develop a markedly positive view of the value of the created order, material and spiritual alike. Here he was helped by his need to out-think the strongly dualistic philosophy of some of his Gnostic opponents. Against their teaching that spirit was good and matter evil, Irenaeus affirmed, for christological and pneumatological reasons, the goodness of the whole of the created order. He is particularly strong on the eschatological dimensions of creation, and an affirmation that all the creation, not just mind or soul, is to be redeemed. Second, Irenaeus achieved the definitive expression of creation out of nothing. The God who creates through his two hands is utterly free over against that which he creates, and requires no assistance from intermediate beings. This contradiction of a central tenet of Greek philosophy demonstrates that the doctrine of creation out of nothing is a unique intellectual achievement which emerged only as a result of the struggle of the early theologians to affirm the goodness and createdness of matter in the context of Greek culture.[4]

Two other theologians are worth a mention at this stage for their developments of this tradition. The motif of the 'homogeneity' of the creation is developed by Basil in the fourth century. His exposition of Genesis, though by no means free of platonic influence, is important for his denial of the divinity and eternity of the heavenly bodies, as it was taught by Aristotle, and later by the church. The sun is, like other things, corruptible.[5] Basil is insistent that everything other than God is created and contingent, and therefore the same kind of reality. There is no hierarchy of mind and matter. The achievement of John Philoponos, two centuries later, is similar, and important for his influence on Galileo. Not only did his belief in God make possible his anticipation of later discoveries in natural science, but he also reinforced the teaching of creation out of nothing by exposing contradictions in Greek views of the infinity of the universe.[6]

However, the development of the doctrine was by no means as straightforward as the foregoing account may have suggested. All the time there was a pull in another direction, and it has had incalculable effects. Its chief causes are an embarrassment with the form of the opening chapters of Genesis and a tendency to interpret them, *and so the whole doctrine*, platonically. The theologians whose achievements we have noted are significant for their resistance to the Greek dualism which in some way elevates the spiritual or intellectual above the material as a higher order of creation. It was, however, others who set the tone for the main developments in the West until the end of the Middle Ages.

The achievement of Origen and Augustine in the third and fifth centuries was the combining of credal and Greek elements in their theologies of creation.[7] Taking his inspiration from Philo of Alexandria's allegorical interpretation of Genesis, Origen taught that there was a two-stage creation. First of all God created a higher world of spiritual beings, whose fall provided the occasion for the second creation, the material world, as a place of reformation where they could freely learn to return to their maker. While Origen did not deny the goodness of the material world, he saw it as good chiefly instrumentally, as a means for the salvation of the spiritual beings. Although he did contribute to the development of a systematic understanding of the work of divine creation, and particularly of its relation to redemption, this concession to Platonism made at best an ambiguous affirmation of the goodness of the material world. In contrast, Augustine's blending of Platonism and the Christian creed avoided such simplifications, and in the process made major contributions to some of the philosophical problems associated with the teaching of creation out of nothing. On the Greek view that the matter from which creation is formed is eternal, there is no obvious problem about the relation of time and eternity. The demiurge at some time shapes matter and form into *this* particular universe. But the Christian view entailed an absolute beginning, and to avoid the embarrassing suggestion that God is in some way limited by time, Augustine, in anticipation of views contained in Einstein's relativity theory, argued that space and time were created *with* the world. That is to say, space and time are not absolute realities that in some way constrain God, but are the *result* of there being a created universe.

But Augustine's achievement was also at the price of continuing to hold a two-stage and hierarchical view of creation, according to which God first created the platonic forms and then the (lower) material world, which he shaped in the light of the forms. This meant that despite Augustine's determined fight against the heresy of Manichaeism, which held that matter was evil, he was never able to affirm as fully as Irenaeus the goodness of material things. Matter was a means to the higher realm and not fully real and good in itself, and in this respect he deeply affected the thought of the centuries to follow. Because he taught that the material universe was shaped in the light of the previously created forms, Augustine allowed them to displace Christ as the effective framework of the created order. The mediation of creation through Christ had for Irenaeus formed the central argument for his affirmation of the reality and goodness of the material world, a goodness he saw reaffirmed in the use of bread and wine in Christian worship. It is noteworthy that Augustine scarcely appeals to christology in his doctrine of creation.

The effects this had on the future of Christian theology are very great, for it impinged on two central areas. First of all, the relation of creation and redemption is thrown out of kilter. It was due to Augustine that the doctrine of predestination as the choosing of a limited number of people from the mass of the lost came to take hold, and the associated view that salvation meant not the redemption of man in and with the whole created order, but apart from it, sometimes even out of it. Redemption thus becomes a human, not a universal project. Second, creation appears more like an arbitrary act of will than the ordered expression of love. It would not be fair to say that this is the whole story with Augustine, rather that here we have tendencies which deeply affected the future. But what did happen was that christology and pneumatology came to have little substantive effect in the development of the doctrine throughout the Middle Ages, so that it was often treated more as an article of natural theology than as part of the creed. It is surely significant that William of Ockham in the fourteenth century could even refer to the first verses of John's Gospel without mentioning the place of Christ in creation. In his thought the conception of creation as an arbitrary act of will became one of the crucial episodes in the movement of much modern culture to atheism.[8]

But there is another side to a very complicated story, and it can be brought out in a contrast between Ockham and his great predecessor and intellectual opponent, Thomas Aquinas. A major focus of Aquinas' cosmology is his doctrine of causes, by virtue of which he argues that the whole of creation is dependent upon God, the uncaused cause of all. In his system, the Aristotelian doctrine of causes replaces the platonic forms as his way of providing a structuring for the universe, which is understood as a system of interlocking causal agents, hierarchically conceived, requiring explanation by divinity. But the effect is the same, and although Aquinas affirms the doctrine of creation out of nothing, he makes little of it, and certainly not of its determination by christology and pneumatology. The result is that the weight of his doctrine falls on conceiving the universe in terms of its necessary dependence on God. That is to say, Aquinas stresses one aspect of what it means to say that the world is contingent – that it is dependent upon God – but is weaker on the other, that the world is given its own relatively independent being. Some commentators have noted how near this theologian can sometimes come to pantheism.[9]

To Ockham, and to a certain extent to his predecessor Duns Scotus, goes the credit – if it is credit, as many would deny – of clearing away the intermediate world of forms and causes that had dominated medieval discussion and developing a strong doctrine of the contingence of the world understood as the outcome of God's unnecessitated free will. In Ockham we return to a strong assertion of creation out of nothing, in which the world is set free from any logical relation on God, and is simply the outcome of sheer will. But because there is here, also, no christology and pneumatology, the structuring element which had provided the framework for medieval conceptions, the forms and causes, is not replaced by anything else, so that God and the world come adrift, and the way of conceiving their continuing relation comes into question.

Two alternative ways were developed of re-envisaging that relationship. The first was that of Martin Luther and John Calvin, who returned to a trinitarian conception of a kind that clearly assisted the emergence of modern science.[10] Here threads stretching back to Basil and Philoponos are again brought into the tapestry. Because the world is, as a whole, the creation, with no necessary links to divinity, and because it is conceived as contingent, science as the study of the world in its actual rather than logical relations becomes possible. Neither the doctrine of creation nor modern science can be understood without some awareness of their inextricable relation.[11]

But, second, other forces were at work to undermine the link between theology and science, so that the outcome of the development was that the doctrine of creation, or a substitute for it, became in large measure the province of science, and scientists replaced theologians as the authorities for knowledge of the created world. Culturally, we might say, the Enlightenment, which in its own way returned to dualistic ways of thought owed to the Greeks, quickly supervened upon the Reformation as the main determinant of the way we understand the created world. Isaac Newton's distinction between relative and absolute space and time, undermining Augustine's contribution, led to the effective divinisation of space and time and to a dualism between the world as we experience it and something unknown beyond it. This in its turn led to Immanuel Kant's contention that there is no way of moving by thought or argument between this world and that of its supposed Creator.[12]

The chief effect of Newtonianism so far as the doctrine of creation is concerned was that it became a philosophy that precluded any satisfactory conception of the continuing relation of God and the world. The easiest way to understand this is from the central metaphor by which the philosophy of the Enlightenment understood the cosmos, which was as a machine. According to this picture – and it is crucial to remember that it is a picture and not the final truth about the world – it was easier to understand God as the one who made the world and left it to run than it was to conceive of any continuing relations with it. There could be creation out of nothing, but little notion of conservation, providence and redemption. Those who wished to combine this philosophy with Christian belief often appealed to miracles as proofs that God continued to intervene from time to time, but this is unsatisfactory because it conceives the relation of God and the world in so external a fashion. God and the world were pictured in such a way that any continuing involvement became a kind of *tour de force,* and the well known problem of the 'god of the gaps' – God's being driven progressively from the world – developed. Here is one place where the failure to maintain a trinitarian conception of the relation of God and the world through much of Christian history exacted a high price. The processes of criticism had driven out the old Platonic and Aristotelian way of conceiving the structure of the created world, but in their place came a conception which excluded meaningful divine action altogether.

Another hostage had been given to fortune on the threshold of the modern age. In response to pressures from the Reformation and elsewhere, both Catholic and Protestant branches of the Western church had begun to move to a rather literalist interpretation of scripture. However, the literal or absolute truth of Genesis was not a feature of the treatment of the doctrine of creation in the early centuries. Irenaeus, whose concern was for the integrity of the whole of creation in the light of the incarnation, makes little appeal to Genesis, while his more rationalist successors, Origen and Augustine in particular, made much use of an allegorical interpretation of the text. When it is remembered that the Western church had also tended to accept back into theology Aristotle's belief in the eternity of the heavenly bodies, it is scarcely surprising that there was a clash between ecclesiastical authority and Galileo, though secularist propaganda has greatly exaggerated the significance of the conflict.[13]

Worse was to come, for in the nineteenth century further defences of a certain way of understanding the truth of scripture were to make the impact of Darwinism far worse than it need have been. But the controversy did not concern only scripture. Prominent in early worries about evolution was its apparent relegation of the human species to a similar level to that of the animals, undermining teaching of its uniqueness. Again, however, it must be remembered that that is by no means an achievement peculiar to theories of evolution. The real threat to human uniqueness – and so to such personal realities as love and artistic endeavour, as well as rationality and science – came long before Darwin was born, as Coleridge and others had realised. The threat to the personal came from the philosophy which made everything simply the outcome of impersonal mechanism. In one respect, Darwinism represented but a modification of Newtonianism, its impersonal categories applied to the way in which life emerged from that which was not alive.

There is still a dispute between the hard Darwinism which turns Evolution, as a kind of deity, into the sole creative force, and various attempts to combine a theory of evolution with some conception of continuing divine action in the world. That God creates out of nothing does not entail that he creates a world fixed from the beginning; as we have seen, the reverse is the case if creation is interpreted as project. The outcome, however, is that it is widely believed that the doctrine of creation has been discredited by the Galileo and Darwin episodes in particular. It is forgotten that many of the great names of nineteenth-century science, for example Michael Faraday and James Clerk Maxwell, were natural scientists because of their Christian belief, not in spite of it.[14]

THE DOCTRINE OF CREATION TODAY

In the theology of Friedrich Schleiermacher and much of that of the later nineteenth century, the decline of the doctrine of creation continued. Schleiermacher, under the impact of Kant, returned to a kind of Platonism: the world existed in a timeless dependence upon God, so that any particular divine action within the created order became difficult to conceive. While he had good reasons for his attempt to avoid both mechanistic deism and pantheism, his funnelling of all theological statements about the world through the human experience of absolute dependence inevitably brought him too near to the latter. He himself noted that creation is reduced to a form of providence conceived to operate timelessly.

The twentieth century has seen some cautious attempts by theologians to reopen the question, notable among them that of Karl Barth, one not else-where characterised by caution. What Barth felt could not be done, by him at any rate, was to engage with the question of science. What he did, however, was to attempt to reintegrate the doctrines of creation and redemption. According to him, God's relations with the world are determined by his covenant love, which creates, out of nothing, a world in which the covenant can be realised. Barth returned to patristic insights by strongly asserting that the doctrine is not the result of philosophical speculation, but one of the articles of the creed. Creation is, on this account, the external basis of the covenant, the covenant the internal basis of creation. This link between creation and redemption, despite its problems, enabled the two to come into far more positive relation than had sometimes been the case. It also enabled Barth to develop fine accounts of providence, of the human person and of the ethics of creation.

Barth's pupil, T. F. Torrance, has taken major steps towards the renewal of the doctrine, though he has concentrated not so much on the doctrine itself as on a number of features which determine its shape. At the centre are, first, the relation between God and the world revealed in the fact that Jesus Christ is both God and man; and, second, the possibilities for a new openness between science and theology consequent on the overcoming of platonic and Newtonian dualism by Einsteinian science and in the work of philosophers of science like Michael Polanyi. One very important claim is that the notion of contingency, implying that the universe displays rational patterns which are yet open, is both the consequence of the doctrine of creation and reveals parallels between scientific and theological rationality. A substantive and rich treatment of the doctrine of creation has recently been essayed by Wolfhart Pannenberg, whose achievement is notable for its attempt to make christology and pneumatology definitive for his understanding. He argues that the basis of the world's distinction from God is to be found in the Son's self-distinction from God the Father.

Other approaches to the doctrine have been made by scientists whose attitudes to Christian belief are various. Prominent in British discussion are Arthur Peacocke and John Polkinghorne, who represent a continuing tradition of seeing science as itself the source or the basis of the possibility of a doctrine of creation. Developments in such areas as quantum theory, biology and chaos theory are held to signal conceptions of a new openness in the shape of reality which enables theology to conceive not a God of the gaps, but God broadly involved in the formation of the world. In this, encouragement is given by the writings of some scientists, particularly cosmologists, many of whom now engage in varieties of theological speculation.[15]

One urgent need in the present is for an ethic of creation. The domination of earlier centuries by the metaphor of mechanism, allied to the view that the image of God is to be found in human reason, has led to a number of regrettable consequences, particularly in ecological ethics. A theologian to have made this topic his major concern is Jürgen Moltmann. If the universe is treated simply as a mechanism, within the control of human reason and without direct reference to God, those dimensions of it which are not mechanical, and particularly its living creatures, are treated with despite, and react in such a way that our own existence is threatened. This disorder is often blamed upon the Christian teaching about human dominion over the creation, but mistakenly. As Pannenberg and others have pointed out, the crisis has developed as a result of the modern abandonment of a religious view of the world.[16] If we cease to see the world as God's creation, we shall treat it not as a project in which we are invited to share but as an absolute possession to be exploited as we will.

However, one response to the crisis has taken the form of a lurch in the opposite direction, to views which in effect return to a view of the divinity of the universe, as in the so-called 'ecofeminist' theologies.[17] These doctrines tend to assimilate the doctrine of redemption to the doctrine of creation. The creation saves because it is divine process. Against this, orthodox Christian teaching has always held that the whole creation, and particularly the sinful human creation, is in need of redemption by a God who is other than it because, as it is, it fails to achieve its proper end. In any case, the universe without human ordering would simply destroy us. There is a proper human dominion over the creation, which must not be confused with a wrongful domination and exploitation. A garden without a gardener will produce little of the food and other necessities for the life of the one who is, furless and clawless, among the most vulnerable of the world's species. A pantheism in which we are simply a function of the world's process is a world in which our otherness, our capacity to be ourselves, would be taken away. Rather than reacting in this way, we need to move from seeing creation as a mere given to receiving it as gift to be cherished, perfected and returned: as grace evoking gratitude.

The heart of the matter is worship, for it is there that are presented and enacted both the Creator's redemptive interaction with his world and the response of the one in whom the creation becomes articulate. Worship as word and sacrament enables us to not only to understand but to live the relation between creator and creation. That means, in summary, (1) the existence of the universe in distinction from, but continuing dependence upon the Creator; (2) the life, death and resurrection of Jesus Christ as at the centre of God's providential, redemptive and perfecting action in and towards the world; and (3) the action of the Holy Spirit who, sent by God the Father, enables the world to be itself by restoring its directedness to perfection through Jesus Christ, the mediator of both creation and redemption.

Notes

1 Basil of Caesarea, *On the Holy Spirit* xv, 36, 38. Translations of this and most other Patristic works cited in this chapter can be found in the series *The Ante-Nicene Fathers,* eds. A. Roberts and J. Donaldson, reprinted 1977, and *The Nicene and Post-Nicene Fathers*, eds. P. Schaff and H. Wace, reprinted 1989 (Edinburgh: T. & T. Clark; Grand Rapids, Michigan: Eerdmans).

2 It is worth noting that the nearest thing before the writings of Christian theologians to the affirmation of creation out of nothing is to be found in 2 Maccabees 7:28, which derived from the time when Jewish belief in the resurrection of the dead began to take shape.

3 Plato, *Timaeus*, 29.

4 Gerhard May, *Creatio ex Nihilo. The Doctrine of 'Creation out of Nothing' in Early Christian Thought,* trans. A. S. Worrall (Edinburgh: T. & T. Clark, 1994).

5 Basil of Caesarea, *Hexaemeron*, 5.1.

6 Richard Sorabji, 'John Philoponus', in Richard Sorabji (ed.), *Philoponus and the Rejection of Aristotelian Science* (London: Duckworth, 1987), pp. 1–40.

7 For Origen, see *On First Principles*, book 2, chapter 2; for Augustine, *The City of God*, books 11–12 and *Confessions*, books 10–12.

8 Hans Blumenberg, *The Legitimacy of the Modern Age*, trans. R. M. Wallace (Cambridge, Massachusetts, and London: MIT Press, 1983).

9 For example, Adolph Harnack, *History of Dogma*, trans. W. McGilchrist (London: Williams and Norgate, 1899), vol. vi, pp. 184–5.

10 Harold Nebelsick, *The Renaissance, the Reformation and the Rise of Science* (Edinburgh: T. & T. Clark, 1992).

11 An influential expression of this claim is Michael B. Foster, 'The Christian Doctrine of Creation and the Rise of Modern Natural Science', *Mind* 43 (1934): 446–68.

12 Thomas F. Torrance, *Transformation and Convergence within the Frame of Knowledge. Explorations in the Interrelations of Scientific and Theological Enterprise* (Belfast: Christian Journals, 1984).

13 F. J. Crehan, SJ, *The Cambridge History of the Bible*, ed. S. L. Greenslade (Cambridge: Cambridge University Press, 1963), vol. iii, pp. 225–7.

14 For an illuminating story, see Geoffrey Cantor, *Michael Faraday: Sandemanian and Scientist. A Study of Science and Religion in the Nineteenth Century* (London: Macmillan, 1991).

15 See, for example, Paul Davies, *The Mind of God* (London: Penguin Books, 1993).

16 Wolfhart Pannenberg, *Systematic Theology*, trans. Geoffrey W. Bromiley (Edinburgh: T. & T. Clark, 1994), vol. ii, p. 204.

17 See, for example, Sallie McFague, *Models of God. Theology for an Ecological, Nuclear Age* (London: SCM Press, 1987).

Further reading

Anderson, B. W., editor, *Creation in the Old Testament*, Philadelphia: Fortress, 1984.

Barth, Karl, *Church Dogmatics*, translation edited by G.W. Bromiley and T. F. Torrance, Edinburgh: T. & T. Clark, 1956–75, volume III.

Gilkey, Langdon, *Maker of Heaven and Earth*, New York: Doubleday, 1959.

May, Gerhard, *Creatio ex Nihilo. The Doctrine of 'Creation out of Nothing' in Early Christian Thought*, translated by A. S. Worrall, Edinburgh: T. & T. Clark, 1994.

Moltmann, Jürgen, *God in Creation. An Ecological Doctrine of Creation*, translated by Margaret Kohl, London: SCM Press, 1985.

Nebelsick, Harold, *The Renaissance, the Reformation and the Rise of Science*, Edinburgh: T. & T. Clark, 1992.

Norris, Richard, *God and the World in Early Christian Thought*, London: A. & C. Black: 1965.

Pannenberg, Wolfhart, *Systematic Theology*, volume II, translated by Geoffrey W. Bromiley, Edinburgh: T. & T. Clark, 1994.

Torrance, Thomas F., *Divine and Contingent Order*, Oxford: Oxford University Press, 1981.

9 Human being, individual and social

KEVIN VANHOOZER

'Know thyself.' Socrates' exhortation is as urgent, and problematic, as ever: urgent, because the human race at the dawn of the third millennium, following the demise of the Christian paradigm and the break-up of modernity, is suffering from a collective identity crisis; problematic, because it demands the impossible, since to know oneself truly involves knowing *more* than oneself. Humans – the self-interpreting animals – have nonetheless responded to the challenge with creativity and zest, striving for self-knowledge through conceptual schemes and cultural works alike.

A THEOLOGICAL STORY?

What is man, that thou are mindful of him? *(Psalm 8:4)*

To what extent is 'man' the proper study not only of mankind, as Alexander Pope suggested, but of theology as well? Theological anthropology offers a distinctive and decisive perspective on the issue of what it means to be human – a question of no little controversy, and one whose answer has wide-reaching consequences not only for the understanding, but also for the practice, of human being: for debates about genetic engineering, human rights, ecology, sexuality, education and politics. The task of Christian theology is to clarify what is distinctively theological in its account of personhood and to formulate criteria for what is authentically Christian in its accounts of human being.

Theological anthropology: method and significance

For all their borrowings from philosophy, virtually none of the early Christian theologians felt obliged to adhere to Socrates' principle. The human creature enjoys neither metaphysical nor methodological pride of place: humanity comes second both in the order of being and in the order of knowing. Augustine's famous prayer – 'our hearts are restless until they find their rest in thee' – expresses a keen sense of humanity's orientation towards

God. The human creature comes second to God, both in the order of being (namely, creation) and in the order of knowledge (namely, revelation). The human being is a 'metaphysical animal', constituted by a desire for what is greater than itself, for ultimate reality. John Calvin develops Augustine's insight into a methodological first principle: 'Without knowledge of God there is no knowledge of self.'[1] Medieval and Reformed theologians, as well as their creeds and confessions, typically place their discussions of anthropology after the doctrine of God. Theological anthropology is an implicit and derivative, not explicit and foundational, doctrine. We only reach the stage of theological anthropology when we affirm that man is a being who has to do with God, or rather, when we affirm that God is the one who has to do with human being. The primary sources for classical Christian thinking about human being are the doctrine of God and the book of Genesis.

Modern theology, in the wake of the turn towards the subject by René Descartes and Immanuel Kant, reversed Calvin's maxim: there is no knowledge of God except through knowledge of self. 'There is none that can read God aright, unless he first spell Man.'[2] Human subjectivity acquires foundational status; the doctrine of God becomes an implication of some aspect of human being. Friedrich Schleiermacher, for instance, conceives of theology as the science of (human) faith rather than the science of God. For Rudolf Bultmann, theological statements are primarily statements about human existence. Modern theology reverses the polarities between God and human being; anthropology has thus become an 'omnipresent element' correlated with each of the major theological topics.

The turn to the subject has not gone unchallenged in twentieth-century theology. For to begin theology by reflecting on human experience seems only to exchange one mystery for another. Furthermore, though Christian theology clearly deals both with God and humanity, the issue is whether Christian anthropology should be anthropocentric rather than theocentric. Karl Barth, an early critic of modern theology, charged liberal theology with never getting beyond anthropology. Barth modifies Calvin's maxim in one crucial respect: he maintains that there is no knowledge of God or self apart from knowledge of Jesus Christ. In Christ, God reveals his 'humanity', that is, his being with and for the human creature. We may therefore say, in the light of the incarnation, that humanity is a theme of theology, not in spite of, but *because* God is the theme of theology. In sum, theological anthropology is the attempt to think through the meaning of the human story, as it unfolds from Genesis through the Gospels to the Apocalypse and as it is lived out before, with and by God.

Stories and sciences of humanity: non-theological anthropology

Human being is a theme not only of the biblical story of creation, fall and redemption, but of diverse stories, told by scientists, poets, philosophers and historians among others. Which version is authoritative: that which privileges the notions of natural cause and universal law, or that which speaks of nurture rather than nature and of actual existence rather than of abstract essence? What is the relation between the Christian story of human being and the various accounts of the natural and human sciences? On the one hand, it is difficult simply to ignore what the arts and sciences say about human being; on the other, it is theologically inappropriate merely to add a few Christian elements to a non-theological understanding that is left essentially untouched. An alternative approach is for theologians critically to appropriate non-theological anthropologies. Secular descriptions are provisional versions of human reality that need to be deepened, or perhaps disciplined, by explicitly Christian beliefs.

The human creature is, to a large extent, a 'microcosm' of the world as a whole. Human being has a material dimension that is a proper object of analysis by the natural sciences: 'dust thou art, and unto dust shalt thou return' (Genesis 3:19). One can study, for instance, the chemical composition of the human body. The natural sciences, however, taken by themselves, provide only a truncated account of human being. They succeed in analysing the human creature's relation to the rest of the material world, but neither biochemistry nor genetics can adequately explain human behaviour. Adultery, for example, is not simply the 'effect' of a genetic predisposition to sow one's DNA. The physical sciences may account for Nature, but not Freedom. Human action requires at least three more distinct levels of analysis: the behavioural and the social, focusing on individuals and communities respectively, and the spiritual. It is not possible to understand cultural works with categories taken from the physical sciences; the study of human society is irreducible to the language of matter in motion.

Human beings are not only sentient but sapient, able not only to have sensations and experiences but to reflect on and interpret them. What distinguishes *homo sapiens* from other creatures is rationality. Early modern philosophers agreed with Aristotle: to be human is to be a rational animal. The Enlightenment preoccupation with what is universal in the human condition was influenced both by the classical Christian view that what defines humanity is the soul rather than the body, and by the conviction that reason could be used to define the essence of the human animal.

In the nineteenth century, the new 'human' sciences challenged the Enlightenment view that there is a single universal human nature: 'Whatever else modern anthropology asserts ... it is firm in the conviction that men unmodified by the customs of particular places do not in fact exist.'[3] The discovery that human being is nurtured in disparate historical contexts had a tremendous impact on the concept of humanity: 'man is an animal suspended in webs of significance he himself has spun'.[4] Culture is one such web. Wilhelm Dilthey suggested that, whereas the natural sciences seek to explain the world by formulating causal laws, the human sciences seek to understand human being by interpreting what individuals and societies have done. Life – both individual and corporate – is a text, culture a public document. Social anthropologists find it difficult to draw lines between what is universal and necessary in the human condition and what is only conventional and arbitrary. Cultural anthropologists offer 'thick descriptions' of cultures, and so determine the range of the variety of the human species. It is only by charting the historical careers of individual cultures that one eventually begins to grasp what are the parameters that define human nature. The study of culture 'provides the link between what men are intrinsically capable of becoming and what they actually, one by one, in fact become'.[5]

The arts represent another strategy for responding to Socrates' admonition. Human beings are self-interpreting animals.[6] The 'humanities' express both the universals and the uniqueness, the constants and the contingencies of human selfhood. Literature is a laboratory wherein authors study the human condition by exploring the panoply of human possibilities. Aristotle held poetry to convey universal truth and thus to be more philosophical than history. Painters, similarly, seek self-understanding through self-portraiture. Rembrandt's works, it has been said, portray the whole Protestant doctrine of human being. It is perhaps in music above all that humanity flexes its freedom and explores its spirit. Melodies are 'the supreme mystery of man' and have the power to mend, or rend, the heart in ways that are inexplicable by psychology or physics alike.[7] Brahms's fourth symphony, for example, takes us to the very threshold of transcendence and the theological, as do other poetic and painterly renditions of the human condition.

An incoherent story?

According to the novelist Walker Percy, the conventional wisdom of the twentieth century about human being contains two major components, the one owing to modern science, the other representing a rather attenuated legacy of Christian faith. On the one hand, we understand human being 'as an organism in an environment, a sociological unit ... endowed genetically like other organisms with needs and drives'; on the other hand, we view humans 'to be somehow endowed with certain other unique properties ... certain inalienable rights, reason, freedom, and an intrinsic dignity'.[8] Percy believes that most educated Westerners would assent to both propositions, but that these two propositions, taken together, are radically incoherent. It is increasingly clear in philosophy and general culture alike that personhood has become an endangered concept. Modern theories of the self no longer yield self-understanding.

While scientific accounts of human being may be provisional and incomplete, the philosopher's stories struggle with the near incoherence of their subject matter. All animals exhibit various kinds of behaviour, but none so paradoxical as the human. All creatures have an instinct for survival, but only the human creature takes foolhardy risks. All creatures are mortal, but only the human creature dreams of immortality. Only humans are capable both of war and peace, poetry and pornography, rationality and self-deception, greatness and pettiness, heroism and villainy. The challenge to philosophical anthropology is to account, in a coherent conceptual scheme, both for our optimism about humanity's creative possibilities and our pessimism about humanity's destructive potential.

Several postmodern thinkers deny that there is any fixed human nature and question whether *homo sapiens* is really a 'rational animal'. Michel Foucault has rushed, like Friedrich Nietzsche's madman, into the village square to announce not the death of God but the death of Man. The vaunted autonomous 'knowing subject' does not order experience rationally, as Kant mistakenly thought; on the contrary, the subject's experience is ordered by the prevailing cultural and ideological codes. What is falsely called knowledge is not merely pride but power. 'Man', the sovereign subject of knowledge, 'is only a recent invention.'[9] The knowing subject is only a proxy of institutional power. The human sciences should therefore be replaced by cultural studies and ideology critique.

The human creature appears inherently unstable, a tensile being whose existence is paradoxical to the modern mind and an open question to the postmodern. From a theological perspective, however, the disproportion or fault-line that threatens to rip human being apart is not that of body and soul, nor finitude and infinity, but rather the tension between what men and women were originally created and destined to be, on the one hand, and what they have actually become, on the other. Theological anthropology is, in this context, intimately related to the gospel, to the Good News that human life is not meaningless. When the Spirit of God ministers the Word of God, 'the self-understanding of man is not eliminated but penetrated, turned around, brought into a new direction and under a new lordship'.[10]

BEGINNINGS AND ENDINGS: THE CLASSICAL PARADIGM

Christian anthropologies affirm that both the beginning and the ending of the human story, both the origin and destiny of human being, are ultimately to be understood in the light of the triune God's creating, redeeming and sanctifying activity.

Human origins: sources of the self

Three indicative statements – all taken from Genesis, the book of 'beginnings' – form the leading themes in Christian reflection about human beings. Theological anthropology begins with these statements of faith and seeks, through reflection, greater understanding.

Being in the image of God

So God created man in his own image. *(Genesis 1:27)*

Christians ground their affirmation of human dignity and personhood in the special resemblance of the human creature to its Creator. Yet just what it is to be in God's image is a matter of some theological dispute. Is the *imago Dei* something humans have, do or are? To be in the *imago Dei* refers, first, to humanity's unique capacity for communion with God. With regard to all other creatures, God said, 'Let it be', but the creation of human being is prefaced by divine deliberation: 'Let us make.' All other creatures were made according to some generic pattern ('after their kind'), but the human creature was made after the divine pattern ('in our likeness'). Being in the image of God distinguishes the human creature from all others and renders human existence inviolable (Genesis 9:3, 6).

Irenaeus, the first Church Father to offer a systematic discussion of the *imago Dei*, drew a distinction between 'image' and 'likeness'. He suggested that the former refers to humanity's natural rational and moral capacities while the latter refers to the spiritual aspect of the human condition that had been lost through sin but restored through grace. The 'form' of the human consists chiefly in one's intellectual capacities; the 'matter' of the human may be sinful or holy, depending on the extent to which one recovers the grace lost at the Fall. Augustine similarly located the human analogy to God in terms of the mind or soul, though he developed his position on the basis of his interpretation of the Trinity. Human being bears certain vestiges of the Trinity ('Let *us* make'), vestiges which Augustine finds in the human soul, namely, the 'trinity' of memory, intelligence and will. Augustine's psychological analogy, though rooted in the Trinity, tends towards oneness in its concept of God and towards individualism in its ensuing anthropology. This interpretation of the soul as the seat of the likeness to God was the normative view in Western theology until modern times.

Finite creaturely being

God formed man of dust from the ground, and breathed into his nostrils the breath of life; and man became a living being. *(Genesis 2:7)*

Human being is a psycho-physical creature, an embodied soul or ensouled body. That the story of human origins occurs in the context of creation in general suggests that humans, like being in general, are dependent for their energy and matter on a source other than themselves. This dependence on God is not a complication but the theme of the human story, not a degeneration but the original condition of humankind. Finitude is not a problem that has to be solved by religion. 'And God saw what he had made, and behold, it was very good' (Genesis. 1:31). The limitations and givens of human existence and the created order should not be rejected as constraints but accepted as enabling conditions for individual and social being. If human beings no longer feel at home in the world, it is not because the world is an inappropriate environment, but rather because they have polluted it, and themselves, by refusing the divine intention behind the created order.

Classical theology, despite its acknowledgement of the goodness of creation, tended, under the influence of Neoplatonism and other Hellenistic conceptual schemes, to privilege the soul over the body. A dualism of body and soul, in which the two were thought to be separate though related substances, eventually invaded Christian anthropology.[11] The rational soul, which God breathed into human being, was considered the superior part of the human constitution. Indeed, for Augustine the soul images God when it governs the body by using it as an instrument of knowing, willing and loving. It is the individual in his spiritual interiority that corresponds to the one God in his divine sovereignty.

Socio-sexual being

It is not good that man should be alone; I will make him a helper fit for him. *(Genesis 2:18)*

This third indicative sentence states that human being is relational in a way that the other creatures are not. Sexual differentiation and relation are more than matters of biology. When humans are thought to be like God by virtue of their rational souls, however, the differences between the sexes tends not to be thought theologically significant. The history of the church's thinking about the body–soul relation is littered with unhealthy attitudes towards human sexuality. Patristic and medieval writers, with some exceptions, condemned the sensual pleasure of sexual intercourse and made celibacy mandatory for clergy. Yet Adam's loneliness in the absence of a female partner indicates the social, not merely sexual, character of the difference between male and female.

Human destiny: destinations of the self

What is God's final purpose for the human creature? If ethics defines the true end of human life, the 'good' life, then we could say that three ethical imperatives follow from the three preceding indicative statements. These imperatives guide human striving as we make the effort to exist and realise our desire to be.

The image of the Son: righteousness

Put on the new nature, created after the likeness of God in true righteousness and holiness. *(Ephesians 4:24)*

The image of God concerns not only human origins but also human destiny. For Martin Luther and John Calvin, the *imago Dei* is less a matter of static properties than of a dynamic orientation of the whole person towards God. Sin turns the human creature away from its true destiny with God and bends the human creature in upon itself. Calvin continues to identify the *imago Dei* with the soul, but insists that the soul has become corrupt. The true image of God is seen only in Jesus Christ: he is the 'image of the invisible God' (Colossians 1:15); he 'bears the very stamp of his [God's] nature' (Hebrews 1:3). Luther calls Jesus 'God's proper man'. Christ is the true image of humanity: 'mankind's destiny in Christ is precisely the fruition of mankind's origin in Christ'.[12] The first 'ethical' imperative – 'put on the new nature, created after the likeness of God in true righteousness' – thus concerns integration, or better, reintegration: become what you are in Christ; become truly human. Because of the disintegrating effects of sin, reintegration (personal and interpersonal) is less a given of nature than a gift of grace.

The creation–cultural mandate: work

Be fruitful, and multiply, and fill the earth and subdue it. *(Genesis 1:28)*

The second ethical imperative is known as the creation, or cultural, mandate. The human creature, body and soul, must cultivate both 'nature' and 'spirit' in order to become 'co-creators' or 'vice-regents' who rule over creation on God's behalf.[13] Adam's naming of the animals is evidence of his dominion over them (Genesis 2:19–20). However, the Genesis text does not state that dominion is itself the image, but rather implies that it is a consequence of humanity's being in God's image. Moreover, it is far from clear that humankind's dominion over nature should result in a rule of power rather than a rule of peace.

'Be fruitful and multiply.' Man's destiny is to be a communal being, to inhabit and shape the social as well as the natural world. This is the commission to establish civilisation and to develop a God-glorifying culture. Culture is a form of serious play in which men and women, in joining together in rule-governed activities, come to share a world.[14] Human beings structure and give meaning to everyday life through such ritual 'play' in society, politics and even religion. The human task, in both work and play, is to order the natural and social world. But to what end?

Worship and wedding: rest and feast

So, whether you eat or drink, or whatever you do, do all to the glory of God. *(1 Corinthians 10:31)*

The Christian liturgy is a sacred play 'at the center of which is the supper that sums up the ministry and destiny of Jesus and links the created reality of human beings and their social life with their eschatological destiny'.[15] The last word to be said concerning the meaning of human life and of human destiny is not work, but rather rest – and feast. The *Westminster Shorter Catechism*, in response to the opening question, 'What is the chief end of man?', answers 'to glorify God, and to enjoy him forever'. Humans glorify God when they exist in right relationships: with their natural environment, with their fellow human creatures, with the opposite sex and with God. Our destiny is to be the kind of creature that God intended us to be; only then shall we fit into the created order and be agents of harmony rather than disruption. Human beings are not the heroes of the human story, for human destiny is not anthropo- but theocentric. 'Man is destined to praise God.'[16]

Scripture pictures humanity's enjoyment of God in terms of a sabbath rest (Hebrews 4:9–10) and in terms of a wedding feast (Revelation 21). As sabbath rest completes God's creative activity, so resurrection completes God's work of new creation. The end of the story of the human creature is anticipated in Jesus' resurrection and completed at the Day of the Lord, when all things, not only the human heart, find their proper rest in God. 'It is not good for creation to be alone.' The goodness of the marriage relationship depicted in Genesis is an image of the true end of the human creature and the Creator.

THE HUMAN STORY: MODERN AND POSTMODERN COMPLICATIONS

In so far as the classical notion of the person as an individual rational substance was secularised, criticised and finally abandoned, the modern and postmodern chapters of the human story are best recounted under the rubric of the 'rise and fall of the subject'.

Descartes privatised the self by claiming that objectivity and certainty could be had by subjects who knew their own minds. Kant secularised the subject by proclaiming it an autonomous knower and doer. The knowing subject orders the world it experiences with categories of theoretical reason; the moral subject orders its freedom with categories of practical reason. Human consciousness is self-constituting and human freedom is self-determining. Humans are autonomous individuals, able through reason and freedom to transcend body, history and culture. The value and destiny of the human person became in modernity a human affair, a matter of self-transcendence. Modern thinkers sought to establish the dignity and value of human personhood 'from below', that is, independently of appeals to the divine. The second 'Humanist Manifesto' (1973) declares 'we begin with humans not God, nature not deity' and claims that 'moral values derive their source from human experience'. Yet the autonomous self, born with such fanfare in modernity, has increasingly come to be seen as a fiction, if not freak, of the Enlightenment.

A knowing subject?

A first set of objections concerns the autonomy of the *knowing* subject. Enlightenment thinkers believed in the rationality of the human race. As Kant acknowledged, however, human history does not actually confirm this optimistic analysis. In the light of the phenomenon of radical evil, what guarantee is there that the rational animal will continue to use its freedom rationally, that is, for the good? Given the evident corruption of human freedom, Kant could only hope that the end of history would be rational. For G. W. F. Hegel, history is itself the unfolding of *Geist* (Spirit): human freedom, embodied in culture and social institutions, develops with rational necessity. Søren Kierkegaard, on the other hand, saw free choice in terms of radical contingency, the dizzying power of the 'either-or'. The self is unfinished and must choose itself anew at every moment. Human being, for Kierkegaard, is a constitutionally risky project. For the existentialist heirs of Kierkegaard, the problem of concrete being (existence) takes precedence over propositions about abstract being (essence). In the light of actual historical existence, the classification of human being as the 'rational animal' appears somewhat hollow, if not perverse.

A further objection to the notion of the autonomous knower concerns the peculiar conception of rationality to which it gave rise. To be rational or 'objective' is to position oneself over against the world 'out there'. Reason becomes an instrument of the subject's will to power; understanding becomes a means of gaining control over some aspect of natural, or social, reality. Knowledge is a form of mastery. Even friends of modernity have found it necessary to question this notion of knowledge. The philosopher Jürgen Habermas, for instance, notes two conflicting tendencies, both modern but at odds with one another, that follow from this subject-centred version of rationality: on the one hand, modern thinkers have proclaimed the ultimate value and rights of the individual; on the other, the increasingly technological thrust of instrumental reason, which treats all areas of life as regions that require rational management, tends to construe the value of an individual in terms of his or her function.

Rationality in the modern paradigm thus appears as a strategy for acquiring, increasing and securing power over others – human and non-human. Scientific knowledge is 'dominating knowledge'; in grasping the world we appropriate it to ourselves. There is a direct correlation between the Cartesian subject–object dichotomy and the contemporary ecological crisis. The notion of the autonomous knower thus ends up depriving the human creature of its dignity and the earth of its integrity.

A spiritual subject?

In modernity's story, the human subject is 'self-constituting' – able to take charge of itself, of its freedom and its actions. With this theme, modernity has effectively privatised and secularised the classical theological view that privileged soul over body. Searching criticisms have been directed at this concept of the autonomous *moral* subject as well.

Behavioural psychologists, approaching human being 'from below', argue that 'the behavior of man and animal alike must be placed on the same level'.[17] Instincts and environmental conditioning are the keys that reveal the mainsprings of human behaviour. Freudian psychologists, on the other hand, contend that to explain human behaviour one has to probe the unconscious. Both schools agree, however, that human consciousness, that is, the private mental life of the individual, is neither autonomous nor rational. Sigmund Freud's work, along with other 'masters of suspicion' (for example, Karl Marx and Friedrich Nietzsche), began decentring the knowing subject in the nineteenth century. In the twentieth century, socio-biologists have suggested that every aspect of our social lives is but a sub-plot in a broader evolutionary drama scripted by human DNA. The true story of the self is about human genes that seek to survive long enough to reproduce. Altruism is, for instance, a biologically determined strategy by which some genes are sacrificed for the greater good of the gene pool. On this view, human values are reduced to biological facts: 'inevitably values will be constrained in accordance with their effects on the human gene pool'.[18] Nature swallows up freedom.

Is the self able to be responsible for itself, as Enlightenment and existentialist thinkers have generally maintained, or is its behaviour determined? Do the genes that we inherit predispose certain humans to alcoholism? to altruism? Is it possible to save human freedom and dignity, to preserve the person, and if so, on what grounds?[19] Arthur Peacocke offers the salient reminder that the issue 'is whether or not the theories ... and concepts formulated in one science operating at its own level can be shown to be but special cases of, that is 'reduced to', the theories, etc., formulated in some other branch of science'.[20] Why should one think that human beings are 'nothing but' atoms and molecules, egos and ids, genes and DNA? From a theological point of view, what constrains our genetic make-up places on our nature is simply the 'given' within which freedom is to operate. 'Human being' covers a complex hierarchy of 'systems' (for example, biological, chemical, psychological, social, etc.), each with a science appropriate to its level. Is there any compelling reason to believe that electrons are 'more real' than, say, the emotions of a human person, a social fact or even divine election? It follows from an acknowledgement of different levels of reality that no one description at any one level should be granted absolute status. Indeed, it is the very need for multiple levels of description – including the properly theological (for example, the capacity to relate personally to God) – that distinguishes humanity from the other species.

An individual subject?

The autonomy of the self has been questioned not only by the natural sciences but also by recent cultural studies. The latter claim that the material processes by which knowledge and values are culturally transmitted can be every bit as deterministic on the intellectual level as DNA is thought to be on the molecular level. Determinisms of 'nature' (for example, socio-biology) and 'nurture' (for example, socio-linguistics) alike cast doubt upon the independence and individuality of the subject. According to structuralist anthropologies, the individual, far from being self-constituting, is rather born into cultural systems which, like languages, are organised into a series of binary oppositions (for example, body/soul; male/female; orthodox/heretical; fact/ value) that predetermine how the subject experiences and interprets the world. Jacques Lacan, invoking Freud, suggests that 'the unconscious is structured ... like a language'.[21] Thinking, behaviour and language are largely shaped by prevailing cultural codes. And, from a Marxist point of view, the individual's conscious thought is governed by an underlying ideology: 'all ideology has the function (which defines it) of "constituting" concrete individuals as subjects'.[22] The self becomes a function of the system.

Poststructuralists question the universality and 'givenness' of cultural and linguistic structures. Jacques Derrida and Michel Foucault undo, in different ways, the authority of linguistic and ideological structures or systems by interpreting them as social expressions of Nietzsche's 'will to power'. According to Nietzsche, human being is the 'not fully defined animal'. Derrida agrees, and proceeds to 'deconstruct' all attempts to assign a definition or stable meaning to human being. Derrida exposes all cultural and conceptual structures (that is, systems of differences) as always only conventional, never natural. Far from representing the nature of things, language is rather a means of imposing order on to them. Habitual forms of language so dominate history, culture and politics that Foucault proclaimed the end of the human sciences. The 'I' is not the speaking subject, only an 'effect' of language. 'Man', the autonomous knowing subject, is dead. What is left of the subject in postmodernity are multiple fragments of a de-centred self.

In summary: the human story as told by traditional Christianity was a divine comedy, an account of how individual human subjects – souls – are saved by God. Enlightenment thinkers transformed the human story into a secular romance: the adventure of the human subject in a world whose natural and social orders can be 'mastered' by instrumental reason. Later existentialist stories, on the other hand, were largely tragic, for the subject is both protagonist and antagonist, alienated both from the world and from authentic human existence. Finally, postmodern accounts are mainly ironic: the modern subject has been exposed as a fiction, its self-congratulatory story undone. It remains to be seen whether or not the dissolution of the classical paradigm of the subject marks the end of the human story or only a promising new beginning.

THE HUMAN STORY: CONTEMPORARY THEOLOGICAL INTERPRETATIONS

Rahner: theological anthropology 'from below'

Karl Rahner accepts modernity's turn to the subject and claims to discover therein the conditions for the possibility of God's self-communication. The ability to experience the transcendent, to 'hear' God, is the defining characteristic of human being: 'man is spirit, that is, he lives his life in a perpetual reaching out to the Absolute, in openness to God'.[23] The human creature, in its *natural* constitution, is 'a being who has to do with God'.[24] Human nature simply *is* the capacity for self-transcendence, that is, the capacity for God. The turn to the subject need not be a turning in upon oneself.

Christology is decisive for Rahner's understanding of theology and anthropology alike. Christ 'is the union of the historical manifestation of the question which man is and the answer which God is'.[25] On the one hand, Christ represents the culmination of human openness, the realisation of humanity's capacity for receiving God's self-communication. When God assumes in Christ the mystery of human capacity for the infinite mystery as his own reality, human existence reaches the very point towards which it is always moving by virtue of its essence. On the other hand, Christ shows us what God becomes in the culmination of his self-communication *ad extra*. The incarnation is the historical culmination of God's gracious self-communication to nature. The ultimate definition of man is that 'he is the possible mode of existence of God if God exteriorizes himself to what is other than himself'.[26] Christ is thus both the total openness of humanity to God and the total self-communication of God to humanity.

Barth: anthropology 'from above'

Karl Barth believes that revisionist attempts, such as Rahner's, to ground theology in human subjectivity are ultimately unable to speak either of God or of humanity correctly. Barth reverses the direction characteristic of liberal theologies: human beings must understand themselves in the light of God, not vice versa. Barth undertook a massive reinterpretation of Christian theology, including anthropology, on the basis of God's self-revelation in Christ. Instead of christology being a predicate of anthropology (for example, christology as 'transcendent' anthropology, as in Rahner), Barth sees anthropology as a predicate or subset of christology. Christology alone lays the proper groundwork on which to consider the human creature, both in its relation to God and in its relation to others. The proper study of mankind, Barth might say paraphrasing Pope, is Christ: 'the existence of this one man concerns every other man as such'.[27]

Jesus' life is absolutely decisive: 'the fact that we are with God is not merely one of the many determinations of our being ... but the basic determination, original and immutable. Godlessness is not, therefore, a possibility, but an ontological impossibility for man.'[28] It is not that Jesus is the completion of humanity but rather that he constitutes true (as opposed to false, or fallen) humanity: 'this man is man'.[29] The identity of Jesus' person is less an expression of universal human subjectivity than it is a matter of Jesus' particular history.[30] Jesus is not simply an intense expression of the common human experience of 'God-consciousness'; nor is christology simply anthropology writ large. Humanity is related to God not on the basis of transcendental consciousness – by nature, as it were – but on the basis of God's free decision to elect the human creature as his partner – by grace.

The incarnation reveals God as the one who is with and for humanity ('Emmanuel': 'God with us'). This 'cohumanity' that defines God also pertains to human nature in general, and is best seen in the differentiation of the sexes. Barth observes that in Genesis 1:26 there is a plural pronoun ('Let *us* make man') and then a reference to man as 'male and female'. The male–female relation images God's free orientation towards another. In God's being, as in human being, there is differentiation and relation between the 'I' and the 'Thou'. To be a self is to be able to sustain relationships with what is not oneself: 'Man never exists as such, but always as the human male or the human female.'[31] Sexuality, and the male–female duality in particular, becomes an image for the difference-in-relatedness that characterises human, and divine, being in general. It is therefore impossible to speak about humanity apart from 'cohumanity': the human person is both irreducibly individual and constitutionally interrelated.

Pannenberg: anthropology 'from the end'

Wolfhart Pannenberg, like Rahner, interprets humanity's openness to the world in terms of an openness to God. God is the horizon of the whole implied in every act of human self-transcendence. Yet the whole is not an implication of human existence, as in Rahner, but a matter for the future, for the end of history. Human existence is 'ecstatic' in so far as the present is lived in an awareness, either implicit or explicit, of the future. Pannenberg claims that this implicit awareness of wholeness is a structural universal in human being and accounts for the universality of religion. He is aware of the danger of beginning with anthropology (that is, we may never get beyond ourselves to God) and insists that theology should not appropriate non-theological anthropologies uncritically. He is not, therefore, searching for a 'point of contact' between Christian and non-Christian self-understanding. His aim is rather 'to lay theological claim to the human phenomena described in the anthropological disciplines'.[32] Theology demonstrates its validity and universality by exposing the incompleteness of explanations of human experience that stop short of a consideration of this ultimate horizon. This is particularly clear in history, the discipline that Pannenberg believes both sums up the human story and yet ultimately fails to complete it; the historian fails to grasp the whole of human reality precisely because the whole is incomplete.

While methodologically Pannenberg argues 'from below', he accords 'material primacy' to the eternal Son. Human destiny – the full flowering of the image of God – has already been realised in Jesus' resurrection. Only through Jesus Christ do the general concepts of human nature and destiny, as well as of God and the Logos, acquire their true content. In the historical life of Jesus, the eternal relation of the Son to the Father takes human shape. Theological anthropology understands the human creature neither from its past nor from its present, but above all from the perspective of its future destiny – fellowship with God – manifested by Christ. Jesus is the eschatological man who, as the last Adam, reveals the true nature and meaning of the first.[33]

Theological anthropology 'from the three': persons as relational

Theologians have recently discovered new resources in the doctrine of the Trinity for determining both the systematic structure of Christian dogmatics and the content of all its parts. That the font of all reality is three-in-one enabled the Greek Church Fathers to correct the ontology of the ancient Greek philosophers. One need not choose between Parmenides' monism and Democritus' pluralism. There is a Christian alternative to the problem of 'the one and the many', namely, the *three in one*. By affirming that Jesus was *homoousios* with the Father the Church Fathers established a radical new ontological principle: 'that there can be a sharing in being'.[34] The Trinity – three persons in communion – defines the very being of God, and provides an ontological foundation for thinking about human personhood and interpersonal relationships as well. God is neither a monistic substance nor an autonomous subject, but a 'being in communion'. That is, God's being is identical with his acts of communion: begetting and being begotten, sending and proceeding.[35] The one being of God is a being in threefold relation: Father, Son and Spirit.

Several implications for theological anthropology follow from this trinitarian conception. Most importantly, personhood, not substance, comes first in the order of being. Second, persons are not autonomous individuals. Whereas individuals are defined in terms of their separation from other individuals, persons are understood in terms of their relations to other persons. This reverses Aristotle, for whom relation is subordinate to substance (that is, relations are what take place between individual substances). Aristotle presupposes that the individual substance is already complete, already potentially what it is, irrespective of its relations. On this view, relations are not constitutive of being. A trinitarian view, on the other hand, affirms that persons are what they are by virtue of their relations to others. For instance, I am a child in relation to my parents, a husband in relation to my wife, a father in relation to my children, a neighbour in relation to those who live near me, a teacher in relation to my students, a creature in relation to God and a disciple in relation to Christ. Some of these relations are free: I chose to marry my wife and I chose to become a teacher. Other relations are involuntary, for example, my being created by God and being born to my parents.

In the Augustinian tradition, one's relation to oneself was constitutive of one's personhood. We speak, for instance, of 'knowing one's mind'. Yet these internal relations alone do not define the person. Persons are embodied, and thus are partly constituted by their 'external' relations to others as well. All human beings are born into particular families, cultures and communities which have their own traditions, histories and language. At the same time, persons are individuals, and not merely cogs in a vast social machinery. Even in the intimacy of a marriage relationship, persons do not lose their individuality but strive for a unity which respects differences. The human creature is neither an autonomous individual nor an anonymous unit that has been assimilated into some collectivity, but rather a particular person who achieves a concrete identity in relation to others. Human being is inherently *social*.

A trinitarian approach to theological anthropology avoids defining persons as relations, however, for such a definition would make it difficult to speak of relations *between* persons. The person is rather an irreducible ontological reality that cannot be defined in terms of something else. Perhaps the best way to render persons is to describe, in narrative rather than concept, how they typically relate and what they characteristically do. One of the primary ways in which humans relate is through language. Human being as communion is largely a matter of being in communication.

THE SELF AS SPEECH AGENT

In the poem, in the prayer, in the law, the reach of words is made very nearly equivalent to the humanity in man. (George Steiner, *Real Presences*, p. 189)

The model of the self as speech agent may prove to be particularly fruitful for theological anthropology in so far as it specifies the nature of personal relatedness (namely, being-in-communication) without collapsing the person into the process. Humans are uniquely human when they engage in various kinds of speech acts: telling stories, making promises, asking and answering questions, praying and praising. To speak of the human creature as a speech agent is not to single out one attribute but to provide an integrative model that responds to the call for a non-reductive analysis of human being as relation. Language specifies the means and medium of personal relationships; agency specifies the role of human persons within these relationships. Persons are neither determined by language nor self-constituting, but rather agents able to initiate and respond to communication.

John Macmurray argues that we can understand the nature of personhood better by starting from the 'I do' rather than from Descartes' 'I think'. Indeed, 'Our knowledge of the world is primarily an aspect of our action in the world.'[36] To act means to take an initiative, to begin, to set something in motion. In thinking the mind alone is active; but doing engages both mind and body. Strictly speaking, only a person can 'act', that is, initiate and realise purpose by doing something that affects the world. Human action takes place within a web of relationships, which condition but do not determine the action. Conversely, what the human agent does affects the web. To be human is to have the dignity of agency: 'A life without speech and without action ... is literally dead to the world; it has ceased to be a human life because it is no longer lived among men.'[37]

The self as communications centre

To be a person is to be a communicative agent in a web of communicative relationships with others.[38] These dialogical relationships take place in larger social, cultural and political contexts: 'We become the people we are as our identities are shaped through the patterns of communication and response in which we are engaged.'[39] On this view, the self is thoroughly relational (for example, 'socialised') yet retains its individual integrity. Individuality refers not to some underlying substance so much as to one's particular and typical pattern of communicative relations: 'Personal identity refers to the communicative form (the stance in relation; the form taken in call and response) which a person habitually takes.'[40]

A focus on the self as speech agent effectively counters a number of contemporary attempts to undo the human subject. In philosophy and the human sciences, language has become the primary field of conflict in disputes about the nature of human being. Jacques Lacan's socio-linguistics is every bit as deterministic as socio-biology: it is not Nature but *'langue'* (namely, a language system) that stifles *'parole'* (namely, speech agency). When speakers are determined either by the language or by the genes they inherit, the possibility of acting freely and responsibly disappears, and personhood with it. Language can indeed become an instrument of power; the fragile process of communication is easily distorted. It is for this reason that the 1989 Manila Declaration of the World Association for Christian Communication affirmed communication as a human right and need as fundamental as food and shelter.[41] To deny people a voice is to deny them their personhood. To deprive persons of speech agency is ultimately to dehumanise them.

Divine speech agency

Is the notion of self as speech agent a properly theological view of the human creature, or is it imported from non-theological comparisons between, say, humans and non-human creatures?[42] A theological account of the self as speech agent should form its notion of speech agency in the light of distinctively Christian beliefs. The communicative agency which defines our identities and bestows our role is God's self-communicative activity in creation, Christ and Pentecost. To paraphrase Barth: God's being is a being-in-communicative-act. The triune divine communicative activity is prior to any creaturely response. God seeks in the created order a being similar enough to himself to be able to speak back to him. Humans are communicative agents like God because God is the one who goes out of himself in communicative action (for example, the incarnate Word) for the sake of entering into a dialogical relation with another.

Scripture puts a special emphasis on men and women as communicative agents. Adam's dignity as crown of creation expressed itself in his naming of the animals and in his ability to speak with God. Fallen human beings have the image of God formally (for example, the capacity to communicate with God and others) but not materially (for example, this capacity is not functioning correctly); there are patterns of distortion in our communication with God and others, and with ourselves. Non-theological thinkers recognise distortions in patterns of communication, but only theology names these communicative distortions *sin*. Indeed, the most dangerous member of the body may be the tongue (James 3:5–10). Distorted patterns of communication eventually lead to a deformed or misshapen self. Hell is not others, as Jean-Paul Sartre wrongly maintained, but rather the inability to relate to others.[43] John Milton's Satan was nearer the mark: 'Myself am Hell.'[44] The attempt to be without God and others (sinful autonomy) leads to autism, that shrivelling of the self to the point of total self-absorption. Spiritual autism thus characterises a kind of solitary self-confinement that stems from the inability, or the unwillingness, to communicate with others. It is precisely to such a hell that deconstructionists and nihilistic postmodernists consign human being by denying that the self is capable of communicative agency. If the human creature is not a speaker but is spoken by language systems, then neither dialogue nor understanding – indeed, no healthy communicative relation – is possible. Deconstruction denies what the scriptures affirm of the human creature, namely, that speakers are responsible for their words.

Imago Dei

The paradigm of communicative agency is well suited to preserve the traditional emphasis on the image of God as rationality as well as the newer emphasis on the image of God as relatedness. Humans are like God in their ability to go out of themselves and enter into personal relations through communicative activity. The etymology of the Latin term for 'person' is instructive: *per-sonare* literally means 'to sound through'. What it means to be in the image of God is best grasped by an auditory rather than a visual analogy. The human creature is not so much ikon as an *echo* of the divine being and of the trinitarian communicative relations.

It is in the human face that the organs of communication are gathered together: 'Face and discourse are tied. The face speaks.'[45] Biblical wisdom literature recognises hearing as the root of true humanity: 'It is the hearing

... above all, that makes man ... the being able to answer.'[46] Moreover, self-knowledge comes about not through reflection but through responding to the call of God. Nor does the human creature live by bread alone, but 'by everything that proceeds out of the mouth of the Lord' (Matthew 4:4). Words are nourishing because the human creature is a communicative agent. 'Thus the mouth, which expresses what ear and eye had perceived, becomes the organ which distinguishes man above all other creatures.'[47] No other part of the human body is associated with as many activities unique to humankind as the mouth: commanding, teaching, blessing, singing, crying, praying, to name but a few. Communicative agency thus refers to something the human creature is and does. Communicative capacity corresponds to the 'formal' image which constitutes the human creature as human; communicative excellence – right relatedness with others and with God – corresponds to the 'material' image by which the creature is conformed to the image of Christ.

AUTONOMY RECONSIDERED

The traditional view of the person as an autonomous knowing and moral subject gave rise to significant problems. How might the paradigm of the self as speech agent respond?

An autonomous knowing subject?

The paradigm of communicative agency responds admirably to criticism of the self as a solitary thinker. Habermas locates rationality not in subjective consciousness but in the processes of intersubjective communication.[48] Implied in every act of communication are three validity claims – to truth, rightness and sincerity – that cannot be imposed but must be agreed. Habermas contends that coming to a rationally motivated mutual understanding is implicit in the very structure of language. By emphasising communicative rationality, we may retrieve part of the classical theological tradition, albeit in a new key. What was misleading about the classical identification of the image with 'reason' was the individualistic and instrumental notion of rationality that accompanied it. Rationality is neither individualistic nor disembodied, but rather a corporate communicative process.[49] It is less a quality located in human nature than in the communicative process between persons: 'Come, let us reason together' (Isaiah 1:18).

An autonomous moral subject?

The body–spirit dichotomy has traditionally generated questions about the nature of human freedom and morality. If there is no separable 'spirit' that supervises one's bodily actions, then how are freedom and morality possible? Again, speech agency provides a helpful corrective to the classical story about the self in so far as it encourages us to conceive of the human person as psychosomatic unity in terms of being-in-communicative-act.

The biblical narratives depict human persons in terms of their being towards God's covenant. What matters is not merely outward behaviour nor, on the other hand, merely the dispositions of one's heart, but rather one's whole-person response to the Word of God and the total pattern of one's historical existence. The particular form that a person's communication takes is the 'spirit' of the individual. The human spirit is not some self-same unchanging substratum of the body so much as the underlying pattern of response that emerges in communicative action. 'Spirit' is the appearance of communicative freedom in history – human being in communicative action. Accordingly, 'spirit' is not to be understood in terms of a Cartesian dualism between spiritual and spatial substances, but rather in terms of that which makes possible both consciousness and culture, namely, communicative agency. If the body is the *field* of communication, spirit is communication's guiding *force*. When speech is denied, so too is spirit. This concern lay behind Kierkegaard's attempts to help his readers grasp the importance of speaking in their own voices: 'Not until the spiritual is posited is language invested with its rights.'[50] When we no longer view ourselves as speakers but as spoken by language, we call spirit itself into question and begin to disappear as persons. Kierkegaard's critique of modernity is concentrated in his charge that the modern self is spiritless.[51]

The human creature, as speech agent, is both animal and spirit.[52] Those activities and actions that are distinctively human are those that are communicative. Humans, of course, engage in other activities – eating and drinking, hunting, playing, procreating – but these activities are not distinctively human. The presence of speech transforms those activities we share with the non-human animal world: 'we humans dine, an activity which is the occasion for conversation, and we human beings procreate ... within the covenant of marriage, a covenant enacted by speech'.[53] Human being inhabits a material condition which is the condition for, but not the explanation of, human speech.

An autonomous individual subject?

Lastly, the model of the self as speech agent puts to rest the mistaken notion that persons are autonomous individuals. We come to know ourselves and others by participating in forms of life. Ludwig Wittgenstein's preoccupation with describing concrete forms of life was intended as 'a kind of anthropology' that makes us aware 'of the kinds of creature we are'.[54] A person's individual identity is formed through communicative interactions with others. Individuals are called into being, that is, into communicative action, by others. A person is a centre of communications in a social context. Personal identity is enacted as one puts the socially governed communication system into motion and initiates speech acts that interact with others.

THE CHRISTIAN STORY: THE PERSON AS COMMUNICATIVE AGENT IN COVENANTAL RELATION

The person as evoked and acknowledged

God creates human persons by calling them forth out of nothing to the dignity of fellowship. To know oneself is to know oneself as evoked and summoned by God. Creation and redemption alike are the results of trinitarian self-communication: in the beginning was the communicative act. The human creature was bespoke by God and gifted with speech. According to Hans Urs von Balthasar, the human creature is one to whom and through whom God is able to communicate, and therefore may be reckoned a 'word of God'.[55]

To be human is to have the capacity to be called and so to enter into covenantal relation with another. The self is summoned by many others – parents by children, husbands by wives, friends by friends and neighbours, etc. – and achieves its particularity in its response. Christian faith declares that, over and above and *through* these encounters with others, the self is also called by God. Indeed, the self-knowledge which Socrates pursued is only possible when one is *acknowledged* by God. Eberhard Jüngel argues that the point of the doctrine of justification by faith is that humans do not and cannot define themselves by their own works. Rather, we only become human when we know ourselves to be recognised and acknowledged as human by God. We cannot achieve humanity – recognition in the sight of God as a dialogue partner – by our works.[56] Speech agency, far from being an autonomous power exercised in an arbitrary context, is rather a divine gift that enables communion and community.

The person as self-conscious

What distinguishes humans from all other creatures is the ability to say 'I'. Human beings are not only sentient but sapient, not only able to have experiences but to reflect upon them. At the heart of our personhood is our ability to speak in the first person, the ability to initiate speech acts and to recognise our own voice as responsible for responding to the call of God and neighbour. It is largely through language, and through the use of the pronoun 'I', that the self is able to relate to itself and so attain a degree of self-consciousness. However, I can only say 'I' when I can also say 'you'. To be a speech agent is to be and relate 'as an I which is "called out" . . . as a dialogue partner'.[57] Most importantly: we only recognise ourselves as singular subjects of communicative action through a social process in which others call us by name, call us to response and responsibility and so call us to ourselves. 'I' am 'indexed' (for example, shown, located) by others who call on me. The pronoun 'I' signals our self-awareness, that is, our awareness of ourselves as responding and responsible communicative agents.

The person as temporal

It is primarily the relation of the person to his or her words that gives the human creature a sense of temporality. Personal identity can be conceived in two different ways. It could mean, first, the self-sameness of substance, where the person is characterised by a list of unchanging properties. Like Oliver Twist, the human person remains essentially the same throughout its adventures; what happens in time is of no consequence. Alternatively, personal identity could mean self-constancy: identity on this view is not a matter of being an unchanging substance but rather a faithful subject. The self is more like David Copperfield, who only knows whether he will be the hero of his own life-story by recounting his personal history. Personal integrity is less a metaphysical (for example, mind–body) problem than an ethical one that pertains to how we relate ourselves to our word. Personal identity is a matter of constancy in one's communicative relations; personal integrity a matter of being true to one's word. Humans are creatures of covenantal discourse, communicative agents that are able to make, break and keep promises. 'The constancy of faithful speech finds its paradigm in the spirit of the biblical God whose word . . . endures forever.'[58]

Communicative freedom

Is the way a self develops predetermined? Does biology or sociology, one's nature or nurture, so condition the self's responses as to deprive it of free agency? In the Christian story, one's 'yes' or 'no' is one's own 'yes' or 'no'. We may not always enjoy freedom of movement, but we retain the power to consent. What humans say is not simply a function of their place in some 'system'. God's intention to create persons who can respond to his communication establishes an ontological structure of freedom. 'God's address determines the structure of human being as response without determining the form of that response.'[59] Speakers, for instance, inherit language codes, but they are able to put these codes to various kinds of use as well as modify them. It is through the preaching of the gospel, for example, that persons are set free. Indeed, it is pre-eminently God's Word that breaks open closed situations and creates, through this 'interruption', the opportunity of free personal response.[60]

Communicative responsibility

Human persons relate to others primarily through communicative activity. The relations in which the self is involved and constituted as personal are not merely internal (for example, memory, choosing, thought) nor merely external (for example, material, causal), but rather communicative. The promise, above all, is the place where the self relates itself to itself and to others through its words. Promising makes manifest what is the case in all speech acts, namely, that speech agency is a matter of giving one's word to another. The self is thus responsible for its words; our word is our bond. The 'I will' that seals the marriage covenant is a promise, not a piece of rhetoric. It is only in this context of interpersonal relationships (promise and commitment) that the sex act becomes communicative rather than merely instrumental. Marriage is a communicative action (for example, promising) that constitutes a privileged and exclusive interpersonal relation. The human creature is social in so far as its life is regulated by various patterns of communicative action and responsibility. The self is entangled in 'webs of interlocution'.[61]

Communication and covenant

The human person is a communicative agent in various covenantal relationships. We need not follow Nietzsche and those postmodernists who view human beings in terms of the will to power; that way madness lies. The desire to assimilate things, and other humans, to oneself, is a deformity of the human creature. From the perspective of Christian faith it is more accurate to see the human creature not as a centre of power but of communications. The purpose of communicative agency is to relate and to participate with others, not to appropriate or possess them.

Christian existence is a matter of the relation a speaker bears to his own words. Faithfulness may be defined as the religious relation to one's own words; the life of faith is the life of faithful speech. 'Aesthetic' speech, on the other hand, speech in which the speaker does not 'own up to' his words, is a way of avoiding responsibility for oneself, and ultimately of denying one's true personhood.[62] God evokes human creatures through his creative, saving and sanctifying activity and calls them to faithful fellowship. Humans, as communicative and covenantal creatures, respond to this call, sometimes appropriately (for example, the obedience of Abraham), sometimes inappropriately (for example, the unfaithfulness of Israel). The church too exists as a gathered people by virtue of the divine call (*ekklesia* = 'called out of'). To be human is to participate in the covenant of divine discourse as a faithful hearer and speaker.

CONCLUSION: HUMAN BEING AS VOCATION

... lead a life worthy of the calling to which you have been called.
(Ephesians 4:1)

We are in the image of God in so far as we are able to respond to the call of God, of others and of our own conscience. But it is God's address to us in Jesus Christ that draws us forward eschatologically towards our destiny as human creatures.

The vocation of being human follows from God's prior evocation. We are called into existence through the triune God's self-communicative activity. Being human thus involves both indicative and imperative dimensions: what we should do follows from the kind of creatures we are. Personhood is a vocation. Being human means being summoned: to be male or female, to be free and responsible, to live well with others in justice and peace, to glorify God. Human personhood is both privilege and responsibility. Other creatures fulfil their vocation unconsciously: 'The heavens declare the glory of God.' It is the special privilege accorded the human creature to do so freely and gladly. All that the human creature does – whether eating, drinking, marrying, working, etc. – should be oriented to the glory of God. Such is the measure of the human vocation.[63]

The human creature is called above all to be a witness. It is the vocation of human being to be echoes of God's evocative creative, reconciling and redeeming action.[64] To know oneself is to know oneself as summoned, as evoked from nothingness for the purpose of witnessing to and fellowshipping with the one in whom is hid the fullness of being. The 'glorious exchange' is a pre-eminently communicative act: Christ is the Word of God who expired on our behalf and sends the Spirit to inspire; the breath that animates human being should, in turn, be used to give glory and praise back to God. The goal of vocation is fellowship and the essence of vocation is witness. Humanity's 'chief end' – to glorify God and enjoy him for ever – is thus an eminently communicative one.

Jesus Christ is paradigmatic both of the divine communicative initiative and the human communicative response. Christ's communicative agency so corresponds to that of the Father that he is identified as God's Word. God's faithfulness to his Word proves God to be true and Jesus to be the truth. The story of Jesus, from incarnation through resurrection, is the supreme instance of what it is to bind oneself to one's Word, to oneself and to others. The gospel summons the self to its proper vocation – faithful speech agency – as well. 'It is a declaration. And as it comes to us, it is an address, promise and demand, a question and answer ... It encounters us, speaks with us, addresses us in terms of I and Thou.'[65] It is primarily by virtue of this dialogical relation that human being is summoned to its truest self.

'Know thyself.' From the perspective of Christian faith, there is no self-knowledge apart from the knowledge of God in Christ. To know oneself, as one whose individual and social being has been decisively shaped by Jesus Christ, is to accept gratefully one's vocation as a responsive and responsible communicative agent who exists in covenantal relation with oneself, with others and with God.

Notes

1 John Calvin, *Institutes of the Christian Religion*, ed. John MacNeill and trans. Ford Lewis Battles (Philadelphia: Westminster Press, 1960), book I, ch. 1, section 2, p. 37.

2 Francis Quarles, *Hieroglyphics of the Life of Man* (1638), i, 1.1.

3 Arthur Peacocke, *Theology for a Scientific Age* (London: SCM, 1993, enlarged edn), p. 35.

4 Clifford Geertz, *The Interpretation of Cultures* (London: Fontana, 1993), p. 5.

5 *Ibid.*, p. 52.

6 See Charles Taylor, 'Self-interpreting Animals', in *Human Agency and Language. Philosophical Papers* (Cambridge: Cambridge University Press, 1985), vol. I, pp. 45–76.

7 George Steiner, *Real Presences* (Chicago: University of Chicago Press, 1989), p. 197.

8 Walker Percy, *The Message in the Bottle* (New York: Farrar, Straus and Giroux, 1975), p. 20.

9 Michel Foucault, *The Order of Things: An Archeology of the Human Sciences* (New York: Vintage Books, 1973), p. xxiii.

10 Otto Weber, *Foundations of Dogmatics* (Grand Rapids, Michigan: Eerdmans, 1981), vol. I, p. 544.

11 There were, however, some important exceptions to this rule. Second-century Christian apologists argued, in opposition to the Gnostics, that the body too was fully part of God's good creation. And Justin Martyr stressed, against Plato, that the soul was created, neither pre-existent nor independently immortal.

12 Philip E. Hughes, *The True Image: The Origin and Destiny of Man in Christ* (Grand Rapids, Michigan: Eerdmans, 1989), p. viii.

13 Gerhard von Rad, *Genesis*, Old Testament Library (Philadelphia: Westminster Press, 1961), p. 60; D. J. A. Clines, 'The Image of God in Man', *Tyndale Bulletin* 19 (1968):101.

14 See J. Huizinga, *Homo Ludens: A Study of the Play-Element in Culture*, trans. R. F. C. Hull (London: Routledge Kegan, 1949).

15 Wolfhart Pannenberg, *Anthropology in Theological Perspective*, trans. Matthew J. O'Connell (Philadelphia: Westminster Press, 1985), pp. 337–8.

16 Hans Walter Wolff, *Anthropology of the Old Testament* (Philadelphia: Fortress, 1981), p. 228.

17 J. B. Watson, *Behaviorism* (New York: W. W. Norton & Co., 1930) cited in Pannenberg, *Anthropology*, p. 29.

18 Edward O. Wilson, *On Human Nature* (New York: Bantam Books, 1978), p. 175.

19 For theological approaches to this problem, see Arthur Peacocke, *God and the New Biology* (San Francisco: Harper & Row, 1986); Ronald Cole-Turner, *The New Genesis: Theology and the Genetic Revolution* (Louisville, Kentucky: Westminster/John Knox Press, 1993); Ted Peters, *Sin: Radical Evil in Soul and Society* (Grand Rapids, Michigan: Eerdmans, 1994), ch. 10.

20 Peacocke, *Theology for a Scientific Age*, p. 40.

21 Jacques Lacan, *Ecrits*, trans. Alan Sheridan (New York: Norton, 1977), p. 234.

22 Louis Althusser, 'Ideology and Ideological State Apparatuses', in *Lenin and Philosophy and Other Essays*, trans. Ben Brewster (New York: Monthly Review Press, 1971), p. 171.

23 Karl Rahner, *Hearers of the Word* (New York: Herder & Herder, 1969), p. 66.

24 Rahner, 'Person', in *Encyclopedia of Theology: The Concise Sacramentum Mundi* (New York: Crossroad, 1986), p. 1221.

25 Rahner, *Foundations of Christian Faith* (New York: Crossroad, 1987), p. 225.

26 Rahner, 'Man (Anthropology)', in *Encyclopedia of Theology*, p. 893.

27 Karl Barth, *Church Dogmatics*, ed. G. W. Bromiley and T. F. Torrance (Edinburgh: T. & T. Clark, 1960), vol. III, part 2, p. 134.

28 *Ibid.*, p. 135.

29 *Ibid.*, p. 43.

30 See Hans Frei, *The Identity of Jesus Christ* (Philadelphia: Fortress, 1974).

31 Barth, *Church Dogmatics*, vol. III, part 4, p. 117.

32 Pannenberg, *Anthropology in Theological Perspective*, p. 19.

33 Pannenberg, *Systematic Theology*, trans. Geoffrey Bromiley (Grand Rapids, Michigan: Eerdmans, 1994), vol. II, p. 317.

34 Colin Gunton, *The Promise of Trinitarian Theology* (Edinburgh: T. & T. Clark, 1991), p. 8.

35 John D. Zizioulas, *Being as Communion: Studies in Personhood and the Church* (London: Darton, Longman and Todd, 1985), p. 17.

36 John Macmurray, *The Self as Agent* (London: Faber & Faber, 1957), p. 101.

37 Hannah Arendt, *The Human Condition* (Chicago: University of Chicago Press, 1958), p. 176.

38 This thesis has been admirably argued by Alistair I. McFadyen, in *The Call to Personhood: A Christian Theory of the Individual in Social Relationships* (Cambridge: Cambridge University Press, 1990). Communicative agency develops what Gunton terms 'the alternative tradition' for thinking of the person, namely, the self as agent (*The Promise of Trinitarian Theology*, p. 90).

39 McFadyen, *Call to Personhood*, p. 7.

40 *Ibid.*, p. 27.

41 'Communication is God's unique gift to humankind, through which individuals and societies can become more truly human. Genuine communication is as essential to the quality of life as food, shelter and health care' (cited in Michael Traber and Kaarle Nordenstreng, *Few Voices, Many Worlds: Towards a Media Reform Movement* (London: World Association for Christian Communication, 1992), p. 33).

42 On the question of whether speech distinguishes human beings from other animals, see Mary Midgley, *Beast & Man: The Roots of Human Nature* (London: Methuen, 1980), ch. 10.

43 That 'hell is other people' was the conclusion to Sartre's play *Huis Clos* (*No Exit*).

44 John Milton, *Paradise Lost*, book 4, line 75.

45 Emmanuel Lévinas, *Ethics and Infinity* (Pittsburgh: Duquesne University Press, 1985), p. 87.

46 Wolff, *Anthropology of the Old Testament*, p. 74. Cf. von Rad: 'Constitutive for man's humanity is the faculty of hearing' (cited in *ibid.*, p. 76).

47 *Ibid.*, p. 77.

48 See Jürgen Habermas, *The Theory of Communicative Action* (Boston: Beacon Press, 1984) . Trinitarian theology provides ontological grounding for the notion that personal being is being-in-communicative-relation. Some critics believe Habermas is vulnerable at just this point, for he has no means of showing that communicative rationality is fundamentally prior to instrumental rationality.

49 See Niels Thomassen, *Communicative Ethics in Theory and Practice*, trans. John Irons (London: Macmillan, 1992).

50 Søren Kierkegaard, *Either/Or*, trans. David Swenson (New York: Doubleday & Co., 1959), vol. I, p. 66.

51 See Ronald L. Hall, *Word & Spirit: A Kierkegaardian Critique of the Modern Age* (Bloomington: Indiana University Press, 1993), p. 5.

52 See Fergus Kerr's review of David Braine, *The Human Person: Animal and Spirit* (London: Duckworth, 1993) in *New Blackfriars* (July/August 1993): 333–7.

53 Hall, *Word & Spirit*, p. 61.

54 The point is Norman Malcolm's, as recounted by Fergus Kerr, *Theology after Wittgenstein* (Oxford: Basil Blackwell, 1986), p. 74.

55 Hans Urs von Balthasar, *Man In History: A Theological Study* (London: Sheed and Ward, 1968), p. 228.

56 For an extended treatment of this point, see Eberhard Jüngel, 'On Becoming Truly Human: The Significance of the Reformation Distinction Between Person and Works for the Self-Understanding of Modern Humanity', in *Theological Essays*, trans. and ed. John B. Webster (Edinburgh: T. & T. Clark, 1995), vol II, ch. 10.

57 McFadyen, *Call to Personhood*, p. 23.

58 Hall, *Word & Spirit*, p. 191.

59 McFadyen, *Call to Personhood*, p. 22.

60 Eberhard Jüngel, *God as the Mystery of the World*, trans. Darrell L. Guder (Edinburgh: T. & T. Clark, 1983), p. 165.

61 Charles Taylor, *Sources of the Self: The Making of Modern Identity* (Cambridge, Massachusetts: Harvard University Press, 1989), pp. 38–9.

62 So Hall, *Word & Spirit*, pp. 74–80.

63 See Gustaf Wingren, *The Christian's Calling: Luther on Vocation* (Edinburgh: Oliver & Boyd, 1957).

64 According to George Hunsinger's reading of Barth, justification and sanctification can be interpreted as the external basis of vocation, 'and vocation as the internal basis or telos of justification and sanctification' (*How to Read Karl Barth: The Shape of his Theology* (Oxford: Oxford University Press, 1991), p. 154).

65 Barth, *Church Dogmatics*, vol. IV, part 3, p. 83.

Further reading

Berkouwer, G. C., *Man: The Image of God*, Grand Rapids, Michigan: Eerdmans, 1962.

Brunner, Emil, *Man in Revolt*, translated by Olive Wyon, Philadelphia: Westminster Press, 1947.

McFadyen, Alistair I., *The Call to Personhood: A Christian Theory of the Individual in Social Relationships*, Cambridge: Cambridge University Press, 1990.

Niebuhr, Reinhold, *The Nature and Destiny of Man*, 2 volumes, New York: Charles Scribner's Sons, 1964.

Pannenberg, Wolfhart, *Anthropology in Theological Perspective*, Philadelphia: Westminster Press, 1985.

Schwöbel, Christoph, and Colin Gunton, editors, *Persons Divine and Human: King's College Essays in Theological Anthropology*, Edinburgh: T. & T. Clark, 1991.

Wolff, Hans Walter, *Anthropology of the Old Testament*, Philadelphia: Fortress, 1981.

Zizioulas, John D., *Being as Communion: Studies in Personhood and the Church*, London: Darton, Longman & Todd, 1985.

10 Redemption and fall

TREVOR HART

The notion of redemption or salvation is a basic constituent in the plot of the story which Christian faith tells about human existence in God's world. The characteristic designation of this story as 'gospel', good news, already bears within it the assumption of a human race in some serious need or lack or crisis, whether it is aware of it or not. To unpick this central thread and seek to remove it in order to accommodate the more optimistic and comfortable stories furnished by the cultures of premodernity, modernity and post-modernity alike, would be to run the risk of the tapestry of Christian belief and self-understanding unravelling, so vital is it to the design and structure of the whole. Humans, Christians contend, need to be rescued from a plight which currently distorts and ultimately threatens to destroy their creaturely well-being under God, but which lies utterly beyond their control or influence. But just what sort of threat is this? And by what means are we to think of it as having been met?

The history of Christian doctrine reveals a remarkable variety and diversity of answers to these questions, and this for two chief reasons. First, the biblical text itself (which furnishes the raw materials for the theological craft) offers a striking kaleidoscope of metaphors in its attempts to make sense of and develop this central theme of the gospel. Second, these images have in turn been taken up, interpreted and developed within a vast range of different social and historical contexts, each bringing its distinctive questions and concerns and expectations to bear upon the text. Not surprisingly, as each age, each socially located group, has interrogated the apostolic tradition afresh, it has found that some parts speak more naturally and immediately to its particular world of meaning, and, understandably, has sought to develop these aspects rather than others in fleshing out an account of salvation relevant to its context.

Particular construals of salvation, then, are closely linked to particular social contexts and human situations, both in terms of their origins and the ways in which they are later taken up and developed. What this amounts to in practice is that some human communities find it easier to identify with a particular element of the human plight as described by scripture – guilt, alienation, impurity, mortality, ignorance, oppression or whatever – than others, and therefore find it easier to own the correlative metaphor of salvation – acquittal, forgiveness, sanctification, bestowal of new life, illumination, liberation, etc. In a sense this is relatively unproblematic, and the cornucopia of biblical imagery provides something for everyone, a gospel to fit all cultural shapes and sizes. If this provides a convenient way for the theologian to lead his contemporaries into the riches of the biblical tradition, then, we might suppose, so much the better. But things are a little more complicated than this, and there are some problems lurking not far beneath the surface.

The plurality of biblical imagery does not seem to be intended purely or even primarily as a selection box from which we may draw what we will according to our needs and the pre-understanding of our community. To be sure there is some evidence within scripture itself of such pragmatic eclecticism; thus the writer to the Hebrews develops at length the imagery of priesthood and sacrifice, and of the Servant of the Lord, while Paul, writing for a predominantly Gentile community, unfolds the gospel chiefly in terms of more accessible cross-cultural concepts. But in general terms what we find is that particular writers addressing particular groups may nonetheless draw within the space of a few sentences upon a wide variety of images, suggesting that the plurality is no mere indication of the cultural diversity of biblical texts, writers and readers, but points to the multi-faceted nature of the redemptive activity of God itself, which no single metaphor can adequately express. In this case, the metaphors are not to be understood as exchangeable, as if one might simply be substituted for another without net gain or loss, but complementary, directing us to distinct elements in and consequences of the fullness of God's saving action in Christ and the Spirit. To select a particular metaphor from among those available, therefore, and to develop it in isolation from or at the expense of others, is to risk a partial and inadequate grasp on the reality of redemption.

This danger is exacerbated further by the fact that the scriptural metaphors do not seem to be intended by the writers as all possessed of equal weight and significance. Some appear to be much nearer to the heart of the matter than others. Thus, for example, to select the theme of redemption as illumination, the bestowal of truth and understanding to remedy ignorance, at the expense of an adequate handling of more personally and morally focused metaphors such as reconciliation and forgiveness, would seem to be to risk a truncated and inadequate account of things. Picking redemptive metaphors to match the felt needs of our culture, therefore, while it may provide a starting point, is unlikely to be sufficient to bear the weight of responsibility attaching to the call to transmit the full gospel of Jesus Christ from one context to the next. There is good reason to suppose that those felt needs themselves may be in need of challenge and broadening in the light of the biblical text.

This leads to a further point; namely, the danger that rather than drawing upon the rich diversity of biblical thinking about salvation in order to speak to our context, we may fall into the trap of tearing biblical images and symbols away from their proper location and the network of cultural and theological associations in the midst of which their primary meaning is to be discerned, and employ them as empty labels which we subsequently attach to perceptions of the human situation and of the meaning of 'redemption' obtained in advance and quite independently of scripture itself. In other words, we allow our own self-diagnostic skills (or those of our culture) to tell us the best and the worst about ourselves, decide what measures must be prescribed to deal with the situation, and then seek suitable biblical terms in which to dress this up as a version of the Christian gospel. This is prone to happen especially when the scandal of the cross and what it signifies meets with a pre-understanding more than usually resistant to the news that God's response to humankind and its achievements involves radical judgement and re-creation rather than basic affirmation and some suggestions for improvement here and there; that redemption is, as P. T. Forsyth observed, more than a mere matter of 'grouting the gaps in nature', and that the spirit of the age should not be confused with the Holy Spirit. Whenever the story which the church tells appears to dovetail neatly and without wrinkles with the stories which human beings like to tell about themselves and their destiny, it is likely that the church is cutting the cloth of its gospel to fit the pattern laid down by the *Zeitgeist* rather than the *heilige Geist*. However much we rightly wish to be open to discern the activity of God outside the church and in the intellectual and cultural currents of the day, historical observation and theological judgement suggest that the gospel faithfully transmitted will always arouse some level of opposition and discomfort. It was not meant to do otherwise. If 'Jesus is the answer' we need, nonetheless, in exploring the themes of fall and redemption, of human need and God's action to meet it, to be constantly reminded precisely what the question is. If we assume that we already know, and approach the Christian tradition looking only for answers that fit with our prior questions, then again we shall be in danger of transmuting the gospel message into something else.

No one metaphor, image or model of God's saving activity has ever been exalted to the status of a formal credal orthodoxy within the church. But this should not be mistaken for a sign that the church has a divided mind where the matter of salvation and its concomitant doctrines are concerned. To be sure, some of the descriptions, when set directly alongside one another, do seem to take us in quite different directions, and even to conflict with one another. Yet, as several recent studies have reminded us, we shall misunderstand the relationship between them if we do not distinguish carefully between the reality of salvation itself and these various symbolic and linguistic representations in which its mystery is approached. If we insist on thinking of the relationship between reality and representation as a precise 1:1 correspondence, a mapping of co-ordinates which in some sense captures and 'speaks' reality as it actually is, then we shall quickly run into insuperable difficulties here. For in this case two divergent accounts can only amount to rival claims to truth. But once we recognise the inherently metaphorical nature of our language in its relation to reality then, while the questions of truth and falsity certainly still arise, we can see things in a different light. The metaphors which are to be found in scripture, and those which are derived from biblical ways of thinking and speaking, may be construed as complementary rather than alternative or conflicting accounts. None grasps and renders forth the reality of salvation in its essence. How could it? Language is language. But each points us beyond itself to some aspect of this saving economy, something which, *mutatis mutandis*, it has in common with a victory, a sacrifice, a bearing of judgement, a purification, a redemptive payment and so on. It is, of course, vital that we seek to discern where the discontinuities between the reality and these various ways of thinking of it lie. Failure to do so has frequently been the cause of unhelpful developments in theologies of atonement.

What the metaphors and models all have in common, if they are faithful developments or translations of the apostolic tradition, is a specific focus in history; namely, the life, death and resurrection of Jesus of Nazareth. They do not drift freely across the plains of history as universal truths of reason, or recurrent religious myths in which the global hopes and aspirations of humankind are expressed. They are rooted here, in the awkward particularities of God's dealings with actual men and women, inseparable from the specificities of time and place to which the Christian scriptures bear witness, although transcendent of these in their significance. There, indeed, is the rub for many whose sensitivities are finely tuned to the wavelengths of modernity with its historical consciousness and relativistic outlook. God, the Christian gospel insists, has acted decisively for our salvation *here* rather than elsewhere. It is in the personal particularities of the story of Jesus, a historically and culturally remote figure for most of the human race, that our own personal stories collide with God's story, that they are somehow taken up into his story and transformed. Here particularity and universality refuse to be prised apart. Scandalous as it may be to contemporary pluralism, this claim is intrinsic to the identity of the Christian gospel. In the fortunes and fate of this historical figure we have to do neither with a convenient visual aid for universal ideas of truth, beauty and goodness, nor a local and culturally contained expression of 'religion', but, the church has always insisted, the fulcrum of God's redemptive activity with respect to his entire creation.

In this volume the subject of christology is helpfully treated in a separate chapter. But there is a sense in which questions about the identity of Jesus and those concerning his work refuse to be separated. The designation 'Christ', we need constantly to be reminded, is first and foremost a title, a job-description which locates this man's life and death within the particular framework of God's dealings with the nation of Israel at a specific stage in her history, and within the broader context of his final redemptive purposes for his creation. And so it is with many other christological titles. The key question in soteriology, we must never forget, is not so much how? but who?: who is this one who acts in this way, who says these things, to whom this happens? The answers which we give to this question will shape our entire understanding of the content of biblical soteriology, and determine the shape of the gospel which we bear into our own context. The hallmark of Christian understandings of salvation, then, may be said to be that they have at their centre not a metaphor but a personal history: the life, death and resurrection of the one whom the apostles referred to as the Christ, the Son of God, the Lord. And within this history it is to the compound event of the death and resurrection of Jesus that particular attention is directed. Here is the heart of the mystery, expressed in the ancient Catholic confession that humankind is redeemed 'by the blood of Christ'. It is in the church's attempts to unpack the meaning of this event, and to relate it to the wider texture and structure of human history and existence under God, that Christian soteriology has its distinctive origin.

BIBLICAL PERSPECTIVES ON SIN AND SALVATION

The New Testament is concerned with redemption from the first page to the last. Attempts to sum up the gist of its message briefly are, however, notoriously difficult due to the bewildering array of metaphors pressed into service by its writers in their efforts to unfold the meaning of God's action in Christ. In general these are drawn from the religious, political and social institutions and understanding of the Jewish nation; not simply because these lay conveniently to hand as illustrative material, but in the conviction that the fact and form of Israel's existence was itself a God-given matrix within human history for the eventual irruption and interpretation of God's redemptive act. But the fulfilment which Jesus' ministry brings is located within a story of divine promise and preparation stretching beyond the boundaries of the covenant people to embrace the whole human race and the wider creation. Thus the secret kept hidden for long ages is at last revealed (Romans 16:25; 1 Corinthians 2:6; Colossians 1:26), the mystery of God's will not simply to redeem Israel, but, in, with and under the fulfilment of the covenant and the establishment of God's kingdom, to gather up all things in heaven and earth in Christ (Ephesians 1:10), and to reconcile them to himself (Colossians 1:20), the Creator, in whom we live and move and have our being, thereby fashioning in his own humanity a new covenant, a new humanity, a new creation. These are the ultimate parameters of the New Testament vision of redemption, the broader horizons within which other metaphors find their place.

First, there are metaphors of release. Thus Christ has come 'to destroy the works of the devil' (1 John 3:8), to break the hold of him who holds the power of death (Hebrews 2:14), a theme reflected in the synoptic tradition and its vivid portrayals of Jesus' struggle with dark and demonic forces from his baptism to the cross where the 'prince of this world' is finally disarmed and driven out (Colossians 2:15; John 12:31). The metaphor of 'redemption' (*apolutrosis*) draws on a similar pool of ideas. Just as a person sold into slavery might be redeemed or ransomed by a blood relative able to pay the price specified by law (see Leviticus 25:47–55), so now Jesus' life, death and resurrection bring release to captives (Luke 4:18–19), constituting a ransom (*lutron*) for many (Mark 10:45; see also 1 Timothy 2:6) which sets them free from slavery to sin (Romans 6:6; John 8:34) and the way in which sin employs the law as a device of restraint rather than blessing (Titus 2:14; Galatians 4:4; Ephesians 2:15; Colossians 2:14; Hebrews 9:15 etc.).

Second, there are metaphors of transformation, of change in the human condition. So, for example, Christ brings healing and immortality through resurrection to transform our sickness and death (1 Corinthians 15:20f; 2 Timothy 1:10; John 5:24). Salvation does not only release us from that which binds and inhibits us, it bestows upon us new and unimaginable blessings: eternal life in union with the Son of God (1 John 5:11), the personal indwelling of God's Spirit within us (1 Corinthians 3:16), the moral fruit of the Spirit in changed and Christlike lives (Galatians 5:22f.), the eventual glorification of our humanity (1 Corinthians 15:43; Ephesians 2:6; Philippians 3:21), and (perhaps the most enigmatic verse in the New Testament) participation in the divine nature (2 Peter 1:4).

A third group of metaphors have to do with the facilitation of a new, confident and joyful access to God for those estranged and separated from him by sin and its consequences (Matthew 27:51; Ephesians 2:18, 3:12; Hebrews 10:19f.), and the provision by Jesus of an atonement (*hilasterion*) which facilitates and secures this. Here the language of both cult and legal code are appealed to. Thus Jesus' life and death are construed in terms of the sacrificial cultus of Israel, likened variously to the covenant sacrifice (Matthew 26:28; 1 Corinthians 11:25), the Passover (1 Corinthians 5:7), and the sin-offering (1 John 2:2). Christ purifies us from the ritual defilement of sin and mediates between the most Holy God and sinful humans (Hebrews 9:15). The theology of sacrifice is notoriously difficult to determine, but it seems clear from prophetic denunciations of *ex opere operato* ritualism that what is manifest in its symbolism above all is the complete self-offering of the participant, and not the death or immolation in and of itself. Thus the atoning thing here has an irreducibly moral dimension: it is the offering of a perfect reciprocal holiness from the human side of the covenant relation, a fulfilment of the demand to 'be holy, for I am holy'. Jesus' suffering and death is also construed as a bearing of divine judgement on human sin (a theme the precise relation of which to that of sacrifice is disputed). Thus the crucifixion is a bearing of the curse of the law (Galatians 3:13) in which Jesus was 'made sin for us' (2 Corinthians 5:21), God nailing the claim of the law over us to the cross of his Son (Colossians 2:14); and his death crucifies or circumcises and thereby does away with the sinful nature (Colossians 2:11; Romans 6:6), the wages of sin finally being paid, and the wrath or judgement of God being dealt with (Colossians 3:6; 1 Thessalonians 1:10). Somehow, in and through his obedient life and his death, Jesus justifies us (that is, establishes us in a right relation to God within the new covenant) and sanctifies us (that is, makes us ritually acceptable as an offering to God). And all this is complemented and qualified by the most intimate and personal metaphors. What God desires above all is that we should be reconciled to him, receiving the forgiveness which he longs to lavish upon us, and, through union with his only begotten Son, embracing the status of sons and daughters, loved with an eternal love in his Fatherly heart. This draws our attention to something vital in the apostolic message: namely, the realisation that God is not the problem from which we have to be rescued; he is the one who graciously gives his all to rescue us. Redemption is his idea, and his greatest gift to us.

The terse statement that 'Christ Jesus came into the world to save sinners' is developed in all these and many other ways in the apostolic writings. The brightly coloured threads of metaphor are woven into an eschatological fabric in which God's saving activity unites past, present and future: redemption is a historical achievement in Christ's life, death and resurrection for us; it is an ongoing activity of the Holy Spirit in us who unites our present with that redemptive past; and it is a future hope yet to be realised and in the expectation of which Christian lives are lived. The New Testament, we should observe, knows nothing of the later careful distinction between objective and subjective aspects of this complex package, perhaps because such terms presume hard and fast individual boundaries, where it takes for granted a relatedness and solidarity among human beings. The apostolic mind seems to assume what Colin Gunton has recently referred to as a *perichoresis* of time and space in which we, as the particular persons that we are, and without ceasing to be particular, are nonetheless constituted as such by our relatedness to all that has been and all that will be, as well as all that is.[1] Thus, for example, for Paul salvation is fundamentally a matter of being 'in Christ'. We *were* in Christ in his historical redemptive acts; we *are* in Christ through faith and the indwelling of his Spirit; and we *shall be* in Christ when the final consummation of all things comes to pass. Salvation, then, is not a commodity which we can obtain at will on the free market, or an assurance policy which we can cash in on the last day, but a matter of our personal relatedness, past, present and future, to the Saviour in whose very person and being it has been fashioned, and thereby to God.

In the rest of this chapter we shall consider some different attempts to make sense of the apostolic claim that Jesus redeems. Each is from a quite distinct historical and cultural circumstance, and each reflects in its own way the struggle to translate the heart of the gospel for a world whose outlook and experience is constantly changing. Each bears the inevitable imprint of its cultural location as well as that of its Christian identity, and offers the fruits of a transaction between the two.

REDEMPTION AS DEIFICATION

Modern histories of doctrine have sometimes suggested that the fortunes of Christian soteriology took a distinct turn for the worse during the four or five centuries which followed the apostolic age. The most notorious construal of salvation among the Fathers is that of the deification or divinisation (*theosis* or *theopoiesis*) of humankind. It is in the insistence that the Son of God 'became what we are in order to make us what he is' that the broad outlines of this distinctive patristic soteriological vision are to be identified. And it is here, above all, that some have wished to identify the most telling evidence of an outright 'Hellenisation' of the gospel message. Here, that is to say, Christian theologians allowed their intellectual context to dictate the sorts of questions to which Jesus was subsequently proclaimed as holding the answer. The result was a manifest departure from the moral and relational focus of the New Testament, and the substitution of physical, metaphysical and mystical concerns only loosely related to the particularities of the biblical story of Jesus and his death for sinners. So, at least, some histories of the doctrine would have us believe.

The theme of 'divinisation', of a divine spark latent within human nature, waiting to be fanned into flame by contemplation or participation in esoteric knowledge, and attaining its end in the ultimate glory of ascent to and union with the Divine, all this is familiar stuff in the Hellenic narrative of human provenance and destiny. It finds expression both in the sophisticated philosophical manuals of Middle and Neoplatonism, and in the rather more earthy and colourful religion of the various Gnostic sects. And, some scholars would suggest, it duly finds its way into mainstream Christianity via a syncretistic apologetic strategy, and emerges, incidentally, as the main driving force behind a particular construal of the person of Christ which has subsequently been adhered to as the touchstone of Christian orthodoxy even though its culturally particular soteriological underpinning has long since dropped away. If Christ's saving work is that of uniting us to God by uniting our nature to himself, then clearly he must himself be God, and that which he unites to himself must be our entire humanity, otherwise, 'that which is not assumed is not redeemed' (that is, deified). Ergo, whenever we wish to think of salvation in these terms, we must affirm the careful christological synthesis which was fashioned in the period between the councils of Nicaea and Chalcedon.

Such a version of things may contain a grain of truth, but in general terms it needs to be taken with a large pinch of salt. There is no need to doubt that the language of deification was drawn into Christian theology due to the familiarity of the idea in Hellenic religious and philosophical discourse. Nor can it reasonably be denied that the way in which this language is employed by some major patristic figures (notably, for example, Clement of Alexandria and Origen) seems to be little more than an enthusiastic and largely uncritical baptising of elements of Middle Platonism. But what is equally evident is that when one turns to other (arguably more significant) deployers of this language, one is immediately aware that one is immersed in a wholly different pool of ideas, and that the language of *theopoiesis* is being used here quite differently. The general timbre of the soteriological tone is biblical rather than Hellenic, and the relationship between perceptions of Christ's person and construals of his work different from that sketched above. Here it is recognition of just who the Saviour actually is that drives the writers to speak in these radical terms about the significance of what he has done for us. That Jesus has granted us a sonship together with him is central to the apostolic soteriological vision. But if, as the early church came to be convinced, Jesus is none other than God himself, the eternal Son of the Father, then what he effectively does by assuming and reconciling our humanity to himself, and in pouring out the eternal Spirit of sonship upon us, is to draw us into the trinitarian life of God itself, enabling us to share in the heart of God's 'being'. This, Irenaeus, Athanasius, Cyril of Alexandria and others believed, is the true scope of what God has done for us in Christ, and it rests not on any Hellenic notion of inherent deity, but on a claim which the Hellenic mind as such could not stomach: namely, that God himself has become what we are, in order to allow us to share in his own divine life as those who know him as Abba. It is for this reason that the terms deification (*theopoiesis*) and sonship (*huiopoiesis*) are virtually interchangeable, for example, in the writings of Athanasius. And, incidentally, it is this soteriological vision which is so closely tied to the christological orthodoxy of the councils. Those who allow the 'emanation and return' myth of Hellenism to shape their thinking tend in practice to embrace non-incarnational christological alternatives.[2]

REDEMPTION AS SATISFACTION

Most Western thinking about salvation is cut from a rather different cloth than that of the Christian East, although it draws on a tradition which is equally ancient. Its roots are to be traced in the writings of Tertullian, Cyprian and Augustine, although it received what is arguably its most sophisticated and certainly its most influential treatment in the Middle Ages at the hands of Anselm of Canterbury. His development of the notion of Christ's death as a satisfaction for human sin fed directly into the mainstream of later (especially Protestant) discussions of atonement, although many of those who have ascribed to him credit for shaping their soteriological understanding have in reality underestimated their own creative contribution, and the essence of his thought as unfolded in the key text, *Cur Deus homo?*,[3] has too often been misunderstood and distorted. It is not uncommon, for example, to find Anselm carelessly listed among advocates of the doctrine of penal substitution,[4] a view which he not only did not hold, but went out of his way to avoid.

In unfolding the metaphor of satisfaction as we find it employed by Anselm we are best to begin with the circumstance of humanity apart from the intervention of the Redeemer as he describes it. He takes the biblical language of sin and alienation, drawn from the religious and social structures of Israel's covenanted life under God, and puts a contemporary spin on it, likening it to certain aspects of the feudal medieval society in which he and his original readers lived. Sin, Anselm tells us, is best thought of as a failure to render to God that which is his due from every creature. The Creator–creature relationship is, he suggests tacitly, in this respect not unlike that between feudal overlords and their subjects. Those who are ruled owe certain dues (taxes, or payments in kind and service) to those who rule. If these are not rendered in a fitting manner then a circumstance arises in which the justice of the ruler is breached and his honour compromised. In such a situation it is expected that some reparation will be made proportionate to the damage done, plus some extra compensation for the personal offence caused thereby. If such 'satisfaction' is not forthcoming, offered freely from the offending party, then the Lord will have no alternative but to act in a punitive manner, extracting what is owed by force.

As it is in Teutonic law so, *mutatis mutandis* (Anselm is not so foolish as to allow the convenience of the analogy to obscure such significant differences as exist) it is also in our human relationship to our divine overlord. What is it, then, that we owe, but uniformly (according to the scriptures) refuse to pay? Anselm develops his metaphor: 'The will of every creature must be subject to the will of God . . . This is the debt which angel and man owe to God, so that no one sins if he pays it and anyone who does not pay it sins . . . A person who does not render God this honour due him, takes from God what is his and dishonours God, and this is to commit sin.' (1.11)[5] Again, the 'fitting' resolution of the injustice and offence caused by this circumstance would be for us to repay God that which is owed to him, plus a supererogatory 'satisfaction' in order to compensate for the offence caused. But here Anselm draws attention to the apparent hopelessness of the human situation. Since we owe God all that we are and have already, and since we have squandered much of what we have and are in our sinful lives to date, and cannot recapture it, he points out, we do not have access to the level of moral capital required to repay God (see 1.20). We cannot make good our recalcitrant past, in other words, precisely because it is already past, and because such obedience and submission as we may render to God from now on is already part of what we owe to him. But there is more to it even than this. Compensation, Anselm argues, must be made proportionate to the size of the offence caused, and this is in turn calculated in accordance with the majesty of the person offended – in this case, God. Therefore, he concludes regarding the supererogatory 'something extra' owed by each human person, 'you do not make satisfaction if you do not return something greater than that for whose sake you were bound not to commit the sin' (1.21).[6]

God (the one whom scripture tells us wills our redemption) therefore faces a dilemma, according to Anselm. He cannot allow sin to pass: it would be unfitting to do so. He must either receive from his creatures an appropriate satisfaction, or else punish them for their sin. Yet, as we have seen, the amount owed by sinners is too great for any even to begin to repay it. It seems, therefore, that punishment, and not forgiveness and restoration, must be the final plight of the creature. Here the dramatic irony in Anselm's account is finally resolved, and the answer to his initial question given. In order for due satisfaction to be rendered, the one rendering it must be 'greater than everything that is not God' (11.6).[7] But 'there *is* nothing that surpasses all that is not God but God himself'. Therefore only God is in any position to make a payment of the requisite value. But in order to do so he must first become human, since 'no one has the obligation unless he is truly man' (11.7).[8] This, then, is the saving course which God pursues. Entering our world as a human he places himself under the self-same obligations to himself as all other humans, and these (unlike all others) he fulfils in a life lived from moment to moment in complete conformity to his own divine will. Thus his life is from first to last a worthy tribute to God, and he has no personal debt hanging around his neck. When, therefore, he eventually freely offers up his life itself in obedience to his Father, Christ offers it not as something owed, but as a voluntary supererogation which in effect places God in his debt, and which God gladly accepts as a sufficient 'satisfaction' for the sins of the entire race.

This is the logic of Anselm's case. It is not, we should note, an attempt to deal with salvation in all its aspects, but specifically to explain what the situation was which rendered the incarnation and the cross necessary. As such its focus is predominantly retrospective. It focuses exclusively on what it is that we are saved from and by, rather than what we are saved for. Doubtless it has its inadequacies even in terms of its own stated remit, but it represents the first thoroughgoing attempt in the West to unpack (by means of a secondary soteriological metaphor) the *ratio* and *necessitas* of the events to which the heart of the gospel tradition bears witness, especially in their moral aspect. As such it has had a very considerable impact on the shape of subsequent thinking about the atonement in the West, not least in the tendency of the latter to construe sin and its consequences primarily and too often exclusively in terms of moral and forensic metaphor. There are, however, some key respects in which the story which Anselm tells differs from much of what has followed in its wake. Notably, the agent in the account which he offers is from first to last a Saviour God who seeks ways and takes steps to secure the redemption of his creatures. There is no possibility of construing Anselm's God as a cosmic sheriff or hanging judge whose interest is only in the exaction of that which an abstract justice demands. For Anselm it is precisely God who acts to save us, and he does so not by bearing the punitive demands of justice, but, alternatively, by making from the side of the creature in both his life and his death that perfect offering of obedience and gratitude which alone satisfies a holy Creator. God, to repeat, is not the problem in salvation, but its solution. If there is a striking omission in Anselm's account of the cross, it is his failure to press beyond the categories of Creator and creature, and to read it as an event in the relationship between a Father and a Son, a dimension which would have provided his basic understanding with an even keener edge, and perhaps set it safely beyond the bounds of misconstrual in terms of a penal exaction model.

REDEMPTION AS SELF-REALISATION

The great strength of the Anselmian model is its firm grasp of one central thread in the biblical portrayal of the human circumstance: namely, the seriousness of the situation created by sin when viewed in the light of God's uncompromising holiness. This same basic theme was picked up by the Protestant orthodoxy of the sixteenth and seventeenth centuries. Here the Pauline language of the justification of the sinner became the central soteriological focus. While, however, the moral and relational categories used were ones which broadly reflected biblical priorities, the metaphor itself was skewed and distorted to some extent by being abstracted from the sociopolitical matrix of Israel's covenant life and from the theological context of an explicitly trinitarian doctrine of God. There was a tendency to conceive of the law in terms of which *iustitia* was to be defined as an abstract code akin to those of the emergent judicial administrations of Europe, and a perception of God as the absolute dispenser of such justice. Sin was chiefly a criminal offence deserving a particular fixed penalty, rather than the rebellious act of a prodigal, provoking the burning anger of a Father's heart which is, nonetheless, never other than a form of his holy love. Whatever the virtue of such forensic imagery, it was all too easy for the death of Jesus to be torn away from the trinitarian dynamic of Calvary, where the Son offers himself in obedient love to the Father in the empowerment of the Spirit. Too often it was viewed instead in cold forensic terms as a forbidding *quid pro quo* in which an innocent third party is crushed by the wheels of an absolute retributive justice in order that the guilty might walk away 'Scot free'.

Already in the sixteenth century the more unacceptable excesses of some renderings of this 'penal substitution' doctrine provoked a strong reaction. Faustus Socinus, for example, rejected it as both irrational and immoral, and offered a quite different construal of Jesus' saving activity.[9] God, he insisted, is more like an absolute sovereign than a human judge, and is able to forgive sins upon the basis of his own decision; he certainly did not need a human ritual execution to persuade him to be gracious towards his creatures. Thus Jesus' crucifixion was not a punishment which propitiated God, but an expression of God's love and forgiveness towards human beings designed to provoke in them the response of obedience and faith, and thereby to 'justify' them (restore them to a right relation with God) by jarring them out of their sinful and alienated existence. The broad contours of this so-called 'moral exemplarist' model of atonement have proven attractive to many others since Socinus, and helpfully embody some of the characteristic emphases of 'modern' readings of salvation.

First, there tends to be a 'subjective' as opposed to an 'objective' focus. The terms are obviously relative ones, and here they refer to the precise locus of the redemptive event or happening. That which saves us, it is insisted, is not some event or transaction which is 'objective' to us, that is, happens outside of us, to someone else in some other time and place, and therefore leaves us basically unchanged in any observable sense. Rather, salvation is what happens to us and within us as God works to change us, confirming us to the pattern he has for human existence, improving our moral and spiritual sensitivities and so forth. Thus, for example, Friedrich Schleiermacher[10] construes redemption as the liberation of a person's 'God-consciousness' from bondage to lower forms of consciousness, and its exaltation to a position of controlling influence in his or her moment-to-moment existence. This is a process which takes place, gradually but noticeably, in particular people as they come under the influence of the perfect personality of Jesus, mediated through the human channel of the Christian community. This sort of account of things finds ready acceptance in an intellectual context in which individualism (salvation, to be significant, must happen to me) and empiricism (must be *seen* to happen to me) have both played a significant role.

Second, the dynamics of salvation are primarily directed towards securing a change in human beings, provoking some response of faith or repentance or obedience. Whatever it is that Jesus does, therefore, he does it not in order to change God's mind or his attitude or his actions, but to transform ours. God, it is often maintained, does not need to be changed from being against us to being for us, or from a condition of alienation to one of forgiving and accepting love. If there is a changed state of affairs in salvation, therefore, the change takes place on the human side.

Third, God's character is confidently represented in terms of the analogy of love, seemingly on good biblical authority. But the concept of love as deployed today is habitually one derived and developed in abstraction from the biblical portrayal of God's character where it is fused together with other equally fundamental characteristics, most notably, perhaps, that of holiness. The category of holiness, when it is employed at all in the modern period, is often redefined in almost aesthetic terms, as a numinous quality with no particular moral content. Many simply dismiss the idea altogether as a piece of primitive mythology better suited to earlier and less refined perceptions of deity. In consequence, the central category of forgiveness, rather than being the remarkable and unexpected good news of the apostolic gospel becomes instead something which humans have come to expect of God. After all, forgiveness is what love does when it meets with resistance or opposition.

To this almost presumptuous perception is closely tied a fourth trait of modern discussions of redemption; namely, the way in which they tend to endorse modernity's optimistic assessment of the human condition and human potentialities. It is not only our thinking about God that has changed, in other words, but our thinking about ourselves. Here we return to the inevitable correlation between construals of salvation and changing perceptions of the depth and nature of human need. Since the Enlightenment Western intellectual life has been dominated by the idea of humans as essentially noble and responsible beings, exercising their free choice in accordance with the guidance of a God-given intellect, and gradually transcending themselves in an evolutionary march towards moral and spiritual perfection. Even Immanuel Kant, who was more realistic than many of his eighteenth-century contemporaries about our apparent radical predisposition towards evil, nonetheless ultimately concluded that it must lie within the range of human *ability* to choose to do the good, even if most of us often do not so choose. Not surprisingly, in such an atmosphere redemption comes to be viewed as something altogether less radical than was once supposed. What is required in order to address our circumstance is something more akin to the improvement or perfection of something intrinsically good, rather than the breaking and complete refashioning of something which, whatever it may once have been, has become incapable of that which God demands of and desires for it. In many accounts it is not even clear in what sense a saviour is needed at all. We have within ourselves the resources for self-transformation and the realisation of our latent potential. Jesus, if he figures directly in the picture, does so only as a stimulus, or a forerunner who shows us the way to do it for ourselves.

Some of these characteristically modern emphases represent helpful translations of the tradition, and recapture things which had become lost or forgotten or distorted in earlier manifestations of it. But others seem to represent an accommodation to the sensibilities of modern culture in which something essential to the Christian story is omitted or refigured in a potentially destructive manner. P. T. Forsyth, one of those whose account of the Christian message frequently found itself swimming against the tide of popular thinking, diagnosed the fundamental problem as a loss of the sense of God's holiness. Only a renewed grasp of the holy God as the moral foundation of the universe, he suggests, will grant us a true perspective on the depths and seriousness of the human predicament; and only within the horizons of such a perspective will the radical nature of God's saving action in Christ become apparent to the church once again.

To say this is not to embrace some Gnostic derogation of the creation or to demonise human culture. Forsyth himself was a great connoisseur of creation and culture, not least in his well-known passion for good music and great art. But it is to take seriously the dark and tragic streak which now, according to the Christian story, penetrates every part of human existence in the world, not rendering it wholly bad or worthless, but affecting every part of it nonetheless. To ignore this dark and threatening aspect, to pretend that it is not there, is not necessarily to render the Christian story more relevant, but may be precisely to render it altogether *irrelevant*. What is needed, therefore, in our day is some serious attempt to grapple with this vital foil to the good news, some attempt to translate and explore afresh the meaning and implications of the doctrines of fall and original sin. And that means beginning again with a consideration of something which so many modern restatements of the doctrine of redemption seem to struggle to find any serious place for: the figure of the crucified Jesus in the radical darkness of whose death, Forsyth reminds us, God 'does not come to grout the gaps in nature, not simply to bless nature, but to change it, to make a new earth from a new foundation in a new heaven'.[11]

Notes

1 See Colin E. Gunton, *The One, the Three and the Many: God, Creation and the Culture of Modernity* (Cambridge: Cambridge University Press, 1993), ch. 6.
2 See further on this T. A. Hart 'Two Models of Salvation in Relation to Christological Understanding in the Patristic East' (unpublished PhD thesis, University of Aberdeen, 1989).
3 See J. Colleran (ed.), *'Why God Became Man' & 'The Virgin Conception and Original Sin' by Anselm of Canterbury* (New York: Magi Books Inc., 1969).
4 So, for example, surprisingly Alister McGrath in *The Making of Modern German Christology*, 2nd edn (Leicester: Apollos, 1994), p. 25.
5 Colleran, *'Why God Became Man'*, p. 84.
6 *Ibid.*, p. 110.
7 *Ibid.*, p. 124.
8 *Ibid.*, p. 126.
9 Socinus' views are contained in his polemical work *De Jesu Christo Servatore*. For a helpful account see R. S. Franks, *The Work of Christ* (London: Thomas Nelson and Sons, 1962), pp. 363ff.
10 See Friedrich Schleiermacher, *The Christian Faith*, ed. H. R. Mackintosh and J. S. Stewart (Edinburgh: T. & T. Clark, 1928), sections 100–12.
11 Peter Taylor Forsyth, *The Justification of God* (London: Duckworth, 1916), p. 77.

Further reading

Fiddes, Paul, *Past Event and Present Salvation*, London: Darton, Longman and Todd, 1989.
Forsyth, P. T., *The Work of Christ*, London: Hodder and Stoughton, 1910.
Franks, R. S., *The Work of Christ*, 2nd edition, London: Thomas Nelson and Sons Ltd, 1962.
Gorringe, Timothy, *God's Just Vengeance. Crime, Violence and the Rhetoric of Salvation*, Cambridge: Cambridge University Press, 1996.

Gunton, Colin, *The Actuality of Atonement*, Edinburgh: T. & T. Clark, 1988.

Hooker, Morna D., *Not Ashamed of the Gospel. New Testament Interpretations of the Death of Jesus*, Carlisle: Paternoster Press, 1994.

MacIntyre, John, *The Shape of Soteriology*, Edinburgh: T. & T. Clark, 1995.

Mantzaridis, G. I., *The Deification of Man*, New York: St Vladimir's Seminary Press, 1984.

Rashdall, Hastings, *The Idea of Atonement in Christian Theology*, London: Macmillan and Co., 1991.

Stevens, G. B., *The Christian Doctrine of Salvation*, New York: Charles Scribner and Sons, 1905.

Stott, John, *The Cross of Christ*, Leicester: Inter-Varsity Press, 1986.

Turner, H. E. W., *The Patristic Doctrine of Redemption*, London: Mowbrays, 1952.

Whale, J. S., *Victor and Victim*, Cambridge: Cambridge University Press, 1960.

11 The church and the sacraments

ROBERT W. JENSON

THE MUTUALITY OF CHURCH AND SACRAMENTS

For this volume, ecclesiology and sacramentology are assigned to one essay. This requires some compression of both topics. The benefit probably outweighs the loss, for it is a decisive insight that shows itself in the pairing: all *loci* of theology are interconnected as nodes of an intricate web, but these two indeed make a systematic couple as most possible pairings would not.

Indeed, ecumenical ecclesiology is now dominated by urgent advocacy of just this mutuality of ecclesiology and sacramentology: we are called upon to interpret the Church by the sacraments that occur in her and the sacraments by the church in which they occur. And we may well take this contemporary mandate as our systematic guide, for, as has often been remarked, it is only in the late-modern period and particularly in the post-World War II ecumenical movement that the church has become an explicit and systematically central object of theological reflection. The structure of the following is thus provided by the contemporary ecumenical problematic; earlier thinking about church or sacraments will be adduced within this structure, in somewhat *ad hoc* fashion.

BODY AND COMMUNION

The second Vatican Council made it a maxim of its teaching that the church is herself *'uti sacramentum'*, 'a sacrament, as it were', or perhaps 'a sort of sacrament'.[1] Later in the document, when misunderstanding had become less likely, even the *'uti'* could be dropped: 'Christ, when he was lifted up from the earth ... sent his life giving Spirit ... and through him he constituted his body which is the church as the universal sacrament of salvation.'[2] This teaching, that the church is herself a sort of sacrament, has become a centre not merely of Catholic ecclesiology but of ecumenical discussion.

The teaching has some background in a particular and controversial strain of preconciliar Catholic theology. But it is the conciliar propositions as they stand that are official Catholic doctrine and have come to shape ecumenical ecclesiology; and the deepest root both of the conciliar doctrine and of its wide influence is Paul to the Corinthians.

'The bread that we break, is it not a sharing [*koinonia*] in the body of Christ? Because there is one bread, we who are many are one body, for we all partake of the one bread' (1 Corinthians 10:16–17). Paul then accuses the Corinthians of violating the body of Christ by their behaviour to each other in the meal-assembly (1 Corinthians 11:17–27). We want to ask: is the violated body the church, or is it the bread and cup on the table? But plainly Paul intends both at once: the bread and cup are the body of Christ and the assembly is the same body of Christ. A closer mutuality of church and sacrament is hardly conceivable.

We should note the intertwining of two concepts in the first passage: *soma*, body, and *koinonia*, communion. John of Damascus' exegesis of the passage, summarising patristic interpretation, displays this with an extraordinary phrase: 'As we all eat of one loaf we become one Body and one Blood of Christ and members of one another; we may be said to be *co-embodiments of* Christ [*sussomoi tou christou*]' (emphasis added).[3] Noting this, we are led to the other centre of current ecumenical ecclesiology, also at least co-sponsored by Vatican II: the so-called '*communio*-ecclesiology'.

A consensus-document of East–West ecumenical dialogue provides a crisp statement of this ecclesiology: 'The one ... church is a communion of many communities and the local church a communion of persons.'[4] The concept of communion is successively applied: *a* church is persons in communion, and *the* church is churches in communion. It is particularly the latter point which is advanced by Vatican II: 'In and from ... particular churches there exists the one ... catholic church.'[5]

The mere proposition that the church is pervasively communal could be trivial. It becomes pointed for our concern when we note that in our Pauline passage it is not the assembly merely as such but the assembly's sacramental act, of eating the loaf together, that is 'a *koinonia*' – and that Paul is here indeed thinking sacramentally is guaranteed by the immediate context of the passage. Thus again church and sacraments are assimilated to each other.

This chapter will be built not only around the mutual interpretation of church and sacraments, but also around the concepts of body and communion in their Pauline intertwining. We will interpret each of church and

sacraments by each of the concepts of body and communion, thus developing four material sections. We will see that the four lines of interpretation
constantly cross; and indeed this phenomenon is itself a chief point of the
chapter.

THE CHURCH AS THE BODY OF CHRIST

Paul's teaching that the church is the body of Christ can be exploited for
the similes it enables and Paul so exploits it, but his proposition is not itself a
simile or other trope. That is, 'is the body of' is a proper concept also where
Paul uses it of the church and Christ. Or we may look at the matter so: whether
Paul's 'The church is the body of Christ' is a 'metaphor' or not depends
entirely on what you mean by 'metaphor'. In those senses of 'metaphor'
under which Paul's proposition might reasonably be called one, calling it
that makes no difference to the point here to be made. Of course the church
is not an organism of the species *homo sapiens* and so not what we now will
first think of as a human body. But Paul was not so ontologically inhibited as
are we.

'You are the body of Christ' (1 Corinthians 12:27). The field of similes
opened by this proposition provides Paul with a way of expounding the
variety of gifts in the church. But precisely to do this, the proposition must
itself be an ontological identification, like the regularly paired 'You are the
community of the Spirit.' We are the body of Christ, according to Paul, in
that we have been 'baptised into' it (1 Corinthians 12:13). And what we have
been baptised into is simply 'Christ' (1 Corinthians 12:12). Again, we are 'one
body' in that we do something that can equivalently be described as 'sharing
in the body of Christ' and partaking 'of the one bread' (1 Corinthians 10:
16–17). It is impossible to specify a tropic construal of 'body' in the complex
of these passages that does not make mush of Paul's arguments.

But what *does* Paul mean, if not that the church is very like a body and is
Christ's church? He means that the risen Christ as a complete living human
person has a body and that the church is this body. But how can he say such a
thing?

The suggestion does not seem far to seek: he speaks of the 'body of Christ'
in much the same way as he speaks of his own 'body' or the 'bodies' of his
readers. Nor are these Pauline usages themselves obscure to us. Most generally and centrally in Paul's language, someone's 'body' is simply the person
himself, in so far as this person is *available* to other persons and to himself,
in so far as the person is an *object* for other persons and himself. It is in that

Paul is a body that persecutors can mark him as Christ's (Galatians 6:17); it is in that Paul is a body that he can be seen and interrogated by one of his congregations – or be remote from this possibility (1 Corinthians 5:3); it is in that Paul is a body that he can discipline his own self (1 Corinthians 9:27). In Paul's ontology, such personal availability may or may not be constituted as the biological entity moderns first think of as 'a body'; for Paul, a 'spiritual' body, whatever that may be, is as much or more a body as is a biological body (1 Corinthians 15:44).

That the church is the body of Christ therefore means that the church is the object as which the risen Christ is available to be found, to be responded to, to be grasped. In the assembly of believers, where am I to direct my intention, in order to be intending my Lord? The first answer is: I am to look around me, at the assembly itself.

This answer must not remain the only answer. Protestants have rightly feared any theology that so identifies the church with Christ as to leave the believer with no way to distinguish between them in experience. Catholics have oppositely feared a Protestant tendency to reject Paul's truth along with the suspected error; perhaps the historically most common way of doing this has been to locate the 'real' body of Christ somewhere else, in 'heaven', and interpret the church's identity with it by tropes. Again Paul to the Corinthians shows how the Protestant concern is properly to be satisfied. The churchly assembly is the availability to me of Christ *in that* what constitutes the unity of the assembly is the presence and use within it of something distinct from it, the bread and cup – as that very same availability of Christ.

Why can I, in order to intend Christ, intend the community of believers to which I belong, without appalling hubris? Because we jointly intend Christ not as ourselves, but as the sacramental objects in our midst. Using a famous distinction of modern sociology, the church as a *community* is the body of Christ in that the church as an *association* is confronted within herself by the body of Christ – the same body of Christ that she as community is.

Finally on this line of thought, we should note the actual *teaching* of Vatican II and not only its concepts. The teaching is a *missionary* teaching.[6] The church as Christ's body is 'the universal sacrament of salvation'. She is 'the sacrament – as it were' of 'intimate union with God and the unity of all humanity'. The church is not there for herself but for God and, precisely as sacrament, for the world. What is the body the *world* can intend to be intending Christ? Where can the world find him? The world can find Christ as the assembly of his faithful around his sacraments. The church is the body as which Christ confronts his world.

We must of course pose the prior question: why does Christ need to be embodied for us? Few have pondered this question with such religious passion as Martin Luther. According to his teaching, God embodies his presence among us in order that it may not simply pass into our individual or collective subjectivity, for this would make our participation in it what he and the other Reformers called 'works'. Christ's presence is ours by 'faith', that is, it remains 'external', something to which we must cling: at the same time that Christ enters our subjectivity he remains an object *for* our subjectivity; at the same time that Christ is in me and I in him he is the other on whom I utterly depend. So Luther on baptism: 'Faith must have something that it believes: So faith here hangs on the water . . . however "outward" it may be. Indeed, it must and shall be outward.'[7] The disembodied data, 'You are accepted for Christ's sake', can be integrated into my subjectivity and then used by me for my inevitably self-determined purposes; the stream or bathtub will not go in.

It should not be so surprising as it perhaps is, to find the most powerful single analysis of the underlying structure in G. W. F. Hegel's *Phenomenology of Spirit*, for Hegel after all regarded his philosophy as an exposition of Christianity's inner logic. The famous section on 'domination and slavery'[8] has been the inspiration of many things, some very bad. But taken theologically as Hegel wanted it to be, it makes the precisely necessary point. If in our mutual relation, I am a subject of which you are an object, but withhold myself from being reciprocally an object for you, you are in so far enslaved to me. Only if you are able to intend and deal with me as I do with you, can we both be free. Thus a disembodied personal presence cannot bless but only curse other persons.

Were the person in question God, the slavery would be absolute. Were Christ not body as and for the community in and as which he is present, were his presence merely 'spiritual' in the infra-biblical sense of disembodiment, of invisibility and intangibility, his presence would mean the community's damnation. The pair to Luther's constructive doctrine is his horror at encountering a merely 'spiritual' presence of God: 'Don't give me any of *that* God!'[9]

Finally we must ask how it can be *true* that the church with her sacraments is the human body of the risen Christ. The answer is very simple, if conceptually revolutionary in ways that stretch far beyond this chapter. The church with her sacraments is truly Christ's availability to us because Christ takes her as his availability to himself. Where does the risen Christ turn to find himself? To the sacramental gathering of believers. 'Who am I?' he asks, and answers, 'that community's head', 'the subject whose objectivity is that community'.

For it to be simply and straightforwardly true that the sacraments and their community are Christ's body, all that is required is that the risen Christ's self-understanding determine what is real, that is, that he be the *Logos* of God. We need not think of two metaphysically different bodies, one the risen body in heaven and the other the churchly body, somehow coming together. And as to why we are to intend Christ in and as the church, and not elsewhere, a slightly supplemented version of a traditional answer is thus final: that is where he looks to find himself and so where he tells us to look to find him.

The teaching of Vatican II, that the church is *'uti sacramentum'*, was intended as an ecumenical contribution. It was intended to take Paul's teaching that the church is the body of Christ with ontological seriousness while avoiding the kind of identification of Christ and church that underlies ecclesial triumphalism. For in classic sacramental teaching a sacramental sign both is related to and is that which it signifies; so here the church points *to* Christ and so – and only so – *is* Christ. It must be noted that the offering has been churlishly received, largely, one fears, because the sacramental life of many Protestant churches has so collapsed that its spokespersons are unable to understand Vatican II's language, and take the council to be making precisely the triumphalist claim it disavows.

The cross-purposes are a disaster, for in the council's recurrence to Paul's 'body of Christ' concept lies the possibility of an ecclesiology that is simultaneously deeply Catholic and fully concordant with the Reformation's critique. Protestants have insisted that the church must so be conceived and practised as always to be open to reform. And surely it is Christ who reforms his church and not the church who reforms herself – though Protestantism has not always been so clear on *this* point as would be desirable. If the risen Christ, like all living persons, is his body and yet has his body as his object, what might be called a christological–ascetic understanding of churchly reform emerges: the risen Christ like all living persons must direct and discipline his body, and his body is the church.

THE SACRAMENTS AS THE EMBODIMENT OF CHRIST

Turning now more specifically to sacramentology, the Western tradition has insisted above all on two points. First, sacraments *mean* something. In the terminology Augustine made standard, they belong to the class of *signa*, 'signs', things that point to something other than themselves; what they point to is then the *res*, the 'something' in question, the 'matter' of the occasion. 'Sacraments' are those signs whose *res* is the grace of Christ.[10] Thus sacraments belong to the *discourse*, the 'word', that is Christ's self-interpretation to and in his church.

But second, sacraments *do* something; and what they do is the very thing they mean. We may put it so: in pointing to their *res*, these signs do not point to any other event than themselves. The Council of Trent adopted a phrase of lapidary metaphorical precision: sacraments 'contain the grace they signify'.[11] For – and Protestants should surely affirm the motive – if sacraments pointed us elsewhere than to where they are themselves happening, it would be up to us to get there, and faith would again be replaced by works. Christ must be present independently of our grasp of his call to us; he must be there to *confront* us, in the very event of his call to us.

Thus the paradigmatic decision in the history of Western sacramentology fell in the ninth century when the emperor Charles the Bald asked the theologians Radbertus and Ratramnus:[12] 'Is ... the body and blood of Christ there only as symbolised or in fact ... ?' Radbertus answered, 'Both', and the church declared him right.

But how can both be right? Precisely in that the sacraments *embody* Christ for the church. For someone's body is – again – that person himself as an object for other persons. A bodily presence is a presence that is both substantive, even a sort of 'thing', and personal. A bodily presence is an objectively given personally meaningful presence; it is *both* there as a *res*, an irreducibly given fact, and means for me what the person means.

It is therefore not only the Supper that may and should be interpreted by the concept of body, though it is chiefly by Paul's discussion of the Supper that the interpretation is introduced. Thus, to take the other chief sacrament, it is ecumenical teaching that Christ himself is the agent of baptism; he personally does to the candidate whatever baptism does.[13] The bath is the necessary embodiment of his action, the externality, in the case of baptism, of our meeting with him. 'Where am I to find my Saviour?' the new convert asks, and is answered, 'He will meet you in the water.'

Scholasticism reduced these teachings to a conceptual set that is perhaps a bit too abstract for its matter but is nevertheless helpful. The *signum* or *signa* of a sacrament, also called the *sacramentum*, are the objects we can directly intend. The *res* is some aspect of Christ's personal grace. And ontologically between the two is reality that is both *signum et res*, *res* to that which is purely *signum* and *signum* to that which is purely *res*. In the case of the eucharist, this is the body and blood of Christ, signified by the bread and cup yet there for us as the bread and cup that signify them, and themselves the binding sign of Christ's personal grace. In the case of baptism, it is initiation into the priesthood of believers, signified by the bath and therein granted to the initiate as a permanent fact about himself to which he can point, and just so the sign of priestly access to God.[14]

It is apparent that the way in which this chapter has interpreted sacraments must tend to relativise the old disputes about 'how many sacraments there are'. Most broadly and, one may perhaps suggest, most appropriately, 'sacrament' may denote any embodiment *within and for the church* of that Christ whose embodiment *for God and the world* the church herself is. At least when the church is lively, such events occur in unpredictable profusion. If we then speak of 'the' sacraments or 'a' sacrament, the article selects from this profusion identifiable rites that are repeated through time, embodiments of Christ's presence that can be repeatedly recognised.

How many of these latter are there? If it is simply a matter of recognising rites that are in fact continuous in the church's life and that in one way or another embody Christ in the church, there are still very many; we may then think, for example, of the sign of the cross or the making of processions or the ritual reading of scripture as sacraments. But when the church has made lists, and so discriminations, it has generally been the notion of necessity for sanctification that openly or hiddenly has controlled churchly discourse. This notion is itself treacherous, but if for present purposes we abstract from its difficulties, we may say that – yet again – it depends: necessary for whom? If the answer is simply, for believers, we will come up with something like the Reformation lists of two or three. If the answer is, for certain believers and for believers in certain circumstances, we will come up with something like the Tridentine list of seven. And if we ask how we know what is necessary in either connection, all parties in one way or another begin to quote scripture and authoritative tradition.

Thus Philip Melanchthon got it right in the *Apology of the Augsburg Confession*; theologians and churches should not be eager to argue about the number of 'the' sacraments. What is important is that we know what things God wants done in the church; that we know what blessing he in each case intends; and that we obey. Afterwards we may sort out the terminology.[15] And if we look at it that way, there is in fact notable ecumenical agreement: eucharist and baptism (the latter including 'confirmation') are necessary for all, and the remaining rites on the Tridentine list are surely necessary for some.

THE CHURCH AS COMMUNION

We turn back to the church. And we move to interpretation of church and sacrament as communion.

'The local church [is] a communion of persons.' It is ecumenically both confused and disputed whether 'the local church' is the 'diocese', that is, the internally complex congregation whose pastor is a 'bishop', or the 'parish', that is, the geographically and structurally simpler congregation whose pastor is a 'presbyter'. In view of the history of these entities and ministries, the matter probably is dogmatically insignificant and practically negotiable; the following discussion can anyway be adapted to either structure.

Within Western modernity it may seem platitudinous to call the local church a community. It will be taken for granted that first there are believers, and that because of the communal nature of human personhood, these believers of course come together to make a believing community. But as scripture speaks of churchly communion, it happens exactly the other way around, and what is asserted that way round is far from platitudinous.

Above all the Johannine theology displays the intrinsic order: 'that you may have *koinonia* with us; and our *koinonia* is with the Father and with his Son Jesus Christ' (1 John 1:3). 'As you, Father, are in me and I am in you, may they also be in us ... [May they] be one, as we are one' (John 17:21–2). The communion that is the church is not primally the communion of believers among themselves; it is primally God's communion with us in the incarnate Christ; and because the God who thus admits us to communion is in himself a *koinonia*, the *perichoresis*, the 'mutual inhabiting', of Father, Son and Spirit, we are drawn also to mutual love of one another. The Fathers were very clear on this point; so, for example, Athanasius, who in exegeting John 17, represents the Son as saying to the Father, 'My work is completed in that men ... *having been* divinised, have in each other, *by* [emphases added] looking at us, the bond of love.'[16]

Thus church and sacrament again come together: the communion that is the local church is itself sacramental, constituted in God's gift of communion with himself. Baptism initiates the community of the church; as the liturgical scholarship of all confessions has repeatedly emphasised, baptism is primally a rite of initiation, a 'liminal' step into a new communal reality with its new possibilities and obligations. The communion of the church is then actual as the eucharist; the eucharist does not merely enable or manifest the communion we call church, it *is* that communion. Here an ancient concern of Orthodoxy determines ecumenical *communio*-ecclesiology. So, for example, an early Orthodox–Anglican consensus document: 'The Church celebrating the Eucharist becomes fully itself: that is *koinonia*... The Church celebrates the Eucharist as the central act of its existence, in which the ecclesial community... receives its realization.'[17]

The communion of the church is grounded in the communion of the triune God. Insistence on this insight is a chief feature of the *communio*-ecclesiology. Again we may cite ecumenical consensus between East and West: 'The church finds its model, its origin and its end in the mystery of the one God in three Persons ... [The] mystery of the unity in love of plural persons... constitutes... the trinitarian *koinonia* which is communicated to human persons in the church.'[18] According to this document it is '*because* [emphasis added] the one and only God is the communion of three Persons' that the one church is 'a communion of many communities and the local church a communion of persons'.[19]

So we are led to the other part of the *communio*-ecclesiology, its doctrine of the one church. But before we turn to that, we need some systematic clarification and limitation of the doctrine just stated. We need to ask: *how* does the communion of the church derive from the communion of the Trinity?

Perhaps the best category for the foundation of the church's being is the category of *anticipation*, if we eliminate any idea that anticipating is an action that the church herself is to achieve. The church is community, but this community cannot gather as one until the last day; thus this community's binding spirit is that Spirit whose very reality among us is 'down payment' (Ephesians 1:14). The church is the Body of Christ, but she is the body of that Christ whose bodily communion with the Father involved precisely a bodily departure from his disciples and whose return in like fashion we still await. The church is what she is just and only as anticipation of what she is to be.

What then is she to be? She is to be a communion within the communion that is the life of the triune God. The patristic concept of *theosis*, deification, is doubtless a risky one; just so it is appropriate to the enormous hope that must here be stated. The triune God is not a monad; he is the life of the Father and the Son in and by their Spirit. Thus he is in himself a *communio*, and so has room for others to share his life, if he so chooses. Father, Son and Holy Spirit are real precisely as poles of their fellowship; as the great scholastic formula has it, a triune 'person' is 'a relation ... in the fashion of a substance'.[20] By God's free choice, he does in fact open the communion he is for created persons, that is, for the church.

The church exists to be taken into the triune community, as the body of the second person of that community – here again our two themes come together. Since this is what the church is to be, she now is nothing different. The church's present reality *is* that she is the body that is to be fulfilled in this way; just so the church is herself *communio*. Many of the Fathers[21] saw the triune reality of God more clearly in one biblical scene than in any other, the scene of Jesus' baptism (Mark 1:9–11). Here the Father lovingly commissions the Son, the Son accepts his commission, and the Spirit appears as the mediator of their discourse. Nothing less than the inner life of the Trinity is here depicted. Even more astonishing, however, is the modification Matthew (3:13–17) makes in the scene: the Father's word is addressed also to those with Jesus, that is, the triune converse opens to include them.

We may dare some drastic propositions. When we speak of 'the word of God' being spoken and answered in and by the church, we say more than perhaps we sometimes know, for when the 'law and gospel' are spoken it is the very address of the Father to the Son that is shared with and in the gathering. When the church prays to the Father, believing the Son's promise that he is there to pray with them (Matthew 18:20), this human gathering participates in the Son's obedience to the Father, the very obedience by which he is in fact God the Son. And all this simply *is* the free action of the Spirit, the very action by which he is the *vinculum amoris*, the 'bond of love' by which Father and Son are free for each other.

Here there is a famous theological decision to be reversed. Peter Lombard, in the work which became the textbook of scholastic theology and indeed set the pattern of most subsequent Western theology, the *Libri Quatuor Sententiarum*, accepted the Augustinian interpretation of the Spirit as the bond of love between the Father and the Son. Then he asked whether this same love is that by which believers love God and one another, whether the Spirit is the bond also of churchly communion in its two dimensions. Peter himself decided in the affirmative, that the Spirit is indeed himself the love by which we love God and one another,[22] but at this point Western theology rejected the opinion of its 'master of opinions'. There have always been rebels against the standard position, including such notables as Martin Luther[23] and Jonathan Edwards.[24] We should, I think, join the rebels.

We turn to the political aspect of the *communio*-ecclesiology: 'The one … church is a communion of many communities.' In that Father, Son and Spirit are but one God, and in that the communion of believers is constituted by participation in the communion of Father, Son and Spirit, there can properly be but one Christian communion, that is, one great eucharistic assembly. But only when this assembly is wholly in God will it meet face to face; after the ascension and before the eschaton, although a local eucharistic assembly must like the congregation whose prayers are recorded in the *Didache* summon believers 'from the four corners of the earth' to her local Eucharist[25] she cannot expect to see them all appear. Each local church must know herself as the one church of God. But before the Fulfilment she can do so only mediately, as she knows herself to be the same one church as all the other churches who know themselves in the same way and with which she will at the End be joined. 'The church is . . . a communion . . . subsisting in a network of local churches.'[26]

Such propositions begin, if they do not complete, a doctrine of church polity drawn from the nature of the church, rather than by analogy from the world's polities among which the church lives. The local church is a communion of persons; the one catholic church is the communion of all local churches; and if there are intermediate levels – patriarchal, regional, perhaps even confessional – these too are communions of communions and embraced in the one catholic communion.

As the local communion is actual as the eucharist, so the one church will finally be actual as a single eternal communion-feast. In the time between the times, this great *communio* cannot yet assemble. Thus each local church can know herself as the same one church with all other local churches only by her openness to that final assembly with them, that is, by 'eucharistic fellowship' with them, by mutual reception at the table and mutual recognition of eucharistic ministers. Between the times, the communion of the one church *is* nothing but universal fellowship in the Eucharist. The point can perhaps be most clearly made by severe statement of the ecumenical mandate: if an assembly of persons claims to be church, and if that assembly recognises another assembly as church, and yet these two assemblies cannot celebrate together, both claims are – at the very best – in extreme jeopardy.

The polity of the church, in so far as it is truly necessary at any time or place, is therefore nothing but the structures by which eucharistic fellowship is enabled and bounded. Therefore, again, the determining part of a church polity is the role and status accorded the ordained ministry, by whatever terminology the latter is denoted or discussed; this is as true of 'free-church' polities as it is of hierarchically elaborated or jurisdictionally defined polities.

There is a broad ecumenical doctrine of ordained ministry that belongs to the *communio*-ecclesiology. As ecumenical consensus-documents often note, the canonical appearance of this institution is in the so-called Pastoral

Epistles. The third-generation leaders to which these documents are addressed are incumbents of established offices, among which the office or offices of 'bishop' and 'presbyter' receive the most attention. It is to the rite by which such office is bestowed that the Pastoral Epistles ask us to attend. So far as the rite and the expectations attached to it can be reconstructed, a charism – itself conceived much in the Pauline way – was understood to be given by invocation of the Spirit and the laying on of hands; and the initiates were charged with preserving and handing on the apostolic teaching.

As ecumenical documents interpret the Pastorals – in my judgement rightly – the content of the bestowed charism is indicated jointly by the general terminology and description of the office and by the charge to guard the apostolic teaching. 'Bishops' or 'presbyters', that is, over-watchers or shepherds, are to watch over or shepherd precisely the church's unity in faith, and particularly her fidelity across time to the teaching of the apostles. Specifically ordained ministry is a 'ministry of unity': the role by which it is defined is that of the *pastor*, of one given to shepherd both the flock's present-tense fellowship, against the centrifugal tendencies of disagreement and unloving behaviour, and the flock's temporal unity as the one church of the apostles, against the disintegrative powers of history.

THE SACRAMENTS AS COMMUNION

In the modern period, the sacraments have often been interpreted individualistically, as 'means' at the disposal of the church – and here it matters little whether the church is conceived in more Catholic or more Protestant fashion – for the benefit of individuals. So baptism is conceived – in almost universal practice also where theory is different – as the means by which the church opens salvation to individuals or by which individuals testify to salvation otherwise gained – and again which of these conceptions operates is beside the present point. So the eucharist is conceived as the manufacture of saving substance for distribution, or as a beautiful ceremony by which individuals come closer to God – and yet again it makes small difference which form of individualism appears.

The New Testament, however, conceives baptism and eucharist, and everything else we might call 'sacrament', very differently. We will explicitly discuss the two 'chief' sacraments, and begin with baptism.

We baptise because we are canonically commanded to do so: 'Go ... and make disciples ... baptising them into the name of the Father and of the Son and of the Holy Spirit' (Matthew 28:19–20). The narrative of the risen Jesus' commissioning appearance presumes that the disciples know what 'baptising' is, as indeed they did. Beyond reasonable doubt, the primal church adapted baptism from the repentance-ritual of John the Baptist, which at least some of the first disciples had themselves undergone. Those whom John's preaching brought to repentance he *washed*; the meaning of the gesture is obvious and its further background need not detain us.

Those washed by John, while they turned from the disobedient aspects of their previous behaviour, did not turn to a new community. Whereas those whom the preaching of the apostles brought to repentance did thereby enter a new community, the missionary church; in the Matthean passage baptism is to 'make disciples'. Thus we may summarise the canonical mandate of baptism so: initiate into the church those whom your preaching calls to repentance, by washing them in the Triune Name.

The blessings biblically attached to washing in the Triune Name exactly correspond to its mandate. The Lukan baptismal kerygma is precise: as baptism is a washing of repentance, it is 'for the forgiveness of your sins'; as it is an initiation into the life of the church, it bestows 'the gift of the holy Spirit' (Acts 2:38). Moreover, the biblical promise is well maintained in theological tradition; so according to Thomas Aquinas, the baptised person 'dies to sins and becomes a member of Christ'.[27] From the third generation of Christians on, the duality of the mandate and of the baptismal blessings has posed a problem which does not come to rest: is the infant of parents already in the community not to be initiated into it, because he or she can hardly be thought to repent? This problem cannot be solved here – and may indeed be permanently unsolvable.

Repentance and forgiveness are events in the lives of individuals. But it is the peculiarity of the Christian rite of repentance and forgiveness, that it is identical with initiation into a particular community; thus if we ask what sin *is*, that is to be repented and forgiven, we can only answer from the specific character of this community. We may therefore turn quickly to the side of the matter that most concerns this chapter: baptism as initiation into the church.

The positive blessings ascribed to baptism in the New Testament are without exception participations in the remarkable privileges claimed for the believing community. In the New Testament, the church is the community of the 'justified' or 'sanctified'; just so, as entry into this community and not the other way around, baptism justifies and sanctifies (1 Corinthians 1:26–31; 6:8–11). The church is a kingdom of priests and a nation of prophets; when the New Testament looks at the church in this way, it sees baptism as the anointing by which priests or prophets are made (Hebrews 10:22; 1 John 2:18–27). The church is persecuted and rescued from persecution; therefore baptism 'saves' (1 Peter 1:3–21). And as the church is the bride of Christ, baptism is her toilette (Ephesians 5:25–7).

Also Paul's great baptismal doctrine in Romans, that we are baptised 'into' Christ so as to participate in his death, burial and resurrection (Romans 6:1–11), works only within his doctrine that the church is Christ's body; here too baptism does what it does by initiating into the church. The doctrine of Romans is clearly intended ontologically, not psychologically: as the church is Christ's body, so what happens to Christ happens to the church, and thus to those encompassed in the communion that the church is.

Since the Holy Spirit is the bond of the church's communion, when we are initiated into the church as the justified community or as the nation of priests or prophets, or into the church as bride or body of Christ, we are initiated into a community made communal by the Spirit. Thus the central and decisive New Testament statement of baptism's gifts is that it bestows the Spirit (Acts 2:38; Mark 1:8; Acts 19:1–7; Ephesians 1:13; 4:30; Hebrews 6:4). And so as soon as this is said, it must be repeated: the Spirit in question is not a mysterious qualification of the individual, he is the spirit in whom the church is bound together as community – as every community is somehow so bound. The only thing to which baptism grants a ticket is life in the church – which is the only ticket creatures can need.

We move on to the other chief sacrament, the eucharist. To make this move we may for conceptual simplicity remain with Paul; if baptism is initiation 'into the body of Christ', and if the continuing reality of that body is that 'we all eat the one loaf', then another compendious statement of what baptism bestows is that it grants the privilege of participation in the eucharist. Baptism initiates into the *communio* that is the church; the Supper is that *communio*.

We cannot make this move conceptually without noting a chief disaster of the Western church, that has in practice undone this connection between baptism and eucharist, on which the experienced meaning of both depends. For most of the church's history it was taken for obvious that baptism and first communion were but one continuous event, whatever the age of the baptised, as it still – perhaps somewhat theoretically – is in the East. But in the West the continuity between baptism and first communion was broken in the twelfth century by a combination of historical circumstances and superstition. That in the West the great majority of the baptised thus go for years without experience of the proper meaning of their baptism, and experience the communion of the eucharist as something *added* to years of a previous supposedly churchly communion, means that the church's *communio* is experientially broken at its centre. No amount of theology, including that of this chapter, can remedy that; only churchly reform can.

That the *res* of the Supper is communion in the church is established ecumenical teaching. So Thomas Aquinas: the *res* is 'the mystical body of Christ', in which we are sanctified 'through union with Christ and with his members'.[28] And so Martin Luther: what the Supper bestows is 'the fellowship of all the saints ... This fellowship consists in this, that all the spiritual possessions of Christ and his saints are shared.'[29]

Also in this connection we must thus speak more of liturgical practice than of any needed new teaching. For centuries, no innocent observer of the Western church's life could have guessed that the eucharist was to bestow and be community. Of catholic and Protestant celebrations alike such an observer would have said: what happens is that one set of individuals create holy objects that are then made available to other individuals on various occasions and for various purposes. Recently, a century's labour by the ecumenical liturgical movement has made some headway against this tradition. But no sooner was this accomplished than an opposite perversion appeared: transformation of the eucharist into a religious social event, celebrating believers' own commitments and feelings for each other.

For here too it must be always remembered: the communion into which baptism initiates and which is actual as the eucharist is first God's communion with us and just and only so our communion with each other. The bond of our fellowship is indeed a usual and powerful bond of human fellowship, that we share food and loving-cup. But *this* bread and cup are the body of Christ. Therefore the bond is not a usual human bond: it transcends time and so transcends also the presence or absence of the usual constituents of association. If my enemy appears with me to celebrate eucharist, I must first seek reconciliation in the terms also of this world; but however well or ill my effort succeeds, if he or she receives the bread and cup my reception of them is a declaration and act of eternal love.

A consistent understanding of sacrament as communion with God in Christ relativises another long-standing occasion of churchly dispute: whether the eucharist may properly be conceived and liturgically practised as the sacrifice of Christ offered to God by the church. The first and enabling point to be made is that everything in the life of the church that may be called sacrament must just so also be called sacrifice, so that the question about the eucharist is only about its *particular* sacrificial character.

Plainly, the acts of churchly communion are all, whatever else they may be, acts performed by the church: the water does not of itself wash the body of the neophyte, the bread and cup must be put on the table, the thanksgiving offered, and the meal shared. In so far as such acts are directed to God, they are what the general language of religion calls 'sacrifice', prayer that is not merely linguistic but is done also by gesture and use of objects, prayer that is embodied. Thus simply to call the eucharist sacrifice must be entirely uncontroversial.

But is the eucharist the sacrifice of Christ? It is at this point that understanding of the eucharist as communion with Christ transcends the old contradictions. For of course the church's communion with Christ, actual as the eucharist, is with the living person, and so must be participation in his own present action before the Father. And that action is very properly described as sacrifice in one specific sense, as it is 'a movement of (self)consecration and renunciation'.[30] So international Anglican–Catholic consensus: 'In the celebration of the memorial, Christ in the Holy Spirit unites his people with himself in a sacramental way, so that the Church enters into the movement of his self-giving.'[31]

POSTSCRIPT

The chapter now concluded says very far from all that is to be said about the church and the sacraments, or the identity in difference between them. It only develops the complex of certain themes suggested by their pairing and by the context of contemporary ecumenical ecclesiology. But this complex, in my judgement, must be somewhere near the centre of any constructive ecclesiology or sacramentology at this time in the history of the church and her theology. Perhaps that may satisfy the mandate of the chapter.

Notes

1 *Lumen gentium*, 1.1
2 *Ibid.*, 7.48.
3 John of Damascus, *The Orthodox Faith*, IV.13.
4 Orthodox–Roman Catholic Dialogue, *The Mystery of the Church and the Eucharist in the Light of the Mystery of the Holy Trinity*, III.2.
5 *Lumen gentium*, 3.23.

6 *Lumen gentium*, 1.1: the council intends to declare 'the nature of the church and its universal mission'.

7 Martin Luther, *Large Catechism*, 'Baptism', 29–30.

8 *Herrschaft und Knechtschaft*. In the paragraph numbering of A. V. Miller's translation, 178–96. G. W. F. Hegel, *Phenomenology of Spirit*, trans. A. V. Miller (Oxford: Oxford University Press, 1977).

9 Martin Luther, *Vom Abendmahl Christi, Bekenntnis*, WA 26, 332.

10 In a nutshell, Augustine, *Epistle* 138:7: 'Signs that pertain to divine things are called sacraments.'

11 Council of Trent, Session VII, First Decree, Canon 6.

12 Centuries of seminarians have striven for ways to remember which of these is which.

13 Thomas Aquinas, *Summa Theologiae*, q.64; q.66.6. Martin Luther, *Large Catechism*, 'Baptism', 10.

14 Thomas Aquinas, *Summa Theologiae*, q.73.1.

15 Philip Melanchthon, *Apologia Confessionis Augustanae*, XIII.1–2.

16 Athanasius, *Against the Arians*, III.23. The author's attention was drawn to this beautifully concise passage by Peter Widdicombe, *The Fatherhood of God from Origen to Athanasius* (Oxford: Clarendon Press, 1994), pp. 243–4.

17 K. Ware and C. Davey (eds.), *Anglican–Orthodox Dialogue: the Moscow Statement Agreed by the Anglican–Orthodox Joint Doctrinal Commission 1976 with Introductory and Supporting Material* (London: SPCK, 1977), p. 24.

18 Orthodox–Roman Catholic dialogue, *The Mystery of the Church*, II.2.

19 *Ibid.*, III.2.

20 Thomas Aquinas, *Summa Theologiae*, 1.q.29.a4.

21 So Tertullian, *Against Praxeas*, xi, 9–10.

22 Petrus Lombardus, *Libri Quatuor Sententiarum*, dis. xvii.2.

23 E.g. the *Disputatio Contra Scholasticum Theologiam*, WA 1:224–8.

24 Robert W. Jenson, *America's Theologian: a Recommendation of Jonathan Edwards* (New York: Oxford, 1988).

25 *Didache*, v, 5.

26 International Roman Catholic–Lutheran Dialogue, *Facing Unity*, 5.

27 Thomas Aquinas, *Summa Theologiae*, 3.q.62.a2.

28 Thomas Aquinas, *Summa Theologiae*, 3.q.73.a1; q.79.a5.

29 Martin Luther, *The Blessed Sacrament of the Holy and True Body of Christ*, WA 2:743.

30 The phrase is taken from the pioneer document of Catholic–Protestant consensus in this matter: Groupe des Dombes, *L'acte sacerdotal du Christ dans l'activité sacerdotale de l'Église* (1962), 3.8.

31 International Anglican–Roman Catholic Dialogue, *Eucharistic Doctrine: Elucidations* (1979), 5.

Further reading

Augustine, St, *The City of God.*

Aquinas, St Thomas, *Summa Theologiae*, iii. qq.60–83.

Dulles, Avery, *Models of the Church*, Garden City, New York: Doubleday, 1974.

Gunton, Colin and Daniel Hardy, editors, *On Being the Church*, Edinburgh: T. & T. Clark, 1989.

Jenson, Robert W., *Unbaptized God: the Basic Flaw in Ecumenical Theology*, Minneapolis: Fortress, 1992.

Luther, Martin, *Great Confession of the Lord's Supper*, 1528.

12 Eschatology

DAVID FERGUSSON

Eschatology has traditionally been understood as the doctrine of the last things (*eschatos* is the Greek word for 'end'). In manuals of doctrine, the four last things were often identified as resurrection, judgement, heaven and hell. The task of eschatology was to elucidate these on the basis of information contained in scripture and tradition. In this way eschatology was the final piece in the jigsaw of Christian belief, and could be set out largely in isolation from the exposition of other doctrines.

One of the hallmarks of twentieth-century theology has been its insistence that eschatology is a central Christian doctrine and conditions every other article of faith. The doctrine of the last things is already embedded within any adequate Christian account of God and creation. One can understand neither the being and action of God nor the purpose of creation without reference to the final end that has been appointed for all nature and history. This eschatological turn in modern theology determines the treatment of scripture, God, creation, Christ, the Holy Spirit and the Christian life.

At the outset it may be worth considering the threat to eschatology posed both by enhanced expectations of the quality of life here and now, at least in the more affluent parts of the world, and also by various theological trends. This has a variety of causes. Progress in medical science has given rise to lower mortality rates amongst children and young adults, while economic growth and technological advance have provided access to material goods and a standard of living almost unimaginable fifty years ago. In this context human aspirations tend to be directed towards life before rather than after death.

Furthermore, the Marxist criticism that hope in the hereafter is a consolation which promotes acquiescence in an unjust *status quo* has been acutely felt within theology. Eschatology as 'pie in the sky when you die'[1] is thus viewed with suspicion. When it distracts from the significance of the here and now, or, even worse, is used to license present sufferings it becomes morally and politically suspect. More recently, Christianity's traditional proclamation of the prospect of a better and more permanent world has raised fears of a theological rationale for environmental complacency or even exploitation. If the physical world is a transient stage for the drama of this life only, then we need not worry unduly about its preservation in perpetuity. Thus environmentally unfriendly eschatologies have been quietly discarded by ecologically aware theologies.

Yet while eschatology has been downgraded or even viewed with suspicion in some quarters, it has proved persistent in other respects. The improvement in living standards has been accompanied by fears of a nuclear catastrophe and environmental degradation. The experience of uncertainty in the present has proved fertile soil for renewed eschatological speculation.[2] In this paradoxical situation, there has been a popular fascination with eschatology in the USA, the richest and most powerful of the nations. In many crude, but highly influential renderings, environmental catastrophe, perhaps through a nuclear war, is anticipated enthusiastically as heralding the millennium. According to Hal Lindsey's best seller *The Late Great Planet Earth*,[3] global trends confirm ancient biblical expectations about a seven-year world war culminating in Armageddon, the second coming of Christ and the establishment of the millennium. Christians, however, are advised that there is an opportunity to avoid this final tribulation through being 'raptured', caught up in the air with Christ and translated to a new mode of existence. Through a bizarre exegesis of biblical passages ripped out of their original context, current events ranging from the establishment of the modern state of Israel, the European Community, the threat of Soviet Communism, ecumenism and drug abuse have all been interpreted as fulfilment of biblical prophecy. The blatant disregard for this world, the avoidance of the cost of Christian discipleship and the implicit anti-Semitism of this vision have all been noted.[4]

Despite the collapse of the Soviet Union (for long the focus of popular apocalyptic concerns) the American interest in prophetic literature continues unabated. In his recent study, Paul Boyer has carefully shown how this has continued with reference to the politics of the Middle East, threats to the environment and the imminence of the year 2000. Those trends which have eroded secular confidence in the future have led to a revival of older religious eschatologies. This is a significant social phenomenon in American society, and is facilitated by a network of seminaries, Bible schools, publishing houses, Christian bookstores and radio and TV programmes.[5]

In face of such trends, the task of a responsible eschatology today is to demonstrate that Christian hope for the future bestows a significance upon the present time and instils a sense of responsibility within the church for the world. Instead of presenting a demobilising ideology, eschatology should enable an effective and sober Christian witness.

ESCHATOLOGY IN SCRIPTURE

For the writers of the Bible, history is a field in which God's purposes are progressively enacted. Although this is not a smooth and unambiguous progress, the future is nonetheless expected as a time in which God's intentions will be decisively disclosed. Eschatology, rather than dealing simply with the last things, can be seen more broadly in the Bible as concerned with important changes in the course of history through God's action. Thus the Old Testament is concerned, at an early stage, with national eschatology (the future of Israel), and cosmic eschatology (the future of the world), but only at a later stage with personal eschatology (the future of the individual).

In much of the imagery used to depict the future, national and cosmic hopes are intertwined. In the celebrated vision of Isaiah 11:1–9 the anointed emissary of God will bring justice not only to Israel but to the whole earth. 'The wolf shall dwell with the lamb, and the leopard shall lie down with the kid, and the calf and the lion and the fatling together; and a little child shall lead them.' Similarly in several of the Psalms, God's restoration of Israel is an act which involves the other nations and even the non-human creation. 'He has remembered his steadfast love and faithfulness to the house of Israel. All the ends of the earth have seen the victory of our God' (Psalm 98:3).

The release of the Jewish captives from exile in Babylon, following the edict of Cyrus in 538 BC, is seen by Second Isaiah as an event which heralds the final salvation of Israel. It is an event, moreover, which is of significance for all the rulers and nations of the earth. 'It is too light a thing that you should be my servant to raise up the tribes of Jacob and to restore the preserved of Israel; I will give you as a light to the nations, that my salvation may reach to the end of the earth' (Isaiah 49:6).

Yet the history of Israel did not entirely fulfil these hopes. The context of Haggai and Zechariah reveals a community sunk in poverty, having squandered the opportunity of better things. The hopes of Second Isaiah are thus projected further into the future. In so-called Third Isaiah there is perhaps the beginning of a notion of a radically new order of creation which God will bring about. 'For behold I create new heavens and a new earth; and the former things shall not be remembered or come into mind' (Isaiah 65:17).

In Daniel, one of the latest books of the Old Testament, there is a movement towards an eschatology in which both the community and its members find fulfilment in a life beyond death. The book of Daniel also belongs to the genre of apocalyptic literature, in which the writer's visions of a transcendent heaven reveal past, present and future trends of earthly history under God's control. The most famous vision is in chapter 7 where four great beasts arise out of the sea. After the slaying of the fourth beast, dominion over the nations is given to 'one like a son of man' who represents in some way 'the people of the saints of the Most High'. In the final chapter of Daniel, the Old Testament speaks unambiguously about a personal resurrection (at least of some) from the dead. 'Many of those who sleep in the dust of the earth shall awake, some to everlasting life, and some to shame and everlasting contempt. And those who are wise shall shine like the brightness of the firmament' (Daniel 12:2–3).

The fusion of the apocalyptic literary genre with Jewish theological themes produces an apocalyptic eschatology which provides the backdrop to much of the New Testament. What are its necessary features? 'Apocalypse' is a form of literature in which a revelation from a heavenly realm is imparted to a human being.[6] This revelation discloses both the coming end of the world, and the nature of the supernatural world. In apocalyptic eschatology we encounter a vision of the end of history which includes not only the Jewish people but all the nations of the earth, and which understands the end of the world as coming about through a sudden irruption of God into the flow of world history. There is thus a radical discontinuity between present time and the future age. In depicting the end time in this way, several typical features of apocalyptic eschatology emerge. There will be a great struggle between the forces of good and evil with the former triumphing decisively over the latter. This results in a pattern of events: crisis; judgement; and vindication.

These themes are developed in Judaism before, during and after the time of the New Testament. For example, in writings from the Pseudepigrapha such as 1 Enoch, 4 Ezra (=2 Esdras) and 3 Baruch apocalyptic–eschatological ideas are prominent and the image of the Messiah assumes greater significance. He brings about the salvation of Israel through the destruction of her enemies. In the final triumph of God's purpose all ungodly forces in the cosmos must be defeated. The kingdom is to be finally established both on earth and in heaven. The power and unity of God over all creation will be manifested in a complete victory which will embrace the whole cosmos and all forces at work therein. Such visions are granted to the apocalyptic writers who stand at the brink of the end times. The outcome of history is for them universal (it determines all nations), decisive (people are judged and the righteous triumph) and transcendent (it depends upon the action of God which intervenes to end the current course of world history).

In the teaching of Jesus people are confronted with a decision that is of eschatological significance. 'The kingdom of God is at hand; repent, and believe in the gospel' (Mark 1:15). The present has now taken on decisive significance, for the future has already begun. The relationship between present and future in Jesus' eschatological message of the kingdom has divided commentators. Is this an eschatology which is realised, inaugurated, historical or other-worldly? Perhaps one can even say that the texts lead in different directions and that the message of Jesus reflects all these aspects. The kingdom of God is to come, but yet it has already begun decisively with the appearance of Jesus. A further question concerns the extent to which Jesus' message can properly be regarded as apocalyptic. While apocalyptic themes are present, there are nonetheless important differences. Jesus' message is preoccupied with what men and women should do now, rather than with heavenly visions of the future. Moreover, his proclamation of God's unbounded mercy towards sinners contrasts with the theme of the punishment of the ungodly. The future is spoken of in terms of eschatological significance and hope, but in Jesus (and Paul) we tend to find eschatology with apocalpytic elements rather than apocalyptic world views with some eschatological elements.[7]

The term kingdom of God (or kingdom of heaven) appears 122 times throughout the Bible. In 99 of these cases, the usage is in the Synoptic Gospels, and, of those, 90 instances are from the words of Jesus. The kingdom of God is a community which lives in obedience to the generosity, forgiveness and righteousness of God. It is a society in which physical handicap and weakness are overcome; in which racial and religious differences are ended; in which there is justice for the poor, the oppressed and the powerless; and in which the dead are raised. The bodily and communitarian nature of the kingdom of God was often lost sight of in Christian tradition, but it is integral to the teaching of Jesus and to an authentic eschatology today. In this respect there is a fundamental contrast between a philosophical account of the natural immortality of the individual soul, and the theological belief in a resurrection of the body by the grace and power of God.

The resurrection of Jesus from the dead, and his subsequent presence in the church through the work of the Holy Spirit, are to be understood in terms of their eschatological and apocalyptic significance. The resurrection is the

sure sign of the general resurrection of the dead; the exaltation of Jesus anticipates his final reign; the Christian life in the Holy Spirit is already the first
fruit of the coming kingdom. The faith of the church is thus irreducibly
eschatological. It cannot be understood except in terms of convictions about
the future, and the role of Christ in that future. The presence of Christ and
the Spirit in the worship, fellowship and witness of the church here and now
carries a necessary reference to a future which is prayed for and expected.
'Fear not, I am the first and the last, and the living one; I died, and behold I
am alive for evermore, and I have the keys of Death and Hades' (Revelation
1:17–18).

ESCHATOLOGY IN THE CHRISTIAN TRADITION

It is sometimes argued that eschatology was replaced by ecclesiology as
hopes for an imminent return of Jesus gradually receded in the early church.
Instead of the last things, emphasis fell upon the role of the institutional
church in the present time. At most this is a half-truth. The institutional
church assumed a growing significance in the history of early Christianity,
yet the church was understood as a vehicle which enabled the believer to
attain everlasting happiness beyond death. The content of eschatological
hopes continued to form the *terminus ad quem* of the Christian life. In the
eschatologies of most of the Church Fathers a pattern emerges from New
Testament sources. At death, all human beings enter some intermediate
state, perhaps sleep or a disembodied existence. This is followed by the
return of Christ (the *parousia*), the resurrection of all the dead, their judgement and final destiny in either heaven or hell. These ideas were elaborated
and systematised in the Middle Ages. The most graphic portrayal of an
eschatological scheme is found in Dante's *Divine Comedy* with its depiction
of the circles of hell and heaven, concluding in its final canto with the vision
of the Trinity and the flooding of the poet's will and desire by the love of God,
'the love that moves the sun and the other spheres'.

At the Reformation, the concentration upon the radical nature of God's
grace towards the believer in Jesus Christ brought some shift in eschatological focus. In the writings of Martin Luther, there is a sense of the urgency
of the times in which he is living and the struggle with the enemies of the
gospel. By equating the papacy with the Antichrist, Luther eagerly expected
the imminent defeat of the powers of darkness. This day would be a time of
deliverance, and therefore was one for which he longed fervently. Thus he
could stand alongside the church of the New Testament and look for the

'dear last day'.[8] John Calvin, while more reserved in his use of apocalyptic imagery – Revelation was the only book of the New Testament on which he did not write a commentary – had a strong sense of the union of the believer with the risen and ascended Lord, particularly in his doctrine of the Lord's Supper. The assurance of salvation with Christ in heaven is here affirmed in a more immediate and particular way.

Throughout the history of the church, however, there have been fringe groups proffering a more detailed and urgent eschatology usually in criticism of the complacency of the established church. Montanus in the second century predicted that the heavenly city was about to appear in a plain in Phrygia. Joachim of Fiore, a twelfth-century monk, claimed that the ages of the Father and the Son were soon to be superseded by the new age of the Spirit when the Christian faith would spread across the earth through the work of the new religious orders. At the time of the Reformation, Thomas Münzer preached the imminence of the *parousia* and Christ's millennial reign. The response for which he called involved a waging of violent war against the rich. In general the church has proved deeply suspicious of such apocalyptic movements on its fringes. Since Augustine interpreted the millennium of Revelation 20 not as some future interim reign of Christ but as the present life of the church on earth, the theologians of the mainstream churches have generally resisted millenarian tendencies, condemning them as fantastic and fanatical.[9]

In the nineteenth and twentieth centuries, the most potent version of this apocalyptic story has come in secular guise. For Karl Marx, history is the arena of a class struggle in which the proletariat are destined to overthrow by revolutionary means the ruling capitalist class. When this happens a communist society will arrive in which alienation is overcome, and human beings will find fulfilment in the fruits of their labour. This society, moreover, will be one which no longer has any need for the ideological consolation of religion. The eschatological tenor of this communist vision of the future of history has often been commented upon. 'Marx's vision of the end-state is of a classless society rising from the ashes of an apocalyptic-type struggle of good and evil forces. Here religious eschatology, mediated in its heretical chiliastic forms, becomes radically secularized. The transcendent becomes immanent, the theological becomes teleological, the hereafter nothing but the postrevolutionary future.'[10]

While the historical determinism of Marx's philosophy was abandoned by many later Marxist thinkers, it is not hard to understand why this vision of the future inspired revolutionary activists. In his three-volume *Principle of Hope*,[11] Ernst Bloch argued that hope is a universal characteristic of human existence from the cradle to the grave. The achievement of Marx's philosophy lies in its relating knowledge to future possibilities. At the same time, all aspirations must be related to realistic prospects. There is thus a close setting of reason and hope in a relationship of mutual interdependence. Although the future must be anticipated in sober thought, the element of enthusiasm should not be suppressed.

This secular eschatology reveals significant points of both contact and difference with Christian theology. The future is eagerly anticipated as a time in which present imperfections and injustices can be overcome. History, and not merely the private destinies of individuals, is charged with significance. Human existence in the present assumes a definite importance in the light of an expected future. On the other hand, for the Christian the coming future is dependent upon the action of God. The present does not contain an intrinsic quality which will inevitably yield a better future. We must await and pray patiently for God's coming kingdom. Until this arrives, the failings of human nature will be manifested in new and unexpected ways. Confirmation of this can be found in the fate of Marxist politics in the former Soviet Union where the overthrow of one unjust order merely created the possibility for new and more frightening forms of tyranny. By sweeping out one unclean spirit, the house merely becomes available to seven more evil spirits (Matthew 12:43f.). From the Marxist side, it may be argued that Christian eschatology is too quietist and provides inadequate support for political change. To place one's hopes only in a final divine irruption is to undermine human effort. To insist that the marks of sin will be manifest until the end of time is to leave people without genuine hope of moral and material improvement. This tension between secular (this-worldly) and theological (other-worldly) eschatologies continues to be felt.

THE REDISCOVERY OF ESCHATOLOGY

In twentieth-century theology, eschatology has been recovered as a central theme. There are several reasons for this. The liberal theology that flourished in Germany at the turn of the century presented an account of Jesus which focused upon an ethical and religious message largely devoid of first-century eschatology. This was part of the husk of primitive Christianity which had to be discarded in the effort to lay bare the kernel of Jesus' life and example. The revolt against the theology of Albrecht Ritschl and Adolf Harnack took various forms.

The historical interpretation of the New Testament could not support the notion that apocalyptic eschatology was an accretion upon the essential gospel. Johannes Weiss and Albert Schweitzer, both New Testament scholars, argued that eschatology belonged to the essence of Jesus' message, and that it could not be understood except in this light. Jesus' words, actions and mission all presupposed the kingdom of God. He summoned others to prepare for God's rule on earth and he understood his own ministry as fulfilling a decisive role in bringing this about. The conclusion of Schweitzer's *Quest for the Historical Jesus* seemed convincing precisely because it was theologically problematic. He could not be accused of presenting a reading of the New Testament to fit a preconceived theological theory. On the contrary, his exegetical conclusions made theologising a precarious endeavour. For Schweitzer, the erroneous nature of Jesus' belief about the final coming of God's kingdom entailed that his mission had to be judged a failure in at least one sense.

> In the knowledge that He is the coming Son of Man He [Jesus] lays hold of the wheel of the world to set it moving on that last revolution which is to bring our ordinary history to a close. It refuses to turn, and He throws himself upon it. Then it does turn; and crushes Him. Instead of bringing in the eschatological conditions, He has destroyed them. The wheel rolls onward, and the mangled body of the one immeasurably great Man, who was strong enough to think of Himself as the spiritual ruler of mankind, and to bend history to His purpose, is hanging upon it still. That is His victory and His reign.[12]

Whether or not Schweitzer's thoroughgoing eschatological reading of the New Testament is conceded, it is clear that eschatology was not an optional extra for Jesus or the early church. The message of the kingdom, the Lord's prayer, the resurrection of Jesus, the sacraments, life in the Spirit – all have an eschatological shape. These can only be understood in terms of a future that is expected and for which human beings must prepare.

The rise of dialectical theology after the First World War also brought a renewed emphasis upon eschatological themes. The notion of a gradual progress of human history towards the kingdom of God had been shattered by the carnage of war, and the theological culture of the 1920s and 30s saw a reaction against liberal theology. This reaction had an eschatological cast. Karl Barth complained that Protestant theology had lulled us 'to sleep by adding at the conclusion of Christian Dogmatics a short and perfectly harmless chapter entitled – "Eschatology"'.[13] What the church needed to hear, however, was an eschatology which spoke of the 'infinite qualitative distinction' (Søren Kierkegaard) between eternity and time, the Creator and the creature. Thus, eschatology was used not so much to speak of a time that lies ahead of us, as the eternal, uncontrollable action of God from above to below.

Barth's theology proceeded from the Romans commentary to speak of the significance of created time in the light of the incarnation, death, resurrection and *parousia*, and thus to offer a more linear account of the theology of history. Rudolf Bultmann, another dialectical theologian, wished to jettison much of the New Testament's 'mythological world view' and to speak only of the significance of the present moment for the individual when confronted by the Word of God.[14] Eschatology is here largely reduced to the encounter of the individual with God in the present time. This encounter calls for faith but not one which can be expressed by a naive theology of history dominated by conceptions of an intermediate state, the *parousia*, the resurrection of the body, etc. These notions are the residue of an outdated world view, and cannot be the preoccupation of Christian faith in the modern world.

The theology of the second half of this century has nonetheless insisted against Bultmann that the apocalyptic and eschatological images of the New Testament should not be so swiftly dismissed. This is largely a reaction against the individualism and ahistorical trend of his anthropology. A human being can be understood only in terms of the community to which s/he belongs, and the history in which s/he is located. Jürgen Moltmann's *Theologie der Hoffnung* (1965) located eschatology at the beginning of theology rather than the end, on the grounds that hope for the future was a fundamental characteristic of faith in the God of the Bible. The resurrection of Jesus is an event which reveals a future for the world, a future which is described by the New Testament in Jewish apocalyptic and eschatological images. Eschatology cannot therefore be abstracted into a timeless encounter between God and the individual. The claim that God's action comes 'from above' to intersect time, rather than 'at the end' to fulfil time leads to a loss of historical and political hope. The mission of Jesus, confirmed in the resurrection, is intelligible only in terms of what is promised. 'His future, in the light of which he can be recognized as what he is, is illuminated in advance by the promise of the righteousness of God, the promise of life as a result of resurrection from the dead, and the promise of the kingdom of God in a new totality of being.'[15]

In the writings of another contemporary German theologian, Wolfhart

Pannenberg, there has been a renewed emphasis upon eschatology. The meaning of the present can only be known in the light of the future. God is the one who must be thought of as the power of the future, and the kingdom of God – the central motif of the teaching of Jesus – is the future that is promised to us. For Pannenberg, the resurrection of Jesus is both the proleptic anticipation of the future of the world and also the power of this future already at work in the present. In this respect, the categories of apocalyptic thought have to be reworked *post resurrectionem*. The eschatological future of God already present in Jesus is the standpoint from which we must understand the world as a whole. Thus even the creation of the world must be elucidated by reference to the eschaton.[16]

Eschatological themes are powerfully advocated by liberation theologies. The context of oppression and the integration of theology with a praxis of liberation provide a strong contrast between the present and the future that is to be ushered in. Yet this must be a future which can in some sense be actualised by political struggle here and now. Liberation theology, like Marxism, is deeply suspicious of an eschatology which so stresses the discontinuity between present and future that it ignores the prospect of improvement in history. The 'eschatological proviso' in traditional theologies is castigated for deliberately dampening hopes for life in this world. Juan Luis Segundo argues that the qualifying of all human work by the Lutheran doctrine of justification by faith relativises every political system. In the end this approach tends towards passivity and to the theologian turning away from politics in disgust.[17]

Reinhold Niebuhr argued that history after Christ is an interim between the revelation and the fulfilment of its meaning. In this eschatological tension the kingdom can be revealed but can never triumph until the end of history. This creates an eschatological reserve whereby no possible state of affairs prior to the end of the world can be invested with ultimate value or can command absolute allegiance. The other-worldliness of apocalyptic thought, with its claim that the kingdom can only be brought about by the irruption of God at the end of history, prevents one from investing any political programme or form of social organisation with ultimate significance. At the same time, the possibility remains for protest and reform in the time that God has graciously given us between the resurrection of Jesus and the end of the world. Yet this may be suspiciously quietist and insufficiently radical for much liberation theology. The distraction of a trans-historical and trans-worldly hope can do little to assist the cause of the oppressed in the present.

ISSUES IN CONTEMPORARY ESCHATOLOGY

The individual and corporate dimensions of the kingdom of God

Within the Christian tradition, the life everlasting has often been conceived as largely a private affair involving the soul's contemplation of God. This has doubtless had something to do with the tendency to consider the immortal soul as the essential person. Once the soul is conceptually detached from the body and its domain in the physical and social world, the communal dimension of human existence is difficult to recapture. Death is pictured, not so much as a translation to a new form of embodied life, but as a release from the imperfections and limitations of the body. The classic philosophical statement of this notion of death as liberation from the body is found in Plato's *Phaedo*.

Nonetheless, the Christian tradition has been prevented by its scriptures from describing the redeemed life in terms of a solitary or disembodied paradise. The God of the Bible has appointed us to a physical mode of existence. This is confirmed by the creation stories of Genesis; by the way in which Hebrew anthropology conceives of the human person as a psychosomatic unity (there is no possibility of a sharp conceptual distinction between body and soul as in Greek philosophy); by the incarnation, resurrection and ascension of Christ as an embodied person; and by Pauline descriptions of the resurrection of the body in the new age. The theme of resurrection as opposed to immortality extends the Old Testament concern with the establishment of God's righteousness on earth. The resurrection of Jesus is both a vindication of his message regarding the kingdom of God and a sign of the full arrival of that kingdom. In the eschatological vision of Revelation 21, the exalted Lamb will illumine the holy city, and in the light of God the nations and kings of the earth shall walk.[18]

The tendency in the Bible, therefore, is to speak of the kingdom of God not as a release from our present mode of physical existence, but as a transformation of the entire created order. The redemption which is promised is one which involves not only human persons, but societies, other living beings and the realm of nature. 'The creation itself will be set free from its bondage to decay and obtain the glorious liberty of the children of God' (Romans 8:21).

Where human existence is understood as essentially embodied, its communal nature also becomes apparent. The physical world with which we interact is also the world of other people. We are dependent upon the society of others for physical sustenance, for affection and for the acquisition of knowledge. The capacity to think and speak is dependent upon our mastery of language in a public world. The call to Israel to enter into a covenant relationship with God requires not only the ordering of their religious life but the ordering of society according to the divine law. The love of God and the love of one's neighbour cannot be separated, and within the community of the church there is the fellowship (*koinonia*) of the Holy Spirit which itself is an anticipation of the greater communion of the coming kingdom of God.

The significance of *koinonia* has been shown in different ways in recent theology. Where the doctrine of the Trinity is allowed to control our thinking about God and the world, the notion of communion will assume greater importance for describing the goal of creation. The end of human existence is to reflect under creaturely conditions the eternal love that is grounded in the life of the trinitarian persons. Ecclesial existence is the manner in which the future is already present in lives of freedom and love redeemed by the Father through the Son in the Holy Spirit. 'The truth and the ontology of the person belong to the future, are images of the future.'[19] The Eucharist is to be understood as a foretaste of the end of all things. As such it is a sacrament in which believers are not only bound to God but also to one another. The Eucharist opens up the vision of the divine rule which has been promised as the final renewal of creation, and is a foretaste of it. Signs of this renewal are present in the world wherever the grace of God is manifest and human beings work for justice, love and peace. The Eucharist is the feast at which the church gives thanks to God for these signs and joyfully celebrates and anticipates the coming of the kingdom in Christ (1 Corinthians 11:26; Matthew 26:29).[20]

At the same time, the emphasis upon community must be seen as the correlative of the emphasis upon the individual. The fellowship of the kingdom of God is an inclusive society which seeks the welfare of both the outsider and the insider. The ministry of Jesus is at least as much concerned with the one outside the flock, as with the ninety-nine inside. In its affirmation of the individual, albeit an individual whose identity is social, Christian theology stands against secular ideologies such as Marxism and Darwinism which tend to sacrifice the interests of individuals to the progress of society or the species. It is partly for this reason that eschatology has understood the work of Christ to be of decisive significance not merely for those who have lived within the influence of the visible church. It reaches backwards in time and outwards in space to determine the destiny of every human being.

The images that are used to describe the eschatological age are at best indicators. They point towards a new quality of existence, but because it is qualitatively different from the present we lack the vocabulary and thus the knowledge to describe it. The words of Luther are worth recalling. 'We know no more about eternal life than children in the womb of their mother know about the world they are about to enter.'[21] Yet the images that are employed provide a direction both for our hopes and for our energies here and now. Hendrikus Berkhof has argued that statements about eternal life should be based on the principles of exclusion and extrapolation from Christian life in the world.[22] The principle of exclusion enables us to speak of eternal life as life without sin, disease, catastrophe or death. The principle of extrapolation, on the other hand, requires us to think in terms of a fuller vision of God centred around Christ who calls forth our praise and gratitude, a perfected oneness with other human beings, an ordering of society in which there is neither fear, hatred nor discrimination, and a lifting up of nature as the world within which this takes place.

The relationship between this world and the next

We have already observed the unease amongst Marxists and liberationists regarding an other-worldly eschatology. In contemporary theology, this is increasingly registered by those concerned with the protection of the environment. The thought that this world is passing away can easily be allied to the notion that its ecosystem is finally dispensable. 'Christendom is surely not accidentally the culture whose holy book happens to culminate in a vision of the imminent devastation of the earth, the culture that has developed the technologies and politics capable of Armageddon, nuclear or greenhouse.'[23]

Is there a way of affirming the apocalyptic notion that the kingdom of God will be fully established only by the divine recreative act at the end of history, without thereby diminishing our commitment to this world? This remains one of the central challenges to contemporary eschatology. The response might begin by noting that the importance of the present has often been most intensely felt by those who expected the end of the world. The promise of the kingdom in the Bible, moreover, acts in two ways. First, it empowers those who are called to serve God in the present. The context of New Testament teaching about the apocalypse is one in which the consolation of the future is never allowed to distract from the present. The eschatological chapters towards the conclusion of Matthew's gospel are fraught with warnings about neglecting the service of God in the present. The Son of Man already confronts us in the poor, the sick and the hungry. The discourse about the end of the world should not be (though it often is) allowed 'to abstract the reader from the challenge of facing the cost of the shadow of suffering and martyrdom'.[24] Second, it instils into that present, despite its miseries and trials, a sense of joy and celebration. This is a quality of Christian existence made possible between the resurrection of Jesus and the end of the world. It is the positive result of the eschatological tension between the now and the not yet of God's promise to us. This is acclaimed as the ecclesial context of recent liberation theology. 'This happy intense hope, despite the tears of yesterday and today, is not a private perspective on life, but reflects the ecstatic spirituality of black liturgy or the celebration of the eucharist in the basic community in Brazil or Central America.'[25]

Universalism or separationism?

Recent eschatological literature has been much exercised by the question of universalism. Will all God's creatures eventually be gathered into the kingdom? Or are there some who will forfeit this privilege and be condemned to a final separation? While the New Testament appears for the most part to assume a separationist position, universalism has not been without its distinguished advocates in the history of the church. Origen believed that God's will must triumph in all his creatures, and that everyone, including even the devil, will return to God. In modern times, writers from Friedrich Schleiermacher to John Hick have contended that anything other than a universalist outcome would be an affront to the love of God. On this scenario divine judgement and punishment must be construed as rehabilitative rather than retributive in intent; hell is an interim state which is coextensive with purgatory. Karl Barth comes close to a universalist position when contending that we must hope for the salvation of all God's people but that this is not something that we can unequivocally assert without impugning the divine sovereignty.[26]

The respective arguments for universalism and separationism can be set out briefly. The universalist can point to various inclusive strains within scripture which may be regarded as more consistent with its essential message of the unconditional love God set forth in Jesus Christ (for example, 1 Corinthians 15:22; Colossians 1:19–20; Philippians 2:9–11; 1 Timothy 2:4–6). It can also be argued that if God's purpose is to redeem the whole creation this will not be frustrated in the long run. The notion of hell as eternal torment is regarded as morally intolerable by universalists, and unworthy of a God whose nature is love. If Jesus teaches us that our forgiveness should know no limits will this not also be true of God? Death should not be regarded as a point in time when the love of God will be withheld, nor should hell be characterised as a place where people are beyond reach of the divine mercy.[27] Universalism is also typically concerned with the destiny of those who have lived before or beyond the proclamation of the Christian faith. Their eternal destiny, it is claimed, cannot be determined by an accident of either history or geography. We must assume therefore something like a post-mortem encounter with Christ which will enable them to enter his kingdom.[28]

The arguments for separationism are simple. It is claimed that this is the clear and consistent message of scripture, and that to deny this involves a strangely literalist reading of a handful of isolated texts. It has also been the mainstream consensus position of the entire Christian tradition. Separationism claims to make sense of the seriousness of our choices here and now, and to do justice to the freedom which God has bestowed upon us. If God had granted us the possibility of accepting his kingdom, this must imply the possibility of a final refusal. Separationism is consistent with the view that most people will be saved, including many who never heard the name of Christ in this life, but it rejects an explicit universalism which teaches that none will finally be lost.

The truth claims of eschatology

How and in what sense can eschatology today be considered true, as opposed merely to inspiring, instructive or consolatory? Much recent theology indeed seems more concerned with the political correctness of eschatological utterance than with its truth. On what basis should eschatological claims be believed as more than the outcome of disappointment with the present? Why should these be entertained as other than the projections on to an ever receding future of the frustrated faithful?

The traditional scriptural images of the end are problematic if we suppose them to be detailed, albeit coded, messages from the future. The apocalyptic images of the Bible are too opaque, too inconsistent and too conditioned by their original *Sitz-im-Leben* (life-context) to be considered cryptic statements about how the world will end. Christian faith and hope, moreover, are predicated upon our ignorance of exactly how the future will be.[29]

Eschatology should be understood as the transposition of fundamental Christian statements about the world, ourselves and God into claims about the form, though not the precise content, of the future.[30] Christian hope in the kingdom of God is based upon Christ crucified and risen. These claims stand or fall with the truth of faith in the mission of Christ, in the God of Israel to whom he witnessed and in the activity of the Holy Spirit here and now. Confidence in the future is not a peculiar esoteric insight. It is a function of faith in God – Father, Son and Spirit – and a way of expressing the significance of that faith for the future of the world. Amidst the presence of injustice, suffering and death, Christian faith until the end of time must take the form of hope for the future. Such a hopeful conviction about the end of the world and its people is demanded by belief in creation's continuing status as loved by God, redeemed by Christ and brought to fulfilment by the Spirit. It is a belief properly expressed not in unwarranted speculation but in prayer, praise and Christian service.

Notes

1 The term comes from a rallying song, 'The Preacher and the Slave' (1911), of the International Workers of the World.
2 A study of church history suggests that eschatological trends may always have affected sectors of the Christian community. Cf. Norman Cohn, *The Pursuit of the Millennium* (New York: Harper & Row, 1961).
3 *The Late Great Planet Earth* (London: Marshall Pickering, 1971).
4 For theological criticism of Lindsey et al. see Daniel Migliore, *Faith Seeking Understanding* (Grand Rapids, Michigan: Eerdmans, 1991), pp. 235–6; Gabriel Fackre, 'Eschatology and Systematics', *Ex Auditu*, 6 (1990): 110–12.
5 Paul Boyer, *When Time Shall Be No More: Prophecy Belief in Modern American Culture* (Cambridge, Massachusetts: Belknap Press of Harvard University Press, 1992), p. 339.
6 I am following here the discussion of terms in Zachary Hayes, *Visions of a Future: A Study of Christian Eschatology* (Wilmington, Delaware: Michael Glazier, 1989), pp. 31ff.
7 Cf. Ben Witherington III, *Jesus, Paul and the End of the World* (Downers Grove, Illinois: IVP, 1992).
8 Luther wrote 'Komm, lieber jungster Tag' (Come, dear last day) in concluding a letter to his wife on 16 July 1540. Cf. *Martin Luthers Briefe*, Zweite Band (Leipzig: Inselverlag, 1960), p. 167.
9 For a helpful survey of eschatology in the history of the church see Brian Hebblethwaite, *The Christian Hope* (Basingstoke: Marshall, Morgan & Scott, 1984).
10 Carl Braaten, 'The Kingdom of God and the Life Everlasting', *Christian Theology: An Introduction to its Traditions and Tasks* (London: SPCK, 1983), p. 287.
11 *The Principle of Hope*, trans. Neville Plaice et al. (Oxford: Blackwell, 1985).

12 Albert Schweitzer, *The Quest of the Historical Jesus: A Critical Study of its Progress from Reimarus to Wrede* (London: Macmillan, 1966), pp. 370–1.

13 Karl Barth, *The Epistle to the Romans*, trans. Edwyn C. Hoskyns (London: Oxford University Press, 1933), p. 500.

14 'The New Testament and Mythology' (1941) is reprinted in Rudolf Bultmann, *New Testament and Mythology and Other Basic Writings* (London: SCM, 1985), pp. 1–43.

15 Jürgen Moltmann, *Theology of Hope* (London: SCM, 1967), p. 203.

16 Wolfhart Pannenberg, *Systematic Theology*, trans. Geoffrey W. Bromiley (Edinburgh: T. & T. Clark, 1994) vol. ii, pp. 136ff. The most succinct statement of Pannenberg's position is presented in 'Dogmatic Theses on the Doctrine of Revelation', in Pannenberg (ed.), *Revelation as History* (New York: Macmillan, 1963), pp. 123–58.

17 Juan Luis Segundo, *The Liberation of Theology* (New York: Orbis Books, 1976), p. 147. For an important discussion of this issue see Dennis P. McCann, *Christian Realism and Political Theology* (New York: Orbis Books, 1981), pp. 172ff.

18 Cf. Christopher Rowland, 'Interpreting the Resurrection', in Paul Avis (ed.), *The Resurrection of Jesus Christ* (London: Darton, Longman and Todd, 1993), pp. 68–84.

19 John D. Zizioulas, *Being as Communion: Studies in Personhood and the Church* (London: Darton, Longman and Todd, 1985), p. 62.

20 Faith and Order Commission of the World Council of Churches, *Baptism, Eucharist and Ministry* (Geneva: World Council of Churches, 1982), paragraph 22.

21 Cited by Paul Althaus, *The Theology of Martin Luther* (Philadelphia: Fortress, 1966), p. 425.

22 Hendrikus Berkhof, *Christian Faith* (Grand Rapids, Michigan: Eerdmans, 1986), p. 540.

23 Catherine Keller, 'Eschatology, Ecology, and a Green Ecumenacy', in Rebecca S. Chopp and Mark Lewis Taylor (eds.), *Reconstructing Christian Theology* (Minneapolis: Fortress, 1994), p. 341.

24 Christopher Rowland, 'Reflections on the Politics of the Gospels', in R. S. Barbour (ed.), *The Kingdom of God and Human Society* (Edinburgh: T. & T. Clark, 1993), p. 228.

25 Theo Witvliet, *A Place in the Sun* (London: SCM, 1985), p. 40.

26 Cf. Richard Bauckham, 'Universalism: A Historical Survey', *Themelios* 4.2 (1979): 48–54.

27 This is advocated by Jürgen Moltmann, *Jesus Christ in Today's World* (London: SCM, 1994) and in *The Coming of God. Christian Eschatology*, trans. Margaret Kohl (London: SCM Press, 1996), pp. 235–55.

28 Cf. Stephen Davis, 'Universalism, Hell and the Fate of the Ignorant', *Modern Theology* 6.2 (1990): 174–86.

29 Modern science suggests that the physical universe will either burn itself out through indefinite expansion or suffer contraction to a point of infinite density. The consequent fate of human life is explored from the perspective of 'scientific eschatology' by Frank Tipler in *The Physics of Immortality* (London: Macmillan, 1995).

30 This is argued in an important essay by Karl Rahner, 'The Hermeneutics of Eschatological Assertions', *Theological Investigations* IV (London: Darton, Longman and Todd, 1966), pp. 323–46.

Further reading

Braaten, Carl, 'The Kingdom of God and the Life Everlasting', *Christian Theology: An Introduction to its Traditions and Tasks*, London: SPCK, 1983, pp. 274–98.

Gowan, Donald E., *Eschatology in the Old Testament*, Edinburgh: T. & T. Clark, 1986.

Hayes, Zachary, *Visions of a Future: A Study of Christian Eschatology*, Wilmington, Delaware: Michael Glazier, 1989.

Hebblethwaite, Brian, *The Christian Hope*, Basingstoke: Marshall, Morgan & Scott, 1984.

Hick, John, *Death and Eternal Life*, London: Collins, 1976.

Moltmann, Jürgen, *The Coming of God. Christian Eschatology*, translated by Margaret Kohl, London: SCM Press, 1996.

Rahner, Karl, 'The Hermeneutics of Eschatological Assertions', *Theological Investigations* IV, London: Darton, Longman and Todd, 1966, pp. 323–46.

Schwartz, Hans, 'Eschatology', in Carl Braaten and Robert Jenson, editors, *Christian Dogmatics*, volume II, Philadelphia: Fortress, 1984, pp. 475–587.

Wainwright, Geoffrey, 'The Last Things', in Geoffrey Wainwright, editor, *Keeping the Faith*, Pennsylvania: Fortress & Pickwick, 1988, pp. 341–469.

Witherington, Ben, III, *Jesus, Paul and the End of the World*, Downers Grove, Illinois: IVP, 1992.

13 Jesus Christ

KATHRYN TANNER

Not all Christian theologies are overtly christocentric; they do not all make Jesus Christ the focal point for their exposition of theological topics.[1] But Jesus Christ is arguably the centrepiece of every Christian theology in so far as beliefs in and about him mark with special clarity the distinctiveness of a Christian religious perspective and have an impact, whether it is a matter for explicit theological notice or not, on an exceptionally wide range of other issues – for example, the Trinity, human nature and its problems, sacraments, church, God's relation to the world and the character of Christian responsibility.

The early church in its ecumenical creeds laboured to establish guidelines for theological discussion concerning the nature of Christ's person and his relation to God. The creed of Nicaea affirmed the full divinity of Christ and the Council of Chalcedon strove to resolve problems that this affirmation of Christ's divinity posed for an understanding of Christ's person: a terminological distinction between 'nature' and 'hypostasis' was enlisted in an effort to clarify the proper way to speak of the very same one, Jesus Christ, who is both divine and human. Without a great deal of innovation on these matters, medieval theology brought both analytic rigour and synthetic breadth to the discussion, often, as in the work of Thomas Aquinas, by setting such an account of Christ's person in the context of a fully-fledged systematic exposition of other theological topics. The medieval period also saw the beginnings of sustained theological attention to the question of Christ's work, that is, the question of how Christ saves us. While discussion of Christ's person from the time of the early church had been fuelled by concerns about salvation – the early creeds, for example, were, indeed, guided in their accounts of Christ's person by the question of what Christ must be like if he is to save us – the nature and manner of salvation in Christ only took shape as a focal topic of theological concern in its own right with such medieval texts as Anselm's eleventh-century *Cur Deus Homo?*[2] Rather rancorous debate about soteriology or the nature and manner of Christ's work, particularly in its effects upon human persons, arrived with the Reformation; at issue, with wide-ranging implications for a number of different church practices, was the relation between Christ's doing and our own in the processes through which we are saved.

The modern period in christology (post-1648), branching out from a European context, makes its own distinctive contributions. For example, the humanistic and this-worldly outlook of contemporary times finds expression in the effort by theologians to recover the humanity of Jesus, a humanity purportedly endangered by the emphasis on Christ's divinity in the creeds and high christologies of the early church. In keeping with an Enlightenment preoccupation with intellectually responsible belief, modern theologies often offer highly critical reassessments of the conceptual adequacy and intelligibility of Chalcedon and its language of nature and hypostasis.[3] This same Enlightenment worry about the conditions under which belief is justified teams up in modern christologies with an emerging consciousness of history to produce historical reconstructions of Jesus' actual words and deeds, for the purpose of either undermining or shoring up church teachings about Jesus – the old and new quests, respectively, for the historical Jesus. Other developments in christology show the influence of the more inclusive, global awareness typical of modernity. For example, Jesus' life and death are increasingly interpreted as a kind of theodicy, in order to address, in particular, the sufferings and struggles of the world's poor and oppressed. The universal relevance and finality of Christ are reconsidered in the face of a newly won respect for the possible religious validity of other religions and out of a recognition of the historical conditionedness of all religious claimants and claims.

THE PROBLEM WITH MODERN CHRISTOLOGIES

The point of this chapter is not to rehearse these preoccupations of modern christology, one by one, but to uncover a basic paradigm shift that underlies at least some of them and to offer thereby a critical perspective on them. Even if the convoluted and confused contemporary debates on modernity and postmodernity remain inconclusive, the advent of the debate – the appearance of the category 'postmodern' – at least means that critical distance has been gained on the assumptions of modernity – for example, the modern turn to epistemology and to a human subject identified as that centre of consciousness according to whose perspective the natural and moral worlds are organised. With the distance afforded by the advent of the postmodern comes clarity; the student of doctrine can now see the characteristic shapes of modern christologies more clearly. With clarity comes the possibility of criticism. Indeed, by way of a few examples, I shall suggest that modern assumptions such as the ones just mentioned have infiltrated contemporary theologies with untoward effects for discussion of Jesus Christ and a number of other theological topics with which christology is most closely logically intertwined (for example, speculation about the Trinity). Such criticism of modern christologies functions, ideally, as an alert to students of doctrine as they embark on their own efforts to think in a sustained way about Jesus Christ and his significance for us. While this chapter provides no blueprint for a way beyond the typical preoccupations of modern christologies, it is offered in hopes that diagnosis is half the way to cure; knowing of the dangers in modern christology, the student of doctrine might be better able to avoid similar dangers in future.

Before providing examples from contemporary christology that make evident the problems at issue, let me more carefully explain the nature of the criticism I am making and therefore the kind of cases in which I will be most interested. Although rather abstract and methodological in nature, these remarks now will help prevent misunderstandings of my project and of the recommendations it entails for students trying to make their way as theologians on the contemporary scene.

First of all, my objection to the way contemporary christologies have been influenced by modernity is not a criticism of them for rising to meet the challenges posed by modern times. Modern times present a whole host of problems for christology which theologians ignore at their peril. Such challenges as these: the loss of self-evidence or presumptive truth for Christian beliefs with the decline of the church's influence and the growth of secular societies; the emergence of disciplines (for example, historical methods) that operate independently of religious beliefs or norms; the contemporary imperative for respectful inter-religious dialogue; the threat of nuclear warfare and environmental destruction; the plight of the poor and oppressed which contemporary liberation movements thrust to the fore; and the need to repent for anti-Semitism which the Holocaust makes an overriding moral mandate.

Theologians, moreover, cannot presume to answer or respond to such challenges without a major reinterpretation and re-evaluation of prior christological thought. My worries, however, surround the way in which such reinterpretation and re-evaluation proceed. Challenges are one thing; dictates another. Modern developments present a problematic influence when they set not simply a requirement of response but also the terms of it.

The mere fact of being influenced by modernity need not mean, however, that modernity is dictating the terms of christological response. In criticising the way they allow modernity to set the terms for response to modern challenges, I am therefore not faulting theologians simply for appropriating modern assumptions – assumptions about, say, the importance of epistemological questions, the priority of human beings in the establishment of meaning and truth, or the character of human identity as a matter of a unitary perspectival consciousness. It is impossible for modern theologians to proceed apart from assumptions like these, as if they were members of another time, and therefore immune from the contemporary terms of intellectual debate. What theologians say – in christology or any other topic of systematic theology – is always influenced by the assumptions of the day; such assumptions inevitably infiltrate theological work. What matters, however, is how they are taken up within theology, whether this is done reflectively and critically, with attention to possible losses, as well as gains. The assumptions of the day should not remain mere assumptions in theological use; they should not retain the taken-for-granted status which they so often have for modern people. Such presumptions should become subjects, instead, for theological revision and re-evaluation, in and through the very process of formulating theological responses to contemporary problems.[4]

The charge that this chapter explores is therefore this: that the assumptions of modernity have not been given the requisite critical scrutiny in christological use, a critical scrutiny much more typical, I believe, of prior periods in the history of Christian thought.[5] Perhaps contemporary theology has been lulled into complacency on this matter, lulled into taking over modern assumptions as they stand, by modernity's own representationalist view of language's inflexibility (the meaning of words is fixed in virtue, it is hoped, of some transparent reference to objects) or by modernity's facile belief in the epistemological privilege of the later (the modern idea of progress). Despite what theology might have customarily done in the past, theology's freedom to reinterpret and revise modern assumptions in particular might have seemed for these reasons both unnecessary and improper. Whatever the reasons for the critical reticence – even if modern theology is no worse on this score than the theology of any other time – the entrance of any new era of thought – in this case the postmodern – enables the assumptions of a previous time to stand out in relief as questionable. The critical analyses of certain moves in contemporary christology, provided in the body of this chapter, will, I hope, have this kind of effect on a small scale, thereby making any future use of such assumptions in theology more self-conscious and self-critical.

Something like the critical stance towards modern assumptions that I am recommending has been going on for quite a while with reference to modern historical methods. One example is Wolfhart Pannenberg's defence of the historicity of the resurrection by way of an attack on historical positivism (an appeal to facts purportedly unmediated by prior normative and interpretive frameworks).[6] Another way of revising the assumptions of modern historical methods is to draw a distinction between different senses of history (for example, between what is historical in the sense of the bare facts uncovered in a historical investigation to determine fact from fiction, and historical in the sense of events of decisive significance for the way one leads one's life). Such a distinction between what is historically factual and what is existentially eventful is often used to undermine the idea that Christian claims about Jesus are dependent upon the results of historical investigation into his life; Christian claims are historical in the latter sense and not the former. By itself, such a distinction may suggest, however, an arbitrarily imposed and therefore intellectually disreputable form of Christian protectionism. As a mere supplement to a modern understanding of factual historicity, such a distinction may also be acceding too much to it. For example, by leaving a modern understanding of factual historicity alone and opting instead for a more existentialist conception of historically decisive events in one's personal life, a christology may have difficulty interpreting Christian eschatology in terms of hope for a temporally future history; the eschatological import of Christ's Word for the human race might amount to nothing more than a call to a subjective process of decision-making in the present.[7] Finally, Ernst Troeltsch's three principles of historical method – the principles of criticism, analogy and correlation – have been the subject of constant and recently renewed critical attention.[8] Troeltsch believed that one should abide by the directives of historical method in the apparently historical affirmations one makes about Jesus – holding such affirmations open to revision in keeping with their relative probabilities (the principle of criticism), judging such probabilities according to the idea that the past was not radically unlike the present (the principle of analogy) and understanding the events at issue in terms of their causal connections with other historical events serving as antecedent conditions or consequences (the principle of correlation). While some objections to the relevance of these principles for theology seem based on a mere obscurantist appeal to the supernatural – the theologian, it is argued, does not have to abide by these principles since the supernatural agency of God is at issue in the person and work of Christ – other objections concern the adequacy and sufficiency of these principles on their own terms.[9] The taken-for-granted character of these principles – their absolute-ness, one might say, as simple presuppositions – is questioned. The principle of analogy in particular has fallen under fairly compelling censure as a prin-ciple of historical method, for failing to be open to the strange and the novel. The demand that the future be like the past is, according to this charge, a form of intellectual hubris; it expresses an unwillingness to learn from or be corrected by what is other.[10]

The modern assumptions that I am interested in making objects of criti-cal scrutiny are not, however, matters of method – historical or otherwise. Theologians in the modern period have by and large been quite self-conscious about method, bringing together for comparative analysis their own theological procedures and those of the modern disciplines. If the latter methods were not questioned, they were always at least question*able* in virtue of this sort of thematic consideration. No need for this chapter, then, to make them so.

What remains unexplored and therefore what this chapter hopes to set in relief are the more unselfconscious ways that christological topics are transposed into modern idioms. Such processes of transposition tend to be unselfconscious because they are part and parcel of the very formulation of theological topics to begin with. For example, in the case I just mentioned, although theologians commonly engage in critical reflection on historical methods, they do not as commonly question the fact of a theological preoc-cupation with method. Yet this is a distinctively modern preoccupation which generally conforms to a modern turn towards the human subject, and the 'how' of its intellectual procedures. It is this very basic level of assump-tion, working its way within the very formulation of theological topics and positions, that requires effort in order to be uncovered.

I pursue this task – the task of uncovering the unselfconscious way in which topics in christology have been reworked in modern terms – by inves-tigating two major issues in contemporary christology – the Jesus of history/ Christ of faith problematic and the identification of Christ with revelation. The first issue concerns the preoccupation of nineteenth- and twentieth-cen-tury christologies with the relationship between Jesus in his earthly career and Jesus as he is proclaimed by Christians on the basis of his post-Easter appearances. The creeds maintain that the risen Christ is the same one Jesus, that particular person who lived and died in a certain time and place, two thousand years ago in Palestine; but does historical investigation into the life and teachings of Jesus bear that claim out? What kind of continuity can be established between the two on historical critical grounds? Are Christian claims about Jesus' significance unsupported, perhaps even contradicted, by the results of historical investigation into his life and death? The second issue, the preoccupation of modern christologies with revelation, goes back to an Enlightenment deist attack on any basis for theological claims – like knowledge of God in Christ – that falls short of the most general arguments from human experience accessible to any rational person. The purported sufficiency and sole legitimacy of natural reason in theology brings the question of Christ as a particular and privileged revelation of God to the fore in modern theology.[11]

Critical analysis of these two cases – because of their centrality in modern christological discourse – has the potential to push christology in a new, postmodern direction. Before launching into an extended treatment of them, however, I believe it is best to start with several rather more brief and more narrowly circumscribed examples from contemporary christology. Taking these examples up first will help clarify what I mean by a transposition of topics into a new idiom and help identify the nature of the modern assumptions that constitute that new idiom.

CHRIST'S BENEFITS

A first brief example, to start us off, concerns the way in which, in the modern period, the logic of what is believed about Christ's benefits is transposed into a kind of epistemological idiom so that it becomes a logic of how one comes to believe. Christologies historically include a discussion of the changes one undergoes by Christ's grace – for example, an account of the stages of Christian faith and love. Such an account is part of what Christians believe; in my terms, it is part of the logic of Christian belief. Perhaps even, as in some forms of Protestantism, such an account of the changes that Christians undergo is central to that logic of belief, providing an organising focus for all the rest of what Christians believe about reality – for example, what they believe about the creation of the world, the fall of human beings, and their redemption in Christ. In the modern period, however, the story of what happens to a believer is taken out of the context of these other beliefs, the context of beliefs that, by way of its organisational logic, gives that story its intelligibility. For instance, within the context of the logic of Christian belief, what Christ does in and for us makes sense as a remedy for the Fall. Now, however, this story of what happens to the believer is interpreted independently of the logic of Christian belief, so that it becomes an account of what has to happen before one can hold any Christian beliefs at all. The preoccupation becomes how one comes to believe, minus any of the other beliefs about the reality of God and world that made an account of the stages of faith initially plausible from a Christian point of view. Minus such a context of intelligibility the question how one comes to believe quickly becomes the question whether one has the right to believe, under what conditions if any – a general epistemological question. Thus, the question whether it would have made sense for Christ to come if human beings had not sinned – a question concerning the logic of Christian belief – becomes the question whether the evidence for human failing gives anyone a reason to believe in the need for Christ; on the English scene in the early modern period, the Westminster Confession, for example, gives way to John Locke's *Reasonableness of Christianity* (1695).

CHRIST 'FOR ME'

One might object that these preoccupations with the logic of coming to believe are simply the natural and appropriate response to a historical context in which Christianity has lost whatever prima facie plausibility it had before. It is therefore uncharitable to explain this trend, as I do, by saying it has its origin in a surreptitious warping of the usual theological preoccupations by way of their translation, without adequate critical reflection on the theologian's part, into the epistemological idiom of the day. Unless this sort of charge is answered now, one might cavil, indeed, with all my examples on the same grounds.

Consider, then, another example of a similar sort – another example of a transposition of a christological topic into an epistemological idiom. This example – like all the remaining ones I will give – is less susceptible to such an objection because in it efforts are clearly being made to remain in continuity with previous theological concerns; the theologian hopes to do what was done before but now in a modern idiom – an idiom which I argue frustrates that intent.

The example concerns the way a Lutheran affirmation that Christ is *pro me* (for me) or *pro nobis* (for us) becomes in contemporary theology a general methodological principle.[12] In Martin Luther's writing, that Christ is *pro me* or *pro nobis* means that Christ has accomplished all that he has – slaying sin, death and the devil – not for his own sake, but specifically for us. The preacher of the Word makes this clear so that one recognises one's own identity and destiny in the gospel stories. What these stories describe has everything to do with us. A proper understanding of the Word should therefore be life-transforming, manifest, for example, in transformed dispositions of trust and gratitude towards God and a new freedom to love others that such new dispositions make possible. Christ therefore answers to the believer who worries 'But where do I stand?': '[All that I have done] is done for you. You must know and take comfort that I have overcome the world not for Myself – for I had no need to descend from heaven, since I was lord of all creation beforehand, so that the devil and the world would certainly not touch Me! But I have done this for your sake ... This is the reason to take it to heart.'[13]

In Luther's writings, this affirmation of the *pro me* makes a specifically christological point. Contrary to the God of our imagination who desires nothing more than to judge us in wrath, Christ shows that God is *for us*, a God of forgiving mercy. Apart from attention to Christ, one can mistakenly think that God demands our own righteousness as a condition of divine favour, and so strive, ultimately haplessly, to establish one's own good standing before God, with the unfortunate dispositional consequences of either terror or deluded self-conceit. A worry about whether Christ is not just for us but *for me* is resolved in the same way: by turning away from self-preoccupations and realising that nothing one has done is an impediment to divine acceptance in and through Christ. In short, the worry is resolved by simply having faith in Christ and what Christ accomplishes.

In contemporary theology, following Immanuel Kant, this affirmation of the *pro me* suffers, one might say, a subjectivist epistemological swerve, which moves it away from its use in Luther. I mean by this, first of all, that God *pro me* or God in relation to me – God for human beings in Christ or Christ's dwelling in those who believe – is now identified with God as a matter of human apprehension. The *pro me* for Luther concerned a dimension of the reality of Christ's working. That Christ accomplished what he did *for us* is part of the reality of the matter; apprehension of the gospel stories that failed to apply them to one's own life would not, then, be true to reality. Now, however, the *pro me* falls simply on the side of human apprehension; it is simply identified with the process by which human subjects make the gospel message their own. The *pro me*, moreover, is no longer a specifically christological affirmation about the character and consequences of God's action in Christ, but a general theological principle about conditions for proper talk about or belief in God – for example, a principle that makes subjective appropriation one such condition. Talking about a God who means nothing to me is no way to talk about God at all. What one believes about God must speak to the human situation and to me personally. It must be a truth that human beings have made their own. Not just something they know in the abstract to be true but something they are sure of in their own hearts and minds.

These new twists to the *pro me* are not simply a response to the modern Enlightenment imperative to think for oneself, but an attempt to carry on the specifically religious concerns of the *pro me* in a new idiom. Thus, the *pro me* in its new form of a general rule for appropriate talk about God is designed to prompt, as usual, the proper Christian dispositions of trust, gratitude and love towards God. Ways of talking about God that do not follow the general rule of making clear the relevance of what is said for us objectify God, suggesting thereby that God (and God's favour), like any object of theoretical knowledge, is subject to human influence and control or a matter of indifference with respect to the basic existential questions of life. The non-objectifying language about God, which the *pro me* as a general rule for talk about God requires, is apparently therefore a precondition for appropriate Christian attitudes towards God.

Unfortunately, however, a general rule for talk about God seems here to supplant the importance of Christ in bringing about the transformations of disposition that mark a Christian life. Appropriate Christian dispositions are not a matter of simply taking to heart the fact that Christ is for us; they are the consequences of a certain manner of talking about or apprehending God, embodied therefore in a rule to which it is crucial that theologians conform. To make the same criticism a little differently: this way of transposing a theological worry about ensuring the proper Christian dispositions into the purely subjective arena of human apprehension – the fact that the nature of that apprehension is to do the work required – sits uneasily with the extrospective attention to Christ, the looking outside oneself to Christ, which continues to be the lynchpin of this theological perspective. According to that extrospective emphasis, one must not look to oneself for one's salvation, to the ultimately untrustworthy character of one's own faith and works, but to God's mercy in Christ. The *pro me* in its earlier formulation conformed with such an extrospective viewpoint because it referred primarily to what Christ did for us. A certain way of talking about Christ for us – proclamation and not some abstract disquisition regarding indifferent facts – was necessary, too, in order to get the point across. But crucial here was the character of what Christ actually accomplished – he saved *us* – by his doings and sufferings. Proclamation was just the recognition of that fact and not itself an independent condition for making Christ one's own. According to that extrospective emphasis, indeed, there are no conditions we have to meet before Christ can become our own; he is already ours in virtue of the character of what he accomplished, and that is just what genuine Christian preaching proclaims. Now, however, with the new twists to the *pro me* emphasis falls on the propriety of one's own manner of talking about or apprehending Christ. One cannot properly attend to what Christ does for one without being concerned at the very same time with oneself and the character of one's linguistic and cognitional processes. Indeed, the emphasis on such subjective processes is so great that Christ need not, it seems, be the subject matter of them. Nonobjectifying language about God, whether Christ is the focus of such language or not, seems to have the desired effects on Christian dispositions.

This example of the Lutheran *pro me* raises subtle issues that usually fall under the Jesus of history/Christ of faith problematic; it raises issues, that is, concerning the relation between what Jesus did and what Christians proclaim about him. We will therefore return to these issues in our more extended treatment of that problematic. But before we begin to tackle that topic, let me give one more, rather less complicated example of what I mean by an untoward, insufficiently critical transposition of a christological issue into a subjective idiom.

WHAT MAKES CHRIST EXCEPTIONAL

The example comes from Friedrich Schleiermacher's christology. Schleiermacher tries to follow the intent, if not the language, of Chalcedon, according to which Jesus is one with God and yet fully human, both at once without separation or confusion. Schleiermacher recognises, first of all, that the exceptional character of Jesus has to do with his divinity; Jesus is exceptional because of the character of the relation to God found in Jesus, his unity or oneness with God. This divinity cannot be identified, however, with any particular empirical aspect of Jesus' human life and experience. Doing so would relegate divinity to part of the spatially and temporally conditioned world; and thereby contravene both Schleiermacher's characterisation of divinity as the Whence of one's feelings of absolute dependence (one cannot be absolutely dependent upon what is itself conditioned) and the naturalistic interpretation of human events (such events are not interrupted by the divine) which Schleiermacher affirms as a modern man. Identifying the divinity of Jesus with any particular empirical aspect of his life and experience would also mean making some exception to the claim of the full humanity of Christ; some aspect of Jesus' empirical existence would not be in fact human but would see the emergence of, and therefore be replaced by, divine properties.[14]

Schleiermacher resolves the difficulties in meeting these conditions of a proper christology by saying that the whole of Jesus' life (without exception) springs out of, has its originating impulse in, his relationship with God. This seems, indeed, to be a fair summation of what Chalcedon recommends with its language of hypostasis and nature, although Schleiermacher believes, for various reasons, that such language is not helpful in conveying it. As Chalcedon suggests with its technical terminology, Jesus, unlike us, enjoys his very existence ('hypostasis' in the sense of independent existence) – his being therefore whole and entire – in the Word; his unity with God is in this sense 'hypostatic'. The language that Schleiermacher himself uses to make this point translates the unity of Jesus Christ with God into terms of human consciousness. Jesus' exceptional relation with God is a matter of his God-consciousness, a matter, that is, of his constant and undiminished feeling or immediate awareness of himself in a relation of utter dependence upon God, a feeling that dominates the entirety of his human existence. One can there-fore say, according to Schleiermacher, that the being of God in Christ – the Word taking flesh – is this being of God in Jesus' immediate self-conscious-ness whereby, unlike what happens in everyone else, all that Jesus says, does or undergoes, is subordinated to or conditioned by it.

The problem here is that God-consciousness is a dimension – albeit a very fundamental one according to Schleiermacher's philosophical psychol-ogy – of human life and experience. It is a modifying feature of that ordinary, if rather subtle, aspect of human consciousness according to which one is unthematically aware of oneself in and through whatever it is that one is thinking or doing or suffering. When Schleiermacher transposes the intent of Chalcedon into this idiom of human consciousness he thereby violates its intent. What is special about Jesus is no longer a relationship with God that leaves the humanity of Jesus' life wholly intact, essentially unaltered by its associations with divinity and therefore identical with ours. The exceptional nature of the unity with God found in Christ is now transferred to a feature of *human* existence – his God-consciousness. Jesus' humanity itself therefore becomes exceptional.

Indeed, the more exceptional that humanity, the more seemingly super-human in its perfection it becomes. Trying to approximate in the idiom of God-consciousness the quite radical claim for the exceptional character of Jesus' person traditionally made by the churches, Schleiermacher is there-fore forced to say that Jesus' God-consciousness is unwavering in its power. Jesus was never even tempted to sin; he never struggled to bring his life and thought under the sway of his immediate self-awareness of dependence upon God. Here the problems, which it was the intent of Chalcedon to help the theologian avoid, return in full measure. As David Friedrich Strauss pointedly expressed it: Jesus cannot be simply human and at the same time stand above everyone else in virtue of his humanity.[15]

Whatever the disadvantages of saying that union with God occurs hypostatically in Jesus Christ, it at least had the advantage of not requiring this sort of elevation of an aspect or dimension of Jesus' human life and experience. What makes Jesus unique is the fact that the humanity of Jesus has its subsistence in the Word. This hypostatic union does not have any particular location in Jesus' life – say, in his immediate self-consciousness. Indeed, the arguable intent of a distinction between nature and hypostasis in Chalcedon was to suggest the impropriety of discussing Christ's unity with God in terms of human nature and its relations with divinity (understood in a general, non-trinitarian way).[16] But this is just what a focus on the relation between humanity and divinity in human God-consciousness does.[17]

THE JESUS OF HISTORY AND THE CHRIST OF FAITH

Let us turn now to our first major case, the Jesus of history/Christ of faith problematic. A very explicit epistemological concern usually funds the problematic: the question to be answered, in other words, is whether an investigation into the life and teachings of Jesus himself, using historical methods and modern techniques of biblical criticism, justifies or undermines what Christians say about Jesus. Such a question has at least a prima facie legitimacy since Christians are claiming that it is a historical person, Jesus, who has such an enormous significance for human history; historians and religiously neutral biblical critics, not just the Christian faithful, should therefore be able to say something about him.

The pertinence of modern modes of historical enquiry is not often, however, taken for granted here. The adequacy of such methods tends, instead, to come under critical theological scrutiny; the Jesus of history/Christ of faith problematic is usually, indeed, the context for the general questions about historical methods mentioned earlier. More specifically, two issues come to the fore in this sort of theological assessment of historical methods: (1) whether it is *possible* to reconstruct a reliable historical picture of Jesus from the gospels, and (2) if so, whether the results are of any theological importance (are there, for example, certain aspects of reality that historical criticism, in so far as it is a limited method, misses; are the character of Christian claims and the manner in which they are held naturally at odds with the conclusions and stance of historical investigation?). Although theologians can of course make mistaken judgements here, they cannot be faulted for a lack of self-consciousness and self-criticism in their approach to historical methods when working through a Jesus of history/Christ of faith problematic. I am concerned, instead, with the way the Jesus of history/ Christ of faith problematic represents a transposition into a new idiom of topics usually included within the logic of Christian belief.

Epistemological questions may influence the transposition at issue but it occurs even among Christian theologians who repudiate the logical or genetic dependence of Christian faith upon historical reconstructions of Jesus; it occurs, that is, even among theologians who do not believe in the theological importance of the Jesus of history/Christ of faith problematic as an epistemological question concerning how to justify or arrive at belief in Jesus Christ. Indeed, the transposition is clearest among Christian theologians of that sort, for whom the distinction between the Jesus of history and the Christ of faith functions within a dogmatics or exposition of Christian faith, and not as a preparatory defence or attack upon what Christians usually affirm about Jesus Christ. The two theologians I shall discuss are Friedrich Schleiermacher and Rudolf Bultmann.[18]

For Schleiermacher, historical investigation is not the appropriate means to arrive at beliefs about Jesus Christ the Redeemer; everything that a theologian needs to know about Jesus can be derived from the nature of Christian piety itself. For Bultmann, only the Christ proclaimed in the New Testament and subsequent Christian witness has importance for theology; historical investigation into the life and death of Jesus, aside from merely confirming the historical fact that he existed, has no place in grounding, validating or adjudicating Christian faith claims. Rather than raising epistemological questions about Christian belief's genesis from or logical dependence on historical investigation, the Jesus of history/Christ of faith problematic represents in their work a way of talking about a variety of closely related christological topics. Thus, the two terms 'Jesus of history' and 'Christ of faith' are used, respectively, to talk about the relation between Jesus and his effects on those he saves (Schleiermacher), or to talk about the relation between Jesus Christ and the Holy Spirit poured out among us (Bultmann). The two terms also stand in for the humiliation of Jesus, on the one hand, and his exaltation, on the other (the earthly Jesus of the crucifixion and the risen Lord).

With this substitution of terms comes a subtle but quite significant theological change. In general, theological discussion of an order in reality is changed into a discussion of the relation between the objective and the subjective – for example, the relation between history and human experience or the relation between fact and human apprehension of it. For example, whereas before one could talk about the work of the Holy Spirit in relation to Jesus Christ in terms of different, interconnected aspects of the real activity by which humans are saved, one now talks about the Holy Spirit's relation to Jesus Christ simply in terms of human *response to or apprehension of* what has *happened* in Christ (Bultmann); what were different aspects of the order of reality by which humans are saved (say, saving acts for us in Christ and their actually becoming ours by way of the Holy Spirit) are now divided up between the objective (the events of Jesus' life and death) and the subjective (the experiential responses to them in human life). Whereas before one could discuss the ways in which Jesus is really both exalted and humiliated in different respects – *qua* human and *qua* divine – one now talks about how the crucified Jesus is exalted by being taken up into Christian *proclamation* about this *event*'s saving significance (Bultmann). Whereas before one talked about the world-shattering efficacy of Christ, one now talks about Jesus as the *fact* responsible for a particular sort of salvific human *experience* (Schleiermacher).

Transposed into the language of human consciousness or self-understanding, the second terms of the aforementioned pairs (the effects of Jesus' saving activity on human consciousness, the Holy Spirit, the exalted and risen Lord) take primacy over the first, objective terms (Jesus as the one responsible for a change in human consciousness, the Word in the flesh crucified). The second set of subjective terms is the sole mode of access for and indeed seems to constitute the first set of objective terms. Thus, Christian consciousness of Jesus as Redeemer (Schleiermacher) or Christian proclamation about him (Bultmann) is the only mode of access to the one in whom Christians believe: Jesus in relation to an altered Christian God-consciousness (Schleiermacher) or self-understanding (Bultmann), Jesus for us, the Christ. Everything that one must say about Jesus as the generative founder of Christian God-consciousness is derived from the nature of that God-consciousness itself (Schleiermacher). It is the risen Lord proclaimed by Christians that makes the earthly existence of Jesus, *qua* crucified, religiously significant (Bultmann). The object of Christian belief *is*, moreover, the Christ present to Christian consciousness or present within Christian proclamation.

Here an epistemological motive seems to infiltrate the dogmatic exposition. This primacy of subjective terms ensures, for Schleiermacher, that Christian discourse about Jesus Christ is self-contained, that it may proceed without the need for any historical reconstruction of Jesus independent of Christian consciousness. The same sort of primacy is what ensures for Bultmann that christology cannot be disconfirmed by historical investigation into the what and how of Jesus' life and teachings. In this mixing of epistemology and dogmatics, Jesus as he is apart from Christian piety or church proclamation is equated, surreptitiously, with Jesus as an object of historical investigation, with what a historian or neutral knower might say about him. Protecting Christian beliefs from the possibly awkward results of such historical investigation therefore requires the sort of primacy I have described for what Christians experience of or claim about Jesus.

The primacy of the second term over the first in these pairs makes it difficult, however, to distinguish the two since the first does not seem to have the requisite independence. The first (Jesus as a concrete historical person) *is* just what the second (Christian piety or proclamation) says it is. The description given of the first terms of the pairs is therefore as much a derivative of Christian religious self-consciousness or Christian proclamation as the second: human subjectivity spans both sides.

The results are problematic for dogmatics. In Schleiermacher's case, where Jesus of history/Christ of faith becomes the modern translation of Christian talk about the relation between Jesus and his saving effects, the inability to distinguish adequately between the terms means that the divinity of Jesus and the human nature of those he affects are blurred. The divine dimension of Jesus' life must mimic (albeit in a perfect form) the character of Christian piety as an experience of him. Jesus has to have in his own right that superiority of God-consciousness which arises in Christian consciousness of him.

The persons of the Trinity, which were distinct in previous theological discussion of the order of reality, also tend now to blur. The Word of Jesus Christ seems impossible to distinguish from the faith that is poured out by the Holy Spirit for the community of Christians; the Word of Jesus Christ seems submerged or dissolved within it. Therefore Bultmann can say that the proclamation of Christians 'has put itself in the place of the historical Jesus; it represents him'. It 'has, as it were, displaced [him]'. 'Then there is no faith in Christ which would not also be faith in the church as the bearer of the kerygma . . . faith in the Holy Ghost.'[19] The Word of Jesus Christ indeed has no saving efficacy apart from the eschatological event of proclamation brought by, and initiating a life lived in, the Spirit. Jesus himself merely promised salvation; it is only with the outpouring of the Holy Spirit, when Jesus is preached, that Jesus saves.[20]

It may be that, contrary to the impression of submergence, the kerygma, or Christian proclamation of the saving significance of Jesus Christ, is salvific here for the very reason that Jesus is present in it; the kerygma saves by making the saving events of the cross present now. But it is still the case that the salvific power of Jesus seems strangely confined to Christian faith and proclamation, the two being closely associated in traditional terms with the Holy Spirit. The cross of Jesus seems to have no saving power in itself; it would be an insignificant fact of past history apart from them.

Moreover, because of the transposition into a subjective idiom, it becomes difficult to distinguish either of these persons of the Trinity from human experience or Christian witness. This is the *pro me* problem again. Although both Schleiermacher and Bultmann strongly affirm the dependence of Christian existence upon the saving action of God, the divine simply does not seem to have room to stand over and against the second term of the pairs being discussed. Thus, the Holy Spirit becomes very difficult to distinguish from the spirit of a Christian form of life once the Holy Spirit is closely identified with subjective human appropriation or response. Objective and subjective moments are divided up between Jesus and the workings of the Holy Spirit respectively so that an objective moment of divine initiative over and against Christian experience or proclamation is hard to discern in the case of the latter. It becomes hard to say that the Holy Spirit has called me to the gospel and mean by that anything more than that one has responded appropriately to the Christian proclamation of the saving significance of Christ (Bultmann). Given the proclamation, appropriate human response seems to be a matter of human decision. The proclamation itself, as we have already implied, seems, moreover, to create the saving significance of the Christ event rather than depend on the inherent saving significance of anything Jesus says, does or undergoes in itself. Christian experience therefore seems to revolve around itself without any opening to the very divine initiative which these theologians nevertheless continue to affirm as the only remedy for human incapacity.[21]

The priority of divine initiative is not therefore a presumption or something that follows as a matter of course in dogmatic exposition, but something these theologians have to labour to show, often at the price of inconsistency. Bultmann, for example, combats the impression in his theology that human beings save themselves by distinguishing between proclamation and faith and insisting on the dependence of the latter upon the former. This is a far cry, however, from a theological position that could affirm confidently the dependence of both faith and proclamation on the workings of Christ and the Holy Spirit. Relying on a distinction between faith and proclamation to show the prior initiative of God merely reinstates the kind of transposition into a subjective idiom that brings along with it the deficiencies we have been exploring.

Thus, Bultmann claims that faith is not a decision under human control because it is an immediate response to the call to faith made in Christian proclamation concerning the saving significance of the cross. The Christian is not in a position to believe whenever or wherever he/she desires, but must await the moment of proclamation which is itself only possible after Jesus.[22] It is not at all clear, however, that the distinction being made here between faith and other less constrained forms of human decision or affirmation is an adequate answer to the question about the dependence of faith on the saving initiative of God. Dependence upon the saving initiative of God does not seem to follow simply from this claim that faith is not a general possibility for neutral consideration but a historical matter, in the dual sense that Bultmann employs – enabled by the historical fact of Jesus' coming and happening in the here and now of proclamation that addresses one's existential predicament. The historical character of faith's dependence upon Christian proclamation will suggest the priority of divine initiative only in case one can show the dependence of proclamation itself on that initiative, only in case, that is, one can show that Christian proclamation is not itself a merely human activity under human control. But such a task simply throws one back to the initial worries about the self-enclosure of Christian proclamation with which we began. Bultmann's putative answer simply returns one to the initial question – the question about the submergence of the Word in what Christians say about it.

Schleiermacher counters this worry about Christian self-enclosure – the worry that Christian piety is in dialogue only with itself – by insisting that Christian piety depends for its emergence on the redemptive influence of Jesus' God-consciousness. The exposition of dogmatics may enforce an always neat correlation between Jesus and Christian piety, since a reference to Christian consciousness spans both sides, but suggestions here of a self-enclosed piety are broken by the claim that none of this is possible apart from the causative influence of the historical figure of Jesus who brings about Christian piety in the first place. According to Schleiermacher, without Jesus as its founding cause, Christian piety is nothing.

This dependence of Christianity on the causative influence of Jesus' God-consciousness is not, however, equivalent to the original question about the saving initiative of God in Christ. At issue in that question of divine initiative is the Christian's absolute dependence on God for salvation, the sort of absolute dependence that Schleiermacher discusses in terms of consciousness of God as the Whence of our feeling of absolute dependence. Schleiermacher's talk of God-consciousness is, indeed, his translation of divine initiative or sovereignty into a modern idiom. It is not at all clear, however, that Christian piety can be absolutely dependent on Jesus in this same way. This Jesus who is the cause of Christian piety apparently exists like any other finite being within the world; that means that, like other finite beings, he is something that conditions and is conditioned by other things within the world. Christian piety therefore cannot be absolutely dependent on Jesus in the way it is absolutely dependent on the Whence of its own God-consciousness; one can be absolutely dependent only on what excludes the activity of others upon it. In short, Jesus cannot play the same role as God in Christian piety. Which is another way of saying for Schleiermacher, who bases everything he says about Jesus on the character of that piety, that Jesus' divinity must be downplayed; Jesus is not God but a human being with a perfectly formed human God-consciousness. But now if Jesus in so far as he is a historical person is not the sort of thing upon which one can feel absolutely dependent, the redemptive activity of Jesus that brings about the development of Christian God-consciousness should have, accordingly, only a relative primacy: those influenced by Jesus should be both free and dependent with respect to him. The dependence of Christianity on Christ would seem to be quite similar, then, to the ordinary dependence of any religion on its founding moment. This, however, is a far weaker sense of dependence than one usually finds in the claim of dependence for salvation on divine initiative in Christ.

Schleiermacher is then in a bind. The translation of divine sovereignty into the subjective idiom of God-consciousness raises the spectre of Christian self-enclosure. The God whom one can be absolutely dependent upon is the God who seems to remain shut up in feeling as the simple expression of this feeling concerning itself.[23] Schleiermacher attempts to answer such a charge by appealing to the Jesus of history; Christian piety is dependent on a historical person who exists independently of it. The very historical independence that is to solve the problem brings, however, its own difficulties: one cannot, according to Schleiermacher, be dependent on a historical person in the way one is absolutely dependent on God. The result is then an unresolved dilemma: absolute dependence expressed in an idiom that seems to contradict it; a possible solution to this problem in the historical Jesus, but according to Schleiermacher's presuppositions such a person cannot exercise sovereign initiative.

REVELATION IN CHRIST

The criticisms of Bultmann and Schleiermacher that I have just made follow those of the twentieth-century theologian Karl Barth.[24] But Barth himself is not immune from similar criticisms concerning illicit transpositions of traditional theological topics into a subjective idiom. The identification of Christ's work with revelation (especially in the early volumes of the *Church Dogmatics*) is a case in point.

The connection of christology with an account of revelation has a long pedigree in Protestant theological traditions, especially those that take their inspiration from John Calvin. Making such a connection is therefore not necessarily in itself an indication of either a modern subjectivist tendency – a modern penchant for making questions of human subjectivity paramount – or an epistemological turn in the way topics in christology are treated. Talking of Jesus Christ as the revelation of God is a way of talking about the operation of God's prevenient grace in Christ as it impacts our knowledge of God. By divine initiative, Jesus Christ is a special medium for a special sort of knowledge of God, unavailable elsewhere. What is unusual in Barth, however – and here he is illustrative of a general trend in Protestant theology after the Enlightenment – is the way the category of revelation becomes the overarching rubric for discussing all that Christ does for us. The relatively unproblematic Christian claim that Christ makes known in a special way the character and purposes of God – unproblematic in that no Christian is likely to deny this – takes centre stage as the expository key for a discussion of all Christ's works and thereby pushes the rest of the account of what Christ achieves in a subjectivist direction. That is, discussion of what God does in Christ shifts away from the character of those acts themselves and what they achieve (for example, healing our wounds, divinising our nature or forgiving our sins), and shifts towards what they communicate to humans thereby (say, the awareness that God is gracious and forgiving, or the recognition of the special relation of Jesus to God that such acts presume). In a kind of subjectivist transposition of talk about God's acts, the conclusions that one can infer about the nature of God from the acts of God in Christ seem now to be the primary reason that God performs them.[25] For example, the actual healing of our infirmities seems to pale in significance before the importance of getting us to see the need for God's help.

While this is a mere shift in emphasis and need not displace interest in the work of Christ that extends beyond the human cognitive or affective spheres, it creates more problems than one might expect. This subjectivist transposition has an odd effect, for example, on a number of other theological topics. The logic of those Christian beliefs with which christology is associated takes a number of untoward turns; once the transposition is made one cannot quite say what one could say before.

This is especially clear in the case of affirmations about the finality or decisiveness of what God has done in Christ.[26] When those acts of God are interpreted with primary reference to the category of revelation, finality or decisiveness turns into exclusiveness: what comes before or after Christ must be disparaged. It is very difficult to see how Christ as the revelation of God can be final or decisive if such revelation is not completed in Christ. The finality or decisiveness of revelation in Christ is similarly threatened the more that knowledge of God is accessible before or independently of Christ's coming.

This development is in rather sharp contrast to what could be said before such a transposition of talk about God's acts into the idiom of revelation. When Christ is not understood under the primary rubric of revelation, the acts of God in Christ can be decisive even if they set in motion a process in which there is more to come. For example, if the work of Christ is understood under the rubric of healing or redemption from sin, Christ can be decisive even if the effects of sin are gradually eradicated over time or the healing process continues into the future. The person who pulls you out of a desperate situation, the medicine that heals your otherwise mortal wounds, can be decisive and of irreplaceable significance even if the recovery is prolonged, even if that recovery reaches new heights by way of additional interventions in future. Similarly, without the subjectivist transposition we have been discussing, the simple existence of divine acts for us elsewhere need not take away from what is done in and through Christ's coming. Whether they do or not depends, for example, on the nature of those acts in Christ and what they alter about the circumstances of human beings in relation to God. God's acts in Christ can be decisive and final in virtue of the character of the transformations initiated by them even if God has been very obviously at work before. The decisive and irreplaceable significance of Christ need not be ensured by a simple contrast between absence and presence as it is when revelation is the primary christological motif.[27]

This difference between christologies with and without the central organising motif of revelation has major theological implications. At stake is the relation between creation and salvation; theologies of the former sort easily provoke a very sharp tension between the two, with unfortunate implications for the relations between the first and second persons of the Trinity. Moreover, the understanding of the relations between Jesus Christ and the Holy Spirit is certainly adversely affected: the Holy Spirit can effect nothing new without jeopardising the finality of Christ. Contrary to the equal status of the persons of the Trinity affirmed in the ecumenical creeds, the Holy Spirit becomes a clearly subordinate player to the Word incarnate in Christ.

A subjectivist shift in the discussion of Christ's works produces, moreover, rather grave internal tensions for the christologies at issue. When the concept 'revelation' takes centre stage in this way, it becomes *more* rather than less difficult to convey the prevenient initiative of God which an appeal to revelation is supposed to get across. First, the compass of God's prevenient activity is compressed in the efforts we have just talked about to retain in this new idiom traditional affirmations about the finality and decisiveness of Christ. Revelation in Christ seems to be not just one place where the gracious prevenient initiative of God is manifest, but the only place. The difference between God's grace and human achievement now cuts between knowledge of God in Christ, on the one hand, and knowledge of God through reason and observation of the world, on the other; whereas before it was quite possible for theologies, like Calvin's, to say that all knowledge of God, whatever its media of communication, had the prevenience of God at its source.[28] Contrary to Barth's intentions, therefore, the world of ordinary experience easily falls under the sway of a merely human-centred secularism; God's initiatives there become invisible.[29]

Second, the prevenience of God's acts in Christ becomes itself more difficult to affirm. Unlike acts of God that would seem to be powerful in and of themselves, whatever human beings make of them, revelation (at least in the ordinary sense of that term) is nothing apart from human apprehension of it. It does not seem to make sense to say that something is a revelation of God if human beings refuse to accept it or remain ignorant of it. The ordinary implications of the term therefore would suggest that God's actions in Christ depend for their efficacy on human reception.

Finally, since human reception is a constitutive moment of revelation, the church – the place where revelation is completed by being heard – is naturally prone to be elevated in status. Once language of God's acts in Christ is transposed into the idiom of revelation, the more one applauds what God has done in Christ, the more one has to applaud the Christians who recognise it. This sort of Christian self-congratulation stands in marked tension, however, with the attack on religion – Christianity included – that is part of Barth's emphasis on divine sovereignty.

Barth tries to get around such internal tensions by an odd use of the language of revelation. He tries to undercut the importance of human reception, which the language of revelation suggests, by saying, for example, that revelation in Christ is self-attesting: 'In Himself [Jesus Christ], whether we perceive and accept it or not, is eloquent and radiant. He does not simply become this when we perceive and accept Him as such.'[30] God's act in Jesus Christ does not stand at the mercy of the free decision of human beings; the Holy Spirit, in a second act of God's prevenient initiative, brings human beings to accept it. The human contribution is evacuated, moreover, of any independent significance by talking of it as a mere recognition or acknowledgement of what has already been achieved by Jesus Christ. It is no more than a subjective repetition of what has been accomplished in fact by Christ, without us.

Here again, however, as we saw in the Jesus of history/Christ of faith problematic, Barth is translating the relation between Jesus Christ and the Holy Spirit into the terms of human subjectivity so that the relation concerns a difference between the objective and the subjective, a difference between what human beings acknowledge and that acknowledgement itself. The concept of revelation, with its subjective and objective sides, indeed, encourages him to make this translation: Jesus has to do with the objective pole of revelation; the Holy Spirit with the subjective pole of human apprehension. Barth simply holds off the threats to God's prevenience to which we have seen such a translation is prone by a secondary theological manoeuvre: he subordinates the subjective moment as much as he can to the objective. Unfortunately, this strategy means that once again his theology has to subordinate quite radically the third person of the Trinity to the second.

One would think that the easier procedure would be to avoid altogether this kind of transposition of theological topics into the idiom of human subjectivity. Although this is suggested by his criticisms of Schleiermacher and Bultmann and is part of Barth's explicit theological programme, we have seen that he does not carry through on it consistently. Although Barth reflects critically on the language of revelation and attempts to alter its common-sense implications in theological use, he does not seem to see that a preoccupation with the revelation of God in Christ already involves a transposition into a subjective idiom. Because he fails to see this, he does not question such a preoccupation to begin with, but merely tries to make do with it.

An epistemological motive thereby infiltrates Barth's dogmatics. Revelation is no doubt highlighted the way it is in response to secular questioning about the legitimacy of Christian beliefs; it is a way of defending Christian beliefs from challenge by claiming a special source for them. In

Barth's case, appeal to revelation, indeed, is a way of arguing against the need for any defence in terms that a wider secular public would accept. Ironically, however, 'the primacy assigned to revelation in his theology means that Christian claims are still being viewed in fundamentally epistemological terms'.[31]

The fact of revelation is not simply presumed and exposited by Barth as it was by other theologians in the past. Simply presuming and expositing revelation would not require the concept of revelation itself to be made such a point of focal centrality in dogmatics. Instead, the constant refrain of appeals to revelation means that an implicit defence against secular criticisms runs throughout the discussion of theological topics. If the arguments that I have presented above are convincing, this sort of mixing of dogmatic and epistemological concerns comes at too great a theological cost.

CONCLUSIONS

What general conclusions can one draw from my analysis of these examples from contemporary christology? I have not shown that the modern idioms at issue are incompatible with what these theologians wanted to say about Jesus Christ. Transposition into modern idioms need not be fatal; lack of watchfulness in the process is. Christians hope that Jesus Christ is a figure for every time and place and therefore they believe that the clothing of contemporaneity will not force Christ's concealment – in modern times any more than at any other time. According to such a hope, it should be quite possible to avoid the theological problems raised in this paper through a more consistent and thoroughgoing critical awareness than yet exists of the way modernity alters the formulation and development of christological topics.

The diagnostic work of this chapter might help along the construction of christologies that exhibit the requisite degree of critical awareness, christologies that use modern idioms with the necessary critical correctives. Two very general theological guidelines result from this diagnostic work; they form methodological prerequisites for such processes of critical reflection on modernity in theology. First, on the basis of a thorough knowledge of the history of Christian theology, theologians need to form judgements about the logic of Christian belief to use as benchmarks for deciding when modernity has become an untoward, infelicitous influence on christologies constructed to meet the challenges of contemporary times. Indeed, in this chapter my own judgements about the logic of Christian belief lay behind the criticisms made of modern christologies. Second, the epistemological worries prompted by modern critical consciousness – are Christian beliefs about Christ justified? Is there any evidence for them? – should be addressed straightforwardly as an independent topic for discussion, and not be allowed to infiltrate a modern redescription of Christian beliefs about Jesus Christ. Besides altering, as we have seen, the logic of those beliefs, that kind of mixing of epistemological and dogmatic concerns exhibits an unseemly defensiveness that is both intellectually and theologically suspect. While creative redescription of the logic of Christian belief in dogmatics provides a kind of defence of the intelligibility of the Christian faith, it is not sufficient to address the more radical epistemological worries about justification typical of modernity. A dogmatics that mixes epistemological concerns into the description of the logic of what Christians believe in order to defend against such concerns merely succumbs to protectionism: it fails to risk itself in intellectually honest argument with modern scepticism about religion. In succumbing to that temptation, such a dogmatics makes, moreover, its own defence of greater importance than the God whose doings in Christ it is to witness to and serve.[32]

The advent of postmodernism might, however, render moot the need to reflect critically on the use of modern assumptions in christology. With the advent of the postmodern, modern idioms lose their plausibility and currency outside a theological context; theologians are therefore less likely to try to transpose christological topics into modern idioms in the first place. Should that be the emerging situation, then the diagnoses to be found in this chapter and the general recommendations of critical reflection that propel it become a warning to a new generation of students of doctrine who will be responsible for developing the postmodern christologies to come.

Notes

1 For example, Karl Barth's theology is Christocentric in exposition, while Thomas Aquinas' is not.

2 See *St Anselm: Basic Writings*, trans. S. N. Deane (La Salle, Illinois: Open Court, 1972).

3 The *locus classicus* for this is found in Friedrich Schleiermacher, *The Christian Faith*, ed. H. R. Mackintosh and J. S. Stewart (Philadelphia: Fortress, 1976), paragraph 96.

4 See Karl Barth, *Church Dogmatics*, ed. G. W. Bromiley and T. F. Torrance (Edinburgh: T. & T. Clark, 1978), vol. I, part 2.

5 See, for example, Augustine's revisions of Neoplatonism, or Thomas Aquinas' revisions of Aristotle.

6 See Wolfhart Pannenberg, *Jesus – God and Man*, trans. L. Wilkins and D. Priebe (Philadelphia: Westminster Press, 1977).

7 For a criticism like this of Rudolf Bultmann, see Jon Sobrino, *Christology at the Crossroads* (Maryknoll, New York: Orbis Books, 1978), p. 250.

8 See Ernst Troeltsch, 'Historical and Dogmatic Method in Theology', in *Religion in History*, trans. J. L. Adams and W. Bense (Minneapolis: Fortress, 1991), pp. 11–32.

9 See Van Harvey, *The Historian and the Believer* (New York: Macmillan, 1966), pp. 14–19. For recent criticisms, see Sobrino, *Christology*, pp. 248–51; and Jürgen Moltmann, *The Way of Jesus Christ* (Minneapolis: Fortress, 1993), pp. 242–5.

10 Moltmann, *The Way*, pp. 244–5.

11 See F. Gerald Downing, *Has Christianity a Revelation?* (London: SCM, 1964), p. 160.

12 See H. J. Iwand, 'Wider den Missbrauch des pro me als methodisches Prinzip in der Theologie', *Theologische Literaturzeitung*, ns 7/8 (July/August 1954): 454–8.

13 *Luthers Werke* (Weimar: Hermann Bohlau, 1883), vol. 46, p. 110. Cited by Ian Siggins, *Martin Luther's Doctrine of Christ* (New Haven: Yale University Press, 1976), pp. 138–9.

14 See Schleiermacher, *The Christian Faith*, paragraph 97.

15 David Friedrich Strauss, *The Christ of Faith and the Jesus of History*, trans. Leander Keck (Philadelphia: Fortress, 1977), pp. 4–5.

16 See Aloys Grillmeier, *Christ in Christian Tradition*, trans. John Bowden (Atlanta: John Knox Press, 1975), vol. I.

17 Note that this criticism of Schleiermacher does not hinge on the charge that God is not really present in God-consciousness as its Whence; I am not presuming that Schleiermacher's account of God-consciousness is reductively psychologistic.

18 Schleiermacher did not explicitly use the language of Jesus of history or Christ of faith, but Strauss popularised the terms in talking critically about Schleiermacher's theological method and christological conclusions.

19 Rudolf Bultmann, 'The Primitive Christian Kerygma and the Historical Jesus', in *The Historical Jesus and the Kerygmatic Christ*, trans. and ed. C. Braaten and R. Harrisville (New York and Nashville: Abingdon Press, 1964), pp. 41, 30.

20 *Ibid.*, pp. 40–1.

21 Proof of such Christian self-containment is found in the express admission that the Word no longer has any critical leverage with respect to Christian proclamation of it. Since the Word is constituted by the church, one cannot

appeal to the Word in order to settle doubts about the church. See Rudolf Bultmann, *Faith and Understanding*, ed. R. Funk, trans. L. P. Smith (Philadelphia: Fortress, 1987), p. 213.

22 *Ibid.*, pp. 138–41, 174–6.

23 See, for this criticism of Schleiermacher, Karl Barth, *Protestant Thought from Rousseau to Ritschl*, trans. Brian Cozens (New York: Harper and Row, 1959), p. 348.

24 *Ibid.*, pp. 331–54; and 'Rudolf Bultmann – An Attempt to Understand Him', in *Kerygma and Myth II*, ed. H.-W. Bartsch (London: SPCK, 1962), pp. 83–132.

25 See Downing, *Revelation*, p. 109.

26 See *ibid.*, pp. 209–15.

27 Besides the work of Downing, see Gustav Wingren, *Creation and Gospel* (New York: Mellen Press, 1979), and *Theology in Conflict* (Philadelphia: Muhlenberg Press, 1958), for criticisms like this of Barth in particular.

28 See Ronald Thiemann, *Revelation and Theology* (Notre Dame: University of Notre Dame Press, 1985), p. 11.

29 See Wingren, *Creation and Gospel*, p. 77.

30 *Church Dogmatics*, vol. 4, part 3, p. 79; see also vol. 4, part 2, p. 123.

31 Ian McFarland, 'Teaching with Authority: Communal Practice and the Logic of Accountability in Christian Belief' (unpublished dissertation, Yale University, 1995), p. 8.

32 See H. R. Niebuhr, *The Meaning of Revelation* (New York: Macmillan, 1941), ch. 1, sections II and III.

Further reading

Barth, Karl, *Church Dogmatics*, translation edited by G. W. Bromiley and T. F. Torrance, Edinburgh: T. & T. Clark, 1975, volume I, part 1.

'Rudolf Bultmann – An Attempt to Understand Him', in *Kerygma and Myth II*, edited by H.-W. Bartsch, London: SPCK, 1962, pp. 83–132.

'Schleiermacher', in *Protestant Thought from Rousseau to Ritschl*, translated by Brian Cozens, New York: Harper and Row, 1959, pp. 306–54.

Bultmann, Rudolf, *Faith and Understanding*, edited by R. Funk, translated by L. P. Smith, Philadelphia: Fortress, 1987.

'The Primitive Christian Kerygma and the Historical Jesus', in *The Historical Jesus and the Kerygmatic Christ*, edited and translated by C. Braaten and R. Harrisville, New York and Nashville: Abingdon Press, 1964.

Downing, F. Gerald, *Has Christianity a Revelation?*, London: SCM Press, 1964.

Frei, Hans, *Types of Christian Theology*, edited by George Hunsinger and William C. Placher, New Haven and London: Yale University Press, 1992.

Grillmeier, Aloys, *Christ in Christian Tradition*, translated by John Bowden, Atlanta: John Knox Press, 1975, volume I.

Harvey, Van, *The Historian and the Believer*, New York: Macmillan, 1966.

Pannenberg, Wolfhart, *Jesus – God and Man*, translated by L. Wilkins and D. Priebe, Philadelphia: Westminster Press, 1977.

Schleiermacher, Friedrich, *The Christian Faith*, edited by H. R. Mackintosh and J. S. Stewart, Philadelphia: Fortress, 1976.

Schweitzer, Albert, *The Quest of the Historical Jesus: A Critical Study of its Progress from Reimarus to Wrede*, New York: Macmillan, 1968.

Thiemann, Ronald, *Revelation and Theology*, Notre Dame: University of Notre Dame Press, 1985.

14 The Holy Spirit

GEOFFREY WAINWRIGHT

God as such is spirit, holy in himself and transcending matter of which he is the Creator. In a graphic way, and in the geopolitical context of the late eighth century BC, the Old Testament prophet brings out the transcendence of the Holy One of Israel over both equine and human creatures, showing the Lord's righteous rule over what he has made: the Egyptians are 'men, and not God', and their horses are 'flesh, and not spirit', and when the Lord stretches out his hand, they will perish together with those who have sought help from them rather than from 'the Holy One of Israel' (Isaiah 31:1–3). Or in the words of Jesus in John's Gospel (4:24): 'God is spirit, and those who worship him must worship in spirit and truth.' Yet beside this more general connection of God with spirit and holiness, the Holy Spirit is the particular name of the third person of the Blessed Trinity, Father, Son and Holy Spirit. The explanation of this apparently ambivalent usage – God as holy spirit, and God the Holy Spirit – requires a historical account of the biblical and patristic developments that will already set us on the road of a more systematic exposition of pneumatological doctrine. Our procedure, therefore, will first be to retrace the self-revelation of God and the corresponding experience, practice and cognitive process of Israel and the early church.

A DISTINCTION-IN-IDENTITY: THE BIBLICAL AND PATRISTIC ROAD

In the Old Testament, 'the Spirit of God' or 'the Spirit of the Lord' indicates a distinction-in-identity that will eventually allow the Christian church, after the coming of Christ and the pentecostal outpouring of 'Holy Spirit', to elaborate its doctrine in a trinitarian direction.

The beginnings of the notion and experience of 'the Spirit of God' or 'the Spirit of the Lord' reside in the wind or in breath, the mundane reference of the word *ruah* in Hebrew. Israel's deliverance from slavery in Egypt had been effected through the parting of the waters of the Red Sea when 'the

Lord drove the sea back by a strong east wind all night' (Exodus 14:21). Reflection on the story of the people's redemption will have affected Israel's understanding of creation. According to the first chapter of Genesis, 'the Spirit of God' moved over the face of the waters at creation (verse 2). Some would want to translate the phrase here as 'an almighty wind'. To stay at that level would be a reductive translation, disallowing the divine reference of the analogy and running counter to the point of the story of creation as God's work. Nevertheless, the figurative connection of spirit with wind remains significant. In the third chapter of John's Gospel, Jesus tells Nicodemus: 'That which is born of the flesh is flesh, and that which is born of the Spirit is spirit. Do not marvel that I said to you, "You must be born anew." The wind blows where it wills, and you hear the sound of it, but you do not know whence it comes or whither it goes; so it is with every one who is born of the Spirit' (verses 6–8). At Pentecost, the Spirit descends upon the infant church: 'Suddenly a sound came from heaven like the rush of a mighty wind, and it filled all the house where they were sitting ... And they were all filled with [the] Holy Spirit and began to speak in other tongues, as the Spirit gave them utterance' (Acts 2:2–4). (At this stage in the chapter, the enclosure of the definite article in brackets means that the article is lacking in the Greek. The point of this nuance will become clearer later.)

In another Old Testament passage to do with creation, the Psalmist says:

By the word of the Lord the heavens were made,
and all their host by the breath of his mouth ...
For he spoke, and it came to be;
he commanded and it stood forth. *(Psalm 33:6–8)*

Here *ruah* is the 'breath' of God which accompanies his creative word.

According to Genesis 2:7, 'the Lord God formed man of dust from the ground, and *breathed* into his nostrils the *breath* of life; and man became a living being'. In this passage, different Hebrew words, the verb *nph* and the noun *n*e*shamah*, are used, but the Greek Old Testament, which the early Christian writers largely depended on, employs the noun *pnoê* which has the same root as *pneuma*, the regular word for spirit. With regard to all earthly creatures, the Psalmist confesses before God:

When thou takest away their breath, they die
and return to the dust.
When thou sendest forth thy Spirit [*ruah*],
they are created;
and thou renewest the face of the ground. *(Psalm 104:29–30)*

In Ezekiel's prophetic vision of the renewal of Israel, the Lord causes *ruaḥ* (wind, breath, spirit) to enter into the dry bones and make them live (Ezekiel 37:1–14).

The Spirit of God is not only the basic source of life. The Spirit of the Lord also comes upon various figures in the Old Testament to equip them for their several tasks and responsibilities towards God and towards Israel. Thus for 'the construction of the sanctuary', 'the Lord filled' Bezalel and Oholiab 'with the Spirit of God, with ability, with intelligence, with knowledge, and with all craftsmanship, to devise artistic designs, to work in gold and silver and bronze, in cutting stones for setting, and in carving wood … to do every sort of work done by a craftsman or by a designer or by an embroiderer in blue and purple and scarlet stuff and fine twined linen, or by a weaver' (Exodus 35:30–36:1). Among the Judges upon whom the Spirit of the Lord came, intermittently (it seems) for particular exploits, were Gideon (Judges 6:34), Jephthah (Judges 11:29) and the mighty Samson. Even while Samson was a youth, 'a young lion roared against him; and the Spirit of the Lord came mightily upon him, and he tore the lion asunder as one tears a kid' (Judges 14:5–6). A similar influx proved useful 'when the Philistines came shouting to meet him': 'The Spirit of the Lord came mightily upon him, and the ropes which were on his arms became as flax that has caught fire, and his bonds melted off his hands. And he found a fresh jawbone of an ass, and put out his hand and seized it, and with it he slew a thousand men' (Judges 15:14–15).

When Samuel anointed David to designate him as king, 'the Spirit of the Lord came mightily upon David from that day forward' (1 Samuel 16:13). Later it would be said of the expected Messiah in David's line: 'And the Spirit of the Lord shall rest upon him, the spirit of wisdom and understanding, the spirit of counsel and might, the spirit of knowledge and the fear of the Lord. And his delight shall be in the fear of the Lord. He shall not judge by what his eyes see, or decide by what his ears hear; but with righteousness he shall judge the poor, and decide with equity for the meek of the earth' (Isaiah 11:2–4).

Moses, the first of the prophets, could wish 'that all the Lord's people were prophets, that the Lord would put his Spirit upon them' (Numbers 11:29). The prophet Elijah had from the Lord a spirit which Elisha could inherit (2 Kings 2:9, 15). The Spirit could enter into the later prophet Ezekiel (Ezekiel 2:2), lift him up (3:12), carry him away (3:14) and fall upon him (11:5).

The Psalmist prayed:

Create in me a clean heart, O God,
and put a new and right spirit within me.
Cast me not away from thy presence,
and take not thy holy Spirit from me.
(Psalm 51:10–11; see also Ezekiel 11:19–20)

And:

Teach me to do thy will,
for thou art my God!
Let thy good Spirit lead me
on a level path. *(Psalm 143:10)*

The picture that emerges from the Old Testament is that of a divine Spirit which is distinct from the Lord and yet equivalent to God's creative and redemptive presence for the sake of life, strength, skill, wisdom and justice, a means of revealing the Lord, communicating his will, energising his work and enabling obedience to him. The Spirit may come upon and enter into a human being, but the Spirit remains God's Spirit.

This pattern persists into the gospel accounts of Jesus' life and ministry, but the christological stamp which it there receives sets in motion certain developments that will lead towards a more defined doctrine of God in which the Spirit is recognised as the third person of the Trinity.

In the Lucan narrative of the annunciation to Mary, the angel says: '[The] Holy Spirit will come upon you, and [the] power of the Most High will overshadow you; therefore the child to be born of you will be called holy, the Son of God' (Luke 1:35). In this specific and particular event, [the] Holy Spirit figures as the agency [or Agent] of Jesus' conception in Mary's womb (see also Matthew 1:18, 20). To speak in terms that depend on the later Chalcedonian definition concerning the person and natures of Christ: the Spirit is thus the divine Creator of the humanity which the divine Son receives from Mary on his entry into the creaturely condition.

At his baptism at the hands of John in the Jordan, Jesus 'saw the Spirit of God descending like a dove, and alighting on him; and lo, a voice from heaven, saying, "This is my beloved Son, with whom I am well pleased"' (Matthew 3:16–17; see also Mark 1:10; Luke 3:21–2; John 1:29–34). 'Full of [the] Holy Spirit' (Luke 4:1), Jesus was then 'led up by the Spirit into the wilderness to be tempted by the devil' (Matthew 4:1; see also Mark 1:12–13; Luke 4:1), and the testing centred on his exercise of the divine sonship. Jesus' answer is to be revealed in his public ministry when, returning 'in the power of the Spirit' (Luke 4:14) into Galilee, he begins by appropriating to himself in the synagogue at Nazareth the passage from Isaiah (61:1–2): 'The Spirit of the Lord is upon me, because he has anointed me to preach good news to the poor. He has sent me to proclaim release to the captives and recovering of sight to the blind, to set at liberty those who are oppressed, to proclaim the acceptable year of the Lord' (Luke 4:18; see also Matthew 12:18). In controversy with his opponents, Jesus declares: 'If it is by the Spirit of God that I cast out demons, then the kingdom of God has come upon you' (Matthew 12:28). Upon the successful return of the seventy disciples from a mission of proclaiming the kingdom of God in face of demonic powers, Jesus 'rejoiced in the Holy Spirit and said, "I thank thee, Father, Lord of heaven and earth, that thou hast hidden these things from the wise and understanding and revealed them to babes; yea, Father, for such was thy gracious will. All things have been delivered to me by my Father; and no one knows who the Son is except the Father, or who the Father is except the Son and any to whom the Son chooses to reveal him"' (Luke 10:21–2).

[The] Holy Spirit is promised by Jesus to those who will ask the Father for the gift (Luke 11:13). After his own death (by which, according to Hebrews 9:14, he 'through the eternal Spirit offered himself without blemish to God') and his resurrection (and in Romans 8:11 Paul speaks of 'the Spirit of him who raised Jesus from the dead'), Jesus told his apostles: 'I send the promise of my Father upon you; but stay in the city until you are clothed with power from on high' (Luke 24:49; see also Acts 1:4–8). In St John's Gospel, this 'promise' takes on a physiognomy which will be very important in the recognition of the Holy Spirit as the third person of the Trinity. In the farewell discourses, Jesus speaks in these terms:

> I will pray the Father, and he will give you another Counsellor/
> Comforter [*Paraklêtos*], to be with you for ever, even the Spirit of truth,
> whom the world cannot receive, because it neither sees him nor knows
> him; you know him, for he dwells with you, and will be in you.
> *(John 14:16–17)*

> The *Paraklete*, the Holy Spirit, whom the Father will send in my name,
> he will teach you all things, and bring to your remembrance all that I
> have said to you. *(John 14:26)*

> When the *Paraklete* comes, whom I will send to you from the Father,
> even the Spirit of truth, who proceeds from the Father, he will bear
> witness to me. *(John 15:26)*

It is to your advantage that I go away, for if I do not go away, the
Paraklete will not come to you; but if I go, I will send him to you. And
when he comes, he will convince the world concerning sin and
righteousness and judgement: concerning sin, because they do not
believe in me; concerning righteousness, because I go to the Father,
and you will see me no more; concerning judgement, because the ruler
of this world is judged. I have yet many things to say to you, but you
cannot bear them now. When the Spirit of truth comes, he will guide
you into all the truth; for he will not speak on his own authority, but
whatever he hears he will speak, and he will declare to you the things
that are to come. He will glorify me, for he will take what is mine and
declare it to you. All that the Father has is mine; therefore I said that he
will take what is mine and declare it to you. *(John 16:7–15)*

While the Spirit is spoken of here in such personal terms (symptomatically,
the masculine pronoun is used, corresponding to *ho Paraklêtos*, not the
neuter that would match *to Pneuma*), the Fourth Evangelist can also revert to
an older conception of the Spirit when he describes the scene with the risen
Jesus and his apostles: 'He breathed on them, and said to them, "Receive [the]
Holy Spirit. If you forgive the sins of any, they are forgiven; if you retain the
sins of any, they are retained" ' (John 20:22–3).

The Acts of the Apostles and the New Testament Epistles hover between
the conception of 'Holy Spirit' as 'the power of God' or 'a mode of God's presence', on the one hand, and the more 'personal' understanding of 'the Holy
Spirit' most clearly apparent in the Johannine farewell discourses, on the
other. In Acts 2, the Spirit comes with the sound of a wind and the appearance of fire, making good the promise of Jesus that his followers would be
'baptised with [the] Holy Spirit' (Acts 1:5) and inaugurating the fulfilment of
Joel's prophecy 'And in the last days it shall be, God declares, that I will pour
out my Spirit on all flesh' (Acts 2:16–18). People are 'filled with [the] Holy
Spirit' (Acts 2:4; 4:8; 9:17; 13:9) and act 'in the Spirit' (Acts 19:21) and
'through the Spirit' (Acts 21:4). Yet, in more personal turns of phrase, the
Spirit speaks (Acts 1:16; 8:29; 10:19; 11:12; 13:2; 28:25), bears witness (Acts
5:32; 20:23), snatches (Acts 8:39), sends (Acts 13:4), thinks good (Acts
15:28), forbids (Acts 16:6), prevents (Acts 16:7), appoints (Acts 20:28), is lied
to (Acts 5:3), put to the test (Acts 5:9) and resisted (Acts 7:51; see also 6:10).
In St Paul's Letters, the phrase 'in the Spirit' or 'in the Holy Spirit' occurs frequently, where the preposition *en* may suggest instrumentality or location
(Romans 9:1; 12:11; 14:17; 15:16; 1 Corinthians 6:11; 12:3, 9, 13; etc.). Yet

again, in more personal terms, the Spirit leads, bears witness, makes intercession, cries, is grieved (Romans 8:14, 16, 26; Galatians 4:6; Ephesians 4:30).

The more the Spirit is conceived as 'the power of God' or 'a mode of God's presence', the less difficulty there is, at one level, of speaking of the Spirit's divinity. But to restrict oneself to that understanding and language, as some in early Christianity did, is to fall into either or both of the two ancient heresies which modern historians of doctrine have labelled precisely *'dynamic* monarchianism' and *'modalistic* monarchianism' (the common term 'monarchianism' reflecting the assumption of a concern for the divine unity). 'Dynamic' monarchianism sees [the] Spirit as divine power 'adopting' the man Jesus in a way that perhaps barely exceeded the Spirit's action on, or inhabitation of, the Old Testament figures or the later saints; it fails to see the Holy Spirit as specifically creating the humanity of Christ from its first moment and constantly accompanying the eternal Word who took flesh at the incarnation. 'Modalistic' monarchianism sees the Spirit as a temporary manifestation of the One God appropriate to a stage in history, a kind of extension of God into the world that will be finally retractable; it fails to recognise any hypostatic distinction (to use what became the technical term for the 'persons') in the Godhead. Neither of those does justice to the personality of the Holy Spirit.[1] On the other hand, the danger in stressing the personality of the Holy Spirit is that, for the sake again of maintaining a certain kind of monotheism, one will this time reduce the Spirit to a creature of the one true God. This is exactly what happened in Arianism, so that the second generation of Nicenes found themselves advancing, with respect to the Holy Spirit, arguments similar to those that had been employed in order to interpret and defend the deity of the Son. The veteran Athanasius, in his Letters to Serapion, stressed the church's practice of invoking the Holy Spirit in the Triune Name at baptism (where the saving gift of participation in God can be given only by God); and in this he was followed by the Cappadocians, who added a consideration similar to one that Athanasius himself had adduced in favour of the deity of the Son, namely the church's practice of addressing worship to the Holy Spirit (an unthinkable case of idolatry, if the Spirit were not God).[2]

For the ecumenical church, the matter was settled by the Council of Constantinople in 381. Whereas the first ecumenical council of Nicaea in 325 had been content to confess belief in the Holy Spirit by the simple affirmation 'and in the Holy Spirit', the second ecumenical council inserted into the creed – a genre having its origins in baptism and catechesis and now geared also more deliberately to serve as a test of episcopal orthodoxy –

certain phrases functionally equivalent to defining the deity of the third person of the Trinity in the way that Nicaea had done in respect of the second, the Son ('God from God, Light from Light, true God from true God, begotten not made, being of one substance with the Father'). For the ecumenically orthodox teaching of the church concerning the Holy Spirit, we may now therefore study the third article of the Nicene-Constantinopolitan creed (or the Nicene creed, as it is more commonly known).

THE CREDAL CONFESSION

The third article of the Nicene-Constantinopolitan creed starts thus:

And [we believe] in the Holy Spirit, the Lord and Life-Giver,
who proceeds from the Father,
who with the Father and the Son together is worshipped and glorified,
who has spoken through the prophets.

It is clear that 'the Holy Spirit' is a Name, or an element in the Triune Name of Father, Son and Holy Spirit in which baptisms took place (see Matthew 28:19). Its use to designate the third person of the divine Trinity governs each part of the compound phrase, 'Holy' and 'Spirit'.

Thus, first, the Spirit's *holiness* belongs to the defining and originating holiness of *God*. The being and character of God define holiness. Whatever God is, is holy. What God is, is specially revealed to the world in Jesus Christ, the incarnate Word, the Son sent to make the Father visible to humankind (John 1:14,18; John 14:9; Hebrews 1:1–3). Towards humankind, then, the Holy Spirit makes known 'the things of Christ', which are in the first place 'the things of the Father' (John 16:14–15). The Holy Spirit can accomplish this mission because he *has his eternal being* from the Father, who is *eternally the Father of the Son*. The Spirit's holiness goes, then, with his divine *nature*; and since it is of the *character* of God to be self-giving to what he has freely made, the Holy Spirit also *imparts* holiness to the objects of God's love.

Now, second, God is spirit (John 4:24). Not every spirit is God, or even 'from God' (1 John 4:4–6): there are created spirits, some of which are sent into the world to serve God's saving purposes (Hebrews 1:14), while others have fallen into opposing God and thus become evil or demonic (Matthew 8:16; 10:1; 12:43–5; etc.). As spirits, they all transcend matter; and this applies also to the human spirit (Romans 1:9; 8:16; 1 Corinthians 2:11; 7:34; etc.), which is and remains God's animating and personalising gift that constitutes a particular creature of flesh and blood as the image of God. *God's* spiritual transcendence of matter, and of all other spirits than himself, is the unique transcendence of their *Creator*. In Christian tradition, therefore, the Holy Spirit may be invoked as the *Creator Spiritus*. The hymn 'Veni, Creator Spiritus', attributed to Rhabanus Maurus (*c.* 776–*c.* 856), reads thus in John Dryden's translation as used in the *English Hymnal*:

> Creator Spirit, by whose aid
> The world's foundations first were laid,
> Come, visit every pious mind;
> Come, pour thy joys on human kind;
> From sin and sorrow set us free,
> And make thy temples worthy thee.
>
> O Source of uncreated light,
> The Father's promised Paraclete,
> Thrice holy Fount, thrice holy Fire,
> Our hearts with heavenly love inspire;
> Come, and thy sacred unction bring
> To sanctify us while we sing.
>
> Plenteous of grace, descend from high
> Rich in thy sevenfold energy;
> Make us eternal truths receive,
> And practise all that we believe;
> Give us thyself, that we may see
> The Father and the Son by thee.
>
> Immortal honour, endless fame,
> Attend the almighty Father's name;
> The Saviour Son be glorified,
> Who for lost man's redemption died;
> And equal adoration be,
> Eternal Paraclete, to thee.

That 'the Holy Spirit', third person of the Trinity, is both 'holy' and 'spirit' in the divine significance of the terms is affirmed in the next two phrases of the Nicene-Constantinopolitan creed. 'We believe ... in the Holy Spirit, *the Lord, the Life-Giver*' (adjectivally in the Greek, *to Kyrion, to Zôopoion*). 'The Lord' (*ho Kyrios*) is the name by which the Greek Old Testament represents the Hebrew Yahweh; it is also the title given to Jesus Christ in the New Testament and figures as such in the second article of the Nicene creed: 'We believe ... in one Lord Jesus Christ, the only Son of God.'

The same sovereignty is now recognised also to the Holy Spirit. Further, the Nicene creed speaks of the Son, 'through whom all things were made'; and this the third article matches when it affirms a 'life-giving' role for the Holy Spirit. As 'the Spirit of Life' (see Romans 8:2), the Holy Spirit energises what is made through the divine Word. Traditionally, the sovereign, life-giving Holy Spirit is hymned as 'the treasury of all good things' in the Byzantine Pentecostarion dating from the eighth century, *Basileu ouranie* ('O Heavenly King'):

> O King enthroned on high,
> Thou Comforter divine,
> Blest Spirit of all Truth, be nigh
> And make us thine.

> Thou art the Source of Life,
> Thou art our Treasure-store;
> Give us thy peace, and end our strife
> For evermore.

> Descend, O heavenly Dove,
> Abide with us alway:
> And in the fullness of thy love
> Cleanse us, we pray.[3]

The Council of Constantinople next confessed that the Holy Spirit 'proceeds from the Father (*ek tou Patros ekporeuomenon*)'. This corresponds to the Council of Nicaea's confession of the Son in the second article as 'begotten of the Father (*ek tou Patros gennêthenta*)'. Although the Nicene watchword is not used, the implication is that the Paraclete also is 'consubstantial with the Father (*homoousios tô Patri*)'. The reference of the 'procession' is to the eternal being of the Godhead, not directly to the Spirit's 'mission' into the world. More will be said on this theme when we come to twentieth-century discussion of the phrase which, in the first millennium already, the Western church added to the Nicene-Constantinopolitan creed and which has been a bone of contention between East and West ever since, namely the *filioque*, which affirms that the Holy Spirit proceeds from the Father 'and from the Son'.

The creed then confesses that the Holy Spirit 'with the Father and the Son together is worshipped and glorified (*to syn Patri kai Huiô synproskynoumenon kai syndoxazomenon*)'. To worship is to regard as divine, and the only proper recipient of worship is the one true God. Here, then, is a further confession of the Holy Spirit's divine being and personal character. Basil of Caesarea, in his treatise *On the Holy Spirit*, expounds and defends the practice of addressing 'co-ordinated' doxologies 'to the Father with the Son together with the Holy Spirit' or, as became more common, quite simply 'to the Father and to the Son and to the Holy Spirit'. Basil explains that all God's gifts reach us from the Father through the Son in the Holy Spirit, and correspondingly our thanks are addressed in the Spirit through the Son to the Father; but underlying the divine co-operation whereby God's works begin from the Father, are mediated by the Son and are consummated in the Spirit, is the mutual indwelling of the three divine hypostases, so that when God is contemplated *in se*, it is proper to address all three persons together. Traditionally, the Christian liturgy has long included the third person with the first two in its doxological ascriptions, while the particular and distinct invocation of the Holy Spirit in direct address is rarer. Dryden's version of the 'Veni, Creator Spiritus' neatly maintains the address to the Holy Spirit even when moving into a closing trinitarian doxology.

Finally, the Nicene-Constantinopolitan creed declares that the Holy Spirit 'has spoken through the prophets'. The principal effect of this clause is to affirm the unity and continuity of God's redemptive history with the world from the election of Israel onwards. As adumbrated by 1 Peter 1:10–11 and 2 Peter 1:21, from a Christian point of view it is precisely 'the Holy Spirit', third person of the Trinity, who was already at work in preparing for the incarnation of the Christ whose day was foreseen by Abraham (see also John 8:56–8) and whose glory by Isaiah (see also John 12:41).

The statement in 2 Timothy 3:16 that 'all Scripture is inspired by God (*pasa graphê theopneustos*)' has traditionally been expanded to include not only the Old Testament but the New. A similar expansion has been made with regard to the apostle Paul's statements in 2 Corinthians 3 on the vital role of the Spirit in the interpretation of scripture. In combination, these two principles lead to the further principle of a Christian hermeneutic that 'Scripture must be read through the same Spirit whereby it was written'.[4] Accepting that it was indeed the Holy Spirit who led the conciliar fathers at Constantinople to interpret the scriptures in such a way as clearly to confess the Holy Spirit as the third person of the Trinity, we may now, in a benignly circular move, reread the witness especially of the New Testament without the pussyfooting brackets around the definite article in order to show the scriptural basis for all those features in the practice of the church and in the experience of individual Christians that are traditionally ascribed precisely to 'the Holy Spirit'.

REREADING THE NEW TESTAMENT

After the presence and activity of the Holy Spirit in the conception, life, ministry, death and resurrection of Jesus Christ, we find the 'other Paraclete' (John 14:16)[5] given to the apostles (John 20:22–3), the 'Promise of the Father' (Luke 24:29; Acts 1:4–5) made good at Pentecost (Acts 2:1–21; see also 33). Henceforward the Holy Spirit will be the Life of the church, itself the 'first-fruits' of God's new creation (James 1:18) and an instrument in God's hands for the achievement of God's purposes among humankind. The Holy Spirit works from the very beginning to constitute and compose the church and its members, coming to them and abiding in them corporately and individually, starting to transform them in the direction of God's kingdom and enabling them to bear witness to the gospel for the sake of its extension.

The Holy Spirit is, in the first place, the power of Christian preaching. It was as among those 'filled with the Holy Spirit' (Acts 2:4) that the apostle Peter first proclaimed the message (Acts 2:14–39; see also 4:8–12). While Peter spoke at Caesarea, 'the Holy Spirit fell on all who heard the word' (Acts 10:44). Similarly, the apostle Paul attributes his own evangelising to the Holy Spirit: 'I will not venture to speak of anything except what Christ has wrought through me to win obedience from the Gentiles, by word and deed, by the power of signs and wonders, by the power of the Holy Spirit, so that from Jerusalem and as far round as Illyricum I have fully preached the gospel of Christ' (Romans 15:18–19; see also 1 Corinthians 2:2–5; 1 Thessalonians 1:5). The Holy Spirit not only energises Christian preaching, but ensures its christological content, for it is the Spirit's function to 'call to mind' and 'declare the things of Christ' (John 14:25; 15:26–7; 16:14).

The Holy Spirit then correspondingly enables the response of faith. It is only 'by the Holy Spirit' that one can say 'Jesus is Lord' (1 Corinthians 12:3). It is as having 'the Spirit of faith' that 'we believe, and so we speak'; and such testimony allows 'grace to extend to more and more people' and so 'increase the thanksgiving, to the glory of God' (2 Corinthians 4:13–15). In his hymn 'Spirit of faith, come down', Charles Wesley characteristically weaves together several scriptural allusions to trace this entire movement:

No man can truly say
That Jesus is the Lord, [1 Corinthians 12:3]
Unless thou take the veil away, [2 Corinthians 3:12–18]
And breathe the living word; [Matthew 4:4; John 20:22]
Then, only then we feel

Our interest in his blood, [1 John 1:7]
And cry with joy unspeakable, [1 Peter 1:8]
Thou art my Lord, my God! [John 20:28]

The initial preaching and response are sacramentally signified in baptism. 'Repent,' Peter preaches, 'and be baptised every one of you in the name of Jesus Christ for the forgiveness of your sins, and you shall receive the gift of the Holy Spirit' (Acts 2:38). Those who 'repent and believe in the Gospel' (Mark 1:15) are 'born again of water and the Spirit' (John 3:3–7). 'You were washed,' Paul reminds the Corinthian Christians, 'you were sanctified, you were justified in the name of the Lord Jesus Christ and in the Spirit of our God' (1 Corinthians 6:11). Baptism is a 'washing of regeneration and renewal in the Holy Spirit, which he poured out upon us richly through Jesus Christ our Saviour, so that we might be justified by his grace and become heirs in hope of eternal life' (Titus 3:5–7).

It is by the personal work of the Holy Spirit, sacramentally signified in baptism, that believers are made holy. The purifying and regenerating activity and indwelling presence of the Holy Spirit have immediate consequences for conduct, as Paul expounds to the Corinthians: 'Do you not know that your body is a temple of the Holy Spirit within you, which you have from God? You are not your own; you were bought with a price. So glorify God in your body' (1 Corinthians 6:19–20; see also 2 Corinthians 6:16–7:1).

In his *Letter to a Roman Catholic*, John Wesley sets out the faith of 'a true Protestant' by means of an expansion on the Nicene-Constantinopolitan creed with which he fully expects his addressee to agree; and in the course of it, he spells out the holiness which the Holy Spirit originates in believers:

I believe the infinite and eternal Spirit of God, equal with the Father
and the Son, to be not only perfectly holy in himself, but the immediate
cause of all holiness in us: enlightening our understandings, rectifying
our wills and affections, renewing our natures, uniting our persons to
Christ, assuring us of the adoption of sons, leading us in our actions,
purifying and sanctifying our souls and bodies to a full and eternal
enjoyment of God.[6]

Such a summary helps us to specify the continuing work of sanctification through the abiding presence of the Holy Spirit in the believer, once the initial response to the gospel has been made and sealed.

The renewal of our minds, hearts and lives in union and conformity with Christ occurs through the abiding gifts of the Holy Spirit, faith, hope and love (1 Corinthians 13:13; see also 12:31; Galatians 5:5–6). These theological virtues, as they are traditionally called, constitute the ongoing transformation of sinners into the likeness of God which the human creature, made in the image of God, was and remains called to become. An old Roman collect prays: 'Give us, Lord, an increase of faith, hope and love.'7 The faith elicited by the gospel is meant to grow into deepening trust and constant fidelity. To borrow another stanza from Charles Wesley's 'Spirit of faith, come down':

> Inspire the living faith
> (Which whoso'er receives,
> The witness in himself he hath,
> And consciously believes), [1 John 5:10; Romans 8:15]
> The faith that conquers all, [1 John 5:4]
> And doth the mountain move, [Mark 11:23; 1 Corinthians 13:2]
> And saves whoe'er on Jesus call, [Romans 10:13]
> And perfects them in love. [1 John 4:17]

As Paul makes clear in Romans, faith produces and is sustained by hope of the final consummation: 'Since we are justified by faith, we have peace with God through our Lord Jesus Christ. Through him we have obtained access by faith to the grace in which we stand, and we rejoice in our hope of sharing the glory of God' (5:1–2; see also 15:13). If 'hope does not disappoint us', it is 'because God's love has been poured into our hearts through the Holy Spirit which has been given us' (Romans 5:5). Love is the 'greatest' of the gifts (1 Corinthians 13:13), because it gives us 'a share in the divine nature' (2 Peter 1:4), allowing us (in St Augustine's phrase) to 'imitate whom we worship'.8

'If we live by the Spirit,' Paul tells the Galatian Christians, 'let us also walk by the Spirit' (Galatians 5:25). The indicative of the Holy Spirit as the source of the Christian life implies an imperative to a conduct of holiness. 'The fruit of the Spirit is love, joy, peace, patience, kindness, goodness, faithfulness, gentleness, self-control' (Galatians 5:22): virtue, we might say, is its own reward, as long as we remember the part played by the Holy Spirit in its creation and that 'righteousness and peace and joy in the Holy Spirit' properly belong to 'the kingdom of God' (Romans 14:17).

Of that kingdom, Christians have been made joint heirs with Christ through their adoption into the Father's family as sons and daughters in the Beloved (see Ephesians 1:5–6). The key passage is Romans 8:14–17: 'For all who are led by the Spirit of God are sons of God. For you did not receive the spirit of slavery to fall back into fear, but you have received the Spirit of adoption. When we cry, "Abba! Father!" it is the Spirit himself bearing witness with our spirit that we are children of God, and if children, then heirs, heirs of God and fellow heirs with Christ, provided we suffer with him in order that we may also be glorified with him.' Amid the trials of this world, and in anticipation of final glory, the present privilege of Christians is to address Almighty God, in the name of Christ (Matthew 18:19–20; John 15:16; 16:23) and by the power of the Spirit at work in them (Ephesians 3:14–21), as 'Abba, dear Father' (see also Galatians 4:4–6). The Christian liturgy classically follows the pattern of Ephesians 2:18: 'Through Christ we have access in the one Spirit to the Father.' The Holy Spirit is the teacher and bearer of Christian prayer: 'The Spirit helps us in our weakness; for we do not know how to pray as we ought, but the Spirit himself intercedes for us with sighs too deep for words. And he who knows the hearts of men knows what is the mind of the Spirit, that the Spirit intercedes for the saints according to the will of God' (Romans 8:26–7; see also 1 Corinthians 2: 6–13).

According to the ancient church order identified as *The Apostolic Tradition* of Hippolytus, the worship assembly is 'where the Spirit abounds (*ubi floret Spiritus*)', and 'where the Spirit of the Lord is, there is liberty' (2 Corinthians 3:17; see also John 8:31f.): believers are delivered from the power of sin in order to be able to serve God (Romans 6), 'whose service' (in the collect from the Book of Common Prayer) 'is perfect freedom'.

The Holy Spirit is the guarantor of the eschatological prospect. The Spirit is said to be the 'earnest (*arrabôn*)' of the final inheritance (2 Corinthians 1:22; 5:5; Ephesians 1:13–14). That notion is coupled with the baptismal image of sealing: 'By the Holy Spirit of God', baptised believers 'have been sealed for the day of redemption' (Ephesians 4:30). In another figure, the Holy Spirit is spoken of as the 'firstfruits (*aparchê*)' of a redemption that will not only reach the children of God but carry consequences of cosmic dimensions (Romans 8:19–25).

The radicality of life in the Spirit depends on the present location of existence between the resurrection of Christ and the general resurrection in which 'we shall all be changed' (1 Corinthians 15:51). The crucial passages for Christian teaching in this matter are Romans 8 (again) and 1 Corinthians 15. Already in Romans 6, Paul has demonstrated the absurdity of continuing in sin, that grace may abound: those who have been baptised into Christ's death are to walk in newness of life, considering themselves dead to sin and alive to God in Christ Jesus, knowing that they will be united with Christ also in a resurrection like his. The new life is 'according to the Spirit' (Romans 8:4–6); and 'you are in the Spirit, if in fact the Spirit of God dwells in you' (8:9). This Spirit of God is also 'the Spirit of Christ' (8:9–10), apparently in virtue of his resurrection, and this will have ultimate consequences: 'If the Spirit of him who raised Jesus from the dead dwells in you, he who raised Christ Jesus from the dead will give life to your mortal bodies also through his Spirit which dwells in you' (8:11). For Christ will turn out to be 'the first-born among many brethren', those predestined to glorification (8:29–30). Then in 1 Corinthians 15, in light of the risen Christ as the Last Adam who has become a life-giving Spirit, Paul develops the notion of a 'spiritual body', by which those who belong to Christ will be made alive in him, raised in power to glory, raised imperishable for immortality, until God will be all in all. Although the human eye has not yet seen, nor the ear heard, nor the heart conceived what God has in store for those who love him (1 Corinthians 2:9), those who meanwhile receive the gifts of the Spirit of God (2:14) and are indwelt by the Spirit of God (3:16; 6:19) are learning to glorify God in their body (6:20) as by the Spirit they are being changed into the Lord's likeness from one degree of glory to another (2 Corinthians 3:18).

The 'fellowship of the Holy Spirit (hê koinônia tou Hagiou Pneumatos)' is the gift of a common participation in the life of God (2 Corinthians 13:13). All believers have been baptised by the one Spirit into the one body of Christ (1 Corinthians 12:13). The same Spirit gives a variety of gifts to the several members for the common good (12:4–11, 14–26). The various ministries that Paul mentions in this context are apostles, prophets, teachers, workers of miracles, healers, helpers, administrators, speakers in various kinds of tongues (12:27–30). Similarly, Ephesians 4 speaks of 'one body and one Spirit', 'one Lord, one faith, one baptism'; and the gifts are 'that some should be apostles, some prophets, some evangelists, some pastors and teachers, to equip the saints for the work of ministry, for building up the body of Christ'; meanwhile the Christians are to 'maintain the unity of the Spirit in the bond of peace'. 'Fervent in the Spirit', the bondsmen of the Lord are to use their different gifts of grace within the unity of the body, in prophecy, in serving, in teaching, in exhortation, in contribution, in works of mercy (Romans 12:4–13). Ecclesiologically, there has often existed some tension within and between churches between a more 'charismatically' and a more 'institutionally' oriented view of ministries. Both the more spontaneous and the more structured conceptions lay claim to the Holy Spirit. The Holy Spirit is invoked at ordinations as well as recognised to fall upon individuals for temporary and particular tasks.

Pneumatology was for long a neglected doctrine in Western Christianity. Whether as cause, symptom or effect of the neglect, treatment of the Holy Spirit tended in the Middle Ages and at the time of the Reformation to be absorbed under the heading of 'grace', where controversies took forms that were only indirectly pneumatological. Not unconnectedly perhaps, subsequent developments in Socinian and deistic directions led to an undifferentiated godhead which finally lost relation with the world. All this may have had roots in the patristic period when different approaches to God opened up between East and West, epitomised in the question of the *filioque*. That, at least, is how Orthodox theologians in the ecumenical twentieth century have persuaded many Catholics and Protestants to view the matter.

Before coming to the description of beneficial Eastern Orthodox influence on contemporary ecumenical pneumatology, however, there is a homespun Western phenomenon to be recognised. In part perhaps as a reaction against the aridity of much church life either of a liberal or a more classical kind, the twentieth century has witnessed the outburst of a Pentecostal movement that has generated an entire new ecclesiastical family (however loose the institutional structures that bind 'Pentecostalist' denominations) and brought 'charismatic' renewal (though sometimes at the cost of division) to many Protestant and Catholic groups and congregations. The classical ecumenist Lesslie Newbigin spotted the emergence of this 'third type' in his book *The Household of God* and prophetically discerned the significance of this ecclesiology of 'the community of the Holy Spirit' alongside those of 'the congregation of the faithful' (characteristically Protestant) and 'the body of Christ' (characteristically Catholic); and he made the trinitarian complementarity – and properly coinherence – of these models even more obvious in his later missiological study, *The Open Secret*.[9]

If the danger of Pentecostalism is pneumatological hypertrophy (and practical 'enthusiasts' have never lacked for conceptually orthodox critics in the history of Christianity), the invigoration brought by the Eastern Orthodox to ecumenical pneumatology in the twentieth century has come from a very deliberately trinitarian context. It has shown itself in several areas: the theology and practice of worship; the doctrine and experience of grace; the constitution and limits of the church; the discernment and depiction of sainthood.

The term *epiklesis* can stand for the influence of Eastern Orthodox pneumatology in the liturgical realm. Meaning 'invocation', its technical reference is to the prayer made for the sending of the Holy Spirit upon the worshipping assembly, its actions and the materials that are employed in its sacraments. Crucial is the eucharistic epiklesis. It runs thus, for instance, in the Byzantine Liturgy of St Basil:

> And having set forth the likenesses of the holy body and blood of your Christ, we pray and beseech you, O Holy of Holies, in the good pleasure of your bounty, that your All-Holy Spirit may come upon us and upon these gifts set forth, and bless them and sanctify and show this bread to be the precious body of our Lord and God and Saviour Jesus Christ. Amen. And this cup the precious blood of our Lord and God and Saviour Jesus Christ, which is shed for the life of the world. Amen. Unite with one another all of us who partake of the one bread and the cup into the communion of the one Holy Spirit . . .

The 'invocation of the Spirit' figured in its due place – after 'thanksgiving to the Father' and 'memorial of Christ' and before 'communion of the faithful' and 'meal of the kingdom' – in the exposition of eucharistic faith and practice made in *Baptism, Eucharist and Ministry* by the Faith and Order Commission of the World Council of Churches;[10] and while some Protestants have difficulty with the invocation of the Holy Spirit upon 'inanimate objects', several official responses to the Lima text by Protestant churches welcomed the move as making clear that 'the sacraments are prayer-actions and not mechanical means of grace' (as the Anglican Church of Canada put it).[11] Many Western churches have, like the Roman Catholic Church, introduced in one shape or form a pneumatological epiklesis into their new eucharistic prayers in ways that also enhance the trinitarian understanding and structure of the action.

Eastern Orthodoxy has also influenced the Western churches towards the recovery of a more personal understanding and appropriation of grace. There had been for many centuries tendencies in the West to view grace somewhat in the manner of a quantifiable fluid and to speak of the doubtless necessary distinctions in the stages and purposes of God's gracious activity in ways that could verge on the impersonal. Eastern Orthodox theology insists that the divine energies by which God shapes creation are trinitarianly personal. This has reinforced the efforts by Roman Catholic theologians in particular to present the transformative work of God in human beings in terms of the indwelling Holy Spirit, whether making the most of such themes in the patristic and scholastic literature of the West[12] or drawing on the experience of the modern charismatic movement.[13]

Ecclesiologically, the Eastern Orthodox have reproached the Western churches, and not only the Roman, with an 'institutionalism' and even a 'juridicalism' that they relate to 'christomonistic' tendencies in the faulty trinitarianism of the West. This criticism, together with a measure of charismatic renewal, has contributed to a certain 'pneumatological correction' that has entered contemporary Western ecclesiologies – including the Roman Catholic – in both theory and practice. For their own part, the Orthodox are starting to seek a theological way of accounting for the presence of Christian faith and life which the ecumenical movement has led them to encounter beyond the canonical bounds of Orthodoxy; and there is a strong tendency to do this in pneumatological terms.[14]

The recognition of instances of conspicuous sanctity beyond the bounds of one's own tradition and community may prove an important stimulus to a rereading of Christian history and a reconfiguration of church relations in the present and future. To recognise the presence and work of the Holy Spirit in another Christian has implications for one's view of the community to which that Christian belongs. Where the Holy Spirit is, can the Tradition be far away? An 'exchange of saints' would make a significant contribution to the restoration of unity; and it is encouraging to notice that some Protestant churches, having recovered the notion and practice of a *sanctorale* in part from Orthodox example, have taken figures from far beyond their own obvious boundaries for inclusion in their calendars.

The depiction of saints in their iconography is, in Orthodox eyes, a pneumatological reality. Paul Evdokimov speaks of the Holy Spirit as 'the divine iconographer'.[15] It is by the Holy Spirit that the painter works; it is by the Holy Spirit that the icon is consecrated for liturgical use; it is by the Holy Spirit that the worshipper approaches the icon in contemplation. The Holy Spirit dwelt in Christ and in his saints who are depicted by the icons; Christ and his saints now make their presence known to the assembly in the Holy Spirit through the medium of the icons. Many Western Christians have started to gain an appreciation of all this. Iconography could contribute to the Christian aesthetic so much needed in the contemporary world. The senses need schooling just as were those of the saints depicted. The beauty of holiness must norm the holiness of beauty. The divine glory compassed a crucifixion (1 Corinthians 2:8; see also Isaiah 53:2–5) before effecting a resurrection (Romans 6:4; John 17:1–5).

All that the West may have learned from the East, and may still learn, is, however, epitomised for the East in the overcoming of the *filioque*. For behind this question may lie the entire doctrine of God as regards the very being of God, the self-revelation of God and the proper approach to God. The Orthodox certainly consider the Western declaration that 'the Holy Spirit proceeds from the Father *and from the Son*' to be the deepest issue between Eastern and Western Christianity. If the hypostasis of the Holy Spirit is not satisfactorily acknowledged (and that is the threat which the East sees in the *filioque*), then the doctrine of the Trinity falls, and with it the personal character of God. Slowly but surely, the question has been taken up again in the modern ecumenical movement.[16]

The chief culprit in Eastern eyes is Augustine of Hippo, author of the most influential Western treatise 'On the Trinity'. The criticism runs roughly as follows. In Augustine, it is difficult to distinguish the person of the Holy Spirit from the common essence of the Godhead which, according to Augustine, logically precedes the distinction of the persons: the Holy Spirit is holy, but so is already the Godhead as such; the Holy Spirit is spirit, but so is already the Godhead as such; the Holy Spirit is the love which 'binds' the Father and the Son, but the Godhead as such is love (1 John 4:8). The problem is compounded by the psychological analogies which Augustine finds and employs, whereby (say) 'memory, understanding, and will' fit rather a 'unipersonal' or (more accurately) a 'super-individual' view of God. For the East, however, the biblical, patristic and orthodox understanding and experience is of God as 'persons-in-communion'. The East makes the Father the hypostatic principle (*archê*), source (*pêgê*) or cause (*aitia*) of deity, communicating being to the Son and to the Spirit. That is what preserves the personal distinctiveness of all three, Father, Son and Holy Spirit (and to make both Father and Son into the 'principle' of deity is to fuse the two and to diminish the Spirit, to boot).[17]

The modern ecumenical discussion has tried a somewhat new tack by phrasing the issue as that of the proper relation between the Son and the Spirit, where attention to their mutual relationship in the history of salvation – such as we traced it through biblical and patristic developments – may help towards the resolution of differences concerning their place in the eternal being of God.[18]

Since the last formal discussion of the *filioque* in Faith and Order, the question has in fact acquired an unexpected relevance beyond that of settling classical differences between East and West; and here the controversial fronts appear to have shifted rather significantly. The seventh assembly of the World Council of Churches was held at Canberra, Australia, in 1991 under the banner 'Come, Holy Spirit: Renew the Whole Creation'. The cosmic title betokened the council's current interest in 'justice, peace *and the integrity of creation*, while events and discussions at the assembly (turning around the fire ritual and provocative address of the Korean theologian Chung Hyun-Kyung)[19] showed that some participants were willing to give a very generous, or undiscriminating (as the case may be), meaning to 'spirit'. The Eastern and Oriental Orthodox representatives issued a sharply critical statement in which they observed that

> some people tend to affirm with very great ease the presence of the Holy Spirit in many movements and developments without discrimination. The Orthodox wish to stress the factor of sin and error, which exists in every human action, and separate the Holy Spirit from these. We must guard against a tendency to substitute a 'private' spirit, the spirit of the world or other spirits, for the Holy Spirit who proceeds from the Father and rests in the Son. Our tradition is rich in respect for local and national cultures, but we find it impossible to invoke the spirits of 'earth, air, water and sea creatures'. Pneumatology is inseparable from Christology or from the doctrine of the Holy Trinity confessed by the Church on the basis of Divine Revelation.[20]

For their part, Protestant Evangelicals, worried also by the loss of evangelistic thrust in the WCC, wrote this in their letter from Canberra:

> As the Assembly discussed the process of listening to the Spirit at work in every culture, we cautioned, with others, that discernment is required to identify the Spirit as the Spirit of Jesus Christ and thus to develop criteria for and limits to theological diversity. We argued for a high Christology to serve as the only authentic Christian base for dialogue with persons of other living faiths.[21]

Classical Roman Catholic voices could be heard in similar vein. One Western defence of the *filioque*, perhaps offered a posteriori, has been its usefulness in keeping the Spirit together with the Word.

CONCLUSION

We have come full circle. Anthropologically, spirit and holiness are practically universal categories; they are found wherever 'religion' is found. Characteristic of Christianity is the belief that God has made mankind in the divine image in order that we may share in the divine life and character. The Holy Spirit who sustains the human creature and sanctifies people by transformative participation is no less than the hypostasis of Love uniting Father and Son from all eternity and to all eternity. Those in whom the Holy Spirit comes to dwell are being conformed to Jesus the incarnate Son. Acquiring the mind of Christ and walking in his way, they join the company which worships the Father in Spirit and in Truth and begin to enjoy the communion in and with the divine Trinity which their gracious creator and redeemer has in store for them.

> *Glory be to the Father and to the Son and to the Holy Spirit:*
> *As it was in the beginning, is now, and ever shall be, world without end.*
> *Amen.*

Notes

1 The continued recurrence of 'dynamism' and 'modalism', often in curiously mixed form, finds instantiation in the works of G. W. H. Lampe, *God as Spirit* (Oxford: Clarendon Press, 1977) and Hendrikus Berkhof, *The Doctrine of the Holy Spirit* (London: Epworth Press, 1965) and *Christian Faith* (Grand Rapids, Michigan: Eerdmans, 1979).

2 The four relevant letters of Athanasius to Serapion on the Holy Spirit have been translated into English and copiously annotated by C. R. B. Shapland (see Further reading); for the argument from worship in favour of Christ's divinity, cf. the letter of Athanasius to Adelphius, 3–4. By the Cappadocians, note Basil, *On the Holy Spirit*, 24–6 (baptism), 71–5 (worship); Gregory Nazianzen, *Oration XL, on Holy Baptism*, 41–2; Gregory of Nyssa, *Sermon on the Baptism of Christ*, and *On the Holy Spirit, against the Macedonians*.

3 Version from the *English Hymnal*.

4 'Omnis scriptura legi debet eo Spiritu quo scripta est.' This formulation of the classic principle by Thomas à Kempis (*Imitation of Christ* 1.5) is twice paraphrased by John Wesley: 'Scripture can only be understood through the same Spirit whereby it was given' (*The Works of John Wesley*, ed. Thomas Jackson (London: Wesleyan Methodist Book Room, 1872), vol. xiv, p. 233); and 'I do firmly believe (and what serious man does not?): We need the same Spirit to understand the Scripture, which enabled the holy men of old to write it' (*ibid.*, vol. ix, p. 154).

5 See 1 John 2:21 for Christ as the 'first' Advocate.

6 *Works*, ed. Jackson, vol. x, p. 82.

7 This was the oration of Pentecost xiii in the Tridentine missal.

8 '*Imitari quem colis*': Augustine's phrase (*De civitate Dei* viii.17.2) is quoted by John Wesley in Sermon 29, 'Upon Our Lord's Sermon on the Mount, ix' (*Works*, ed. Jackson, vol. v, p. 381).

9 Lesslie Newbigin, *The Household of God: Lectures on the Nature of the Church* (London: SCM, 1953); *The Open Secret: Sketches for a Missionary Theology* (Grand Rapids, Michigan: Eerdmans, 1978).

10 *Baptism, Eucharist and Ministry*, Faith and Order Paper No. 111 (Geneva: World Council of Churches, 1982).

11 See Geoffrey Wainwright, 'The Eucharist in the Churches' Responses to the Lima Text', *One in Christ* 25 (1989): 53–74.

12 Gérard Philips, *L'union personnelle avec le Dieu vivant: essai sur l'origine et le sens de la grâce créée* (Gembloux: Ducoulot, 1974).

13 Heribert Mühlen, *Der Heilige Geist als Person: Beitrag zur Frage nach der dem Heiligen Geiste eigentümlichen Funktion in der Trinität, bei der Inkarnation und im Gnadenbund: Ich, Du, Wir* (Münster: Aschendorff, 1963; enlarged edn 1967).

14 See Damaskinos Papandreou, 'Die Frage nach den Grenzen der Kirche im heutigen ökumenischen Dialog', in D. Papandreou, W. A. Bienert and K. Schäferdiek (eds.), *Oecumenica et Patristica: Festschrift für Wilhelm Schneemelcher zum 75. Geburtstag* (Stuttgart: Kohlhammer, 1989), pp. 21–32.

15 Paul Evdokimov, *L'art de l'icône: Théologie de la beauté* (Paris: Desclée de Brouwer, 1972), p. 13.

16 See Lukas Vischer (ed.), *Spirit of God, Spirit of Christ*, Faith and Order Paper No. 103 (Geneva: World Council of Churches, 1981).

17 For hints that twentieth-century theologians in both East and West may have been too readily taken in by the schematic opposition between the patristic East and the patristic West drawn in the Jesuit Théodore de Régnon's *Études de théologie positive sur la Sainte Trinité* (1892–8), see M. R. Barnes, 'Augustine in Contemporary Trinitarian Theology', *Theological Studies* 56 (1995): 237–50.

18 Vischer (ed.), *Spirit of God, Spirit of Christ*, pp. 8–10, 17–18.

19 See Michael Kinnamon (ed.), *Signs of the Spirit: Official Report, Seventh Assembly, Canberra, Australia, 7–20 February 1991* (Geneva: World Council of Churches, and Grand Rapids, Michigan: Eerdmans, 1991), pp. 15–16, 37–47.

20 *Ibid.*, pp. 279–82.

21 *Ibid.*, pp. 282–6.

Further reading

Badcock, Gary D., *Light of Truth and Fire of Love: A Theology of the Holy Spirit*, Grand Rapids, Michigan: Eerdmans, 1997.

Basil the Great, St, *On the Holy Spirit*, translated by David Anderson, Crestwood, New York: St Vladimir's Seminary Press, 1980.

Bilanuik, Petro B. T., *Theology and Economy of the Holy Spirit*, Bangalore: Dharmaram Publications, 1980.

Bruner, Frederick D., *A Theology of the Holy Spirit: The Pentecostal Experience and the New Testament Witness*, Grand Rapids, Michigan: Eerdmans, 1970; London: Hodder & Stoughton, 1971.

Congar, Yves, *Je crois en l'Esprit saint*, 3 volumes, Paris: Editions du Cerf, 1979–80.

Del Colle, Ralph, *Christ and the Spirit: Spirit-Christology in Trinitarian Perspective*, New York: Oxford University Press, 1994.

Fee, Gordon D., *God's Empowering Presence: The Holy Spirit in the Letters of Paul*, Peabody, Massachusetts: Hendrickson, 1994.

Hendry, George S., *The Holy Spirit in Christian Theology*, Philadelphia: Westminster Press, 1956; London: SCM Press, 1957. Revised and enlarged edition 1965.

Heron, Alasdair I. C., *The Holy Spirit*, Philadelphia: Westminster Press, 1983.

Hopko, Thomas, *The Spirit of God*, Wilton, Connecticut: Morehouse-Barlow, 1976.

Kirkpatrick, Dow, editor, *The Holy Spirit*, Nashville: Tidings (for the World Methodist Council), 1974.

McKenna, John H., *Eucharist and Holy Spirit: The Eucharistic Epiclesis in Twentieth-Century Theology*, Alcuin Club Collections No. 57, Great Wakering, Essex: Mayhew-McCrimmon, 1975.

Moltmann, Jürgen, *Der Geist des Lebens: Eine ganzheitliche Pneumatologie*, Munich: Kaiser, 1991. Translated by Margaret Kohl as *The Spirit of Life: A Universal Affirmation*, Minneapolis: Augsburg-Fortress, 1992.

Moule, C. F. D., *The Holy Spirit*, London: Mowbrays, 1978.

Ramsey, Michael, *Holy Spirit: A Biblical Study*, London: SPCK, 1977.

Shapland, C. R. B., *The Letters of St. Athanasius concerning the Holy Spirit*, London: Epworth Press, 1951.

Taylor, John V., *The Go-Between God: The Holy Spirit and Christian Mission*, London: SCM Press, 1972.

Vischer, Lukas (ed.), *Spirit of God, Spirit of Christ*, Faith and Order Paper No. 103, Geneva: World Council of Churches, 1981.

Volf, Miroslav, *Work in the Spirit: Toward a Theology of Work*, New York: Oxford University Press, 1991.

Welker, Michael, *Gottes Geist: Theologie des Heiligen Geistes*, Neukirchen-Vluyn: Neukirchener Verlag, 1992. Translated by John H. Hoffmeyer as *God the Spirit*, Minneapolis: Fortress, 1994.

General index

Abelard 8
Althaus, Paul 243
Althusser, Louis 185
Anselm of Canterbury 8, 15–18, 198–201, 245
anthropology chapter 9
  non-theological 160–1
  philosophical 161–2
  theological 158–9, 171–5
apocalyptic 229–30, 239–40
Aquinas, Thomas 8, 10, 15–18, 27–8, 45,
  52–3, 57, 86, 100, 101, 132–3, 150–1,
  220, 222, 224, 245, 269
Arendt, Hannah 186
Aristotle 8, 27, 37, 148, 152, 161, 174
Arius 128
arts chapter 6, 161
  autonomy 103–4
  constructivism 108–9
  and materiality, physicality 106–8, 110
  as redemptive 111
  responsibility 105–6
Athanasius 54–5, 74, 125, 128–32, 143, 198,
  215, 279
Augustine of Hippo 7, 9, 15, 25–6, 85–6, 101,
  106, 132, 149–52, 158–9, 164, 198,
  212–13, 232, 270, 286, 292
Aulenti, G. 114
autonomy 57

Bach, J. S. 109
Balthasar, Hans Urs von 46–7, 100, 101, 180
baptism 215, 219–23
Barnes, M. R. 295
Barth, Karl xi, 6, 17–18, 21–2, 24, 31, 32–4,
  84, 99, 122, 135–6, 153–4, 159, 171–2,
  176–7, 234–5, 240, 264–8, 269, 270, 271
Basil of Caesarea 142, 148, 151, 283
Bauckham, Richard 243
Bauhaus 113
Beach, Waldo 37
Beckett, Samuel 104
Bell, Clive 117
Berkhof, Hendrikus 239
Bible, the 6, 58, chapter 4
  text's 'final form' 75–8
biblical studies 72–5
  as archaeological 76–7

Biggar, Nigel 39
Bloch, Ernst 232–3
Blondel, Maurice 58
Blumenberg, Hans 156
Boethius 8, 132–3
Bonhoeffer, Dietrich 35
Boulez, Pierre 108–9, 112
Bowie, Andrew 103–5
Boyer, Paul 227
Boyle, Leonard 38
Braaten, Karl 242
Brahms, Johannes 161
Braine, David 187
Bruegel 101–2, 106, 111, 113–15
Brunner, Emil 11
Buckley, Michael 44–5, 58
Bultmann, Rudolf 159, 235, 258–64
Burge, Gary M. 138

Cage, John 104
Calvin, John 10, 28–9, 93, 151, 159, 165, 232,
  264, 266
canonical texts 67–8
  supplementation 77–8
Cantor, Geoffrey 156
Cappadocian Fathers 7, 9, 129–32, 279
Caro, Anthony 104
Carroll, John 61
Chalcedon 245–6, 255–6
Charles the Bald 213
Charron, Pierre 45
Christian canon 76, 84
christology 7, 123–4, 193, chapter 13
  as epistemology 253–5, 257–63
  modern 246–51
  as revelation 264–8
  See also Jesus Christ
church 23–4, 57–8, 112, chapter 11, 231, 291
  as body of Christ 209–12
  as communion 208–9, 215–19, 221
  local 217–19
  as sacrament 207, 210
  universal, unity 217–18
Cicero 44
classic texts 67
Clement of Alexandria 197
Cohn, Norman 242

Index of biblical references

3905